Ethno-erotic Economies

Ethno-erotic Economies

SEXUALITY, MONEY, AND BELONGING IN KENYA

George Paul Meiu

THE UNIVERSITY OF CHICAGO PRESS • CHICAGO AND LONDON

The University of Chicago Press, Chicago 60637
The University of Chicago Press, Ltd., London
© 2017 by The University of Chicago
Published 2017.
Printed in the United States of America

26 25 24 23 22 21 20 19 18 17   1 2 3 4 5

ISBN-13: 978-0-226-49103-5 (cloth)
ISBN-13: 978-0-226-49117-2 (paper)
ISBN-13: 978-0-226-49120-2 (e-book)
DOI: 10.7208/chicago/9780226491202.001.0001

Library of Congress Cataloging-in-Publication Data
Names: Meiu, George Paul, author.
Title: Ethno-erotic economies :
sexuality, money, and belonging in Kenya / George Paul Meiu.
Description: Chicago ; London : The University of Chicago Press, 2017. |
Includes bibliographical references and index.
Identifiers: LCCN 2017007062 | ISBN 9780226491035 (cloth : alk. paper) |
ISBN 9780226491172 (pbk. : alk. paper) | ISBN 9780226491202 (e-book)
Subjects: LCSH: Samburu (African people)—Ethnic identity. | Samburu
(African people)—Sexual behavior. | Sex customs—Kenya—Samburu. |
Samburu (Kenya)—Economic conditions.
Classification: LCC DT433.545.S26 M45 2017 | DDC 306.7089/965—dc23
LC record available at https://lccn.loc.gov/2017007062

♾ This paper meets the requirements of ANSI/NISO Z39.48–1992
(Permanence of Paper).

Contents

A Note on Language

The material discussed in this book is drawn from English, Swahili, Maa, and German. English and Swahili are Kenya's official languages, while Maa is the language of Samburu. Most elderly Samburu spoke only Maa, but many of my other informants—some younger, educated men and women—also spoke fluent Swahili and English. Often, my informants shifted from one language to another or mixed words from these different languages in the same sentence. I translated most Maa and Swahili sentences into English for an easier read. When I offer the Maa and Swahili versions of different words, however, I mark these respectively as *M* or *S*. In addition, when I cite German words I mark them with a *G*.

Introduction

Oh, baby, I come from the totem of Nine Villages. Warriors—growl—no woman can resist us. . . . I am a savage who understands only blood and strength. Will you save me with your tenderness? Send me money to keep my totem alive: if my totem dies, my sex power dies, baby.—BINYAVANGA WAINAINA, "SHIPS IN HIGH TRANSIT"

In June 2011 in Samburu District, northern Kenya, local radio station Serian FM reported that thirteen young men had beaten up elders of their clan in the highland village of Lorosoro. A man in his early twenties had initiated the fight. His name was Meikan, and he was probably one of the richest men in the area. Like many of his age-mates, he had been traveling regularly to Kenya's tourist beach resorts along the coast of the Indian Ocean, some six hundred miles southeast of his home district, to perform traditional dances and sell cultural artifacts. Also like many of his age-mates, Meikan often had sex with women from Europe and North America in exchange for money and other gifts. Recently, he had begun a long-term relationship with a Belgian woman in her late fifties. With the money he received from her, Meikan built two houses in Samburu, one in the town of Maralal and the other in Lorosoro, where his family lived. He also purchased five acres of land, opened a restaurant in Maralal, and started a cattle farm in his village. With an alarmist tone, Serian FM reported that Meikan had enlisted the help of other young men to attack the elderly men of his clan.

I learned more about this conflict a few days later, when I visited friends in Lorosoro. People there told me that Meikan had been driving his Land

Rover when he noticed that his neighbor, a relative and respected elder in the village, had built a fence that slightly obstructed the path to his house. People said the young man had been too proud to discuss the issue with his relative, and instead drove his car over the elder's fence, destroying it. Angered by Meikan's act, the elder contacted the area chief. But before the chief arrived, Meikan had summoned his age-mates and, together with them, went to the elder's house and beat him up. They also beat other senior men and women who were visiting the homestead at that time. Neighbors called the police, and the young men were taken to prison. Among those arrested was Meikan's brother, Korendina, also a wealthy young man in a long-term, long-distance relationship, in his case with a woman from Scotland. Others in their group migrated regularly to coastal beach resorts, but had not yet found foreign partners who would support them with money. In criticizing the situation in Lorosoro, Serian FM pointed out derisively that "beach boys are nowadays beating their elders."

In the next few weeks throughout the Samburu highlands, people commented extensively on the incident in Lorosoro. Some had heard it mentioned on the radio, others by way of gossip. They considered the deeds of the young men an outrage, and their lack of respect for elders a sign of eroding moral values. Samburu and other Kenyans saw elders as repositories of cultural wisdom and moral authorities in matters of rural life. Living in rural communities meant, in one way or another, respecting elders and, to some extent, obeying them. But the man that Meikan and Korendina assaulted was not only an elder. He was also a member of their immediate family, the son of their father's brother. In Samburu, patrilineal descent—that is, relatedness traced through fathers—plays a dominant role in how people relate to each other. In this context, the offspring of one's father's brothers (what anthropologists call paternal parallel cousins) are, in fact, one's own brothers (M: *lalashera*) and sisters (M: *nkanashera*). So from a local perspective, these men committed a double affront: not only had they disrespected an elder, but they also turned against the closest of kin.

"They want to show off how big they are," Jackson, a man from Lorosoro, complained to me of Meikan and Korendina. "When these guys were poor, the father of that elder [that they had beaten] had helped them very much. He had been a soldier in the army. He used to give them small jobs to herd his cattle, and he gave them money." Recalling a history of indebtedness, Jackson suggested that young men's sudden access to cash allowed them to forget past debts and, therewith, future moral obligations to their comparatively poor, rural relatives. Some rural men and women I spoke to emphasized that young men like Meikan and Korendina, who amassed wealth through relationships with foreign women, returned to their home areas with styles and ambitions that others considered undesirable. Not only did these men use their resources to override the authority of elders and kin, locals said, but they also conspicuously consumed the money they had obtained through sex. Some Samburu saw such money as a polluting, unpropitious kind of wealth—money of wrongdoings (M: *shilingini e ng'ok*), they called it. Such wealth, they said, corrupted the character of its owners and threatened the well-being of their families. The fact that such money could buy social influence and authority remained puzzling to onlookers, who often pointed out to me that the prosperity of these men would be short-lived. When locals infantilized these men by calling them "beach boys," they hinted precisely at the seemingly immature and problematic ways in which they mixed sex, money, and kinship.

Jackson told me that Meikan paid some $300 in Kenyan shillings[1] as bail for each one of his age-mates. Soon after that, the district court dismissed the case against these men, prompting elders to suspect that Meikan had bribed the judge. "That is just to show that he has money and that there is no law for him," Jackson emphasized. But residents of Lorosoro did not let the issue rest. Elders imposed their own collective fines. The young men had to pay several cows to those they had beaten, and cash for the property they had destroyed. Even so, some women in Lorosoro thought the sanctions did not measure up to the gravity of the young men's deeds. Younger women threatened to call up Meikan's and Korendina's European partners and reveal to them that the two had secretly married local women. This, they thought, would prompt the partners to end their relationships and cut their financial support. More senior women, however, saw no point in such threats. They were adamant that these men should be cursed to death through a collective ritual.

The scandal in Lorosoro shows how relatively rich young men like Meikan and Korendina positioned themselves in their home communities, and how others positioned themselves in relation to them. When the district court failed to uphold moral expectations of kinship and intergenerational respect by punishing the young men for their deeds, villagers took the matter in their own hands. They reminded young men that being part of the social life of Lorosoro meant abiding by specific expectations of respectability and reciprocity associated with kinship and seniority. However, as I learned during my fieldwork, economic hardships and the scarcity of material resources undermined the ability of many locals to sustain such expectations in their

own lives. In this context, men like Meikan and Korendina, who had significant access to cash, had become patrons of their home villages. Their family
members, clan mates, age-mates, and neighbors turned to them for financial
help with daily expenses, children's school fees, ritual obligations, and much
more. As the money of these men became an important economic and social
resource for people in Lorosoro, locals wondered whether they could really
use money of wrongdoings to build lasting kinds of material wealth and social bonds. Some elders told me that if this money was directed toward the
good of the wider community—rather than consumed individually—it would
lose its polluting qualities. By gossiping about beach boys—their seeming
sexual immorality, bad behavior, and disrespect for their kin and elders—
locals impelled these men to demonstrate their commitment to local values
by sharing their wealth with others. Young men who participated in coastal
tourism desired to be respected at home. They invested in houses and farms
and supported members of their families, villages, clans, and age sets. They
desired to be full members of these social groups. But they were also skeptical of how others expected them to redistribute their wealth, worrying that
their resources would quickly drain out. Treading a fine line between keeping
their money and giving it out, these men then used their wealth to reimagine
and shift the terms and conditions of their belonging. Thus, conflicts ensued
in Samburu over the nature of morally positive labor, wealth, and consumption; the expectations for sex, gender, age, generation, and kinship; or the
significance of being Samburu and the futures Samburu could secure collectively in a globalizing world.

When I began working in Kenya in 2005, I knew little about Samburu
men in relationships with European women. Like most foreigners upon their
first arrival in the country, I was struck by how often I encountered images of
the Maasai and Samburu young male "warrior," or so-called *moran* (in Kenyan
English and Swahili), on Kenyan websites or in public spaces that catered
to foreigners. The stereotypical moran was tall and slim, his body only partially covered with a red loincloth and colorful beads, his long braided hair
dyed with red ocher, and his sharp facial features accentuated with painted
geometric patterns. I encountered this image on postcards, T-shirts, airport
banners, and safari vans, or in the form of wooden statues or metal candle-
sticks in souvenir shops. I also encountered it "live," as it were, as young
Kenyan men dressed in moran attire to welcome tourists in airports, wildlife
parks, and beach resorts. The eroticized silhouette of the moran had become
a popular commodity of Kenya's tourist industry. I wanted to explore how
Samburu themselves used this image to market their traditional artifacts and

dances to foreigners visiting their district. But during my first week in Samburu, something else caught my attention. My interlocutors were debating extensively the moral implications of the growing and controversial trend of young men engaging in various kinds of sex-for-money exchanges with white women. Many of these women, they said, desired morans for their exotic appearance, cultural uniqueness, and sexual otherness. I quickly noticed that in Samburu, this trend generated new allegiances, inequalities, and tensions, raising new concerns over what it meant to belong to the region.

This book explores why belonging comes so saliently into question in northern Kenya with the rise of tourist markets of ethnic culture and sexual intimacy. It shows what happens when postcolonial subjects take their ethnicity and sexuality to the market in order to access resources that would allow them to participate more fully in kinship relations and ethnoregional politics, or in the power structures of the state and transnational circuits of money and goods. I describe how people's everyday struggles to gain recognition and access resources shape and in turn are informed by globally marketable idioms of their race, ethnicity, and sexuality. I use *belonging* to refer to relationships, representations, and practices through which various social actors construct and contest their positions in the world. In this sense, belonging, like citizenship, is a "dual process of self-making and being-made within webs of power" (Ong 1996, 738). Based on "techniques of differentiation," belonging refers to "a set of intertwined practices and collective repertoires for defining, legitimating, and exercising the rights of some bodies against others" (Sheller 2012, 21). Weaving together ties of kinship, ethnicity, civil society, state governance, and market relations, belonging constitutes an ongoing negotiation of who has a right to be included, who may claim such rights, and who might not. I ask: What forms of belonging are possible for Samburu men and women as their sexuality becomes a "hot" global commodity? How does the commodification of their ethnic sexuality shape what it means to be Samburu? What forms of collective consciousness emerge in relation to the marketable sexuality of the moran? How are notions of respectability, prestige, moral personhood, and good life reenvisioned in the conflicts between young men in relationships with foreign women, other men who desire to have such relationships, and their respective kin, agemates, and neighbors? What everyday activities, bodily practices, and material goods signify belonging and social value? How are relations of gender, age, generation, and kinship reshaped, and what subject positions emerge in the process? And what do these historical developments in Kenya tell us about belonging in today's postcolonial world more generally?

I address these questions through an ethnographic study of what I call *ethno-erotic economies*. I offer the framework of ethno-erotic economies to explore the myriad social and economic effects of the commodification of the moran—his ethnicity, sexuality, masculinity, and bodily youth. These effects reach beyond tourist resorts, as money, goods, and persons circulate between multiple locales to shape desires, social attachments, and livelihoods across all these sites. Starting in tourist resorts and moving outward in ever-wider circles into coastal migrant communities and then into Samburu towns and villages, I describe the reach and depth of such circulations and their social and cultural ramifications.

ASPIRATIONS, INNOVATIONS, AND
THE BLESSINGS OF BELONGING

Many Samburu found the violent events of Lorosoro noteworthy. They were outraged that Meikan and his age-mates had assaulted elders. But the issue of young men beating elders was not new. Nor, for that matter, did it involve only young men who migrated to the coast. In the few years preceding these events, I had heard men and women complain repeatedly that the young men's age set, or class of age-mates, was very badly behaved. By the time the Lorosoro incident occurred, elders throughout the district already had been trying to find ways to deal with growing conflicts between themselves and the young men who were morans.

In the rainy season of 2010, for example, Samburu elders were busy preparing a set of ceremonies called *mayan*, or blessing. A sense of urgency drove them. All men aged roughly seventeen to thirty years found themselves in a dangerous, unpropitious state. A few young men had recently beaten and killed individual elders throughout the district. Their deeds made their whole age set susceptible to the anger and curses of others. Elders noticed that men of this age set were dying, for various reasons, in large numbers. So they feared that the whole age set might gradually die off. Organizing a collective blessing was therefore crucial. And elders lost no time. In each village, a senior man hosted the ceremony in his homestead and offered a fat ox to be slaughtered. Elders summoned the morans to the home, blessed them, and invited them to feast on the meat. Through this ceremony, they hoped to make a truce with the young men, foreclose further bad feelings between the two generations, and rejuvenate communal life.

"There were many problems with the Lkishami," Ltarsia, a Samburu man in his late fifties, explained to me, invoking the name of the morans' age set. It was September 2010, and I was visiting him in the highland village of Siteti, fifteen miles north of Lorosoro. Sitting in his compound, Ltarsia told me about the special ceremony that had taken place in his village a few months prior. When I asked him about the purpose of the ceremony, he began complaining about the morans' age set. "This is a bad age set," he told me in a firm voice, pointing to the ground with his wooden club. "So many bad things have happened since the Lkishami were circumcised. That's why we had to do the blessing."

Age sets and age grades are central modes of relatedness in Samburu. An age set (M: *ntowuo* or *laji*) is a named cohort of age-mates who are initiated together into social adulthood and who move together through a number of "age grades," or stages of life. Every fourteen years or so, elders open a new age set, and throughout the following years, young men aged approximately fifteen to twenty-five years are initiated into it through circumcision. This ritual passage marks their transition from the age grade of childhood (M: *keraisho*) to that of moranhood (M: *lamurrano*). Ideally, morans (M: *ilmurran*; sg. *ilmurrani*) may not marry or rely too much on the resources of their families. Although in the past morans went to war and raided cattle, nowadays many herd livestock, attend school, or work for wages. After fourteen years, elders promote morans to elderhood (M: *lpayiano*) and encourage them to marry.

Ltarsia recalled how, when the Lkishami age set had been ritually opened in 2005, elders had made a few mistakes. Choosing the first novice to be circumcised on the sacred mountain of Nyiro as a forerunner of the age set had proved very difficult. This novice had to be of exemplary moral upbringing, with a history of good deeds and perfectly symmetrical bodily features lest he negatively affect the well-being of the entire future age set. As it turned out, the first candidate the elders chose had killed a person and was therefore unpropitious. The second candidate was ideal. But his mother, an Anglican Christian, refused to participate in the ceremony. So with the ceremony rapidly approaching, elders hastily chose another candidate. After the ceremony, they realized that the candidate had "crooked eyes," and so was inauspicious. Then there were issues with the ritual bull, or the *lmong'o*, that had to be slaughtered by way of ritually opening the age set. Like the main novice, the bull had to have propitious physical features and a pure line of descent. However, after the ceremony, people learned that awhile back, the bull had been traded at the market for a donkey. Donkeys, Samburu said, are unclean animals. And people held that something that was traded for another sometimes continued to carry the other's properties. So it was as if, in Ltarsia's words, "the bull belonged to the donkeys." Further, on the day of its slaughter, the bull had walked toward a donkey and mounted it. In hindsight, then, it was as if a donkey, not a bull, had been slaughtered for the age-set ritual. This was a grave error indeed.

But of all the mistakes that started off the age set on the wrong foot, Ltarsia told me, one in particular stood out. According to custom, only four women were allowed to climb the mountain for the ceremony. All four had to occupy very specific positions in terms of descent and kinship, and had very well-defined ritual roles in the ceremony. At the initiation of the Lkishami age set, however, seven white women, all world-renowned photographers and filmmakers from the United States, climbed the mountain to document the proceedings. They offered money to elders in order to be permitted to attend. A major fight then ensued among the elders. Some wanted to chase the white women away. Others hoped to capitalize on the visual spectacularity of their rituals. Eventually, they allowed the women to attend the ceremony. But a few years afterward, more and more elders concluded that their presence had proved unpropitious for the new age set after all. "That's why," Ltarsia said, "so many morans are now going crazy chasing white women on the coast for money." He laughed. Then he turned serious. "Elders say we should not circumcise any more boys in this age set. We should just close it and move on."

In recalling mistakes at the initiation rituals of the morans' age set and criticizing this age set for the misdeeds of some of its members, Ltarsia sought to position himself as a respectable, authoritative elder who defended the moral good of age-set relations. When I first met him in the summer of 2008, however, he was far from being respected. Together with his wife and four children, he lived in extreme poverty. I would often see him drunk on Siteti's main path, and I also heard villagers make fun of him by calling him a beach boy, though by age grade he was, in fact, an elder. I had learned at that point that Ltarsia had spent twenty years at coastal tourist resorts. The sex economy was less prominent in the early 1980s, when Ltarsia—at that time a moran—had gone to Mombasa for the first time. Nonetheless, at least three men from Siteti who belonged to his age set (the Lkuroro) had met European women and made a good life for themselves. Two of them still traveled regularly to Switzerland to spend time with their partners. Ltarsia, however, had been unsuccessful. He returned to Siteti in 2000 with only enough money to buy a few goats and build a small bark-roof hut. By 2008, he had no longer owned livestock and struggled to make ends meet by selling charcoal.

When I returned to Siteti in 2009, however, I learned that things had taken a positive turn for Ltarsia. He no longer drank and had purchased two cows. He was very determined to improve his life. By 2010, he had already owned five cattle and was also paying for his son's boarding school education. When Siteti elders organized the blessing ceremony for its morans, Ltarsia sponsored the event and hosted it in his compound. This was a costly affair. He gave out a fat ox and purchased large quantities of sugar, rice, tea leaves, and other foodstuffs to entertain villagers. Only well-to-do elders could sponsor such a ceremony, so for Ltarsia, having been able to do so was an important achievement. "All the elders of Siteti, all the mamas, and the children came to my homestead for the blessing," he recalled proudly. "It was very beautiful."

By sponsoring the blessing, Ltarsia used his otherwise modest material resources to invest in age-set relations, village sociality, and clan rituals. This, he hoped, would grant him respect and secure him the support of his community in the future. Ltarsia and his age-mates were the ritual patrons of the morans, their "fire-stick elders" (M: *mpiroi*; *lpiroi*) (because they had kindled the ritual fire that brought the age set into being). He sought to become exemplary as a member of his age set and a mentor for the morans. By sponsoring the ceremony, he aligned himself with locally recognized forms of relatedness and sought to belong more fully to local social worlds. Through the collective blessings of elders during the ceremony, he had also hoped to propitiate life force (M: *nkishon*) for himself, his family, and his homestead, thereby augmenting their ability to prosper further in the future.

Like Ltarsia, other elders had high hopes for the 2010 ceremonies. Yet not everything went as expected. In the villages of Siteti and Lorosoro, for example, many young men missed the event. The ceremony took place during the peak of Kenya's tourist season, and many of them were at coastal beach resorts, trying to make money. This does not mean that all these young men disregarded age-set affairs—quite to the contrary. Whenever I visited Samburu friends at coastal resorts, they asked me if I had news about the timing of one or another age-set ceremony. They wished to plan their return trips accordingly. But the current ceremony was a spontaneous innovation of elders in the face of new intergenerational conflicts. It was not part of the mandatory ceremonies through which every age set had to pass. Some morans, therefore, did not consider the ceremony sufficiently significant to warrant making the sixteen-hour bus journey back to Samburu and miss out on the moneymaking possibilities of the tourist season. So they simply skipped it.

Parents and relatives of the absent morans were concerned. Attending the ceremony was necessary for the young men to receive the collective blessings of their ritual patrons and claim their rightful place in the age set. In Lorosoro, Mama Zakayo complained to me that her twenty-year-old son had not attended the ceremony. A locally operating German NGO had assigned her son a sponsorship for his high school education, but he had dropped out of school, determined to make money on the coast. He was good friends with Meikan and Korendina, who were his age-mates and had recently become wealthy. "He was hanging out with these boys a lot," Mama Zakayo recalled. "He started to feel left behind. So one day he just decided to go to Mombasa and try his luck there. But few people who go to the coast succeed in making money nowadays."

Mama Zakayo was the widow of a former soldier in the Kenyan national army. She had raised five children. Four daughters were already married and lived in neighboring villages. The husband of one of them also had an elderly Swiss wife and was quite wealthy. Mama Zakayo understood her son's desire to meet a white woman and have a comfortable life, although she would have preferred that he had finished high school and found employment. As a senior widow, she was now imagining spending her old age caring for her son's future family in Lorosoro. She wanted to help her son to become a respected man, perhaps as his father had once been. To be respected, she thought, her son also had to commit to his age set. A Samburu proverb urges, "God, take away my mother and my father, but leave me my age set," emphasizing the supreme importance of age-set solidarity.[2] Age-mates, Mama Zakayo knew, must be able to rely on one another unconditionally for support. "If you don't have your age set, who do you have?" she said.

In the absence of so many morans, elders and relatives devised another means to incorporate the young men into the mayan ceremony. Normally, for the purpose of the ceremony, each moran would carry his personal wooden calabash with a bit of milk inside. Elders would use this milk to sprinkle young men during the ritual blessing. But in this instance, relatives of the absent morans walked to the homestead of the ceremony themselves, taking along the calabashes of the absent. When the ceremonies began in both Lorosoro and Siteti, some fifty calabashes were lined up along the fences of the compound for the blessing. Standing in front of them, some 150 or so morans held their own calabashes. Mama Zakayo explained to me that in the absence of the novices, their calabashes took on the blessings for them. Samburu saw individually owned calabashes as extensions of the embodied personhood of their owners.[3] As such, a calabash could take on blessings in its owner's absence and could represent its owner in absentia at certain rituals. Thus, as more and more young men sought to make the best of tourism on the one

hand and local forms of relatedness and respectability on the other, the calabash acted as a placeholder that enabled them to be present, as it were, in
two places at once.

The practice of blessing a calabash in lieu of a moran was not new. In the
past, when morans could not attend a particular ceremony, their calabashes
were blessed in their stead. What was new was the scale of absenteeism. One
elder said that in the old days, some five to ten calabashes stood in for absent
morans, whereas now there were about fifty, if not more. Not all fifty morans
were on the coast. Some worked in the capital city of Nairobi or in other
towns, and could not obtain a leave of absence. But the vast majority of the
morans of Siteti and Lorosoro were indeed at Mombasa's tourist beach resorts. At the 2010 ceremonies, the unattended calabashes at once brought
forth their absent owners, claiming belonging on their behalf, and made their
absence conspicuous to those present.

The intergenerational conflicts, moral dilemmas, individual aspirations,
and ritual innovations I encountered in Siteti and Lorosoro speak of shifting forms of belonging. As men and women in rural Samburu tried to craft
respectability in the midst of wider social and economic transformations,
they pointedly contested relations of age, generation, gender, and kinship.
Such relations have long played an important role in how locals related to
each other, to the Kenyan state, and to the market economy. These have also
been central in defining who is "really" Samburu, and what it means to belong to local worlds. Yet now, imagining belonging to age sets, lineages, clans,
and regions also meant dealing with the social and economic ramifications of
young men marketing their culture and sexuality in tourism. Most of these
men returned to Samburu and, over time, reshaped local livelihoods. Rich
young men like Meikan and Korendina sought to override the authority of
elders, kin, and age-mates and produce new forms of privilege and patronage. Poorer men like Ltarsia sought respectability by turning to ritual and
pursuing the egalitarian ethos of reciprocity and mutual support associated
with clan and age relations. Meanwhile, women like Mama Zakayo crafted
respectability in part as mothers, mothers-in-law, wives, and sisters by engaging, in various ways, men's desire for both the cash of coastal tourist resorts
and the recognition of their home communities. And so in Samburu, the
conditions, meanings, and potentials of belonging came sharply into question.

Why, when more and more young African men and women sought to migrate to Europe or North America for better economic opportunities, did

Samburu men only very rarely follow their foreign partners abroad?[4] Why did they return to the economically marginal areas of northern Kenya? Why did they choose to pursue belonging through local worlds of culture and kinship when they often found themselves excluded or exploited by elders and kin? Why did other Samburu work so hard to incorporate these men— if sometimes through their calabashes—in their local ties of relatedness and mutual support when they often disapproved of their making a living through sex? And why did social ties in Samburu rely so strongly on older expectations of kinship, age, and personhood when, in the absence of resources, it was increasingly difficult for many to sustain such relations?

Patrilineal descent, age sets, and village life speak of a particular kind of belonging. They reflect a desire to sustain ethnicity, culture, and autochthony as primary sites of attachment and good life. In Samburu, as I will show, such collective representations gained renewed importance with the advent of global markets of ethnic culture and sex. Many locals turned, in new ways, toward kinship—for them, a kind of guarantee of durable wealth and worth—precisely as they mobilized to seek rights, recognition, and resources through the Kenyan state and the global market. Yet amid conflicts that involved young men, elders, women, age-mates, and kin, relatedness and belonging also took on new, unexpected forms.

SAMBURU MEN IN KENYA'S COASTAL TOURISM

The Kenyan tourist industry has grown spectacularly over the past four decades.[5] In this context, being Samburu moran has become a way of embodying substantial economic value. According to a tourist ad on the website Kenya Cultural Profiles, "the Samburu are a proud warrior-race of cattle-owning pastoralists, a section of the Maa-speaking people, amongst whom the Maasai are the best known."[6] "Proud of their culture and traditions," the ad continues, "the Samburu still cherish and retain the customs and ceremonies of their forebears, unlike most other tribes in Kenya who have been influenced by Western civilization." Many of my Samburu interlocutors, echoing such ads, described themselves as "people of cattle" who inhabit the semiarid savannahs of northern Kenya. They also gestured to the fact that they shared a language and customs with Maasai people of southern Kenya and northern Tanzania, and emphasized that—unlike the Maasai and their other southern neighbors—Samburu "still kept their old culture." I felt uneasy about what to me seemed like essentialist descriptions of ethnic identity. I occasionally pointed out to my interlocutors that such descriptions occluded, for example, the fact that in recent decades, cattle economies declined, a town-based Samburu middle class burgeoned, and many Samburu relocated elsewhere in Kenya. My interlocutors would nod. All that was true, of course. But as one man pointed out, what being Samburu is "really about" is "keeping this old culture." I gradually learned that such descriptions of ethnicity were more than simple attempts to bank on stereotypes that state officials, NGO workers, and tourists readily recognized. They were also strong affective claims to a particular cultural identity and to specific genealogical and territorial attachments.

Morans figured centrally in tourist ads of Samburu culture. The Kenya Cultural Profiles ad details, "The moran, or warriors, are the most striking members of Samburu society and are inevitably attractive to young girls. They enjoy a convivial and relatively undemanding life with permissive sex for roughly 14 years. Most of them will at one time or another have many lovers who demonstrate affection with lavish gifts and beads." The sexualized moran became emblematic of the traditional heritage of the Samburu and other Maa-speaking ethnic groups (such as Maasai and Chamus). For foreigners, he also congealed fantasies of sexual freedom and erotic enjoyment. Moreover, the moran became a core brand of East Africa as an international destination (Bruner 2005, 35; Kasfir 2007, 280).

Beginning in 1979, faced with the challenges of rapidly declining cattle economies, scarce access to land, droughts, rapid population growth, and rampant unemployment, some Samburu men migrated seasonally to coastal tourist resorts. There, they lived in different small towns to the south and north of the city of Mombasa, including Diani, Mtwapa, Watamu, and Malindi (fig. 1). During the day they sold spears, bead necklaces, and bracelets at the beach, and in the evenings they performed dances in hotels (Kasfir 2007, 286–88). Many hoped to meet foreign women for sex or long-term relationships. Most women who had intimate relationships with morans were from Germany, Switzerland, England, Italy, Netherlands, Norway, France, and Belgium (cf. Kibicho 2009, 102). Fewer came from the United States and Canada, and only a very few from Australia and Japan. While some of the women sought the company of morans for one-night stands or for the duration of their vacation, many others desired lasting romantic relationships or even marriages. In the latter case, women visited their partners regularly and, on occasion, paid for these men to visit them in Europe. Only a few women moved permanently to Kenya, and I know of no more than six or seven Samburu men who moved to Europe to live with their partners on a more per-

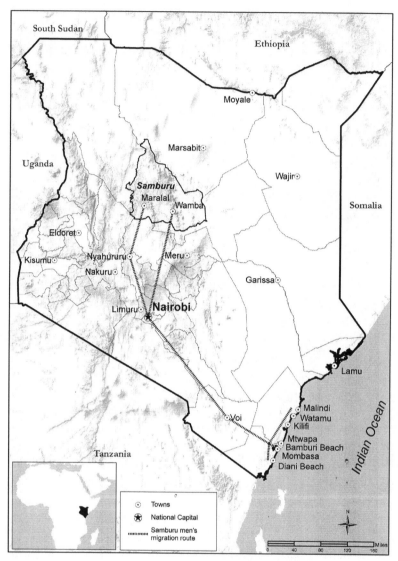

1. Map of Kenya, with Samburu men's migration route and the place-names mentioned in the book. (Map created by the author.)

manent basis. Although most of the women were ten to forty years older than their male partners and a few had children with them, they often sponsored one or more children of their partners' lineages. Most women arrived to Kenya as tourists. But many returned to work for NGOs or start their own businesses. By visiting their partners regularly and establishing affective ties with their families in northern Kenya, these women hoped to escape the apparent artificiality of tourist resorts and foster ties of love and care with local men and their families. Often, but not always, relationships ended when women were no longer able to finance their partners or when they found out that their partners had married local women.

Samburu men desired relationships with tourists for several reasons. They enjoyed spending time with these women, drinking and having a good time in nightclubs, in bars, or on leisurely trips in Kenya or abroad. Many developed strong bonds of friendship, love, and care with their partners. They also eroticized white women as uninhibited sexual partners who often engaged in sexual behaviors—such as kissing, oral sex, and foreplay—that were more rarely practiced in Samburu. But for most men, relationships with foreign women were also pleasurable and desirable in another sense. They held the possibility of rapid wealth. Some women sent their Samburu partners money regularly, through bank transfers or Western Union. With this money, men bought motorbikes, cars, and livestock or built businesses, houses, and farms. Some men also used this money to support Kenyan girlfriends or to pay bridewealth and marry one or two local wives. Others invested in electoral campaigns and secured positions in the government administration. Indeed, during my fieldwork, some of the richest men in Samburu were those in relationships with foreign women. By the same token, however, some of the poorest men were those who had waited unsuccessfully for years to find white partners at beach resorts before returning home without any savings.

The migration of Samburu men to coastal resorts increased significantly throughout the last three decades of the twentieth century. If, in the early 1980s, there were some one hundred Samburu on the coast during the tourist season, by 2010, according to my own estimates, their numbers had risen to over one thousand. This remained a relatively low percentage (approximately 2.23 percent) of Samburu District's total population (approximately 223,947 people in 2009). However, the economic, social, and cultural effects of men's migration came to reverberate far beyond tourism to engulf many other social actors that were not directly involved in the tourist industry as such. Throughout the 1990s and the early 2000s, circulations of people, money, and goods associated with Samburu morans who sold ethnic culture and sex intensified spectacularly.

"MORAN MANIA": MARKETS OF ETHNOSEXUALITY

On December 12, 2004, the Nairobi-based national newspaper *Daily Nation* announced, on the first page of its Sunday magazine, a booming "moran mania" among tourists in the country. In the accompanying article, journalists Oscar Obonyo and Daniel Nyassy note that the moran has become one of the "bestselling images in world tourism," and that now, "numerous young men . . . have embraced the *moran* image to charm and win the hearts of tourists visiting Kenya." "You know," a young man told the reporters, "if you hook up with a white woman, you say goodbye to poverty." According to a local researcher interviewed by the journalists, "some tourists believe that the moran is primitive, unexposed, untouched and therefore a safe and valued sex partner." "Other reasons advanced for the moran's sexual attraction," the journalists say, include "that he is young, tall, athletic and strong." The article points out that "this has become a lucrative business, and scores of morans—genuine and fake alike—flood the coastal beaches to make a living from the trade."[7] But the article also decries the potential effects this touristic "moran mania" would have on Maasai culture and on moran masculinity. As the cover of the special issue illustrates (fig. 2), the journalists find the touristic moran corrupted, devalued, and "ugly," a mockery of what had once been a noble, heroic masculinity (represented here, in the background, as a fading image).

In a similarly sensationalist tone in 2013, New York's news web Vocative announced in a short video feature that "in many ways, the Maasai and Samburu warriors, known collectively as the moran, still live like their tribes have for centuries. But these days, they are hunting very different game: white women from all over the world, who travel here in search of the *moran's* legendary love-making powers—their sexual prowess."[8] In 2014, Afk Travel—a website devoted to travel within Africa—noted that on the Kenyan coast,

> along the waterfronts and shorelines fringed with coral reefs, it is not unusual to see Samburu and Maasai men dressed in red and black traditional garb and beaded jewelry walking and evidently flirting with foreign women as old as their mothers. The mystique of African men, especially 'warriors' from the Maasai and Samburu tribes, has long drawn European women of a certain age. Some are lonely, while others are looking for a distraction. Many have found 'love' in the strong arms of these warriors.[9]

2. "Moran Mania": cover of *Daily Nation's Sunday Lifestyle* magazine, December 12, 2004.

By coupling an anachronistic view of Samburu and Maasai lives with the warriors' "mystique," "legendary love-making powers," and "sexual prowess," these news reports assign radical cultural and sexual alterity to morans.

Romance on the Road (Belliveau 2006), a touristic guide for women traveling in search of sex and love, lists what is specific about Kenya as a sex destination: "Unlike in the Caribbean, where men regale visiting tourists with romantic speeches, [in Kenya] some Masai [*sic*] warriors apparently just stand around looking beautiful while women fall at their feet" (157). Among chapters with titles such as "Caribbean Men: Ready, Willing and Able" and "Instant Sex, Amazon Style," the guide points out that "relaxed views [on sex] make Africa the world's sexiest continent" (167). "Africa," it says, "is where . . . two sexual freedoms from the beginning and end of history converge: the license of the modern Information Age woman and the polygamous, cattle-herding man" (153). What drives white women to Africa, it says, are "the exotic good looks and warrior mystique of many African men, notably the Masai [*sic*] and Samburu in Kenya, the Wollof [*sic*] in the Gambia and Zulus and Xhosa in South Africa" (ibid.). Placing Africa at "the beginning of history" (as Georg Hegel once did) and associating it with stereotypical images of polygamy and cattle herding, the guidebook addresses—we can safely assume—a primarily white global audience. It entangles erotic appeal, sexual freedom, and "warrior mystique" with racial and ethnic difference and ascribes them commodity value. Time figures centrally herein. The further back in time the sexual subject is located, the more authentic and appealing he is (cf. Fabian 1983).

The assumption that people of particular African ethnic groups are radically different—culturally and sexually—informed growing sexual economies in Kenya and elsewhere on the continent (Ebron 2002; Jacobs 2010; Kibicho 2009; Nyanzi et al. 2005). But such assumptions also fueled a certain fascination in newspapers and magazines, on talk shows and reality shows, and in documentary films, blog entries, and social media. African warriors who have sex for money, elderly white women as "sex tourists," and intimacies that cross seemingly natural boundaries of race and culture were indeed the perfect ingredients for a true media sensation. Such discourses produced and imbued with value specific instances of *ethnosexuality*. Drawing on the work of sociologist Joane Nagel (2003), I take ethnosexuality to refer to a homogenous set of sexual drives and erotic qualities assigned in discourse and practice to particular racial, ethnic, or cultural categories of people. In a growing global market of commodified ethnosexualities—for example, Hawaiian hula girls, Amazonian indigenous women, or Rastafarian men on

Caribbean islands—morans also came to occupy positions of essential difference. They embodied fundamental racial, ethnic, and cultural otherness for mostly white, middle-class consumers. Discourses of moran ethnosexuality, as I show in chapter 1, go back to the reformist ideologies of British colonials and missionaries and the development projects of postindependence political leaders. But in the present, such discourses emerged in new ways as some Samburu took their ethnosexuality, as it were, to the market.

A wide range of texts and images focusing on the moran and his sexuality now circulate globally. Since the early 1990s, for example, several European women who had relationships with Samburu men have published their memoirs. The most famous, perhaps, is Corinne Hofmann's best seller *The White Masai* (2005). In this book, the Swiss narrator details how she met a Samburu moran while on vacation in Mombasa in 1986, and how, after selling her business in Switzerland, she moved to northern Kenya to live in her partner's village. *The White Masai* describes the challenges the narrator faced in building a life across cultural difference or dealing with poverty, illness, and the birth of a daughter in "the bush."[10] After its publication in German in 1998, the book became an international best seller and was translated into over eighteen languages. In 2005, the German company Constantin Films released a movie based on Hofmann's memoir. By 2009, the book had also sold in tourist shops, hotels, and airports in Kenya and Tanzania, having become— along with Karen Blixen's *Out of Africa* (1937)—a touristic souvenir emblematic of East Africa. It also became a mythical narrative that enabled tourist businesses to depict East Africa as a place for romance and adventure. Later, Hofmann published two more books about her ties to Samburu, drawing on her fame for being the "white Masai" (Hofmann 2006; 2008).

Hofmann's book was part of a wide genre of texts that eroticized and sexualized Samburu and Maasai morans for global audiences. Less famous and written in a somewhat different vein, the memoirs of British author Cheryl Mason—*White Mischief: The True Story of a Woman Who Married a Kenyan Tribesman* (1995) and *No Ivory Tower* (2001)—are well known among women in relationships with Samburu men. Mason narrates how she sought to escape her deep trauma from having been repeatedly abused and raped as a child and teenager. Through her relationship with Samburu moran Dikola, she hoped to reconnect to the essence of life. Likewise, German author Christina Hachfeld-Tapukai (2004, 2009) describes traveling to Kenya and building a home with a Samburu man as a way to seek new meaning in her life endeavors. White women in relationships with Maasai men authored similar books. Consider, for example, Catherine Oddie's *Enkop Ai (My Coun try): My Life with the Maasai* (1994), Samantha Kimambo's *The English Maasai and Other Truths* (2007), Robin Wiszowaty's *My Maasai Life: From Suburbia to Savannah* (2010), or Mindy Budgor's *Warrior Princess: My Quest to Become the First Female Maasai Warrior* (2013). Overall, these texts speak to a white audience fascinated with radical cultural otherness and with how sex and love may or may not overcome cultural barriers. Rarely, if at all, do the authors reflect on contemporary politics, poverty, or inequality. Rather, they derive authenticity and market value from the white subject's ability to embody and speak for the cultural difference of racial and ethnic others. The Other figures here as the raw material to which the author then adds value through her experience and writing.

Through these books, the experiences of a few European women in relationships with Kenyan men circulated throughout the world, fueling the growth of Kenya's sexual economies. Many of my European interlocutors in Kenya had read several of these books and were familiar with other forms of media that covered the relationships between foreign women and Samburu men. Imaginaries of the sexual moran certainly anchored the market value of such texts. But it is important that we do not think here of moran ethnosexuality as preexisitng "raw material" that these texts packaged for consumers. Rather, as I will show, ethnosexuality, like culture itself, is—to use Kamala Visweswaran's (2010, 3) words—"an effect of the circulation of its descriptions." In the 1990s and 2000s, the circulation of such texts intensified and promoted growing markets of moran ethnosexuality.

SEXUALITY AND ALTERITY IN GLOBAL AFRICA

Africa has long been at the center of global imaginaries of ethnosexuality. From the western European fascination with African bodies during the slave trade, through colonial obsessions with reforming African sexual lives, and to more recent global health responses to the AIDS pandemic, the continent figured as a hub of promiscuity and perversion. Achille Mbembe (2001, 2) argues that "it is in relation to Africa that the notion of 'absolute otherness' has been taken the farthest." Sexuality—understood in the modern sense of an innermost quality of the self, or an orientation or intensity of desire—made a salient argument for such "absolute otherness." "African cultures and sexualities," according to Sylvia Tamale (2011, 19), "were always framed as different, less urbane and inferior to those of the West," thus "justifying racist and imperialist policies." Desiree Lewis (2011, 201) notes that "the legacy of colonialism endures in essentialist attitudes toward African sexuality and corporeal difference." Says Lewis, "Contemporary forms of othering are not always explicitly and recognizably racist," and "might often be presented as positive and ennobling celebrations of the black body" (200). But such "celebrations" of Africanity may also work to naturalize race and ethnicity as categories of pleasure, desire, and subjectivity and sustain hierarchies of global white supremacy.

The idea that people of different races, ethnicities, or cultures embody different sexual drives and practice different sexual customs has long appealed to Western scholars and popular audiences. Earlier generations of anthropologists studied how non-Western people constructed and approached sex differently from Europeans.[11] They often used cross-cultural comparison to problematize Western moral precepts of sex and sexuality and imagine a wider terrain of erotic possibilities. Consequently, they also coupled different sexual mores with specific cultures and ethnic identities. Anthropologists were not alone in this regard, however. Throughout the twentieth century, a certain fascination with the sexual inclinations of others (particularly those marked by race, ethnicity, nationality, culture, class, region, and more) spread globally—albeit with varying implications—through media and commodity consumption. What anchors such fascination is a widely shared premise that sexuality designates a universal realm of biological life; something that we all share in our bodily existence and that revolves, broadly, around genital pleasure. Taking sexuality as a human universal, we then compare and contrast bodily intimacies across lines of social differentiation with various political implications. In a global context structured by white hegemony, the idioms of race, ethnicity, and culture more readily facilitate social classification and moral hierarchization (Chanock 2000; Pierre 2013; Ratele 2007).[12] Thus, the universalism of sexuality and the essentialism of difference represent conditions of possibility for each other. It is more helpful, then, to think of sexuality, but also of race, ethnicity, and culture, not as explanatory analytics but rather as social, historical, and political constructs that act on the world in ways that require explanation.

Anthropologists and historians of colonialism and globalization argue that discursive invocations of sexuality are central channels for drawing and policing boundaries of race, ethnicity, culture, or class (McClintock 1995; Najmabadi 2005; Somerville 2000; Stoler 2002). Drawing on the work of Michel Foucault (1978), they refute the idea that sexuality is a universal realm of bodily and psychic experience that can facilitate straightforward cross-cultural comparison. Sexuality, Foucault argues, is a modern domain of discourse that posits a universal, biological realm in the human body in order to serve modern forms of power. Precisely because it provides a universal

criterion of comparison, sexuality works to produce and normalize hierarchical orders of sameness and difference. It draws lines of exclusion and
embeds them in desire and disgust, purity and pollution, morality and de-
pravity, normativity and alterity. Under late capitalism, the global circulation
of discourses of science and development in matters of health, education,
and rights made sexuality an important category of intervention across the
world. Yet since globalization, systems of oppressive power also have produced difference through sexual ideologies (Boellstorff 2005, 7). As an object of knowledge, for example, sexuality represents a variable for mapping
"ethnocartographies of sexual practice" (Pigg and Adams 2005, 6–7). "Ethnicity and sexuality," Nagel (2003, 1) argues, "join together to form a barrier
to hold some people in and keep others out, to define who is pure and who
is impure, to shape our view of ourselves and others, to fashion feelings of
sexual desire and notions of sexual desirability, to provide us with seemingly
'natural' sexual preferences for some partners and 'intuitive' aversions to
others, to leave us with a taste for some ethnic sexual encounters and a dis-
taste for others."

Africanist anthropologists and historians have recently struggled to dis-
mantle paradigms of sexual alterity that have compromised conceptualiza-
tions of intimacy in African contexts. As Desiree Lewis (2011, 200) argues,
"To explore African sexualities carefully means first exploring how they have
been thought about; it requires what Kwame Appiah describes as a 'discursive space-clearing,' a way of both acknowledging and analyzing how others
have historically been imagined." Reflecting on sexuality in Africa, Signe
Arnfred (2004, 7) suggests, means "thinking beyond the conceptual structure of colonial and even post-colonial European imaginations." For these
reasons, Africanist scholars critique extensively essentialist invocations of
sexuality in Africa and provide deep empirical evidence to counter paradigms
of sexual alterity (Arnfred 2004; Epprecht 2008, 2013; Hoad 2007; Lewis
2011; Tamale 2011). Avoiding stereotypes of African sexuality altogether,
many anthropologists now explore how dynamics of globalization intersect
with sex, intimacy, and love throughout the continent.

But what happens when postcolonial subjects, in Africa and elsewhere,
claim and perform sexual otherness in order to access money and power?
How do they imagine and act on their identities and attachments? And how
do they claim and craft belonging in relation to their ethnosexuality? To find
and understand the answers to these questions, it is not enough to critique
othering representations of sexuality. Nor can we simply look past such
stereotypes. Representations of sexual alterity, far from being only simple

*mis*representations, must also be interrogated as mechanisms of surveillance, marketization, subjection, and empowerment (Lepani 2012; Lorway 2014; Nagel 2003; Stoler 2002). It is important to ask how such representations shape the lives of those they claim to represent. This does not mean that researchers must attend exclusively to people's own meanings of their sexual practices. As Neville Hoad (2007, xxii) argues, "It is not enough to describe the diversity of African sexual practices on the ground," because "description alone, no matter how scrupulous, still produces African sexuality as the object of a prurient Western gaze." While rich ethnography remains invaluable, researchers must also detail how oppressive paradigms of ethnosexuality work on multiple scales at once. We must pay attention to how people come to live *as* Others or *through* and *around* their Otherness in specific contexts.

Samburu District, its people, and its history offer an opportune context in which to study the relations between belonging and ethnosexuality. Here, paradigms of sexual Otherness played a significant role in how the colonial and postindependence administrators and reformists governed Samburu, shaping most intimate aspects of people's lives. Attending to the production and outcomes of ethnosexuality and cultural alterity constitutes, for me, an ethical commitment to the subjects of this book. At the same time, my interlocutors' concrete ways of inhabiting the contradictions of lives lived with alterity offer important insights into the workings of oppressive notions of ethnosexuality—their limits, gaps, and possibilities.

BELONGING, ETHNICITY, AND SEXUAL MORALITY

With growing markets of moran ethnosexuality, many Samburu struggled to imagine how they could claim belonging through the recognition of others—whether the state, NGOs, or foreign donors—when others recognized them precisely for their sexual excesses. In a 2013 blog post, a Kenyan writer, publishing under the pseudonym Obsurvative, decries how "the recent highlights on the news about old white women settling in Kenya and marrying young Samburu men has [*sic*] tarnished the image of the Moran. The new Moran is not supposed to be a lazy young man sitting reluctantly to wait for the woman to provide!" Rather, the blogger says, the "new moran"—having abandoned actual war and cattle raiding—should remain a heroic figure "waging war against the adversities of life's struggles." "Unfortunately," he notes, "taking short cuts has become the order of the day and the new Moran, mischievously has run away from his responsibilities and invested his manhood into a god-forsaken business. The young warrior has resigned to . . . have sexual relations with women of far much old[er age]." The writer worries that morans who sell sex undermine not only their own respectability but also "African" ideals of assertive, independent masculinity that morans had once epitomized. Defending values that he sees as essential to being African, the writer addresses a conservative middle-class audience that is likely to share some of his views. "How then," he asks, "do we accept this heinous act of a young African man evading his duties to marry a white woman 20 years older (a whole generation mark you) than he is, then sit, languor and be provided for?" He concludes (echoing the title of a 1990 novel by Maasai writer Henry R. ole Kulet) that "the Moran is no more!"[13]

Samburu men and women I spoke to invoked, if in different ways, the rhetoric of such criticism when they complained that "men are no longer men," family values have eroded, and that instead of hard work, youths now chose "shortcuts." In their view, morans who had sex for money jeopardized the respectability of Samburu more generally. What happens, then, when young men seek respectability and moral recognition primarily through the commodification of ethnosexuality, that is, through ways others deem immoral? What happens when, in the eyes of others, men selling sex couple their ethnicity with sexual perversion? And how are Samburu to gain recognition in a wider world when the global media coverage of the "moran mania" relies on stereotypes of their sexual immorality?

Such concerns emerged from specific political aspirations in the present. Around 2010, many Samburu suddenly began talking more intensely of ethnicity or tribe (S: *kabila* or M: *lorere*), anticipating new political possibilities. Throughout the previous decades, some Kenyan leaders and civil society groups had advocated for the devolution of the state into a form of ethnoregional federalism called *majimboism*, hoping that this system would allow for a more just distribution of national resources. Then, following promulgation of a new constitution in 2010 and its implementation after the 2013 elections, Samburu District became a self-governing *county*. That is, for the first time, locals rather than the central government appointed their leaders through elections. In anticipation of this moment, in 2010 a growing number of Samburu politicians hoped to turn the county into an ethnic corporation of sorts and market wildlife safaris and ethnic cultural heritage to foreign tourists. Others hoped to open NGOs and attract foreign donors to invest in regional development. Many rural Samburu had long been marginalized by leaders of more powerful ethnic groups who considered them primitive and backward. Now, they hoped that once their district leaders were Samburu, they would benefit more directly from government resources. As they envisioned autonomy, Samburu sought to rearticulate what it meant to belong locally, who was really Samburu, and who was therefore entitled to partake in forthcoming political and economic opportunities. In this context, some spoke out more vocally against Turkana and Somali refugees or against Kikuyu, Luo, and Kamba migrant settlers, who were minority groups in the area. Others inspected more closely who had sustained ties of patrilineal descent and age set in the region and who did not. Ethnicity and morality played important roles in their attempts to define belonging.

In recent decades, a preoccupation with belonging and autochthony has been common throughout the world. In *The Perils of Belonging*, Peter Geschiere (2009, 6) argues that in Africa, for example, "democratization and decentralization, the two main issues on the neoliberal agenda, have the paradoxical effect of triggering an obsession with belonging." Questions such as *who belongs?* and *how can one establish belonging?* become central concerns as communities reorganize themselves continuously in relation to new flows of global capital. In this context we witness, among other things, a "return to the local" or a rise of "localist thinking" (6, 27), varyingly expressed through the idioms of autochthony, ethnicity, indigeneity, or culture. In a similar vein, a central paradox of localist belonging is that it promises primordial, natural, and therefore safe and durable membership, while at the same time heightening concerns over who is *really* entitled to belong and who is not (38). So as new economic opportunities arise, Geschiere argues, "local communities are tending to close themselves and apply severe forms of exclusion of people who had earlier been considered fellows" (21). The stakes are high, for "struggles over local belonging are closely intertwined with the desire to be recognized as a citizen of the world" (27).

In Kenya, ethnicity represents a dominant mode of autochthonous belonging. Since the country's independence in 1963, ethnic categories that the British colonial administration have solidified through its politics of indirect rule now shaped competitions over state resources, access to land, and political authority. Larger ethnic groups, such as Kikuyu and Luo, but also Kamba and Kalenjin, dominated state governance and the distribution of national resources and development (Lynch 2011; Oucho 2002). Patron-client relations along lines of ethnic belonging as well as between the leaders and populations of different ethnic groups partly dictated the geopolitical distribution of wealth. Hence, electoral practices—as well as, for example, the election violence that took place most recently in 1997 and 2008—have been anchored in networks of patronage based on ethnicity (Mwakikagile 2001; Oucho 2002). Janet McIntosh (2016, 6) argues that in Kenyan public discourse, "entitlement to belong and to own land increasingly hinges on having deep ancestral roots in local soil." Ethnicity is a dominant mode for claiming such "roots" of primordial attachment through descent.

Kenya's ethnicities were, however, anything but equal. National and international development discourses concurred with colonial and postcolonial hierarchies of identity to depict some ethnic groups as modern, developed, and entrepreneurial, and others as traditional, underdeveloped, and backward. In this ideological order, Maasai, Samburu, Turkana, Pokot, Rendille, and other "pastoralists" figured as culturally conservative Others of the nation. Political leaders in Nairobi often saw these groups as undeserving of modernization, development, and national resources, and thus denied them the benefits of full citizenship. In Samburu, for example, the government had long invoked cultural backwardness to postpone building infrastructure and incorporating locals more fully in the labor economy. Yet since 1980, as populations grew rapidly, livestock holdings declined, and the effects of structural adjustment programs further limited government spending, some Samburu (and Maasai) have found new ways to subvert Kenya's ethnic hierarchy. Whereas in Kenya they occupied a basal and marginal position, on the global market, they soon found out, their identity was highly valued as more authentic and more exotic than those of other Kenyans. With otherwise limited access to resources, they consequently turned their marginality into a new source of capital.

In the past three decades, an increasing number of postcolonial subjects have found new venues to wealth through their ethnicity, in the process rediscovering the value of their identity and belonging in new ways. In *Ethnicity, Inc.*, John and Jean Comaroff (2009, 1) argue that following the effects of market liberalization, in Africa and other parts of the world ethnicity does not disappear but rather becomes "more implicated than ever before in the economics of everyday life." Seeking new ways of accessing resources, people commodify ethnicity or turn it into corporate enterprises. This trend, the Comaroffs argue, has raised new challenges for belonging. On the one hand, it "opened up new means of producing value, of claiming recognition, of asserting sovereignty, of giving affective voice to belonging" (142). On the other, the commodification and incorporation of ethnicity "may also entrench old lines of inequality, conduce to new forms of exclusion, increase incentives for the concentration of power, and create as much poverty as wealth" (52). As ethnicity offers new entrepreneurial possibilities, "the question arises . . . of who benefits from ethno-branding, the incorporation of identity, the accumulation of capital. And what impact it has on belonging" (108). Herein, ethnicity is increasingly anchored in hegemonic imaginaries of genetics, an imagined immutability of blood (38–46).[14] But questions of morality are also key in establishing the right to belong.

The commodification of Samburu ethnicity through moran ethnosexuality brought sexual morality to the forefront of struggles over belonging. That sex and sexuality are central sites of moral anxiety and uncertainty over belonging is nothing new. This has long been the case. But in the present, this also plays out in new ways. Paul Amar (2013) describes the emergence of a new obsession with sexuality throughout the global South with the rise of "human-security governance," a form of power sustained, among other things, by moral rehabilitation and the policing of "perverse" sexualities. In East Africa, the allegedly perverse sexualities of gays, lesbians, transvestites, prostitutes, and beach boys have been made, in recent years (if to different extents), to *both* congeal *and* bear responsibility for the failures of hegemonic expectations of family, kinship, and community. And this at a time when market reforms and social transformation often rendered such expectations unsustainable. Legal reforms and violent suppressions targeting homosexuals in Uganda and Kenya since 2008, more recent attacks on "loosely dressed" women in the capital cities of Kampala and Nairobi, and the daily police harassment of prostitutes and beach boys exemplify moral battles fought in the name of citizenship. Under these circumstances, invocations of the sexual immorality of morans directly challenged the belonging of Samburu to the nation-state and made their entitlement to national resources and state security questionable. Sexuality, as we shall see, increasingly defined entitlements to belonging and ethnicity, albeit in contested ways.

ON FIELDWORK, ITS ATTACHMENTS, AND ITS DETACHMENTS

I carried out a total of twenty-five months of field research in Kenya between 2005 and 2015. My shortest research trips were of two and three months' duration, and my longest (in 2010–11) was fifteen months. Most of my fieldwork was based in Samburu, in Maralal town and in two highland villages that I call Siteti and Lorosoro.[15] I also paid shorter visits to two other highland villages and two lowland villages. In addition, I undertook three months of research in the districts of Kwale and Mombasa at the Indian Ocean as I joined Samburu men in their seasonal migration to coastal beach resorts. There, I rented an apartment in the town of Mtwapa and also visited Samburu in Bamburi, Watamu, and Diani.

At the beginning of my fieldwork, I carried out a total of seventy-four household surveys in Siteti, Lorosoro, and two other Samburu locales. I wanted to understand the social and economic context of life in the district. I asked men and women about their family's economic pursuits, genealogy, and kinship relations, as well as about their plans for the future. These conversations also allowed me to learn about struggles and desires that preoccupied my interlocutors. Gradually, I began to sit down with them for longer, open-ended interviews about their life trajectories, their challenges, and the kinds of respectability and belonging that they desired. I recorded sixty-six such interviews with Samburu men and women and European women. Throughout my stay in Samburu, I helped organize and also participated in formal events such as clan ceremonies, weddings, funerals, disco parties, political rallies, and tourist shows. I also followed up through informal conversations on things I had seen or heard. Between scheduled interviews and formal events, I spent much time socializing with men and women while herding cattle, working in gardens, selling in shops and bars, or hanging out on street corners or at the beach. Having become part of my informants' lives over the years, I had the opportunity to document their oftentimes rapidly shifting life trajectories.

Most of my interlocutors knew that I was from Romania, an Eastern European country with many political and economic problems that were quite similar, in some regards, to those in Kenya. But they also knew that I lived, studied, and worked in the United States, and that I had more money than most rural Samburu families. Consequently, numerous interlocutors sought to anchor me in their own relations of kinship and care as a patron and sponsor. Over the years, I have agreed to support several close friends with gifts in cash and kind. But I also resisted numerous such demands so that I could sustain my research and living budget. A Siteti elder, for instance, was quite upset that I refused to marry his daughter (whom I did not know) or help him rebuild his mother's house. To him, it was clear that I was, in fact, refusing not only his gift of affective kinship but also his economic clientage that would have been intrinsic to such a relationship. Working in coastal sexual economies proved even more difficult, as I had to figure out how to politely divert requests to participate in sex-for-money exchanges while spending many hours talking to people about such transactions. Although in many of these circumstances I preferred to remain unattached, these were key learning experiences. After all, many of my interlocutors—both Samburu and European—shared similar daily dilemmas.

In a context in which sex, ethnicity, and belonging were highly controversial topics, one of the greatest challenges of my field research was to navigate between groups of people who had strong and divergent views on these issues. Men who traveled to the coast, their European partners, village elders, and urban middle-class youth and traders did not always share similar aspirations and goals, and at times distrusted one another or kept one another at a distance. During my first trip to Kenya, I lived near Lorosoro in the house of a Samburu elder named Francis. Francis was an Anglican missionary who was fluent in English. I had met him in a roadside restaurant in the town of Maralal, when I had just begun to learn Maa language and was making little progress with my research. We became friends, and he invited me to stay in his homestead. His sons, who were the same age as I was, introduced me to herding cattle and to life in Lorosoro. Locals quickly associated me with Francis's family, with his clan (the Lorokushu), and with the age set of his moran sons. That would have been alright with me if locals hadn't also assumed, as they did at first, that I, too, was a missionary, probably from the American church that sponsored Francis. Furthermore, as I became more interested in working with young men who migrated to the coast, Francis disapproved of my being friends with beach boys. He considered them disrespectful, sexually promiscuous, and vain in their pursuit of wealth. This he told me frankly. While we remained on friendly terms, I gradually detached myself from him and made other, closer friends in Lorosoro. Making friends across such lines of distrust and disregard, without really belonging to any one category of people as such, was difficult. But my socioeconomic status doubtless allowed me to attach or detach myself more or less as I pleased, while many of my informants did not have this privilege, at least not to the same extent.

On another occasion, I lived for a few months in the compound of a rich Samburu man married to a woman from Germany. Although many of my friends and research interlocutors disregarded my landlords for various reasons, I liked my apartment and explained to others that I was merely a tenant in that homestead. Soon, however, my landlords told me that they did not want me to receive visits from beach boys or "paupers" from town (I explore this incident in chapter 4). So, contrary to the old anthropological lore on the value of deep fieldwork immersion through kinship, I decided that the best way to sustain companionships with people of different backgrounds was to live on my own. I rented a small house with a garden and a chicken coop on the outskirts of Maralal. From there I traveled by foot or motorbike to spend the day or the week in different villages.

MONEY, LOVE, AND DILEMMAS OF INTIMACY

"If you want money, you should go ask my co-wife," Denise, a woman from France, recalled telling her Samburu father-in-law. "Just go to her," she said, her voice trembling with anger. "She's the one who has been eating all my money, all these years." Then she took a deep puff from her cigarette and looked at me. "These people are impossible, *bwana* [S, man]."

It was July 2008, and I was visiting Denise at her house on a hilltop outside Maralal. Over a cup a tea, she told me of what had occurred in May that year. Journalists from a Nairobi television station had asked her and her husband, Masian, to appear in a feature about marriages between Samburu men and white women. Denise and Masian had separated four years prior. But the journalists did not know that. Because they offered to pay, Denise and Masian concealed their separation. They took the crew to Lorosoro, where Masian's family lived, and pretended to be happily married in the "bush." That, they thought, was what the journalists wanted to see. "We drove to the village with different cars," Denise recalled. She was laughing. "We got out of the car and played the greatest lovers ever. We held hands, walked around. . . . Then we got back in our cars, drove back, and never spoke again since." What angered Denise was that after the crew had left, Masian's father followed her to the car and asked her for money. "I can't stand it," she said. Then, referring to Samburu elders more generally, she explained, "For them, the *mzungu* [S, white person] means money. Behind your back, they tell their sons, 'Where did you find this one? She is so old. She is so fat.' And to your face, they will say [endearingly], 'Oh, nkerai ai, nkerai ai' [M, oh, my child, my child]. I hate it."

I had met Denise in 2005. A friend from Maralal recommended that I interview her. So one day, I went to her house to introduce myself. She lived in a spacious, luxurious villa with three bedrooms, fully equipped kitchen and bathrooms, and a beautiful flower garden. Denise was very talkative and outspoken, but also funny and welcoming. She had a passion for business and was quite entrepreneurial. (I was not surprised to learn later that she performed for the Nairobi TV crew in exchange for cash.) But she was also very contemplative, and spent long hours reading romance novels, writing poems, and listening to Leonard Cohen's music. Over the years, we became friends. We visited each other, exchanged books and movies, and had long conversations. "Here is another contribution for your research," she would preface the spiciest of her stories. "This one is perfect for your book," she would say.

Denise moved to northern Kenya in 1996, after she married Masian. She had met him on her first visit to the country in 1991, while on vacation at an all-inclusive beach resort in Malindi. Before moving to Kenya, Denise visited Masian once or twice per year. One time, she also paid for him to visit her in Paris, where she worked in the administrative office of a transportation company. "I cannot say that I had a bad life in France," she told me. "I had a secure job, I was living in the capital. . . . If I have chosen Kenya, it is first of all because of my relationship with Masian. Perhaps, if I had fallen in love with a man of another country, I would have moved somewhere else." Denise spent much money to buy land and build a house and commercial spaces to rent. She wanted to live a comfortable life. She also financed Masian to start a cattle farm in Lorosoro. Things went smoothly at first.

"He seemed to be a very quiet man," she recalled. "He was ready to discuss any decision with me, to listen to my advice. . . . He considered me more educated. And he was very concerned with the financial aspects of our life. He was not willing to spend money for stupidities or to listen to the requests of the members of his community or those of his family. Also, he was spending a lot of time with me. It was very romantic."

But money quickly became a matter of conflict between them. Said Denise, "My ex-family always had reasons to ask me for money: the children were sick, the animals were sick, they needed medicines for the livestock. . . . Also, the family was not limited to the father or the mother, which I could accept and understand. But the brothers, the married sisters, the uncles, and cousins were all at my gate almost every day to request my help. I couldn't help them all. So Masian became very aggressive and abusive with me." She sighed. "I realized that to be a white woman in this community meant that I was there to solve all their problems."

Denise was concerned about the extent to which money enabled or corrupted, for her, the possibility of genuine love, intimacy, and affective attachment. Ongoing requests of money prompted her to question her ties to Masian and his family. She was aware, of course, of the discrepancy between her wealth and theirs. So, early in her married life, she had decided to pay for the education of Masian's younger brother and to bring into her house and care for a young boy of his lineage. This she enjoyed doing. But she was hurt to think that Masian and his family saw her primarily as a source of money. For her, love, friendship, and family did not foreclose material support. But the frequency and quantities of others' demands troubled her. Denise often told me that "Samburu beach boys ripped off sex tourists in Mombasa." But, living in Kenya, she did not see herself as a tourist—much less a sex tourist—nor did she think of her marriage as a commodified exchange.

So she struggled to understand why Masian and his family felt entitled to her resources.

Eight years into their marriage, Denise found out that Masian had married a second wife, a young Samburu woman from Lorosoro. She felt cheated. In her view, Masian and his family had lied to her, because they were interested in her wealth. "The power of money has affected my marriage," she told me. "Masian bought the silence of the elders, forcing them to hide the second marriage he made without my consent. This is in total contradiction with the rules of the Samburu community. Polygamy exists, but the first wife is always aware of the arrival of a co-wife, and she is supposed to give her consent." Denise and Masian separated immediately. When Masian's father intervened to settle the dispute, Denise accused him of concealing his son's second marriage. Then, four years later, Denise was hurt once again when the elder came to ask her for money during her visit to his village. She now thought that for her father-in-law, her money had always meant more than her affection and kinship.

Unlike Denise, most European women I met in Kenya continued to live abroad and maintained long-distance relationships with local men, but they shared some of her struggles with money and love. Was the money they gave their partners appreciated as a *gift*, or was it expected as part of a *commodified* exchange? Did their desire for intimacy imply material obligations toward their partners? And if so, did they also have to support their partners' families? And what could they expect in return? Preoccupied with the authenticity of intimacy—whether it was "real" or "false"—these women tried to figure out proper boundaries between money and intimacy. Their concern was part of what Viviana Zelizer (2005, 3) describes as a wider Euro-American obsession with "finding the right match between economic relations and intimate ties." Love and money could mix, but only in specific ways.

European women were not the only ones struggling to understand the monetary requests of the ones they desired and loved. Kenyan men and women faced similar challenges, though they dealt with them differently (Mojola 2014). In many African contexts, love and intimacy have long been imbedded in material exchanges (Cole 2009, 2010; Hunter 2010; Magubane 2004; Nyamnjoh 2005; Thomas and Cole 2009; L. White 1990). What, then, was distinct about such entanglements of sentiment and cash in the present? Certainly, commodification, or the process whereby exchange value is assigned to an object or service, was no longer about straightforward market exchanges. Rather, the logics of exchange value, investment, and risk now inflected domestic relations and familial attachments more intensively.

European women might not have always purchased ethnosexuality explicitly. There wasn't always something one can easily recognize as "sex work" or "sex tourism." For this reason, I also do not find such categories analytically productive for my purposes throughout this book. But the underlying exchange value of ethnosexuality shaped, in myriad ways, women's attachments to their long-term partners and husbands, and to their families. With the commodification of moran ethnosexuality, as we shall see, money infused intimacy and affective attachments, while the logics of kinship and belonging shaped how money circulated in both intimate and public domains.

ETHNO-EROTIC ECONOMIES

This book describes how the money and wealth produced at tourist resorts circulate in coastal migrant communities and farther, to Samburu District, in the north of the country. I offer the framework of ethno-erotic economies to conceptualize how the commodification of ethnosexuality is deeply entangled in processes whereby postcolonial subjects craft belonging. In the global economy of the late twentieth century, fantasies of ethnosexuality defined more intensively the exchange value of sexual labor, pornography, tourist destinations, and popular culture (Jacobs 2010; G. Mitchell 2015; Nagel 2003; Steven 2007; Stout 2014). Such fantasies, in turn, shaped postcolonial subjects' various forms of belonging and their claims to recognition, rights, and resources (Partridge 2012; Sheller 2012). I imagine ethno-erotic economies as extensive circulations of money, goods, and desires that, while anchored in the commodification of ethnosexuality, move far beyond sexual transactions as such to shape subjectivities, identities, and social worlds. Mapping ethno-erotic economies means showing how wider historical and political domains produce the kinds of eroticized and sexualized forms of Otherness available in tourism. It also means showing how such forms of alterity condition the ways in which those deemed Other can craft collective futures and carve out for themselves positions of political recognition and economic profit in the current world order.

Thinking through the framework of ethno-erotic economies, I problematize classic Marxist conceptual divisions between realms of economic production and social reproduction, an *inside* and an *outside* to the market (e.g., tourist market). For this reason, it is important to bear in mind that what I call ethno-erotic economies is not to be reduced to the tourist industry or, for that matter, to explicit sex-for-money transactions. Ethno-erotic economies entail both familial moments in rural homesteads and public encounters on tourist beaches, both intimate affairs of kinship and trans-

actional affairs of sex—all inflected more and more by the logics of commodification. Ethno-erotic economies are therefore a specific instance of *intimate
economies*. Ara Wilson (2004) coins that term to show how private spheres of
life that we usually think of as noneconomic are central sites of capitalism.
Wilson points out that although "modern capitalist systems of production
and marketing are considered less embedded in social life and less inflected
with local cultural meanings and identities," in fact they "are predicated on,
and continue to interact with, these local social realisms" (20). Ethno-erotic
economies are, then, intimate economies anchored in the production and
consumption of ethnosexuality.

A study of ethno-erotic economies moves beyond an anthropology of
tourism that is focused mainly on the relations between "hosts" and "guests"
in tourist sites. Such a narrower focus, I argue, occludes larger social arenas
of exchange, intimacy, and belonging that shape and are shaped by the ethnosexualities marketed in tourism. While focusing primarily on how ethnicity
and culture are matters of representation, performance, and commodification, anthropologists of tourism and cultural commodification paid little
attention to how representations of alterity materialize their effects, over
time, outside the immediate contexts of their performance and transaction.
In stark contrast to this trend, some anthropologists recently began exploring how the tourist commodification of sex shapes intimacies outside
tourist resorts. Noelle Stout (2014) shows how, with market liberalization in
post-Soviet Cuba, queer youths draw on tourist ads and international porno-
graphic productions that eroticize their bodies in order to commodify sex
and intimacy in tourism. As some Cubans sell sex and intimacy, Stout notes,
domestic relations between family, friends, and dependents are increasingly
framed like commodity exchanges, giving rise to complex moral dilemmas.
Stout understands these moral struggles as intricately linked to sexual commodification and as part of an "erotic economy" that entails tourist sites
along with domestic arrangements, consumptive practices, and more. I build
on Stout's work to show how ethno-erotic economies intensified the commodification of intimacy, ritual, and kinship in Samburu; how they generated
paradoxical temporalities and subjectivities; and how all these came to transform notions of respectability and good life inherent to belonging.

Ethno-erotic economies are not closed or static systems of exchange but
complex *circuits* that can be mapped in different ways, from different vantage
points. In this book, I choose to explore how the commodification of moran
sexuality shapes the lives of Samburu. However, one can take other routes by
following, say, Maasai of southern Kenya and northern Tanzania or even non-

Maa-speaking Kenyan men as they commodify moran sexuality and imagine futures; Kenyan women who make lives performing different ethnosexualities—Kamba, Kikuyu, Giriama—for African, European, and, more recently, Chinese and Russian men; Kenyan men and women who move with their partners to Europe; and so on. At different times throughout this book, I offer glimpses of some of these diverse bifurcations of Kenya's ethno-erotic economies. However, I focus mainly on how Samburu craft belonging.

MY POSITION IN ETHNO-EROTIC ECONOMIES

During my fieldwork, I often found myself to be the object of erotic speculation and the subject of ethnosexualization in ways that are significant to understanding the somewhat odd position from which I began to map ethno-erotic economies. Take the following example. It was in the midst of my fieldwork, sometime in January 2011. The dry season had begun with a torrid heat that rapidly paved the way for a short but harsh drought in the Samburu highlands. It was late afternoon, and I was resting in the shade of my house in Maralal, exhausted from a six-mile walk to and from an interview. I found myself looking indifferently in the direction of my chicken coop. There, a rooster was mounting chickens. That was when Mama Jacinta, a neighbor, walked into my compound. Mama Jacinta and I had been good friends for many years. She was a widow in her fifties who enjoyed cooking at my house, chatting, or relaxing when she had too much trouble with her teenage children. Over time, we established a joking relationship of sorts, laughing about things that people would normally not discuss across gender and age divides. She caught me by surprise watching the rooster.

"What are you seeing that is so interesting?" she asked with a smile.

"Well, this shameless rooster has no boundaries," I joked.

Mama Jacinta laughed, embarrassed by what I had said, and yet, feeling licensed by my vulgar joking, proceeded to joke further.

"You know something, George?" she said with a playfully harsh tone. "Go in the house, work on your studies, and let the rooster have his fun. You must not get angry with him, just because you're not getting any."

Although Mama Jacinta's remark made me feel uncomfortable at that moment, it caused me to reflect on how my friends and research collaborators sexualized my presence in ways I had not anticipated. For many of my interlocutors, it was inconceivable that a white man with more money than many of them and with the status of studying and working in North American universities would travel alone without also consuming sex. What is more, during my fieldwork I was in my twenties and early thirties, an age span when men were expected to be sexually active, often with multiple partners. In the case of the young men I worked with in Samburu, their access to money was sometimes made visible to others through the conspicuous consumption of expensive goods and sex. However, as neighbors and friends like Mama Jacinta carefully observed my every move, it soon became clear to many that even my rooster was having more fun than I was.

I preferred to maintain an asexual presence during my research; as a person who identifies as queer, my choice had to do with issues of safety at a time when outbursts of homophobic violence had become more common in Kenya than previously. In addition, I was hoping to avoid gossip that could affect my ability to move between different social categories of interlocutors. Yet gossip proliferated nevertheless. Locals saw my emerging friendships— if in different ways at different times—through stereotypes that were anything but new. Mama Jacinta, for instance, avoided going shopping in town with me, anticipating that people might read sex into our otherwise platonic friendship. One time, when I stopped to greet her in town and took a few steps along with her, another woman called out in front of others, "Mama Jacinta, you got yourself a *mzungu* [white person]?"

Mama Jacinta and I often joked about this incident, even though from then on we avoided walking together. However, my research assistant, Anna, was less concerned about what people said when they saw us together. Anna was a teacher, wife, and mother in her midthirties. When the elders of her native clan began addressing me as *lautani*, a kinship term meant for in-laws, or when her husband became very jealous of our friendship, she kept dismissing them to me as "backward people" who could not see that nonsexual friendships could exist between nonrelated men and women. Anna earned good money from her salaries and several businesses, and she also paid for her husband's education, somewhat undermining his claims to authority as a husband. So she kept working with me even after her husband expressed his dissatisfaction. Anna and I were close friends. We walked together to interview women, we ate in local restaurants, and we spent long hours discussing local social issues. Soon our friendship came to be understood by others as an adulterous affair. That I liked a married woman was okay. Many young men did. But that she was a married woman spending so much time with an unmarried younger man was not. Her husband became very jealous, and elders of their community had to intervene to calm him down. Eventually, he said, he understood that we were just friends. But the town did not. When, before I left for the United States in 2011, Anna organized a surprise party for me with over a hundred guests and cried uncontrollably at the end, people had no doubt that this had been a passionate adulterous relationship. Mama Jacinta, too, with her usual expressive smiles, was happy to realize in the end that, like my rooster, I did have my share of fun on the side, even if it was with other men's wives. Although I remained uncomfortable with such sexual speculations throughout my fieldwork, I also realized that they were not only inevitable but—more important—central to how people imagined and shaped the circulations of sex, desire, and money that characterized the wider ethno-erotic economies I was exploring. In this context, the anthropologist and his interlocutors did not come onto the social scene with fully formed subjectivities, but as they positioned themselves with each other, they claimed and contested subject positions in countless ways. Notions of race, class, gender, and sexuality played an important role in the articulation of such subject positions.

OVERVIEW OF CHAPTERS

Ethno-erotic Economies is divided into six chapters. The first two chapters provide the necessary background for understanding the contemporary effects of the commodification of moran ethnosexuality. Chapter 1 offers a historical overview of how the moran emerged as a figure of discourse in government, missionary, and developmental reforms, from the early colonial period until the present. Representations of the moran and his ethnosexuality played an important ideological role in the growing geopolitical and economic marginalization of Samburu regions and population in Kenya. Since the mid-twentieth century, the moran congealed the ambiguity of a central contradiction: on the one hand, he embodied a morally problematic, excessive sexuality; on the other hand, his eroticized bodily appearance became emblematic of nationalist ideals of assertive masculinity and tourist imaginings of exotic African warriorhood.

Chapter 2 outlines the social and economic conditions that gave rise to various practices of cultural and sexual commodification since the 1970s. I introduce the reader to how Samburu imagined respectability, and to how kinship, age-set relations, and ethno-regional belonging, more generally, have been strained in various ways by economic and social transformations. As the effects of landownership reforms and structural adjustment programs intersected with the outcomes of droughts, declining cattle economies, and rapid population growth, people devised all kinds of new ways to make a living. In this context, some men and women increasingly sold both culture and sex—either separately or together—to earn money.

Relationships between Samburu men and European women became

common in this context. Chapter 3 explores how men and women imagined and negotiated intimacy and the authenticity of moran sexuality at
Kenya's coastal resorts. Detailing how Samburu men performed moranhood and ethnosexuality, what European women expected from their relationships with morans, and how partners negotiated their respective expectations with each other, this chapter maps a set of paradoxes of intimacy
and commodification. Women desired both the cultural difference for which
morans stood as well as the possibility to transcend that difference and live
out romantic fantasies. Men sought their partners' financial support at the
same time that they perceived their partners' attempts to control their
whereabouts as undermining their masculinity. And partners contested how
money threatened the authenticity of sex, intimacy, and romance, thus producing new configurations of intimate commodification. Situating these encounters within the wider sexual economies of coastal Kenya, I show how
such intimacies were inherently slippery, prompting social actors to fix and
stabilize racial, ethnic, and cultural difference as a condition of their ethno-
erotic exchanges.

The following three chapters return to Samburu to show how circulations of money, styles, and desires generated in coastal economies shaped
belonging in northern Kenya. Chapter 4 describes how men who returned
with wealth from Mombasa became the object of salient gossip and moral
criticism; how these men reevaluated their life trajectories and produced
new subjectivities; and how local men and women contested what they saw
as morally dubious forms of production that involved sex, sorcery, theft, and
AIDS and that polluted wealth and, through it, the social world. So-called
Mombasa morans, or men who return from coastal towns with money,
wanted to convert their wealth into local recognition and respectability.
Meanwhile, locals desired the material support of these men while deriding
the sexual pursuits in which their wealth originated. What ensued was a
complex dialogue—often indirect exchanges through the performance of
style, consumption, gossip, songs, and everyday encounters—through which
Mombasa morans and local men and women renegotiated the meanings of
reciprocity, sociality, and kinship.

In chapter 5, I describe how, as men involved in tourism tried to convert
their wealth into the social value of ethno-regional belonging, they often subverted its cultural logics. Representations and practices associated with descent, age sets, age grades, marriage, and bridewealth promised to anchor
moral persons and collectivities in local social worlds. But some of these men
invested money in weddings, elderhood rituals, or polygynous families way

ahead of time, while others struggled to catch up on meeting expectations associated with their life course. This prompted people throughout the district to reimagine the meanings of specific social attachments. Exploring salient subject positions such as the young big man, the beach-boy elder, and the madman, this chapter demonstrates how subversive events and desires worked to transform respectability and belonging, sometimes in unexpected ways. These transformations then opened new future-making possibilities.

Chapter 6 details how impoverished rural men and women in Samburu used clan rituals as the means for challenging their growing alienation and marginalization as well as the patronage and authority of new local elites, including men enriched in tourism. The *lopiro* ritual complex, organized once every fifteen years, dealt with the effects of adulterous sex and foreign commodities on everyday life in Samburu as well as with the myriad effects of ethno-erotic commodification. Because rural families understood new dynamics of sex and commodities as underming ideals of morality, respectability, and propitious life, through the rituals of *lopiro*, they hoped to anchor sex in lineage relations and to domesticate foreign commodities. In this context, "being Samburu" became a matter of also positioning oneself morally in relationship to recent historical dynamics of sexual commodification.

Ethno-erotic Economies claims that a dialectical relationship exists between the global commodification of moran ethnosexuality on the one hand and the ways in which Samburu craft belonging in northern Kenya on the other. It describes how men and women struggle to reconcile older expectations of respectability, morality, and good life with the social and economic transformations that have arrived with tourist markets of ethnosexuality. It shows how, as these struggles unfold, new forms of exclusion and empowerment, inequality and respectability emerge, along with new ways to belong and build a future.

1. Moran Sexuality and the Geopolitics of Alterity

The question of identification . . . is always the production of an image of identity
and the transformation of the subject in assuming that image.

—HOMI BHABHA, *THE LOCATION OF CULTURE*

"Sexually transmitted diseases aren't a pleasant conversation or a source of pride for many Kenyans. . . . But, today, in Samburu County, there are some who consider getting an STD a rite of passage." So began a special feature story broadcast on Kenya Television Network (KTN) on October 4, 2014. The fifteen-minute reportage was entitled "A Moran's Cold." The morans it depicted were Samburu. And their "cold," it turned out, was gonorrhea. "Many morans will not use condoms," the young female reporter explained, "and, because of this, there is a growing concern about the number of gonorrhea infections in Samburu County." Over footage of morans in colorful attire singing and dancing, she noted that "gonorrhea is on the rise among morans," and that these young men take pride in acquiring the infection, as it "establishes their manhood." "The culture of sharing lovers is nothing new, and it is also seen in modern society," she concluded as she stood in front of a Samburu settlement. Whereas, she explained, people in "modern society" know how to protect themselves from sexually transmitted infections (STIs), in Samburu, "change has to start with the simple recognition that gonorrhea, like other STIs, is not merely a common cold."

Part of a series suggestively entitled *The Other Kenya*, this KTN feature story highlighted the depth of Samburu cultural otherness through a focus on moran sexuality. It spoke to an imagined audience that considers sexual promiscuity and unprotected sex socially irresponsible. Its narrative drew on a long-standing paradigm in Kenya, according to which Samburu sexual lives figure in moral opposition to the Christian notions of sexual propriety that anchor middle-class aspirations. Such aspirations and their moral opposites have played a central role in the imagination and articulation of national citizenship. The logic of the televised feature story was forthright: in sharp contrast to respectable Kenyan citizens—who would be embarrassed to talk about, let alone acquire, STIs—Samburu morans proudly assert their "manhood" by getting gonorrhea. In this narrative, what distinguishes Samburu from "modern society" is their lack of knowledge about sexual matters. Morans, so the argument goes, act on instinct rather than reason and thus spread gonorrhea, unaware of its severity. According to this logic, morans fall short of the demands of moral, rational citizenship because of their alleged ignorance and libidinal excess.

The KTN segment may have ridiculed Samburu morans in order to entertain its imagined audience of middle-class Kenyans, but it also expressed nostalgia for the morans' masculine assertiveness and sexual indulgence. As the reporter explained:

> [Morans] are the foundation of the Samburu community. They roam the lands, revered by all, yet answerable to no one. They only pledge allegiance to members of their own age sets. Because they stay segregated from the rest of the community, morans are allowed to take lovers. When he sees a girl he wants, the moran will sing a song. And in most Samburu clans, if a girl agrees, she is given beads as a sign that she belongs to a moran. . . . When the relationship is over, they are both free to find new lovers, and that's where the problem lies.

In Samburu, the KTN journalist discovered a protosexuality unburdened by risk and responsibility, and an assertive masculinity unthreatened by diseases. "Revered by all" and "answerable to no one," morans lead lives of sexual freedom. In ways that echo a long history of both romantic nostalgia and moral derision, morans figure here as the nation's "bad boys" (cf. Waller 2010). This narrative on moran sexuality was widely shared in the Kenyan national media and more generally in Kenyan public discourse.

Why have morans become so central to discourses of respectability, moral responsibility, and sexual propriety in Kenya? How has the national media come to assign sexual and cultural otherness to Samburu morans? How have such discourses shaped the material realities of political belonging in the region? And how have locals positioned themselves historically in relation to discourses about morans and their sexuality? Answering these questions is crucial if we are to understand how and why moran sexuality later became a best-selling commodity in Kenya's tourist industry. Colonial and postcolonial discourses of ethnosexuality were complexly entangled in the growing political and economic marginalization of Samburu regions and populations throughout the twentieth century. The emergence of the discursive category of moran sexuality and its subsequent transformations relate, as we shall see, to how colonial leaders built ethnic regions and sought to reform social life. They also relate to how development ideologies, Christian values, and middle-class aspirations shaped moral hierarchies of ethnic and regional belonging in the postcolonial context.

STEPPING BACK IN TIME: ETHNOREGIONAL MARGINALIZATION IN SAMBURU

Those who travel for the first time from Kenya's capital city of Nairobi to Samburu, in the northern part of the country, often describe their trip as a journey back in time. The impression is understandable. As the green hills of the Rift Valley gradually give way to semiarid savannah plains, towns become smaller and smaller, and cultivated farms slowly morph into dense bush with occasional sightings of zebras, giraffes, and sometimes even lions. Eventually, you begin to spot small settlements of mud dwellings with thorn fences and people dressed in colorful fabric with bead decorations. To many, this is a world so saliently different from that of central Kenya that Kenyans and foreigners alike venerate the north as a place of traditional African culture. But they also see it as a hub of poverty and underdevelopment.

One hundred forty miles north of Nairobi, the tarmac road ends abruptly. For the remaining hundred miles, the journey continues on a dusty dirt road. It may take nine hours to reach Maralal, the administrative headquarters of Samburu. During the rainy season, the journey might take even longer, as vehicles get stuck in the mud and struggle to escape. Safety is an issue, too. At times, when rains destroy the road, armed carjackers ambush vehicles, demanding money and cell phones. "Six days traversing Samburu," writes a Kenyan journalist, "and the experience was like stepping back in time. Roads are in a pathetic state. This pastoralist community seems forgotten."[1] Another journalist traveling on the same road in 2015 recalled how "the driver of the . . . shuttle that I boarded to Nyahururu . . . thought I should have my head examined when I told him my final destination." "You may die of any-thing," the driver warned, "cold or heat, animal attack or bandit assault."[2]

My friends and acquaintances in Nairobi and Mombasa wondered why I chose to do research in Samburu. There, they would say, "people lived like they did a hundred years ago." Although most of these interlocutors had never traveled to Samburu, they described the region as "primitive" and "backward," borrowing from the rhetoric of Kenyan media and state devel-opment. Some of them blamed poverty in northern regions on politicians who had neglected these areas. Others blamed it on the northerners them-selves and their alleged reluctance to abandon archaic cultures and embrace modernization. No matter who is to blame, however, middle-class Kenyans often invoke dominant discourses of socioeconomic progress to place Sam-buru and other pastoralists in the nation's past. In doing so, they perform what anthropologist Johannes Fabian (1983) described as a "denial of tem-poral coevalness" of the Other, that is, a denial of a shared contemporaneity between the speaking subject and the cultural others invoked. As a Nairobi businesswoman explained to me, trying to convince me of the backwardness of my research site, "Those kind of mud houses that they have in Samburu, those haven't existed in central Kenya for many, many years. Those Sambu-rus are left behind." In this sense, southern Kenyans often perceive traveling to Samburu as a way to displace themselves temporally, to step back in time. Euro-American travelers, writers, and development workers who visit the re-gion often agree with this modernist narrative of unilineal temporal mobility. On her way back from Samburu to Nairobi, Swiss writer Corinne Hofmann (2006, 143) noted how "the road improves as we approach civilization." Ken-yans and foreigners alike invoke this paradigm of temporal displacement to situate Samburu regions and populations at a distance from "civilization," the capital city, and middle-class values. Thus, through what historian Anne McClintock (1995, 30) describes as a common modernist trope, the road to Samburu is for many "proceeding forward in geographical space, but back-ward in historical time."

This temporal paradigm of cultural Otherness offers Kenyans and for-eigners a meaningful narrative for grasping the sharply unequal regional dis-tribution of wealth and privilege in Kenya. However, this paradigm is also deceptive in that it occludes its own ideological complicity in the very pro-duction of marginalized regions and populations. Since the advent of British colonialism, administrators have invoked social disorder and radical cultural difference to marginalize northern regions. They argued that cattle raids and intertribal wars were frequent in the north, and that the region had no marketable resources. British administrator Lieutenant Lytton made this point bluntly with regard to Samburu in 1924. "The Samburu are economically unsound (from the Imperial point of view)," he said, adding that "it is therefore best to confine an unprofitable people to as small an area as possible."[3] The colonial state relegated Samburu, along with other pastoral tribes, to the Northern Frontier District, a region kept separate from Kenya's markets and requiring special access permits (Simpson 1994). The colonial government then postponed building infrastructure and initiating modernization projects in the area. After Kenya's independence in 1963, politicians continued to use stereotypes of Samburu and other northern pastoralists as disobedient and irrational people in order to keep delaying investment in the region.

Over the course of the twentieth century, northerners came to understand their position within the Kenyan state as marginal. Many thought that relative to southern ethnic groups, they were—as they would put it—"lagging behind" (S: *kubaki nyuma*) in achieving development (S: *maendeleo*), or that they needed to "catch up" or "push forward" (S: *kuvuta mbele*). This developmental notion of progressive time came to play an important role in how they understood their relationship to the state. When considering the relative absence of infrastructure, the lack of proper schools and health care facilities, rampant unemployment, and poor security in their district, they questioned their belonging to the state. Samburu have articulated this perceived exclusion by suggesting that Kenya lay elsewhere, south of their district, in the capital city of Nairobi and its environs (Holtzman 2004, 64–65). Since independence, political leaders from other ethnic groups, such as Kikuyu, Luo, or Kalenjin, have controlled the distribution of state resources. Many northerners see these ethnic groups as being ahead (S: *mbele*) of them on an imagined path to development, and emphasize their own alienation at the hands of these political leaders. This mode of temporal hierarchization of ethnicities not only shapes national belonging but also sustains and legitimates the unequal distribution of resources. Some Samburu would describe themselves as the nation's Others, because they feel they have been cheated out of their share of the state's resources.

While some Kenyans imagine Samburu to inhabit a backward past, Samburu themselves draw on similar notions of time and development to articulate their respective positions in the district. Jon Holtzman (2004, 71–76) shows how Samburu distinguish between those of them living in the lowlands (M: *lpurkel*) and those living in the highlands (M: *ldoinyio*). Both highlanders and lowlanders generally perceive the lowlands as backward spaces, in which people have little access to resources and live in harsh conditions. That fewer people in the lowlands went to school, had access to employment, or wore modern clothes enhanced their image of backwardness. On our first research trip to lowland villages, my research assistant, a highland resident, remarked in English, "These people are very primitive, surely!" By contrast, the highlands are seen as a space of development and economic possibilities. In the highlands, many people own farmland, live in modern houses, have some education, and occasionally benefit from informal work opportunities. While lowlanders see themselves as marginalized in relation to the highlanders, highlanders also think of the lowlands nostalgically as "a bastion of true Samburu culture," where people have a "greater sense of respect and social responsibility" (75). During my research, Ldereva, a Samburu elder from the lowlands, had moved to the highland village of Siteti to live on his brother's land. He told me he wanted to make money. "I saw with my own mind," he said, "the difference between the lowlands and here." As if to make his point more strongly, he switched from Maa to Swahili, a language he used more often in his daily dealings with traders in Maralal's markets. "Here is the forefront of the Samburu [S: hapa ni mbele ya Samburu]. I cannot return there, backwards [S: siwezi kurudi huko nyuma]." For Ldereva, moving between the lowlands and the highlands was thus a way to travel in time, to move forward on a path to development and prosperity. Ldereva's name translates as "driver," a choice that, he said, reflected his parents' desire for their son to become a rich big man and own a car. Although Ldereva owned no more than two cows and thirty goats, he stayed true to his parents' desire by moving to the highlands to seek personal development. For him, as for Kenyans in general, development came with belonging to regions that offered security and economic prosperity.

For the past century, Samburu have seen the road connecting their district to Nairobi as a key idiom for the creation and contestation of their belonging to the state and a world beyond Kenya. During conversations with elderly Samburu, I learned that for many of them, the road still prompts memories of violent extraction of material resources and labor. They remembered how, in the first half of the twentieth century, colonial administrators forced morans to join labor camps and build the main road of the district. Traders from other parts of the country traveled along this road to Samburu to purchase livestock and hides at lower prices than in the south and import foreign commodities at much higher prices. As a result, they used and perpetuated the relative geopolitical marginality of the region to maximize their own earnings. It was along this road, too, that several generations of morans migrated to southern Kenya to sell their labor. As more and more young men migrated down country and returned with money and goods, Samburu came to see this road as an avenue to a land of riches and heightened economic possibilities. And so, for many of them, the deplorable conditions of the road became iconic of their peripheral position within Kenya. Generations of southern political leaders came to power by promising to tarmac the road, improve infrastructure, and intensify the economic linkages between the south and the north. Yet little has happened so far.

Instead, northern Kenya has become a zone of relative legal and fiscal deregulation that allows myriad shadow economies to flourish. Take, for example, cattle raiding. Often portrayed in the national media as an archaic practice of traditional pastoral tribes, cattle raiding, in its current form, represents an instantiation of the neoliberal economy (Roitman 2005). Collaborating with local morans, politicians and businessmen have generated new modes of speculation and entrepreneurialism. Through violent raids, they sometimes extract thousands of cattle from local economies to be transported to the south and sold on the national beef market. Meanwhile, the media, in depicting these raids as archaic interethnic feuds, ideologically erases the historical context of these shadow economies and legitimizes exceptional measures for policing and securitizing the region.

To read the trip to Samburu as a way of stepping back in time is to miss how developmental ideologies work to shape regions, their material conditions, and their modes of belonging to the state. It is to miss how political leaders and reformists use linear ideas of progress and modernization paradoxically to include Samburu as exceptional and inferior within networks of state patronage and the market economy. It is also to miss how geopolitical and ethnic marginality synthesizes and instantiates long-standing contradictions between the discourses of the powerful and the lives of those on the fringes of the state.

The figure of the moran has played a central role historically in both shaping geopolitical marginality and creating venues of empowerment in Samburu. Narratives of Samburu cultural difference and temporal Otherness often focus extensively on the moran, his visual image, and his behaviors. Journalists, missionaries, administrators, and a wider Kenyan public depict the predisposition of morans to fight, raid, and kill, as well as their alleged sexual promiscuity, as cultural remnants of a precolonial past. Violence and sex have been at the forefront of public discourse and disciplinary interventions since the advent of British colonialism. In depicting morans as agents of sexually transmitted disease, the KTN segment I described in the opening of this chapter drew on ideas about moran sexuality that were deeply rooted in Kenyan public discourse. To understand the meanings of the television segment, its audience had to think of Samburu as cultural and moral Others of the nation, and of morans as key representatives of their culture. Only then could viewers find the segment noteworthy and perhaps even entertaining. It is important, then, to explore the logics of these discourses as well as their origins, in order to understand the historical role the moran has had in the making of Samburu ethnosexuality and alterity.

MAA MORANS AND THE ORIGINS OF AN OTHERING IMAGE

In 2008, while interviewing men who traveled to the Kenyan coast, I asked what it meant for them to be Samburu. I should have known that by implying an essentialist identity, my question inevitably called for a reductionist response. Despite my oversight, their answers struck me in one regard. Most of them invoked, in one way or another, a singular image of the moran. "Being Samburu," one man suggested, "is to keep this culture of the moran, with the red ocher [M: *lkaria*] and the long hair [M: *lmasi*]." "It is about wearing these beads and feathers," another man explained, pointing to his moran attire. Their answers gestured specifically to the visual appearance of the moran. Moranhood has long been emblematic of tradition in Samburu (Holtzman 2009, 169). And the moran's style and bodily appearance also play an important role in the region (Kasfir 2007, 201–35). But tourism, no doubt, has accentuated locals' perception that the moran's visual image is a most valuable aspect of their culture. Consequently, schoolchildren in the district often dress up as morans and perform moran dances in regional festivals and contests; local businesses—including radio stations, honey retailers, and restaurants—adopt the image of the moran as their main brand logo; and the fundraising ads of Samburu NGOs often display pictures of morans.

But the story becomes more complex here. While some Samburu embrace the moran image as an object of cultural pride, foreigners and Kenyans from down country do not always recognize morans *as* Samburu. When they encounter young Samburu men dressed in traditional attire in Nairobi, on the coast, or on the television, they often assume they are Maasai. Indeed, I observed that these young men sometimes introduced themselves to tourists as Maasai. So I asked Saitoti, a man I interviewed in Watamu in 2011, to explain why this was so. "Let me tell you the truth about our history," he offered.

> The Samburu are just Maasai. But, long time ago, they separated. Samburu stayed north, and the other Maasai went south, even into Tanzania. . . . But, you see, the tourists don't want those Maasai from the south, because they have lost most of their culture. Us, the Samburu, we still have the old Maasai culture. If you look at us and you look at them, you will see that they don't wear those beads around the neck like we do.

Saitoti referred to the bead decorations of the morans. "That is the original culture," he said. "That is what tourists want to see." For Saitoti, Samburu were the more original Maasai, and the visual image of their morans a more authentic version of Maasai culture. While many Maasai would surely disagree with Saitoti's description, it is important to note how he claimed relatedness to Maasai to articulate the market value of Samburu culture and morans. Saitoti's claim, though, is not his alone. Nor is it new. Rather, it has long colonial roots. As morans became emblematic of both Maasai and Samburu throughout the twentieth century, colonials and Kenyans alike coupled these identities to invest morans with radical cultural Otherness.

In the present, the image of the moran is emblematic of Samburu ethnicity, even when Samburu are seen as Maasai. However, at the turn of the twentieth century, this had not been the case. When I began archival research, I expected to find numerous images of Samburu morans from the early colonial period. But I did not. References to morans were sporadic and thin, and the young men did not appear in any lithographs or photos from the turn of the twentieth century. In stark contrast, other East African people and their respective warriors figured prominently in the colonial archives.[4] I later learned that there were at least two reasons for this absence. First, at the turn of the century, Samburu lost people and livestock in very large numbers to war, disease, and droughts. Even today, elderly Samburu I spoke to referred to this period as a time of disaster (M: *emutai*), and did not recall any heroic stories about the age set that went through moranhood at that time. In order to survive in relative safety, Samburu—then no more than three thousand people—settled among neighboring ethnic groups. During this time, they lost, if only briefly, any strong sense of collective cohesion.[5] So for travelers, Samburu of those days did not have any of the glamour and aura they were to acquire half a century later. Second, in the late nineteenth century, moranhood was not associated with Samburu exclusively. Warrior age grades were very common in precolonial East Africa. They played an important military role in securing access to cattle, land, or clients (Fadiman 1976; Waller 1993). At a time when wars and ecological crisis had weakened Samburu, the warriors of other tribes appealed to travelers more. Take, for example, the Maasai. Maasai morans stood out, from the very beginning of colonial rule, as the most fearless and dangerous yet noble of the East African warriors (Hughes 2006; Sobania 2002). Having dominated the Rift Valley for over half a century, Maasai were, according to John Lonsdale (1992, 19), "the lords of the Rift." So while early travelers and colonial administrators focused extensively on Maasai morans, their Samburu counterparts received relatively little attention.

But it was at this time that the very category of a pan-Maa people gradually emerged to include Maasai, Samburu, and Chamus. This, of course, is not to say that these different groups did not recognize similarities between themselves, in custom, language, or descent, prior to colonialism. Indeed, they had invoked common cultural grounds for a variety of purposes, and people had moved between these identities at different times. But the classification of tribes by cultural, linguistic, and phenotypic traits, for purposes of governance, was something new. And, quite interestingly, it was by looking at the bodies and decorations of Samburu morans that explorers and administrators classified, for the first time, Samburu as part of the family of Maa people. As one traveler to northern Kenya explained at the turn of the century, Samburu "are not yet definitely classified by ethnologists" (Hardwick 1903, 210). But they "are very like the Maasai or the Wakafi of Njemps [Chamus] in appearance, wearing their hair in pigtail in the same manner, while their clothing and ornaments are very similar" (223). When approached by a group of one hundred Samburu morans, another traveler noticed: "They exactly resembled Masai [*sic*] warriors, wore their hair in the same style of tonsure, and were armed in identical manner" (Chanler 1896, 306). It is unclear to what extent Samburu themselves invoked relatedness to Maasai at that time. We only know that they despised and feared the Maasai (Hardwick 1903, 241). But their classification as Maa people was to become central to how modern Kenyans hierarchized ethnicities, and later, as Saitoti pointed out, to how tourists assessed the value of their culture.

Once explorers established the resemblance of Maasai and Samburu, they also described Samburu morans using stylistic motifs that earlier travelers had employed with Maasai. Nineteenth-century descriptions of Maasai morans combined details of their cruel murders and brave lion hunts with erotic descriptions of their delicate bodily features (Hughes 2006; Kasfir

2007, 39). At the end of the nineteenth century, explorer William A. Chanler (1896, 281) wrote of Samburu morans in similar terms:

> The men were really fine-looking fellows; and I was at once struck with the fact that their features were entirely different from those of any other natives of East Africa whom I had seen. They approached near the Somali type—having regular features, full-rounded chins, and fine bold eyes. In colour, they were brown rather than black. The lobes of their ears were stretched, after the Masai fashion. Upon each side of the breast, they bore a crescent-shaped scar, which started at the point near the shoulder and ended near the lowest rib.

It is important to keep in mind that at the turn of the century, such descriptions of African bodies were common beyond Maa-speakers and involved both African men and women as objects of white men's erotic contemplation. But what emerged at this time, within this vast discursive field of eroticized bodies, was the resemblance between Samburu and Maasai, based primarily on a process of visualizing the bodies of their morans. What was new was the figuration of moran bodies as central sites for such colonial comparisons and, in turn, for the production of ethnic hierarchies.

By the early twentieth century, the emblematic quality of the Maa moran had already crystallized. As the warrior age grades of south-central ethnic groups either dissolved or were reduced to minimal ritual significance, the moran became quintessentially Maa (Tignor 1976, 73–93). A map of the British East Africa Protectorate—today's Kenya—from 1910 marks each region of the colony with an icon the cartographer deemed representative: a camel caravan for the northern deserts, a train for the Taita-Taveta Hills, a sculpted door for the island of Lamu, and so on. Over the Samburu region, the map depicts a moran—tall, slim, standing on one leg, and holding a spear. This suggests that the moran already tied Samburu and the geography of their region to the symbolic image of the young warrior.

SEXUALITY, SECURITY, AND COLONIAL REFORMS IN SAMBURU

Emblematic of Samburu and Maa-speakers, the moran soon came to represent excessive sexuality as well. Throughout the first half of the twentieth century, British administrators believed that morans posed a great security threat to the colonial state. They considered morans violent, disobedient, and likely to revolt against the government (Simpson 1996; Tignor 1976, 73–93). To maintain order, administrators considered it therefore imperative to reform young men. For them, controlling Samburu—and, for that matter, Maasai—meant controlling their morans. And reforming morans meant, in one way or another, containing their impulsive desires.

Colonials thought that morans engaged in cattle raids and homicide as shows of bravery to impress girls and young wives and gain their sexual favors. Samburu elders agreed with this supposition, and at times helped colonial administrators to deal with the morans. At different times, they prohibited the performance of songs and dances—such as *ntoo* and *baringoi*—through which young women teased morans to prove their bravery and young men excited themselves into doing so.[6] On February 20, 1936, the *New York Times* announced that "the taunts of native girls, who tell their admirers first to get blood on their spears before courting, has been responsible for fifty murders in the Samburu district in recent months." Displacing responsibility for the murders onto girls, the article implied that morans are, in fact, captives of their own uncontrollable longings to be desired by young women. This presumption informed colonial reformist policies targeting morans. The same year, after a new age set (the Lmekuri) had been initiated, a British district commissioner in Samburu informed the colonial government that "elders, entirely on their own initiative issued orders forbidding the eating of meat in the bush, or the giving of beads to the maidens by the new morans." "Both of these practices," he explained, "cause the frenzy which the young warrior works himself into before going to blood his spear." At meat feasts, he went on, "a lot of young warriors . . . begin to brag and outdo one another with tales of daring until some of them, worked up in the required state of frenzy . . . go off to foreign lands, and murder follows. In the other case, a young warrior gives beads to his girl, she sings about him, she taunts him to deeds of bravery and so he goes off to blood his spear."[7] The desire to assert oneself before age-mates and gain women's recognition through sex generated—or so the administrator thought—the "frenzy" necessary for the morans to murder. Therefore, to avoid triggering violence, intimacies had to be carefully surveilled. Bans on meat feasts and bead gifts remained relatively inefficient. But attempts to reform morans cemented, in discourse, the association of these men with excessive desires for sex and violence.[8]

Discourses that posited moran sexuality as the cause of violence in Samburu worked ideologically to sustain an imperial monopoly on the very definition of order. Colonial administrators would not readily recognize, for instance, that the social institution of moranhood was based on complex notions of moral personhood, discipline, and endurance that each moran had to cultivate if he was to be respected by others (Spencer 1965, 103–11).

By depicting morans as men driven by desire and emotion rather than reason and self-control, colonials placed them outside—indeed, opposite of—Western-defined order. Notably, however, in the absence of adequate military personnel, colonial armies often depended on alliances with these same "barefoot warriors" from different ethnic groups (Lonsdale 1992, 17, 27). But if such warriors acted on their own rather than on behalf of the colonial government, administrators at once construed them as criminal forces of disorder. For a wider imperial public, colonial descriptions of morans' sexual excesses made reformist interventions in Samburu a moral imperative.

But such descriptions of moran sexuality contained their own erotic excesses. Their telling was enjoyable, entertaining, and, at times, amusing. "The moran indulge in free love with the nditos [girls, from M: *ntito*, pl. *ntoyie*] of their section [clan]," said a British official in 1936, ostensibly shocked to learn that these were passing relationships and that morans rarely ever married women they took as lovers.[9] Anglican missionaries of the Bible Churchmen Missionary Society (BCMS) were concerned about the morans' practice of "free love." They had built a church and a school in the Samburu highlands in the early 1930s. In 1951, as they prepared to add dormitories to the school, they reported back to their headquarters in England that "in view of the fact that free love amongst young people is a recognized part of Samburu tribal life," they "would strongly deprecate a policy which would locate boys' and girls' dormitories on one mission station."[10] The missionaries' efforts amused district commissioner Charles Chenevix-Trench (1964, 199). "The BCMS Girls' School was, alas, bedeviled by sex," he said. "The *moran*[s] approved of the school, which they thought was established solely for their benefit, collecting together thirty or forty girls of an interesting age, far from parental control but conveniently accessible to local Lotharios." Accordingly, sexually mischievous morans—pictured here quite sympathetically through the Don Quixotian reference—made frivolous the missionaries' struggles to bring morality and modernity to the district. What amused the commissioner was that the missionaries were unaware how pointless their efforts were in the face of a population that, he thought, would not change its ways.

If Chenevix-Trench, one of the last colonial administrators of Samburu, seemed to have given up on reforming morans and their sexuality, in earlier days, administrators had put a great deal of energy into such reforms. Most of these reforms focused on transforming the desires—sexual or otherwise—of the morans. Documents I consulted at the colonial archives in Nairobi show that beginning in the 1920s, field administrators produced extensive intelligence in order to control morans. They compiled detailed descriptions of initiation ceremonies and customary rules associated with moranhood. They also sent each other confidential telegrams reporting on the whereabouts of morans, hoping to anticipate possible raids and violence. Because of the cultural similarity among Maa-speaking people, strategies colonialists devised to control Maasai morans in southern Kenya and northern Tanzania were later adopted in and adapted to Samburu.[11] For example, they appointed "moran chiefs" (M: *laigwanak lolmurran*) for each clan in an attempt to obtain information about moran cohorts and gain influence over them (Gavaghan 1999, 170). They also campaigned to disarm morans, by banning and confiscating spears (Kasfir 2007, 102–3). (Between 1931 and 1936, administrators in Samburu collected some five thousand spears.)[12]

But colonials knew that if they were to be efficient, repressive policies would not be enough. They also had to transform the bodies and desires of morans. To make morans into docile subjects, administrators sought to alter the moranhood period as well as the daily routines of young men. First, throughout the interwar period and shortly thereafter, local administrators tried to persuade elders to hasten the initiation of morans into elderhood. They thought that the fourteen or so years that young men usually spent as morans, without being allowed to marry, opened a window of opportunity when—lacking any responsibilities—they were free to misbehave. By reducing moranhood to no more than two or three years, administrators hoped to hasten young men to marry and settle down. But elders were largely unwilling to rush rituals associated with moranhood. For one thing, reducing the time of moranhood interfered with elders' own interest in sustaining polygyny. If young men were allowed to marry earlier, elders reasoned, that would reduce the number of women available to elders themselves as second or third wives (Spencer 1965, 95–99). As we shall see in chapter 5, in the late 2000s, morans in their early twenties who made money through European women took it upon themselves to shorten the time they spent as morans before becoming elders. If colonial administrators had thought that abandoning moranhood would make young men modern, some morans later on also came to invoke the importance of "saving time" by marrying early as a way "to be modern." The time of men's life course remained central in claiming modernity as a condition of citizenship. Indeed, if Samburu were to join the path to progress—an ideological trajectory that, as we have seen, legitimized their geopolitical marginalization in Kenya—they had to subscribe to a modern life course.

Second, Samburu also had to subscribe to modern ways of time valorization. Whatever the actual duration of moranhood, administrators also sought to transform the concrete ways in which morans spent and regulated their daily time. They wished to inculcate modern routines of labor and leisure as a way to turn morans into "responsible"—or, rather, subservient—subjects. In the 1940s, they initiated so-called labor programs in Samburu. Under pressure from the colonial administration, the so-called Local Native Council passed the Communal Labor Resolution, obliging morans to undertake three months of communal work per year. Morans had to reside in labor camps, where they were fed but not paid. During this time, they worked on the construction of roads, administrative stations, and water dams.[13] In both Maasai and Samburu, administrators turned to sports, especially running competitions and soccer games, to offer an alternative context for young men to outdo each other and prove their bodily strength (Gavaghan 1999, 184). Thus, reforms sought to redirect morans' excessive desires for violence and sex through the disciplined rhythms of labor and leisure. Things did not work out as planned, however. Labor campaigns proved extremely unpopular with the morans, and only young men who already collaborated with administrators and missionaries actually cared much for sports.

Yet if construction work did not interest morans, many grew fascinated with building careers as soldiers. Joining the colonial army, young men reasoned, would grant them honor, prestige, and access to cash. Colonial administrators drew on their own stereotypes of Samburu men as brave, fearless warriors to enlist morans as soldiers into the King's African Rifles (KAR). Three hundred and forty-eight Samburu men entered the Second World War as soldiers of the British Empire. They represented a total of 17 to 20 percent of all the Samburu morans of that time (Spencer 1975, 164). In 1952, a district administrator noted, "If one had the time and the money I feel that the Moran as a whole could be molded into very good material, as has been proved by many morans who have entered the KAR."[14] For Samburu men, working as soldiers became a respectable alternative to moranhood (fig. 3). And colonials cherished this outcome. For them, the moran was the embodiment of primitive desire and disorder, while the soldier—thereafter the moran's doppelgänger—was a modern, disciplined, and dignified subject. If one type belonged to an anarchical past, the other pointed to a modern future. These masculine subject positions then continued to shape possibilities of making a livelihood for Samburu men for decades to come. During my fieldwork, many men worked in the national army, on the police force, for UN peacekeeping missions, or for private security firms. Meanwhile, in coastal tourist economies, Samburu migrants sometimes supplemented

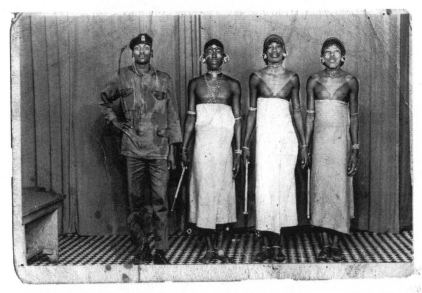

3. Four brothers (a soldier and three morans) pose for a photograph in a town studio in the early 1960s. (Author's collection.)

their incomes at the beach by also working as watchmen and security guards for families and firms in the region.

The colonial politics of moranhood shaped the position Samburu would occupy thereafter within Kenya and globally. Invoking security reasons, colonial administrators placed morans at the forefront of disciplinary interventions and made them into key representatives of Samburu. Meanwhile, administrators' concern with the morans' excessive carnal desire and practices of "free love" made these men into embodiments of an ethnosexuality that was excessive and dangerous. Note here that ethnosexuality is not something that morans' bodies *had*—some preexisting quality they congealed—but rather something that colonial discourses and practices invested them with. Imperial discourses of race, ethnicity, sexuality, and masculinity intersected in the figure of the moran to mark him and the ethnic group to which he belonged as essential Others. However problematic such colonial stereotypes might be, in hindsight they cannot be sidelined as mere racist misrepresentations. That they certainly are, but it is important to explore how such representations also materialized their effects in the conditions of life in Samburu, and how they set parameters within and around which Samburu crafted belonging for decades to come.

By the mid-twentieth century, discourses about the moran had continued to proliferate, yet now more pronouncedly along two distinct lines. On the one hand, photographers, filmmakers, nationalist intellectuals, and tourists aestheticized and eroticized, if in different ways, the bodily image of morans. On the other hand, development workers, religious leaders, and Kenyan elites sexualized the moran further as a morally problematic embodiment of libidinal excess. To grasp what fascinates tourists and other foreigners about morans in the present, it is essential to understand these seemingly opposite narrative threads as two sides of the same coin. The eroticization of the moran's appearance and his hypersexualization work together to inscribe ethnosexuality onto young, male, Maa bodies.

MORAN BODIES AND THEIR "PHOTOGRAPHIC VALUE"

The nostalgic idea of a rapidly disappearing warrior tradition—a last vestige, as it were, of an ancient African culture—is a long-standing romantic motif in the depiction of Samburu in colonial Kenya. But by the 1950s, the moran had become much more pronouncedly an object of visual contemplation to be displayed, admired, photographed, and filmed. More than ever before, postcards, photographs, movies, and folk dance shows displayed moran bodies for Western audiences and an emerging African middle class. A colonial administrator of the late 1950s noticed that morans had recently become "complacently conscious of their photographic value" (Chenevix-Trench 1964, 233). Similarly, anthropologist Paul Spencer, who carried out research in Samburu between 1958 and 1960, told me that at that time, morans were already familiar with photography and film. One moran who had featured in a movie instructed Spencer to wait for the clouds to disperse and the sun to come out before he photographed him (Spencer, personal conversation, February 19, 2011). A few years earlier, in 1952, district commissioner Terence Gavaghan enrolled one thousand morans in the making of the Hollywood movie *Mogambo*. He negotiated with the film director to set the movie in Samburu and promised him "up to 1,000 warriors armed with spears on location." In exchange, he asked for "3½ yards of best quality red silk cloth per man present on site, plus twenty-five shilling each for the 1,000 spears made by our metal workers and 7 pounds of meat per man per day" (Gavaghan 1999, 202).[15] Henceforth, said Gavaghan, "the Samburu became something of a cult for photographers and Hollywood film makers" (203). And Samburu themselves, especially young men, became aware of the commodity value of their bodily appearance.

Famous European photographers and filmmakers visited Samburu throughout the second half of the twentieth century. They included Wilfred Thesiger, a British explorer whose travel writing and photography of the Middle East was renowned in England; Leni Riefenstahl, a German photographer and filmmaker controversial for her early participation in Nazi propaganda;[16] Mirella Ricciardi, the daughter of an Italian settler in Kenya; Nigel Pavitt, a former colonial army officer;[17] Angela Fischer and Carol Beckwith, who together published numerous coffee table books on nomadic African tribes; and others. Their photographs vary greatly in style and technique. However, they also share a set of similarities. They depict primarily young bodies of great symmetric perfection and ignore fat, short, ill, and, to some extent, aging bodies. They romanticize culture by excluding men and women dressed in clothes, or engaged in tasks, deemed nontraditional. And they often depict undressed bodies in scenes of bathing, bodily grooming, or even circumcision.

As if to rescue the image of the moran from the potential stigma of primitivity and pornography of Western coffee table books, African nationalists, mostly educators and folklorists from Nairobi, reworked that image into national cultural heritage. A more fully dressed version of the moran was to feature in folk dance performances, school competitions, and political rallies. The Bomas of Kenya, a national theme park of folk architecture located in Nairobi, hired youths to dress as morans and perform dances for Kenyan urbanites (Bruner 2005, 77–83). Here, the moran was to support a vision of national integrity, divorced from ethnic politics, the social reality of cattle raiding, and excessive sexuality. Instead, by making the moran into an aesthetic phenomenon, a spectacle of culture, elite Kenyans hoped to promote a more dignified image of their national identity and past. In a process akin to "the invention of tradition" (Hobsbawm and Ranger 1983), nationalist intellectuals sought to refigure morans into insignias of a cultural heritage to be performed and consumed by modern Kenyans.

If the moran was part of Kenya's national heritage, so the logic went, he could also figure centrally in the country's tourism industry. Tourism grew spectacularly throughout the second half of the twentieth century, becoming, along with coffee and tea exports, one of the country's major sources of foreign exchange. Wildlife safaris and beach tourism represented the primary attractions for tourists visiting Kenya. Cultural tourism added an important component to tourists' experiences while on safaris or at the beach.[18] Sydney Kasfir (2007, 46) argues that the "Kenya Ministry of Tourism as well as Nairobi-based safari companies incorporated the Samburu into their advertisements about the unspoiled African bush much as they had used the core Maasai to advertise the popular southern game reserves of the Maasai Mara and Amboseli." In the 1970s, the Mayers' Ranch, home to an ex-colonial British settler family in the town of Limuru, near Nairobi, was one of the few places in the country where tourists could watch, photograph, and film Maasai and Samburu moran dances (Bruner 2005, 33–100). The Mayers had long employed Maasai and Samburu men and women to work on their farm as cattle herders. They built a *manyatta* (Maasai moran village) and asked the young men working for them to perform dances for tourists (40–41). During the tourist season, minivans filled with foreigners arrived daily at the Mayers' Ranch for visits of no more than a few hours. Tourists attended moran dances, purchased handicrafts in the cultural village, and, at the end, drank tea and ate cookies on the lawn of the Mayers' house. The Mayers' Ranch, anthropologist Edward Bruner (2005) suggests, appealed at once to the tourists' nostalgia for colonialism and to their fascination with "tribal peoples." In return, the Mayers paid performers a weekly salary and provided them with food (43). The performers lived together on the ranch during the tourist season and afterward returned to their respective homes to invest their wages in livestock (44).[19] After the Mayers' Ranch closed, the morans moved to the coast to work in beach tourism.

By the late twentieth century, the Maa-speaking morans had become valuable visual icons of a culture on the verge of disappearance. On display in shows, films, photographs, and postcards, morans offered a primitive spectacle to the nostalgic gaze of Europeans, Americans, and middle-class Africans who contemplated and celebrated an "Africa" they thought would be no more. But at the same time, morans had another side, one that middle-class Kenyans saw as an embarrassment to their nation. And this other side of the moran also made international headlines.

DEVELOPMENT, SEX SCANDALS, AND MIDDLE-CLASS VALUES

On May 11, 2011, CNN broadcast a short report on how Samburu children are "given beads as gifts before rape." The film shows CNN reporter David MacKenzie, Samburu activist Josephine Kulea, and two Kenyan soldiers driving to a Samburu village on a "rescue mission." Upon arrival, amid the puzzled faces of the villagers, MacKenzie reports, "They call it beading, and what happens is that a close family relative will come to the mother and father with Samburu beads and then bead the girl, place it over her head, and effectively the adult men can have sex with girls as young as six." The report ends dramatically as the activist, with the help of the soldiers, pushes two crying girls into a van. The girls are to be taken to an orphanage. "Staying," the activist assures the audience, "would be a worse fate."

The practice of "girl beading," which once troubled colonial officials and local elders who believed it drove morans into raiding, now troubled development workers and their national and global audiences, because it purportedly signaled a violation of children's rights. "In the beading ritual," declared Kenya's *Daily Nation*, "Samburu *morans* identify little girls as brides by making them wear a beaded necklace. Child rights activists in Samburu say that beading can happen any time a moran meets a girl, irrespective of her age. . . . During the beading, *morans* are free to have sex with the innocent girls."[20] "It's a national shame," said an opinion column in the *Daily Nation*, "that at a time when the Constitution has given children all manner of rights, girls as young as nine in the Samburu community are turned into sex slaves."[21] Reports also vilified elders and married women for collaborating with the morans in upholding this tradition.

Young women encounter various forms of sexual violence and oppression, in Samburu as elsewhere, and I by no means seek to diminish or deny that fact. In the context of such sensationalist reportage, however, what I want to highlight here are the discursive logics at play. It is significant that activists, NGO workers, and state actors invoke the immorality of Samburu sexual culture to legitimize interventions into the intimate affairs of impoverished households. Described as turning girls into "sex slaves," morans become rapists, embodiments of a radical sexual alterity that has now become criminal. And as development ideologies resignify intimate practices as sexual crimes, young women are understood solely as victims who lack agency and need (Western or middle-class) rescue and empowerment. However well intentioned, these logics speak at once to the sensibilities of transnational feminist development and those of a Kenyan middle class.

In Kenya, notions of sexual propriety associated with Christianity, nationalism, and development are criteria of middle-class belonging and, by extension, moral citizenship.[22] Daily, the national media features instances of sexual "perversion"—incest, adultery, bestiality, and rape—as inherent threats to middle-class respectability, life course, and family values. Government officials, development workers, and religious leaders debate issues such as whether youth are victims of the perversions of globalization; whether sex education leads to premature child sexuality; whether poor parenting is to blame for the growing numbers of teenage pregnancies and early marriages; whether legalizing abortion encourages promiscuity; whether the fertility and sexual vitality of young men are declining thanks to unemployment, alcoholism, and pauperism; and whether gay rights threaten to undermine "African cultural values." Addressing and producing a public of middle-class aspirations, these debates also point to a set of concrete sexual peripheries. Samburu are one such periphery, an example of moral decadence. Meanwhile, these public discourses notably exclude the voices of those deemed peripheral subjects.

Morans are held up as representing a denigrated state of underdevelopment. According to this logic, not only are they rapists of young girls, but their irresponsible sexual behaviors also put their communities at risk for disease. Since the nineties, Kenyan and international discourses on the prevention of HIV and other STIs have invoked with alarm the sexual alterity of morans. Recall the television feature described at the beginning of this chapter, ridiculing morans for treating gonorrhea as if it were "a common cold." Because morans—so the story went—were ignorant of safe sex practices yet highly promiscuous, they were responsible for the rapid spread of the disease among Samburu. On March 3, 2011, *Citizen News* announced that "ignorance is proving to be a bit expensive for the residents of Samburu. . . . With an illiteracy level of ninety percent, ignorance is threatening to push HIV prevalence, which stands at 6.9 percent in the County, even higher." The Christian AIDS Bureau of Southern Africa (CABSA) reported in 2010 that "high levels of poverty, illiteracy and cultural practices like polygamy and early marriage have led to high levels of HIV infection among the Samburu."[23] Not incidentally, CABSA offered the example of a moran: "John Lokolale, 21, a Samburu Moran (warrior), said he did not know what the word condom meant until recently."

Images of morans figure widely on posters for adult education, health, and family planning, where they represent the sexual ignorance and irresponsibility of what developers regard as backward people. One poster I saw on the wall of a bar in Maralal in 2015 depicted a moran herding his goats. Next to him, the English text read: "A TRUE MORAN is hardworking; is of responsible behavior; has self-control; respects the rights of other people; respects the girls; abstains or uses condoms" (fig. 4). The poster's very existence implied the need to remind morans of such expectations and reeducate them as responsible citizens. Similarly, a billboard that has stood at the entrance to Maralal since 2010 points out that it is only through self-containment and abstinence that the relations between morans and young women will eventually render the fruits of a "happy family," a "good career," and "celebrity" (fig. 5). By contrast, their promiscuity, implied here by the image of a moran

A TRUE MORAN

- ♦ Is hardworking
- ♦ Is of responsible behavior
- ♦ Has self control
- ♦ Respects the rights of other people
- ♦ Respects the girls
- ♦ Abstains or uses a condom

 European Union  NOPE Building Capacities, Changing Lives   AMURT

The Printing of this communication material has been supported by EU through the JAMII BORA Project

4. Sex education poster in Maralal, Samburu, 2015. (Courtesy of National Organization of Peer Educators [NOPE], Kenya, in partnership with Ananda Marga Universal Relief Team [AMURT], with funding from the European Union under the Jamii Bora project implemented in Samburu County.)

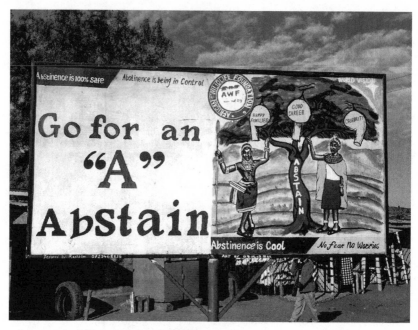

5. Sex education billboard in Maralal, Samburu, 2010. (Photo by the author.)

and a girl in the "bush," threatens to jeopardize their very futures. As most of these iconographic representations are usually accompanied by texts in English or Swahili, they speak mainly to educated men and women, in turn displacing the risk, blame, and promiscuity associated with STIs onto rural morans and girls.

"It is mainly the morans from the villages who are the carriers of these diseases, like STD," a nurse I interviewed in Maralal in 2008 explained.

> You know, when you go to dance in the forest and meet young girls. . . . And, you know, the young girls are free. They are not prevented by their parents to sleep with the morans. So they sleep apart. When they go grazing the goats and cows, that's where the young girls meet the morans. Some of the girls, you know, have been infected with STD from several morans. The girls would distribute [the disease] to about twenty or twenty-five men, because the men would give the little girls some amount of money in order to sleep with them.

Echoing widely held middle-class assumptions about the promiscuity of morans, this health worker presented the morans as embodiments of an excessive sexuality that, in turn, made them "carriers of these diseases."

If, for colonials, the excessive sexual practices between morans and girls carried the potential of disorder and violence in the district, for contemporary health workers the same practices are seen as perpetuating sexual violence, disease, and underdevelopment. It is not by coincidence, I think, that such discourses proliferated, for example, in 2009 and 2010, after the Kenyan government leased land in eastern Samburu to Chinese oil companies, requiring numerous Samburu families to be forcibly removed from the area. It is difficult, of course, to posit a causal link between land alienation in Samburu regions and national discourses of Samburu ethnosexuality. But, regardless of whether their timing was coincidental or not, such discourses work, through middle-class ideologies of sexual morality, to delegitimize the claims of rural Samburu to full national citizenship, an important aspect of which is landownership.

A NATION'S SHAME: MORANS AS BEACH BOYS

With the growing participation of young Samburu men in coastal tourist economies and rising numbers of European women seeking relationships with these men, morans have become the topic of yet another sex scandal in Kenya. Generically referred to as Maasai, Samburu morans at Mombasa's tourist resorts attract, every now and then, the attention of Nairobi journalists. "A few years ago, it would have been unimaginable to think of Maasai moran[s] as beach boys," observed *Sunday Magazine* in 2008. "Now, they have flocked beaches at the Coast lured by riches they could make out of tourists, a trend that has left the elders worried. Dressed in their traditional shukas [body cloth] and armed with rungus [clubs], some have taken the controversial move to sell themselves to the highest bidders."[24] Shocked that morans who "sell themselves" to tourists by taking the humiliating, "unimaginable" move of becoming beach boys, the article romanticizes an imagined status quo of the morans. "They are expected to be courageous and endure many things, including killing a lion with bare hands." The article decries the emasculation of morans who turn into beach boys to become clients to foreign women.

The moralistic tone of these journalistic texts reflects a more general attitude toward morans-cum-beach boys in Kenya. Thanks to the national media, Kenyans throughout the country know of the relationships between European women and Maasai or Samburu morans. Whenever I told people in cities like Nairobi or Mombasa about my research project, they invariably laughed at the actions of morans and cautiously advised me that the subject of my research is an embarrassment for Kenya. It was as if the emasculating transformation of morans into beach boys reflects the failures of a nation which is now itself trying to "entice," as it were, foreign donors as a survival strategy.[25] The country's economic dependence on the World Bank and the International Monetary Fund posits a threat to state sovereignty that many see mirrored in the perceived perversion of Africa's (once) brave warriors. Though the moran has long been an icon of assertive masculinity and a hall-mark figure of national heritage, his engagement in sex-for-money exchanges in tourism has more recently raised questions about the status of the Kenyan state in the world more broadly.

But the moran remains a deeply ambiguous figure. On the one hand, he indexes an antiquated culture that threatens children's rights and people's health. On the other hand, he embodies the nation's masculine indepen-dence, whose prostitution in female sex tourism offends nationalist sensi-bilities. Either way, moran sexuality remains emblematic of the geopolitical alterity of Samburu and an important ideological mechanism for sustaining political and economic marginality in the region. As we shall see, however, for some Samburu, moran sexuality—turned into a commodity—also became a source of wealth and power, even as it further excluded others.

::::

As figures of discourse, Samburu morans, their erotic aura and sexual alterity, are historical products of the twentieth century. The making of the Maa moran into a brand of East Africa as a tourist destination involved long, com-plex processes, through which various European and African actors imag-ined and contested the making of the Kenyan state and how Samburu were to belong therein. As morans became emblematic of Samburu ethnic identity more generally, moran sexuality provided an instance of the radical cultural Otherness of Samburu and thus made a case for their geopolitical margin-alization. In this sense, discourses of ethnosexuality and the material con-ditions of social life in Samburu informed one another, if in different ways at different times. Yet the moran remained inherently ambivalent—at once desirable and derided—in ways that fascinated tourists and other foreigners and made him the foundation of Kenya's growing ethno-erotic economies. It is in this context, as we shall see, that some Samburu turned an image of alterity and an ideological alibi for their marginalization into a new source of wealth and power.

2. Livelihood and Respectability in Hard Times

A sense of respect is an attitude which is inculcated into persons of both sexes from an early age. It is . . . the keystone of Samburu morality. All social obligations which form part of the Samburu moral code may be expressed in relation to it.
—PAUL SPENCER, *THE SAMBURU*

"You know these are hard times," Mama Seiyina, a woman from Siteti, told me in July 2009. "You do what you need to do to find food. But what these boys do—the ones who go to Mombasa—that is very shameful. Going with old mamas for money and taking that money to your parents to eat, that is a shameful thing." She paused. Then she said, "But it's common nowadays." Mama Seiyina suggested that "hard times" prompted people to find unusual means to make a living. To a certain extent, this was understandable. To provide for one's family was a moral imperative and a respectable pursuit. But for her, young men who had sex for money took things too far. Whether selling sex was indeed dishonorable or merely a desperate means to a noble end— a new pathway to respectability, as it were—was an issue people debated at great length during my research in Samburu. And while not everyone would have agreed with Mama Seiyina's perspective, locals generally shared her perception that the present was a time of exceptional economic hardships. For them, the exceptionality of the times rendered the limits of respectability more readily negotiable. But what were the "hard times" Mama Seiyina talked about? And what had generated the circumstances that led young men to the seemingly paradoxical strategy of selling sex to gain respectability?

Since the late 1970s, it has been a particular social and economic context that prompted young Samburu men to turn to the older, colonial figure of the sexual moran and perform it in new ways for foreigners. This was a time when the effects of landownership reforms and structural adjustment programs intersected with the outcomes of devastating droughts, declining cattle economies, and rapid population growth to strain livelihoods in the district. This was a time when suddenly, older avenues to respectability had become—once more—untenable. As people could no longer expect to follow easily normative life trajectories, everyone negotiated more saliently what it meant to be respectable and to build lives locally. It was also in this context that people devised many new ways to access resources. For example, more and more Samburu now marketed their culture to Euro-American and Kenyan audiences. Yet opportunities for cultural commodification remained relatively sporadic and not readily available to everyone. Instead, many families made a living through petty trade in goats, sheep, charcoal, sugar, alcohol, and other commodities. Under these circumstances, some men and women also exchanged sex for money and goods more frequently. In exploring the links between respectability and recent economic transformations in Samburu, we shall understand why, over the past few decades, young men have migrated in ever-larger numbers to coastal resorts. We shall also understand their attempts to commodify moran ethnosexuality as part of a wider context in which people increasingly sold both culture and sex—sometimes separately, sometimes together—in order to imagine futures.

CULTURE AS COMMODITY, CULTURE AS RESPECTABILITY

"Our culture is very beautiful. We, the Samburu, are a people of cattle. You wear all these beads. And you drink milk and blood." Mama Seiyina offered me this romanticized narrative of Samburu culture when I visited her for the first time in Siteti in June 2008. I had begun working in her village only a few weeks prior (fig. 6). A friend from the town of Maralal, where I was living at that time, had recommended Siteti to me as an ideal place to find men who migrated to coastal tourist resorts. The village, I later learned, was indeed one of ten or so highland settlements whose residents have participated in Kenya's beach tourism for almost thirty years. To help me gain the trust and support of locals, my friend introduced me to Lteipan, a man in his

6. View of Siteti, Samburu, 2008. (Photo by the author.)

early thirties who lived in Siteti. I hired Lteipan as a research assistant, and together we started carrying out household surveys in his village. Mama Seiyina had seen me visit her neighbors on previous days, and Lteipan had told her that I studied "Samburu culture"—a phrase he liked to use often (using either the English words in Maa language or the Maa phrase *lwenet lolokop*) when introducing me to locals. Once Lteipan and I sat down in Mama Seiyina's house, she began talking about pastoral people, bead decorations, and diets of milk and blood in ways that she knew were popular with white foreigners. But such stereotypes sat uneasily with the realities of contemporary life in Samburu. Mama Seiyina's family, among others, did not own cattle, subsisting primarily on cultivating maize and trading alcohol, charcoal, and, more rarely, goats and sheep.

After she poured hot tea into two enamel cups and offered them to us, Mama Seiyina turned toward a large iron-sheet box that was standing on a small table near where we sat. She opened it, took out what looked like a small notebook, and handed it to me. It was a Kenyan passport. She smiled, urging me to look inside. The passport carried her picture: her face looking into the camera rigidly, her neck lacking the many strings of colorful beads she usually wore, like many rural Samburu women, in her daily life (because in pictures meant for national documents, one was not allowed to wear markers of ethnicity). "I went to South Africa to play in a movie," she told me. She smiled. "We went there by plane. It was very beautiful. We took our beads and the morans took their spears, and we showed our culture just as it is. People there liked it very much." Mama Seiyina had been among some one hundred Samburu men and women who had flown to South Africa in 1992 to play exotic African "tribesmen" in the Hollywood movie *The Air Up There* (Hollywood Pictures, 1992).[1] For many rural Samburu, a passport was a prestigious item that was otherwise difficult to obtain, especially because few of them owned national ID cards (Kasfir 2007, 344n6). Mama Seiyina's passport—though expired by the time she showed it to me—clearly remained a treasured token of her ties to a world beyond Kenya. It introduced her as someone who had represented Samburu internationally and was therefore a recognized connoisseur of her culture.

Since the early 1980s, residents of Siteti have been variously involved in marketing Samburu culture. Throughout the past thirty years, morans of three consecutive age sets have migrated to the coast to sell artifacts and dance for tourists. Throughout the past twenty years or so, several women from Siteti have made traditional beadwork for sale in the Maralal market, where Kenyan art traders from Nairobi and Mombasa purchase their handicrafts. In 1995, thirty morans from Siteti and neighboring villages traveled once more to South Africa to play in another Hollywood movie, *The Ghost in the Darkness* (Paramount Pictures, 1996).[2] And more recently, three or four times a year, a local tour guide has paid villagers to perform dances for small groups of development workers visiting the area. Market and state reforms have conspired with local environmental, economic, and demographic transformations to strain livelihoods in the district. But within this context, many Samburu have discovered that their culture is marketable, on different scales and at different times.

Regardless of whether one earned money by selling culture or through other means, romanticized visions of culture, like those Mama Seiyina narrated to me, spoke to many of the good life of an imagined past and of a possible avenue toward a better future. Samburu knew that foreigners and Kenyan urbanites were interested mainly in particular aspects of their culture—their traditional dances, attire, and artifacts. They also knew that journalists and development workers condemned other aspects of what they saw as Samburu culture, including sexual promiscuity, girl beading, or female genital cutting. However, for many Samburu, culture, or *lwenet*, was about much more than what foreigners wished to recognize. For them, *lwenet* also entailed the so-called *lkeretita* (sg. *lkereti*) that English-speaking Samburu translated as "the normal ways of doing things," or more loosely as "traditions." More specifically, lkeretita refer to normative expectations associated with ritual and everyday relations. These include expectations associated with age-set relations and the life course, relations of patrilineal descent and marriage, notions of pollution and the divine, and much more. Expectations associated with lkeretita informed people's desire and actions, if in different ways, as they pursued respectability and anchored themselves in local social worlds.

As recent economic transformations significantly undermined the ability of many to produce and sustain relations informed by such normative expectations, ideals of individual and collective respectability were pointedly contested. Respect (M: *nkanyit*) had long been an object of concern and conflict in Samburu (Holtzman 2006; Ott 2004; Spencer 1965). The moral expectations that informed respectability have never been static, of course, but changed over time. Under new economic and social circumstances at the time of my research, questions of respectability and belonging also involved long debates about the moral implications of selling culture and sex.

CRAFTING WEALTH, WORTH, AND WELL-BEING

I visited Mama Seiyina many times in the following years. Her homestead was located centrally along Siteti's main path, between the primary school and a public water pump recently built by a German NGO. Villagers passed by her homestead every day as they fetched water, herded livestock, or walked to and from Maralal or the forest. Taking advantage of her homestead's location, Mama Seiyina earned money brewing and selling a type of alcohol made from fermented grains called *chang'aa*. In the late afternoon, when men and women returned from their daily chores, some stopped by her compound and purchased chang'aa by the cup. They drank together and talked.

Mama Seiyina's family lived on a five-acre plot of land, neatly subdivided with fences of wooden posts, branches, and wires into a maize garden, a goat and sheep kraal, and a main living compound. There were four houses in the compound: a small traditional house of branches that belonged to Mama Seiyina and her husband; two similar houses for her mother-in-law and sister-in-law (who had run away from her marriage in a different village) respectively; and a three-room stone house with an iron-sheet roof that belonged to Mama Seiyina's brother-in-law. Because the latter lived in Nairobi, where he worked as a police officer, Mama Seiyina received her guests in his house. The house was spacious, accommodating some eight to ten visitors at a time.

What is more, its style and furniture were more prestigious than those of the other, more traditional houses. The sitting room contained two armchairs, a sofa, and several wooden stools. Mama Seiyina's teenage children had decorated the room's red-clay walls with white chalk drawings and posters of Jean-Claude Van Damme, Jesus Christ, and Kenyan politician Raila Odinga (then the prime minister and opposition leader). I spent many hours in that room, listening to locals complain about recent landgrabs and the rising prices of foodstuffs or gossip about how so-and-so's daughter had become pregnant in school or how so-and-so's moran son had been disrespectful toward elders. I listened to them plan events or sing songs associated with different age sets from the past. Thus, I began to learn how people made their livelihoods, how they converted their resources into respectability and moral good, and how they spent their free time in each other's company.

Discussing, in such contexts, events and everyday occurrences and comparing the actions and desires of my interlocutors in Siteti with those of people I met in Lorosoro and other villages in the district, I came to learn about respect and its role in defining local belonging. I also learned about respect from how locals expected me to behave, and occasionally by making mistakes of my own, of course. For example, when conversations in Mama Seiyina's house lasted for hours, I often stood up and left before anyone else, as I was in a rush to catch up on field note writing or attend to other research-related work. I did not understand at first how my rushing off might affect my relationships with others. I learned soon enough that leaving in this way communicated a desire for individual fulfilment and personal gain over time investment in furthering social relations. Ideally, a person had to balance rushing and dwelling in skillful ways. Locals with employment or private businesses also rushed in some situations, but they also made sure to spend their evenings socializing open-endedly with others. Once I realized what was at stake for respectability and belonging in the rhythms of everyday sociality, I made a conscious effort to dwell more and pass time, as it were, in others' company.

Over the years, I distilled at least two main overall frameworks for imagining respectability. One had to do with an ideology of reproduction and growth, the other with a set of hierarchies of prestige and "development." Both informed centrally, albeit in contested ways, locals' attempts to produce durable kinds of material wealth, moral worth, and a sense of the "good life." I understand these frameworks to represent what anthropologists call "templates of social value," that is, guiding formulas or generative schemata through which people represent and assess the potential outcomes and moral significance of their concrete actions (Graeber 2001, 44–45; Munn 1986, 15, 121). I discuss each template here in turn.

The first template pertains to sustaining a certain generative power or life force. My interlocutors tried to find the best ways to grow (M: *a-bulu*), or make their material properties, families, and lineages prosper in ways that were propitious. To put it differently, they sought to increase their wealth in people and kind by following particular moral guidelines that allowed wealth to sustain itself and expand in time. In Maa language, to say that a herd, a family, or someone's wealth is propitious or self-perpetuating is to say that "it is alive" (M: *keishu*). More precisely, the verb *a-ishu* means "to give," "to give birth," or "to give life" (Straight 2007a, 216–17). This verb also constitutes the root of the noun *nkishon*, or life force.[3] Of individuals, families, and herds that are healthy, grow, and prosper, people say that they "give life," that is, they thrive with life force. By contrast, of those individuals whose actions are unpropitious (M: *kotolo*), people say that they "don't give life" (M: *mei-shu*). A person, a lineage, or an age set might be wealthy and in good health at a certain moment in time. But if it is deemed unpropitious—whether by a curse or by immoral actions—it is expected that it will "not give life," or that it will be unable to project itself into the future. Those that lacked life force did not prosper or reproduce. They would eventually become sick, and—sometimes after many years—they would die. The ability of individuals, families, or whole communities to perpetuate themselves over time depended as such on the presence and specific qualities of life force.

Which actions fueled life force and which depleted it were matters of constant debate. Often, men and women interrogated new styles, pursuits, and social relations in terms of their ability to give life or sustain life force. However, as an elderly ritual specialist once told me, "it is only time that tells if a new thing is good or if it is bad." Unable to tell what only the future can prove, people generally considered ancestral norms and practices—the so-called lkeretita—safe pathways to a propitious life. Marriage and offspring were important ways of "growing" families and lineages. Men desired to acquire resources and make bridewealth payments for one or more wives. Women sought to raise many children as a way to gain respect and authority in their communities. Men and women aging without families and children were often the subject of harsh ridicule, and were said to lack fertility and life force. To refuse to have children was to refuse to grow socially. I learned this the hard way, when I told a friend—more or less jokingly—that I did not wish to have children. "So what do you want to do?" she said. "You just want to eat your wealth all by yourself?" Eating one's wealth alone was a way to consume without expanding one's name and self in time and space; it was a way to make wealth worthless. Here, a reproductive ideology was at the foundation of propitious life and thus a normative expectation for the moral evaluation of people's life choices. But propitious life could not be reduced to the facts of reproduction and growth. Though one's ability to reproduce and grow signaled to others the temporary presence of life force, it was ultimately the durability of wealth and well-being—their ability to last over time—that proved their propitiousness. In other words, a family that went extinct—along with its wealth—was as good as no family at all (I explore this in chapter 4).

Rural Samburu believed that participating in and sustaining relations of descent and age set was a sure way to propitiate life force. Patrilineal descent—or descent drawn through male filial relations—was based on various nested categories, including the exogamous clan (M: *lmarei*) and its component parts based in the lineage (M: *ntipat*).[4] Each section had its own stories of origin and complex relations to other units of descent. Despite actual hierarchies of wealth and power, members of descent groups imagined themselves as equals and encouraged each other to circulate resources among themselves.

Cutting across vertical relations of descent were horizontal age-set relations. As I pointed out in the introduction, age sets were organized cohorts of people moving together through a number of age grades. For men, such age grades comprised boyhood, moranhood, and elderhood, whereas for women they encompassed girlhood and wifehood. Although women were not initiated as part of an age set per se, they adopted the names of the morans with whom they danced and, as wives, became part of the age set of their husbands.[5]

In addition, lkeretita referred to ritual practices associated with relations of descent and age. Rituals played a crucial role in growing wealth and worth. As I once heard an elder say of a clan ceremony, ritual (M: *ntasim*, meaning also "medicine") is a womb or stomach (M: *nkosheke*) that "gives life"—it regenerates the life force for individuals and the groups of which they are part. Samburu living in urban areas concurred with many ideals of lkereti, often returning to their rural homelands to participate in rituals and sustain relations of reciprocity with kin and age-mates.

A second template for the making of respectability was about prestige, fashion, and hierarchies of material wealth. If life force needed time to prove its presence, what people referred to as development (M: *maendeleoni*) was a more immediate source of social influence and recognition. People used the idiom of development to speak of various kinds of wealth. Drawing on state discourses, they associated development with the ability of individuals, families, or communities to acquire resources and become self-sufficient (Holtzman 2004, 70–71; Straight 2000, 238). Samburu said of rich families and communities that "they have development" (M: *keata maendeleoni*), that "they developed themselves" (M: *keendeleayaki*); or that "they acquired development" (S: *wamepata maendeleo*). If development and material wealth, in general, were partially synonymous, development also referred to a specific set of styles, goods, and properties that were more prestigious than others. Carolyn Lesorogol (2008a, 127) describes how Samburu men and women who, as part of a research project, were asked "to draw what they thought of as development . . . invariably, across more than thirty communities, . . . drew . . . things like corrugated iron roofs on houses and buildings in towns, schools, Western-style dress, vehicles, electricity, tarmac roads, and farms growing crops." There was prestige in such styles of dress, housing, working, and mobility. In towns, men and women who acquired a significant amount of prestigious wealth were referred to as big (wo)men (S: *wakubwa*) or respectable people (S: *waheshimiwa*) and were the patrons of others.

Samburu borrowed a unilinear temporality of progress from state discourses of development to hierarchize specific styles and goods by placing them on a continuum, from the most traditional to the most modern. At the beginning of my household surveys in Siteti in 2008, my research assistant, Lteipan, drew in my notebook the four main types of houses that, according to him, existed in the district. He chose to order the different architectural types on an evolutionary scale, from the most traditional to the most modern. Like Lteipan, my informants described these houses as originating in different time periods and congealing different levels of prestige and value. One of the oldest types still common in the highlands was the *nkerashai*, a rectangular structure of thin wooden beams plastered with a mixture of clay and dung, and covered with a flat roof of clay and soil. The most modern and prestigious type of house was the so-called iron-sheet house (M: *nkaji e mabati*). Built predominantly by labor migrants, iron-sheet houses are rectangular structures of thick wooden posts or stone bricks covered with roofs of corrugated iron sheets. When I once asked a woman in the lowlands whom she wanted her daughter to marry, she responded, "The ones of the mabati" (M: *loomabati*), that is, rich men with iron-sheet-roof houses. A similar hierarchy worked to distinguish different types of gates, fencings, and compounds. It also worked to distinguish between locals who traveled on foot and those who owned bicycles or, more prestigiously, motorbikes or cars; between those who lived in the lowlands and those who lived in the highlands; between those who lived in the town of Maralal and those who lived in rural areas, also known as the "reserve"; and so on.

Nevertheless, acquiring prestige was not about moving progressively from one style or type of wealth and residence to another in any straightforward way. Tokens of prestige and development were recombined in complex ways with other forms of wealth and respectability to fit specific needs and desires. For example, although houses with iron-sheet roofs were the most prestigious, people's actual housing preferences varied (Straight 2007a, 57). Many informants told me that mabati houses were large and, therefore, difficult to heat up in the rainy season, while nkerashai houses were warmer and cozier. Chris, a police officer in Nairobi, had a large mabati house in his village. He equipped the house with expensive furniture, an electric generator, a TV, and a DVD player. But he preferred to sleep in his mother's nkerashai house in the same compound. "I like these traditional houses better," he told me when I asked why he did not sleep in his own house. Often, different types of houses existed in the same compounds, indexing a family's level of wealth and development in relation to one another. Chris's mother might "still" have lived in a nkerashai, but her nkerashai house had been resignified through its juxtaposition to a more prestigious house in the same compound. And once Chris had produced the tokens of development and prestige, he could choose to sleep in the house he liked best. Like Chris, many Samburu expressed desire for development by combining traditional and modern objects and styles according to their possibilities. In so doing, they performed what James Ferguson (1999, 106–7) describes as myriad "cosmopolitan" and "localist" styles along a vast continuum.

While prestige did not carry life force in and of itself, tokens of development demanded the respect of others. Beyond that, respectability hinged on what people *did* with their prestige, how they recirculated their resources, and how they positioned themselves in relations of descent and age by participating in ritual and everyday obligations over longer periods of time. Being respectable meant carefully balancing between achieving prestige and development and ensuring one's ability to grow, in space and time, through work and social reproduction.

In learning how these templates of social life and respectability informed people's desires and actions, I also understood that for the most part, they remained precisely *ideal*—and not *actual*—ways of doing things. Yet the fact that people talked about them and reiterated them convinced me that these were, in fact, very important for how they thought to navigate present times of economic hardships. On the one hand, new economic transformations undermined ideals of respectability and belonging, as we will see. On the other hand, these transformations also gave new salience and currency to such ideals. In this context, young men began migrating to coastal tourist resorts as a way to both obtain resources and respond to expectations of respectability and good, propitious life at home. The following sections outline these economic transformations and their implications for respectability. They provide the background necessary to understand what prompted men to migrate to the coast.

"HARD TIMES": PREDICAMENTS OF LAND, LABOR, AND LIVESTOCK

In the last three decades in Kenya, as elsewhere, the growing mobility of cash, goods, and people; the erosion of state boundaries; the decline of the welfare state; the increasing significance of consumption, speculation, and entrepreneurialism; and the effects of structural adjustment programs, among other things, generated new circumstances of livelihood.[6] Since the mid-1970s, Kenyan leaders applied repeatedly to the International Monetary Fund and the World Bank for loans. International lenders, in turn, asked the Kenyan state to implement structural adjustment programs in agriculture, industry, finance, export development, and education. These programs quickly fueled inflation and rampant unemployment, but they also generated new possibilities for accessing resources and making a living (Haugerud 1997; Smith 2008).

In Samburu, these new economic challenges conspired with local social, environmental, and demographic problems to transform how people made their livelihood. Although previous decades had been hardly stable, locals now remembered them nostalgically as a time of good living and prosperity. By contrast, they perceived the last four decades as a time of hardship, or, as one elder put it to me, a time of disaster (M: *emutai*). (It was not by accident that the elder chose this word, for *emutai* more commonly refers to a time in the late nineteenth century when war and famine killed off many Samburu.) A set of concrete economic transformations informed this perception. These transformations included the aftermath of land adjudication and the declining national labor market, as well as rapid population growth and droughts, and their effects on cattle holdings in the district.

In Samburu, land adjudication began in the mid-1970s. It took place primarily in the highlands on the Leroki plateau, the only region in the district suitable for agricultural production. In embracing market liberalization, the

Kenyan state devised new modes of land management in order to stimulate agricultural entrepreneurialism. Policymakers thought to divide land into collectively or individually owned holdings and encourage owners to invest in small-scale farming projects.[7] They hoped that in Samburu, freehold title deeds would prompt highlanders to engage in farming and sell their products—mostly beef—on the national market (Fumagalli 1978, 55–56; Perlov 1987, 38–87). However, the policymakers also believed—quite stereotypically, perhaps—that pastoralists preferred to manage their land collectively. Therefore, they invented "group ranches." The group ranch was a form of collective landownership that gave a set of people joint rights over the wider territory in which they lived. Siteti, for example, was part of a group ranch with three other neighboring villages, and the inhabitants of all these locations were "shareholders" in the ranch. Shareholders could use their land as collateral for bank loans and to initiate microfinance projects (Lesorogol 2008a, 45).

The process of land adjudication produced sharp inequalities throughout the district. A first set of inequalities emerged between the residents of the highlands and the residents of the lowlands. Whereas in the past, people had migrated back and forth between different parts of the district in search of pastures, adjudication initiatives excluded lowlanders from the more fertile lands of the Leroki plateau by making these the property of highlanders.[8] With diminished access to the territories of the highlands, lowland families had less mobility in times of drought and famine. In the absence of roads, cellular coverage, or police, lowlanders also became more exposed to armed cattle raids. Furthermore, because the territories of the lowlands were de facto the property of the government (or, as British colonials called them, "No Man's Land"), lowland residents, who did not legally own the land they inhabited, were often forcibly evicted from certain areas when these became appealing to investors.[9]

Another set of inequalities emerged within the highlands between people who obtained individual land title deeds, members of group ranches, and people who did not own land at all. The deed holders were usually men who had gone to school and worked either in the army or for the government as chiefs, councillors, or civil servants (Lesorogol 2008a, 60). These men knew how land adjudication worked and how to go about obtaining individual title deeds. They often drew on their ties of clientage to government officials and secured private ownership of large farms. Meanwhile, members of group ranches shared ownership of farmlands. But contrary to the expectations of policymakers, they subdivided land among themselves, fencing family plots and using them for individual farming, gardening, or pasture. Their plots were conspicuously smaller than the large farms of private owners. Lesorogol (54) shows, for example, how in the area of Mbaringon, five individuals had obtained individual title deeds for a total of 1,500 hectares, which represented as much as "36 percent [of] the size of Mbaringon group ranch, which had 307 registered members." Because members of group ranches initially lacked experience with state bureaucracy and the land privatization process, they were unable to object to the alienation of land by a few influential men. Throughout the 1980s and 1990s, people became aware of this problem and began seeking individual title deeds (71). During my research, however, group ranch shareholders still had not obtained individual deeds. Meanwhile, families who had settled in the highlands late had a worse fate—they were rarely able to claim any land whatsoever. They lived on government-owned land, including forests, where they were not allowed to build permanent dwellings or engage in agricultural work and where, like lowlanders, they risked being evicted at any time. In this context, land became an important prerequisite for respectability and belonging in the district.[10]

Emerging conflicts over access to land were aggravated by the decline of the national labor market following structural adjustment programs in Kenya. International lenders emphasized that in Kenya, "[government] spending had to be cut down to a smaller number of 'core' projects" (Swamy 1994, 21). As the state enforced budgetary cuts and numerous state enterprises shut down, people lost jobs. Although Samburu district never underwent a process of industrialization and most wage earners had migrated to other parts of the country, the decline of the national labor market affected locals significantly. Like elsewhere in Kenya, education had expanded in Samburu throughout the 1970s (Holsteen 1982, 27). But in the early 1980s, with the recession of the labor market, what was probably the largest generation of educated youth in the district graduated to face chronic unemployment. Consequently, many school graduates entered the informal sector or the so-called *jua kali* (S, lit., "hot sun"), engaging in petty trade. Many others returned to their rural homes, seeking to make a living on their families' lands. In this context, competition over the resources of lineage farmlands grew. Interestingly, large numbers of men continued to migrate to Nairobi, Nakuru, and other major cities to work in a growing security industry as watchmen and guards. But these were low-paid, unskilled jobs that fell short of delivering the promises of development.

Rapid population growth also played an important role in heightening competition over land and diminishing employment opportunities across

7. Moran with cattle herd at a well in the lowlands, 2010. (Photo by the author.)

the country. Throughout the 1980s, Kenya's population grew at a rate of 3.8 percent annually, while the population of Samburu District increased by 3.92 percent annually (Fratkin 1994, 56, 67). Also in Samburu, the population grew denser in areas with better economic possibilities, such as the highlands and areas near towns such as Maralal. As a result, individual farmlands sometimes became overcrowded, placing increased pressure on local resources.

Severe droughts created additional strains on economic life, as they decreased the number of cattle in the district. From 7.4 cattle per capita in 1962, cattle holdings decreased to 1.7 by 1984 (Sperling 1987, 4). Following land adjudication and rising population densities in the highlands, most cattle owners had less mobility in times of drought, and therefore their cattle died more quickly. Meanwhile, cattle ownership became more stratified than it had been in the past. On the one hand, rich landowners kept hundreds of cattle on their spacious private farms, sometimes transporting their herds on trucks to the lowlands in times of drought. On these occasions, they hired security patrols, which accompanied the trucks by car or—in the case of Samburu who were members of Parliament or leaders in the national army—even helicopter to prevent attacks from cattle rustlers along the way. On the other hand, overcrowded group ranches could no longer sustain large herds. Elders who lived on group-ranch land often sent family members to reside with the livestock in the lowlands (fig. 7). But in the lowlands (and in the western parts of the highlands), people often lost entire herds to armed cattle raiders. In this context, the poor became even poorer. Household surveys I carried out in Siteti, Lorosoro, and two lowland areas near Barsaloi and South Horr, respectively, show that by 2010–11, the number of cattle in these locales had decreased to an average of 3.43 head per household. At the same time, goats and sheep offered a more viable economic alternative to impoverished families (13.43 head per household).

Economic reforms pertaining to land and labor, together with rapid population growth and the transformation of cattle economies, produced new inequalities and strained livelihoods in Samburu. Because many families in the district found it increasingly difficult to earn a living through cattle husbandry, labor migration, or farming, they devised additional, alternative sources of cash and goods.

CHANGING LIVELIHOODS:
CHARCOAL, CHANG'AA, AND CHARITY

In 2008 for the first time, I visited the farmland of the Lekenyit lineage in Siteti. Telekwa Lekenyit, a senior elder of the lineage, became one of my key informants. He was a skilled storyteller who enjoyed spending many hours with me talking about the history and politics of the district. Telekwa belonged to the Lkishili age set (initiated in 1960 and in moranhood until 1976). I first visited him because he had been among the first men of Siteti to travel to the coast and work in tourism in 1982, although he was already a junior elder at that time. Throughout the following years, I visited him several times and also spent time with his brothers and their wives to learn about their lives.

Telekwa and his brothers were born in the northern part of the district, in the lowlands, in the early 1950s. When they were in their teens, devastating droughts reduced the family's herd to five cows. This convinced their father, Ltipiyan, to move to the highlands and settle in the forests near Siteti. In 1967, the local government evicted families from the forest and resettled the Lekenyits on the territories of today's Siteti. In the mid-1970s, Ltipiyan registered as a shareholder in the emerging group ranch. When group ranch members unofficially subdivided the land among themselves, he obtained a two-hectare plot on the slope of a hill. Before Ltipiyan died in the mid-1980s, his sons had begun marrying and having children. As heads of their own families, they quickly subdivided their father's plot into multiple small farms (fig. 8), each with its own homestead, garden, and in some cases kraal. Lakate, the eldest brother, lived on the southern part of the farmland; Ltingesi, the second-born brother, had died by the time of my research, but his wife, Ngarami, and their children lived on the southeastern edge; Telekwa,

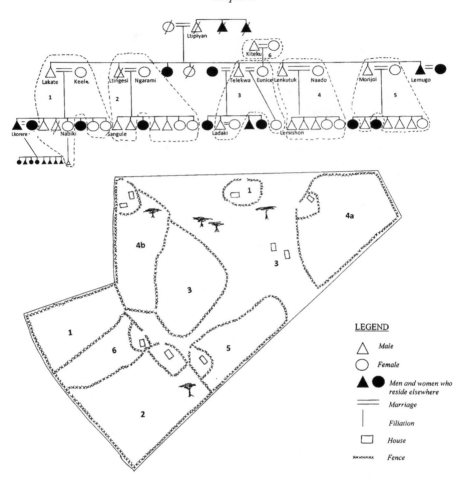

8. Kinship chart of the Lekenyit lineage and a map of the division of its farmland, Siteti, Samburu, 2010. (Documented and drawn by the author.)

the third-born, lived in a yet-unfenced homestead in the middle of the plot; Lenkutuk, the fourth brother, lived at the top of the hill and had also secured a homestead and a garden for his firstborn son, Lemishon, at the bottom of the hill; and Morijoi, the fifth brother, lived along the eastern boundary. Because each Lekenyit elder had some five to eight children, some of whom also had their own children, competition over an already overcrowded farmland had become intense.

All Lekenyits cultivated maize, beans, potatoes, and kale, but their overcrowded farmland did not produce enough food for subsistence. Nor did it have adequate space for livestock rearing. They had lost their livestock repeatedly to droughts throughout the past three decades. At the time of my research, only Ngarami, the widow of the second-born brother, owned cattle. With the help of her son, Sangule, who worked for a bank in Maralal, she had bought three cows. The rest of the family owned only small stock. (Telekwa owned some thirty goats and sheep, which he kept at a second residence in the lowlands, under the care of his first wife and their children; Lenkutuk owned four goats; Morijoi owned three.) Their livestock did not produce sufficient quantities of milk for the survival of the whole family. And although two sons of the lineage were formally employed, only one sent monetary remittances to his parents, and this money was not always enough to be shared with the lineage. Consequently, most Lenkenyits depended on charcoal making (fig. 9), alcohol brewing, and charity for a living.

All the brothers and most of their moran sons went to the forest several times a week to make charcoal to sell in Maralal. Since the 1980s, charcoal has been an important means of subsistence for people who lived in the vicinity

9. Telekwa Lenkenyit with his second wife, Eunice, and their baby in front of their nkerashai house. Telekwa was on his way to Maralal to sell charcoal; note the wheelbarrow with a sack of charcoal on the left. Siteti, Samburu, 2008. (Photo by the author.)

of towns. My surveys show that in Siteti, 80 percent of households relied, among other things, on charcoal for a living. Early in the morning, men of all ages went to the forests, cut dry trees, and sliced them into small pieces. Then they placed the wood in a pit dug in the ground, lit a fire, and let it burn for a few hours. Later, they placed the charcoal in raffia bags and, using a wheelbarrow, transported it to town. A sack of charcoal sold for KSh (Kenyan shilling) 200–300 (US$3–$4 at that time), money that was immediately spent on food. But charcoal making was extremely risky. It was illegal to cut trees from government-owned forests, and Kenya Wildlife Service rangers imprisoned those they caught with charcoal. Others, like Morijoi and Ngarami, also cut timber, made posts, and sold them to people constructing houses in their area. This practice, too, was illegal and therefore risky.

Lakate's wife, Keele, and Lenkutuk's wife, Naado, brewed chang'aa several times a week and sold it to neighbors. Chang'aa has been popular in the district (and throughout Kenya) since the 1980s (Holtzman 2005, 88). Women sold chang'aa for five or ten cents a glass, obtaining no more than KSh 200 (US$3 at that time) for a batch. Like charcoal and timber trade, however, domestic brewing was illegal, and had to be carried out discreetly. Police officers at times walked through villages seeking bribes from brewers. Women who did not bribe them stood by as officers broke their brewing pots.[11]

In addition to charcoal and chang'aa, relief food had also become an important, if only occasional, source of livelihood. Donated by charitable organizations from the United States and brought to Kenya by ships, this food consisted of monthly "rations" of maize flour and cooking oil. (In the lowlands in 2011, for instance, rations included ten kilograms of maize flour and two liters of cooking oil per month per household.) Whereas storage administrators sometimes sold charity foods to local stores at wholesale prices, villagers devised ways to claim double rations and sell the surplus for a profit. A man once pointed out to me how, despite the message in English printed on the flour sacks—"This is a gift from the American people. Do not sell!"—charity food had become an important source of cash. In addition, access to foreign patrons or sponsors—or charity in a more generic sense—played an important role. The presence of German, Dutch, and British NGO workers, Italian and Colombian missionaries, or various volunteers from Europe and North America has increased in the district since the early 1980s, fueling a growing sense that the best way to produce a future was no longer through flows of capital from the state but by establishing direct connections to an imagined abroad (M: *nkampo*) through clientage and kinship to foreigners.

Beginning in the 1980s, it was through such connections that some Samburu educated their children or built houses with iron-sheet roofs.

Charcoal, chang'aa, and charity food generated small amounts of cash that were immediately used to purchase sugar, rice, vegetables, milk, soap, and other goods for daily consumption. Only rarely did people manage to save cash. Nevertheless, they thought that these activities would in time bring them development. Some men hoped that one day, they would to be able to abandon charcoal making and do business with small stock (M: *bia-shara oo suom*), as quite a few people in Siteti and Lorosoro did. They bought goats and sheep cheaply in the lowlands and sold them for a better price in the highlands. Similarly, some women desired to be able to open shops. They would buy sugar, maize flour, and other commodities in towns and resell them more expensively to fellow villagers. For this purpose, they would build small kiosks at the gates of their homesteads or along village paths. Ultimately, both men and women hoped that in the future, they would obtain cattle, own land, and live better lives. While a few people actually managed to climb this imagined ladder of development from charcoal and chang'aa, to small stock and shops, and finally to cattle, most often the success of the few informed the desires of a majority that continued to live in poverty.

ENTRUSTMENT, RECIPROCITY, AND PRECARIOUS RESPECTABILITY

"Charcoal came to divide our families," I heard Telekwa say as he stood up to speak at a group ranch meeting held in November 2010 at Siteti's primary school. "There is nothing to keep us together anymore." Then he went on to explain: "The elder goes to make charcoal by himself. The mama goes to make charcoal by herself. And our children go to make charcoal by themselves. We each make our own money and eat our own share separately. There is nothing left to bring us together. The children no longer listen to their fathers and their elders." Telekwa's words evoked how limited resources and the necessity to act individually instead of collectively have erased distinctions of gender and generation. Such distinctions were otherwise important parts of lkeretita, or "the normal ways of doing things" (cf. Holtzman 2006). In a somewhat similar vein two months earlier, Lenkutuk, Telekwa's younger brother, had lamented the effects of chang'aa consumption at a meeting of the elders of the Maraato subclan (part of the Masula clan), to whom the Lekenyits belonged through patrilineal descent. "Chang'aa makes us hate each other," Lenkutuk said. "When a person is drunk, he knows nothing. He does not distinguish between an elder and someone of his own age. He can even abuse a senior person. This is shameful for the Maraato. Let us stop this shame, because we are the most senior subclan of the Masula clan and we are known by all of Samburu."

Respectability came sharply into question as people perceived that ideal relations of age, generation, gender, and kinship were eroding in the face of changing livelihoods. Not only did people struggle to produce the material resources meant for the production of respectability and prestige, but the new economic routes they had chosen often proved unpropitious. Some men and women I interviewed told me that money of chang'aa (M: *shilingini e chang'aa*) or money of charcoal (M: *shilingini e kuni*) did not last, because these currencies lacked life force. Selling chang'aa was profiting from people drinking and losing their collective vigor, while selling charcoal was profiting from burning living trees. People recognized that desperate times called for desperate measures, but they also agreed that certain modes of generating cash were relatively inauspicious.

As Telekwa pointed out, producing charcoal and chang'aa were individual economic activities that did not involve cooperation beyond—or sometimes even within—the household. Nevertheless, I observed during my field-work that cooperation between families, households, and kin groups *did*, in fact, gain new importance. People constantly took loans from neighbors and relatives, bought food on debt (M: *silen*) from local food stores, or organized themselves into entrepreneurial cooperatives to request bank loans. Entering debt (M: *ajing silen*) became a common mode of survival. For example, the so-called Maendeleo ya Wanawake (Development for Women) program started microfinance projects, offering women loans to open shops, raise chickens for sale, or make and trade bead decorations. Ngarami, the Lekenyit widow, was part of this group, which had gathered wives of different homesteads and lineages and generated new relations of cooperation between them. As elsewhere in Kenya, in Samburu, too, cooperation, credit, and entrustment gained renewed importance (Shipton 2007).

Relations of reciprocity within one's own lineage also gained renewed significance during this time. Customary claims to land appeared and disappeared continuously as sons and daughters established, severed, or remade ties of care and material support to their parents and kin. Young male wage earners sought to maintain access to land in order to have a place to return to in case they lost their jobs. Meanwhile, because remittances from their wages were indispensable to rural livelihoods, sons who had severed ties of material support with their lineages gradually lost their ability to claim land on lineage farms. The Lekenyit elders told me that their youngest brother, Lemugo, married a Swiss woman he had met in Mombasa and moved to Switzerland in the 1990s. He never came back. And because he had not supported his brothers financially over the years, they said that he could no longer claim a share of their farmland. Similarly, Lakate's firstborn son, Lkorere, who lived in the city of Nakuru with his wife and their eight children, could no longer claim land from his kin, because, as his father complained to me, "he never sends us anything." By contrast, Lenkutuk's son, Lemishon, had long supported his lineage with remittances from his salary as a soldier, so the Lekenyit elders unanimously agreed to give him a separate share of their farmland. Land was used strategically in this regard to establish and claim belonging while also ensuring the circulation of other kinds of resources.

Although in theory lineage daughters could not claim land from their father and brothers (for they were expected to live on their husband's land), in actuality, daughters who supported and cared for their parents and brothers could live and cultivate gardens on the farmlands of their father's lineage indefinitely. Lakate's daughter, Nabiki, who had borne a child without marrying, supported her father with money she obtained through daily work in Maralal, and thus continued to live on her father's land. Similarly, landless men could sometimes claim usufruct rights in land from the lineages of affinal kin by supporting them with money, labor, or other things. When Telekwa decided to take a second wife, for example, he no longer owned cattle. Meanwhile, the family of Kiteku, the father of Telekwa's prospective wife, Eunice, owned neither cattle nor land. So Telekwa and his brothers gave Kiteku a piece of their farmland, asking in return for one of their daughters in marriage. And while access to land did not replace the obligatory bridewealth payments as such, it gave Telekwa a good argument for deferring the payment of bridewealth indefinitely. At the same time, Telekwa's father-in-law told me that he looked forward to receiving bridewealth for his daughter, though he could not expect it anytime soon. "When we will get the bridewealth cattle," he said, "we will feel comfortable. Then we will not make charcoal anymore. We will not make chang'aa again." "And when will that be?" I asked. He sighed. "Only God knows."

MIGRATION AND RISING MARKETS OF CULTURE AND SEX

It was in this social and economic context that more Samburu than ever before turned to selling culture in order to make a living. Men and women who sold culture in northern Kenya included "mamas of the market," or women who traveled from villages to market towns to sell beadwork to retailers or travelers, and "plastic boys," young men who dropped out of school to sell souvenirs and act as tour guides for travelers. Yet none of them could depend exclusively on selling culture. Because the tourist presence was mostly concentrated at Kenya's coastal beach resorts and southern safari parks, only a few tourists, travelers, and backpackers ventured to northern Kenya. Until 1997, when cattle raiding and carjacking became more common in the north, some tourists had stopped in Maralal on their way to Lake Turkana and the northern deserts. Others booked safaris in the Samburu Game Reserve. But for the most part, Samburu remained out of reach for tourists, and thus saw cash from foreigners only sporadically. Moreover, such money when available was only enough to get by for a week or, at most, a month. Recall Mama Seiyina, who had traveled to South Africa and played in a Hollywood movie, yet had so little to show for it. Her payment was low, and she spent it all on food and clothes for her family. By contrast, young men who migrated to affluent tourist sites on the Kenyan coast typically made more money in a shorter time.

Samburu men began migrating to other parts of Kenya to sell culture in the early 1970s. At that time, as I showed in chapter 1, the Mayers' Ranch, in the town of Limuru, near Nairobi, was one of the few places in the country where tourists could watch, photograph, and film Maasai and Samburu moran dances (Bruner 2005). In 1977, Pollman Tours and Safaris built a cultural village in Mwapala, south of Mombasa, and recruited many Maasai and Samburu dancers from the Mayers' Ranch to work on the coast. Some one hundred men and women lived there, performing dances, posing for pictures, and selling beadwork to groups of tourists that visited them daily during the tourist season. However, the cultural village closed after one year. My informants recalled that most performers returned to their respective home areas at that time. But a few Samburu morans (of the Lkuroro age set) remained on the coast, trying to sell souvenirs at the beach in order to make a living on their own. During this time, hotel managers became very eager to integrate Samburu dances—often advertised as Maasai—in their hotels' evening schedules. Thus, Samburu performers began obtaining contracts. In addition, they also performed in entertainment parks (Marina Cultural Village, Ng'omong'o Cultural Village, and others) that hosted traditional houses and performers from Kenya's different ethnic groups. In the early 1980s, as the number of migrants to the coast grew, a Samburu diasporic enclave quickly emerged in the small town of Mtwapa, north of Mombasa (Kasfir 2007, 290–91). Samburu communities also emerged in Diani, Watamu, and Malindi.

Selling souvenirs and dancing for tourists allowed many of these men to save money, buy livestock, and sometimes build a house back home. Most of the elders of the Lenkenyit lineage of Siteti had participated in coastal tourism when they were young men. Telekwa, for example, joined the morans on the coast between 1982 and 1986. At that time, his parents had lost all their livestock to droughts and cattle diseases and were subsisting primarily on selling chang'aa. Seeing how men of his village returned from the coast with money, Telekwa decided to join them. He recalled:

> I saw there were lots of problems that were eating people at home. The problems were eating us. So I decided to go to Mombasa so that I can run up and down to find food to take home. I could see there is not enough food for people. One didn't normally go to Mombasa to make a living. That is, it was only problems that took us there. I used to sell spears so that I can eat. Whenever I got a little money, I ran back home.

Throughout the 1980s and 1990s, Telekwa's brothers Lenkutuk, Morijoi, and Lemugo also migrated to the coast. At the end of every tourist season, they returned to Siteti. With money obtained in tourism, they bought sheep, goats, and a few cows. Morijoi also built a three-room house with an iron-sheet roof on his share of the lineage farmland. And Lemugo married a Swiss woman and moved to Switzerland.

As a young boy, my research assistant, Lteipan, grew up near the Lekenyits. He witnessed the relative success of his neighbors. So after his initiation as a moran in 1992, he, too, went to the coast to make money. Lteipan recounted:

> You know, when I was circumcised, my family was very poor. We had only a few goats, but no cows. So when I was a moran, I said it is better for me to leave all this. I left my family with the goats, and I went to Mombasa, because I have seen my friends, they went to Mombasa and they came back and bought goats. And they bought cows. I talked to my friends, and they told me, "There, [in Mombasa], life is not as hard as it is here. Because later on, we want to marry; everyone wants to have a wife. And you see now, you have no cows, you have no goats . . ." That's why I went to Mombasa: to work and get something.

So Lteipan set off, hoping that like his friends, he would be able to acquire livestock and, once a junior elder, be able to marry. Poverty was therefore an important factor that prompted young men to migrate. But it was not the only one.

In addition to poverty, men I interviewed also invoked urgent personal problems and conflicts as their main reasons for going to Mombasa. Lteipan told me later on that although he had contemplated traveling to Mombasa for a long time, it was something else that prompted his final decision to leave—namely, the discovery that his girlfriend was pregnant. The woman's brothers threatened to beat Lteipan if he did not pay a customary fine and promise to marry their sister. But Lteipan's family had no means to pay the fine (usually one cow). So Lteipan ran off to Mombasa to make money to pay his fine and support his child and future wife. Several other men I interviewed had been in similar circumstances, preferring to run away to Mombasa rather than lose respectability at home. Still other men invoked conflicts with their fathers and lineage elders. Such conflicts involved fathers who drank excessively or elders who wanted their sons to engage in charcoal making, which some young men considered demeaning.

Yet other men explained that they went to Mombasa to make money to pay for their education. Sakaine, whom I interviewed in 2008, was a man in his early twenties who lived in Siteti with his widowed mother. She supported him and his five siblings by brewing chang'aa and selling charcoal. The District Education Office had assigned Sakaine a foreign sponsor to fund his education. But one day, when he was in high school, his teacher fraudulently reassigned the sponsorship to one of his own children. "I needed to find some way to get money fast to finish school," Sakaine recalled. "I loved school a lot, and I wanted to go back. That is why I went to Mombasa. I said I will go, make money, and then forget all about it."

Personal problems and conflicts led some young men to go to the coast at a particular moment in time. But many chose the coast—as opposed to other places in the country—because they desired the spectacular riches they believed they could obtain through relationships with European women. If selling souvenirs and performing dances allowed many men to buy livestock, pay fines for impregnating girls, and pay tuition fees, it was ultimately gifts of cash from foreign partners that enabled others to become some of the richest men in the district. They acquired large plots of land, livestock farms, villa-type houses, expensive cars, and private businesses. "I have seen people who came into whites [in Mombasa], and they built houses," one man explained to me. "I saw they have a good life, so this is why I decided to go to the coast." Another informant recalled, "I had heard that if you get a white woman, you will never lack anything again. My family was poor, so I went to Mombasa to try my luck."

Sex-for-money exchanges were very common in Samburu at the time of my research. But most of the time, they involved men offering gifts of cash—in addition to perfumes, soap, or creams—to women. This was not prostitution in any conventional sense. Although some young women indeed worked as prostitutes in towns, there was a more general sense that men had to offer women gifts of money and goods as tokens of love, care, and appreciation when engaged in extramarital sex. This was a common perception throughout Kenya (Mojola 2014). Samburu refer to sex as *mboita* (meaning, literally, "conjoining") or, more vulgarly, *nara* (fucking).[12] Most of my informants understood sex as benefiting, in principle, both men and women in equal manner. However, Christian, developmental, and consumerist notions of gender and sexual propriety also inflected these imaginaries of sex with gender asymmetries. Thus, occasionally, men depicted themselves as active beneficiaries and initiators of sex and women as more passive means of sexual satisfaction. For example, when talking among themselves, men used the verb *a-am*, meaning "to eat," to refer to their engagement in sex, while referring to their female sexual partners in the passive voice, as "being eaten" (M: *a-tamaki*). According to this logic, young men benefited from sex more, and therefore had to offer gifts of money and kind to their sexual partners. Meanwhile, some women strategically invoked such seeming gender asymmetries to demand gifts.

In sharp contrast to these gendered expectations of sex-for-money exchanges, men too could be recipients of gifts from women. What is more, on the coast, they obtained much more money than women engaged in sexual exchanges in Samburu while also at a safe distance from the eyes of kin, neighbors, or schoolmates. I shall return to this issue at greater length in chapter 3. Here it will suffice to point out that young men's engagement in sex for money was part of a wider sexual economy, both in Samburu and on the coast. Over time, Samburu men who traveled to the coast coupled a market of culture with a market for sex.

For many young Samburu men, traveling to the coast offered them the possibility of spending time with age-mates, away from kin and elders, in a place where, as one well knew, one could become rich overnight. In July 2011, Jackson, a young Samburu from Lorosoro, complained to me that his younger brother, Sempele, had decided to go to Mombasa, although, as an elder brother, Jackson had advised him not to go. Jackson had lived on the coast himself for several years, and joined me on a recent research trip to Mtwapa. From his experience on the coast, he concluded that life there had become more difficult than in the past. Now there were over one thousand Samburu men on the coast at the same time. Meanwhile, beach tourism had yet to recover from the postelection violence of 2008. During this time, competition for tourist attention was fierce among traders at the beach. Meanwhile, Jackson pointed out, many young men fell prey to drugs and prostitutes. But Sempele would hear none of it. When I met him, he was angry with his brother. "What does that idiot know?" he said. "He got his white woman, he got his house. . . . Why should I not try my luck also?" Indeed, Jackson was in a relationship with a German woman who sponsored him to build a house. But Jackson was not alone. Sempele's closest friends and age-mates in Lorosoro had already gone to Mombasa, as he explained:

> You know the sons of [our neighbor]? They are of my age set. We have been in school together. They both went to Mombasa two years ago. One of them got a Scottish lady, and he already has a house and a car. The other one has a French lady. He is rich. He has two houses: one in Maralal and one in Lorosoro, and he also has a business in town. And a car and a motorbike . . . And we are of the same age. What do I have? Nothing.

Sempele explained to me that he felt "left behind" relative to other men of his age set. While these men spent most of their time having fun, Sempele illegally cut timber posts from forests and sold them to people building houses. So he wanted to catch up with his age-mates and friends and also enjoy his youth at coastal resorts.

In addition to wealth and prestigious commodities, then, young men like Sempele also desired to travel to the coast as a way to hang out and have fun. On the one hand, this continued an older custom. The time of moranhood had long been a time for young men to detach themselves from household economies and enjoy life away from the controlling elders. On the other hand, fantasies of life in Mombasa and the promise of fast riches also informed these men's desire to hang out on the coast rather than somewhere else. For others, having a white girlfriend was in itself a marker of prestige, as white women represented the promise of a better future and a good life sustained by access to resources. Telekwa said:

> Some [morans] go [to Mombasa] for white women, and some go there only for business. . . . And for that matter, even the one who doesn't want a white woman will get one, because it is his luck. And they like it. They like it because they say they bring money to us. They say they like it because they bring food to us.

Fantasies of fast enrichment through relationships with European women made hanging out at coastal resorts a pleasurable pastime. A common phrase people in Samburu used to refer to the lives of Mombasa morans was "Mombasa raha"; that is, Mombasa is happiness or comfort or fun, all entailed in the Swahili noun *raha*.

Men who went to Mombasa sought solutions to poverty and hard economic times, and ways to escape and solve personal problems and conflicts. But they also sought the pleasures and enjoyments of life in a place where they believed they could become rich and respected overnight.

::::

Since the early 1980s, economic transformations in matters of land, labor, and livestock have produced new inequalities in Samburu. While a few families came to own large farmlands and hundreds of cattle, the vast majority of people struggled to sustain livelihoods by devising alternative economic activities. For many, these times of rapid economic transformation challenged older templates of respectability. Whereas a few rich families continued to perform weddings, bridewealth exchanges, and other life course ceremonies on time, in the absence of resources, impoverished families deferred these markers of respectability and belonging indefinitely (see chapter 5). In this context, some people marketed culture to become respectable. Elderly men and women I met in Siteti and Lorosoro took great pride in what had become globally marketable elements of their culture—their bodily appearances, their dances, beads, and spears. But they were more skeptical, sometimes even embarrassed, about the growing trend of morans engaged in sexual exchanges. Like Mama Seiyina, whom I cited in the beginning of this chapter, many Samburu considered a man having sex with older women or sharing with his family money obtained through sex as acts closely associated with adultery and incest. Prostitution, incest, and adultery were also perceived to be on the rise in the district, undermining older lines of deference and respectability anchored in boundaries of age and kinship and notions of propitious life. How were men and women to use money produced in sexual economies? Could such money be converted into local forms of respectability and prestige? And what would happen to a globally marketable Samburu culture, if young men now coupled it with sex? Such questions now figured centrally in struggles over respectability and belonging in Samburu.

3. Slippery Intimacy and Ethno-erotic Commodification

By taking on sexuality as its assistant, exchange value transforms itself into sexuality.
All manner of goods are enveloped by its surface, and this background of sexual
enjoyment becomes the commodity's most popular attire.
—FRITZ HAUG, *CRITIQUE OF COMMODITY AESTHETICS*

On a Sunday morning in August 2010, Elise stopped by my house in Maralal to invite me to spend the day with her in the village of Lorosoro. When I met her one year prior, Elise, a German, had just broken up with her Samburu partner of two years. But she had many friends in northern Kenya, and returned often to the region. She stayed in a small lodge in Maralal, and during the day took road trips and visited friends. Once in a while, she stopped by my house to drink coffee and talk. I enjoyed our time together, so I gladly accepted her invitation to join her in Lorosoro. That morning, Elise was in a rush. She wanted to go to Lorosoro to visit her friend Helga. Helga, I knew, was one of Elise's dearest friends. She, too, was from Germany. But they had met while on vacation at a beach resort in Kenya. As I followed Elise to the car, she explained why she wanted to see Helga. A few days earlier, Elise met an Austrian woman named Johanna, who had come for the first time to Samburu to visit the family of a moran she was dating. Because Johanna worried about the future of her relationship and desperately needed some advice, Elise decided to take her to Helga. She explained that Helga had lived with her partner for nearly one year, and they seemed to get along well. Johanna and her partner, Rasta, joined us in the taxi Elise had hired for the trip. Though Rasta was not aware of the trip's purpose, he seemed concerned. He was quiet, somewhat displeased. He reminded me of Samburu friends on the coast who preferred that their white girlfriends not hang out with each other lest they compare relationships and start fighting with them.

"How beautiful it must be to live here in the bush, in the middle of nowhere, with such a lovely landscape around you," Elise said as our car pulled up in front of Helga's homestead. "She lives like a real Samburu. I would move here tomorrow, if I could."

But Johanna was not impressed. "Oh, my God," she said in German so Rasta would not understand. "She lives in a traditional homestead? I am horrified."

Elise was disappointed by Johanna's remark. "Well, you better get used to it," she said, smiling. Later, Elise told me she wondered about Johanna's real intentions. "Does she come here because of the beauty of the country? Or does she come here for men and sex?"

Helga lived in a small compound with two traditional nkerashai houses. One belonged to her and her partner, Jackson, the other to Jackson's mother and younger brother. The arrangement was temporary. Helga was financing the building of a large house with modern amenities nearby, and had to live in the small mud house until the new house was ready. As I bent down to enter through the low doorway, Johanna waited outside, hesitating to enter. "Say, can you see anything in there, or is it all dark?" The dim light came mostly from a small, round hole in the wall and from an oil lamp hanging from the ceiling. But I could see fine. The house had two rooms. The first had a hearth on the ground enclosed by three rocks, and a few wooden benches that were placed along the walls. The second room, where Helga spent most of her time, was much livelier, though it was no larger than thirty-two square feet. Blue linoleum with geometric patterns covered the earth floor. Colorful pillows, blankets, and sheets adorned the traditional bed, or *ruat* (a wooden platform raised one foot above the ground). And floral-patterned green fabric hid some of the rough surfaces of the mud walls. There was a small coffee table with some plates, cups, and a candlestick in the middle of the room, and a cabinet covered with a white tablecloth stood by the wall. Clean glasses and cutlery hung from a metal frame on the cabinet.

Helga wished to keep her room clean, so she asked us to remove our shoes. She was very happy to have guests. She sliced a sponge cake she had bought in town and put some biscuits on a plate. Rasta talked with Jackson in the other room while Jackson's mother prepared tea. Elise, Johanna, and I sat on the floor in Helga's room. We spoke in German, though every now and then, Helga slipped English and Maa words into her sentences. "It's been so long since I have spoken German," she explained. "I'm beginning to mix things up." She talked at length about her relationship with Jackson and his mother, and said that she was very happy with their love, support, and understanding. "They are my family now."

Johanna listened carefully. Suddenly, she interrupted Helga.

"Listen, I don't know what to do." She leaned forward on her knees and looked Helga in the eye. "My man is nothing like yours. I have problems with him. He wants me to buy him everything." She went on to describe how Rasta asked her to pay for his family's expenses, and how he asked her to build him a house and buy him land. He told her that his friends laughed at him, wondering how it was that he had a *mzungu* girlfriend but no money. "I don't want to see him stressed about his family and his friends," Johanna said.

"It's your own fault for showing him that you have money," Elise interrupted. Then she turned to Helga: "Yes, she gave him 1,000 euros for her trip from Mombasa to Samburu. Who does that? You can come here with only twenty euros." Elise turned once more to Johanna. "I saw you telling him about your trips to Jamaica and all over the world. Then you pay so much money for everything. Of course, he thinks that you are rich."

Johanna sat quietly, staring at the dark ceiling.

"You cannot do this!" Helga protested. "He will use you. He will only be there with you because of your money. How will you know if he loves you or if he just likes your money?"

Johanna looked puzzled. Tears started running down her cheeks. "What shall I do now?"

"Don't give him any more money!" Helga replied. "Just tell him there is no more money until he goes and works for himself!"

Then Johanna explained that Rasta had threatened to leave her and return to Mombasa if she refused to support him with cash.

"Oh, is that so?!" Helga said, her eyes widening and her voice taking on a cynical tone. "He wants to go back to Mombasa because his other client-machines [German: *Kundenmaschienen*] are coming. What is wrong with you, my sister [G: *meine Schwester*]? Can't you look the truth in the eye? We are not stupid. We women are not stupid. He only wants your money. This is not love. I am sorry I have to tell you this, but you must end it immediately. These are just male *malayas* [S, prostitutes]. These are beach boys. I live here and I know them. They have six women at the same time. Leave him and don't ever get yourself a beach boy again!" Helga paused. For a few seconds she just stared at the wall. "I also live with the Samburu and I don't have these problems," she then said. "My family understands if I don't have money."

As Johanna began to feel more comfortable in Helga's presence, she also confessed that Rasta had stolen money from her twice, and that on one occasion, when she helped him with his email account, she had discovered messages he had sent to other foreign women. She read them in secret. She discovered that Rasta had told all these women that he loved them and that he wanted to marry them. He also asked them for money, invoking illness in his family or other urgent matters. Helga and Elise nodded with sneering smiles. Their suspicions had just been confirmed. Helga then said, "My love, end it now, before it is too late. He only wants your money, nothing else."

Johanna's dilemma and her conversation with Elise and Helga were premised on a deep-seated cultural assumption that relations based on love and relations based on monetary exchange were incompatible with each other. While love belonged to the realm of romance, money belonged to the realm of the market. As Viviana Zelizer (2005, 27) notes, it is a common Euro-American belief that "money and intimacy represent contradictory principles whose intersection generates conflict, confusion, and corruption." Helga, Johanna, and Elise echoed this belief when assuming that Rasta's interest in Johanna's financial support was incompatible with the possibility of love and romantic intimacy. For Helga, only "beach boys" or "prostitutes" asked for money in exchange for love, romance, and sex. According to her, a desire for money prompted beach boys to cheat tourists into believing that they loved them. She thought that real romance, by contrast, rested beyond money and markets. Because Jackson was working as a driver when Helga had met him on the coast, she claimed he had never been a beach boy. In other words, he had not yet been corrupted by a lust for easy money. What is more, having moved with Jackson away from the touristy coast—a place that, as both foreigners and Kenyans saw it, enticed young men to become beach boys—Helga thought that she evaded the possibility of further monetary interests and demands. Other European women I interviewed also held that tourism corrupted Samburu, who would otherwise not desire money—or at least not to the same extent. This culturally othering notion of Samburu as a people who existed outside the market economy was not merely a stereotype but a condition of possibility for women to desire authentic intimacy. But just as many European women I met in Kenya were familiar with young men's expectations for money, so men like Rasta were also familiar with women's expectations for love and romance, as we shall see. Therefore, they actively tried to dissociate their requests for money from sex and intimacy, justifying them by invoking personal problems.

Negotiating the role of money in relation to intimacy and fantasies of cultural difference and ethnosexuality was an important aspect of the relationships between Samburu men and European women. Such negotiations also informed how women socialized with one another, and how they asserted or undermined the authenticity of one another's intimate relations. I was surprised at first to see how quickly Helga and Johanna bonded that day, despite having never met before. Their shared language or their somewhat similar social positions as white girlfriends of local men might have been part of the reason behind their instant connection. After all, Helga addressed Johanna as "my sister." But white women in relationships with local men did not always seek each other's company; on the contrary, many felt that the presence of other white women undermined the authenticity of their experiences and relationships in Samburu. Thus, they preferred to avoid each other altogether. Helga, however, took a different approach. Adopting an authoritative voice in relation to Johanna, she not only claimed intimate knowledge of local expectations and practices, but also presented herself as someone who had gained the real love of a Samburu and his family, a love untainted by money. In the years that followed, I became very close to both Helga and Jackson, and learned that they had many relationship problems of their own, many of which did in fact involve money. But Johanna's relationship to Rasta—tenuous as it might have been—offered Helga the possibility of performing and claiming a certain difference from other white women, a difference she felt she had achieved by living like a Samburu and in familial relations with locals.

After we returned to Maralal that afternoon, Elise and I dropped off Johanna and Rasta in front of their motel, and we all agreed to meet for dinner at a local restaurant. Later that evening, when Johanna and Rasta entered the restaurant, it was clear that they had quarreled. Johanna was shaking with anger. She walked up to me and told me—in English this time—that Rasta had asked her again to build him a house because, while in Lorosoro, he had seen that Helga was also building one for Jackson.

"Please, George, tell him what Helga said," Johanna cried. "Tell him how her man never asks for any money. He does not want to believe me. Maybe he will believe you. Tell him how that guy [Jackson] works hard to earn his own money and doesn't ask her for anything. Please tell him." Embarrassed by Johanna's angry outburst in the middle of the restaurant, Rasta walked out. Elise and I tried to calm Johanna down. We suggested that she talk to Rasta calmly and decide what was to be done. When Rasta returned and we finally sat down for what was a rather awkward dinner, Johanna asked me again for my opinion on her relationship as compared to Helga's. I tried to avoid this difficult situation by saying that each couple is different, so comparing oneself to others is not always helpful. However, such difficult situations remained common throughout my field research. Men and women who agreed to collaborate with me and share their problems sometimes expected my advice and help. They would not accept my being a passive observer at all times. So I gave my opinion as I thought right, without divulging what I knew about other couples in similar situations. That evening, Johanna and Rasta promised to have a serious discussion. Two days later, they broke up. Johanna left for Austria, and Rasta rejoined his age-mates on the coast.

Intimacies between Samburu men and women from the global North constitute circuits of desire and monetary exchange that I call *ethno-erotic economies*. I speak of intimacies to refer not just to sex but more broadly to everyday ways of being in each other's company while variously expressing and contesting desires and affects. As Neville Hoad (2007, 2) argues, "The term *intimacy* is useful in that it suggests relations between bodies that are not reducible to identitarian or psychoanalytic notions of sexuality." Although intimacies remain in excess of sexuality (a set of discourses and practices associated more specifically with erotic desire and pleasure), in the contexts I describe here, fantasies of ethnosexuality and logics of exchange value informed intimacies in myriad ways. It was through intimate moments—encounters at the beach, in hotels and discos, or during trips to northern Kenya or Europe—that Samburu men sought to appeal to women's fantasies of them as sexual morans. And it was through such intimate encounters that the bodies of young men achieved the difference of race, ethnicity, and culture that granted them their potential value as commodities. Samburu men discussed these intimacies with each other while on the coast, by way of learning "what mzungu women wanted." And women like Helga, Elise, and Johanna also discussed such intimacies at length, seeking to distill meaningful experiences of love, romance, and authenticity and foreclose what they saw as ties of material exploitation.

Open to contingency, intimacies were often slippery. As men and women sought to grasp their encounters and shape them to their expectations, their intimate lives shifted, took new, unexpected turns, and sometimes dissolved as suddenly as they had emerged. I use the phrase "slippery intimacy" not to suggest that intimacy can ever be fully stable, but rather to emphasize how my interlocutors perceived the fragility of their intimacies to have wide-ranging consequences for their lives. To understand what anchored ethno-erotic economies and transformed ways of belonging in Samburu, it is crucial to examine intimacy, social actors' investments in its durability, and its links to commodity logics and ethno-erotic fantasies. How did men and women envision and act on these links? What did they expect from their intimacies? And how did they make them last, despite the constant prospect that they would fail?

INTIMACY AND THE LOGICS OF COMMODIFICATION IN LATE CAPITALISM

Concrete intersections of intimacy, fantasy, and money—their performance, contestation, and renegotiation in practice—continuously complicate and expand possible ways in which sexuality emerges as a commodity. It is therefore important to ask how such moments could push us to understand what *commodification* means when talking about ethno-erotic economies in their late-capitalist instantiation. It is also important to understand how attempts to render cash through intimate moments are not ways of simply packaging a preexisting ethnosexuality but rather key modalities of producing it. The kind of "labor" that goes into the production of the ethno-erotic commodity involves performances driven by fantasies of cultural and sexual alterity and a constant preoccupation with their authenticity as part of intimate moments. Such intimacies can therefore reveal what is new about sexual commodification in the present.

Since the late 1970s, market liberalization, the retraction of the welfare state, and the diversification and intensification of consumerism have led, among other things, to new forms of sexual commodification. Sociologist Elizabeth Bernstein (2007) argues that a new model of sexuality emerges with postindustrial capitalism in the global North. This is a "recreational sexual ethic" that is distinct from older models of "procreative" or "companionate" intimate arrangements, and infused more substantially with the logics of market exchange and the rising service industry. "Instead of being premised on marital or even durable relationships," Bernstein writes, "the recreational sexual ethic derives its meaning from the depth of physical sensation and from emotionally bounded erotic exchange" (6). She calls this "bounded authenticity," a form of exchange whose spatial and temporal boundaries are clearly defined, and whose value rests with the quality of the bodily encounter. This is the kind of sex exchange that takes place, for example, in gentlemen's clubs or brothels (Allison 1994; G. Mitchell 2015). Yet bounded authenticity also may represent a more figurative idiom for understanding how market logics suffuse the private realms of sex and sentiment in the present. For example, a woman from, say, England who has sex with a Samburu moran for money during her vacation at a coastal tourist resort seeks, without any further ties, a kind of "bounded authenticity" whose commodity status is clearly defined within the space and time of her vacation. So, too, as we shall see, does a Samburu moran who—having acquired money from a European woman—hires the sexual services of a young African woman for his own pleasure. But such sex-for-money exchanges also work relationally to imbue with implicit commodity value sexual intimacies for which one would normally not have to pay (sex between long-term partners, for instance).

Bounded authenticity, then, is not the only form of intimate commodification that is somehow representative of neoliberal capitalism. For it does not explain why, in fact, so many Samburu men and foreign women desired to produce long-lasting relationships that extended beyond tourist resorts. With the intensification of migration and transnational mobility in the past four decades, intimacies that sustain flows of affect, care, and money over time while connecting different socioeconomic centers to various peripheries are also increasingly important. Hence, durable relationships of love, kinship, and care have also become more intensively commodified (Constable 2009). Yet within these contexts, commodification is often less overtly transactional and more implicitly animated by value speculations. It is important, then, to explore precisely the coexistence of these two opposite kinds of intimate exchanges—one bounded and the other more durable and expandable—and the ways they inform the making of ethno-erotic commodities.

In many African contexts, past and present, intimacy has been imbedded, in complex ways, in material exchanges.[1] Jennifer Cole (2004) argues that various forms of "transactional sex," that is, sex-for-money exchanges, have long animated African sexual economies. These include not only what is conventionally understood as prostitution but also "more long-term liaisons characterized by the exchange of sex and caring services for material support, sometimes ending in formal marriage" (597). Following market liberalization, Cole shows, transactional sex became a common source of money. For example, some women in urban Madagascar pursued means of respectability and reproduction through transactional sex and transnational marriages with men from France. Mark Hunter (2010, 218) argues that with deindustrialization and rising unemployment in South Africa, "certain aspects of intimacy have come to play a more central and material role in the 'fleshy, messy, and indeterminate stuff of everyday life'" (4). Hunter maintains, "Sex has not become commodified in the sense that it is traded impersonally for money, instead it is enmeshed in new forms of emotion and reciprocity— exchanges more akin to gift relations" (180). Yet the distinction between commodity and gift may not be as stable a criterion of analysis as Hunter seems to suggest. Rather, the workings of commodification in relation to intimacy may also shift at this moment in time; commodification possibly expands beyond "impersonal" transactions to encompass also relations that, at first sight, don't seem transactional as such. For in late capitalism, as Jean Comaroff (2007, 213) argues, sexuality and intimacy, like other realms of life, are "inflected more and more tightly by the logic of commodification in both its productive and dystopic forms." And so, as the conversation above be- tween Helga, Elise, and the Johanna suggests, the boundaries between inti- macy and commodity become themselves obscure.

To understand such historical reconfigurations of intimacy and sexual commodification, it is not enough to focus solely on tourism. Studies of tourism, more generally, and the anthropology of tourism, more specifi- cally, have long been characterized by a relatively exclusive focus on tourist sites or "host" and "guest" encounters at the expense of the wider social worlds of which such sites and encounters are part.[2] This analytical focus has prompted scholars of sex tourism to ask mostly comparative questions. For example, a recurrent problem for these studies is whether female tour- ists reproduce or undermine structures of domination inherent in touristic forms of sexual consumption that are typically associated with men. Some scholars argue that "female sex tourists" are indeed occupying the same ex- ploitative positions as their male counterparts (Albuquerque 1998; Kempa- doo 2001; Phillips 1999; Sanchez Taylor 2001). Others claim that women are doing something else, less exploitative—something called "romance tour- ism" (Dahles and Bras 1999; Jeffreys 2003). However, for me this question essentializes gender and dehistoricizes intimacy in ways that are quite prob- lematic (Meiu 2009). Such comparative questions cannot explain how, for example, ex-tourists and locals craft intimate lives, together and in relation to others, when not involved in tourism as such, and how such intimacies in turn shape tourist encounters. The assumption here is that we already know what sex and its commodification are, and that they can either invert binary gender relations or not. I wish to challenge this assumption by opening up the meanings of intimacy and the commodity to ethnographic interrogation.

Sex-for-money exchanges on the Kenyan coast and in Samburu reached far beyond the realms of tourism. Samburu migrants participated in such exchanges with both African and European women in ways that drew on and reproduced various ethnosexualities and sustained flows of cash. Rather than undertake an anthropology of tourism, then, tourism remains for me only one—albeit important—part of the wider ethno-erotic economies that I map throughout this book. The framework of ethno-erotic economies reveals how tourist encounters are the product of—and in turn generate— intimacies and relations that reach far beyond the here-and-now of tourist locales and their social actors. Throughout these contexts, ethnosexuality emerges through but also expands the logics of the commodity form as men and women negotiate how bodies, intimacies, and performances relate to money and exchange value.

The following sections explore how Samburu male migrants entered sexual economies in coastal Kenya; how they performed moran ethno-sexuality as part of their intimate encounters with tourists; what European women expected from their relationships with Samburu men; and how part-ners negotiated their intimacies. I situate these intimacies within wider cir-cuits of sexual speculation and patronage in Kenyan coastal communities, and describe how Samburu men sought to safeguard their relative advantage in markets of ethnosexuality through ethnic enterprises registered with the state. These historical developments, I argue, were premised on a central irony. While intimacies were highly fragile and uncertain, growing markets of ethnosexuality gave rise to all kinds of attempts to fix and stabilize such slippery intimacies as a condition of value production. Yet in the end, such attempts themselves became driving forces of intimacy's slipperiness.

SEXUAL ECONOMIES ON THE KENYAN COAST

Six hundred miles from Samburu in the town of Mtwapa, thousands of mi-grants from various parts of Kenya made a living in the informal economies that had emerged with the rise of beach tourism. Numerous discos, pubs, and restaurants, some with German names, lined the Mombasa-Malindi highway that passed through the middle of Mtwapa, along the shore of the Indian Ocean. Every evening, these locales hosted foreign and domes-tic tourists, travelers, businessmen, and expatriates, who drank and danced alongside comparatively poor Kenyan youth. For young men and women, sex with foreigners was a way to access cash while also enjoying the pleasures of urban life and consumption. Some of them desired to marry foreigners and migrate to Europe. They hoped that they would find employment overseas and lead better lives. Others wished to sustain long-distance relationships with European partners as a way to build houses, open businesses, and live luxuriously in Kenya. While waiting for such life-transforming encounters, many entertained clients of the opposite or same sex, while others sought the patronage of rich, more senior Kenyan "sugar daddies" and "big mamas." In the vicinity of the clubs, men and women of all ages had found means of livelihood in and around the sexual economy. They worked in supermarkets, restaurants, lodges, furniture and leather workshops, butcher shops, gas stations, and cybercafes. Some opened secondhand clothing shops or CD and DVD kiosks, while others sold roasted maize, fruit, vegetables, and newspapers on the sidewalks. Still others sold love magic and sorcery services, promising their customers intimate partners of their choice, whether foreign or local. At different times, some of these traders also moved in and out of sexual exchanges.

Contemporary sexual economies are not new phenomena. When Samburu men began migrating to coastal towns in the late 1970s and early 1980s, they came to inhabit social spaces in which sex and ethnicity had long been at play in exchanges of money, pleasure, and care. While exchanges of goods for sex have long existed in various forms in East Africa, the production of sex as a commodity intensified with monetization, labor migration, and urbanization throughout the early colonial era. By the 1920s, Mombasa and Nairobi had become important centers of employment in Kenya, attracting high numbers of male workers from across the colony. The international port of Mombasa brought thousands of labor migrants to the coast (Cooper 1987). Young women migrated to urban areas to sell sex to African laborers, European settlers and administrators, Indian and Arab businessmen, and foreign travelers (L. White 1990). Young African men also engaged in sex-for-money exchanges with "johns" (S: *majoni*), that is, male European sailors and marines, but also with African and Arab male clients.[3] As Luise White (1990) shows for female prostitutes in colonial Nairobi, the same was true for Mombasa: prostitutes—male and female alike—often accumulated large amounts of cash, bought houses, and became landlords. White (26) argues that "prostitution was essential to the smooth running of a migrant labor economy." The colonial government had initially prohibited wives from joining their husbands in towns as a way to sustain a cyclical migratory system of cheap labor. In this context, prostitutes offered male laborers access to sexual pleasures and domestic services in ways that recaptured some of "the comforts of home." In a letter to the Municipal Council of Mombasa in 1966, three years after the end of colonial rule, a Muslim leader complained that male prostitutes "make a lot of money." "There are many of them," he wrote, "who have bought houses and expensive furniture and other[s] are spending lav-ishly without paying any taxes."[4]

Sexual economies, however, extended beyond the transactions of prosti-tutes and their clients. They included various relations of patronage, client-age, friendship, and kinship. In the 1960s, rich male prostitutes who had sex with men in Mombasa sought girlfriends among the daughters and wives of the most respected Swahili elders. The same Muslim leader I quoted above complained that girls and women "are being spoiled by these male prosti-tutes by being offered huge sums of money and/or gifts of the kind that they have not seen or [been] given . . . by their husbands and parents."[5] So-called male prostitutes often converted their riches into forms of kinship and power that local elders found worrisome. Other examples of transactional sex on the coast in the 1960s and the 1970s include "kept men" and "tem-porary wives." Kept men were poor young men who took rich, single, older African women as their patrons. Many of these women had become wealthy selling sex. Kept men typically performed tasks deemed feminine, such as cooking and cleaning, and also had sex with their patrons in exchange for cash, clothes, and other goods (Gachuhi 1973, 7). Meanwhile, temporary wives were women who resided with male labor migrants for a few years. In addition to sex, these women provided men with housekeeping labor. In ex-change, they received cash and other gifts.[6]

Girlfriends of male prostitutes who had sex with men, kept men, and temporary wives do not fit neatly in the essentialist, ahistorical category of sex workers. Rather, these actors played central roles in what Jennifer Cole (2004, 579) describes—in this case, for urban Madagascar—as "a com-plex sexual economy with many different ways of using sex to create rela-tionships." Sexual economies thus understood are animated not necessarily by sex workers but rather by myriad subjects engaged in different forms of "transactional sex" or sex-for-money exchanges (573). From this vantage point, purchased sex and sex between long-term partners or spouses were not that different. That is to say, prostitutes often also provided food, care, and affection to their customers, while spouses and long-term partners also engaged, if sometimes indirectly, in sex-for-money exchanges. Mark Hunter (2010, 178–90) refers to these multifaceted material aspects of transactional sex as "the materiality of everyday sex," that is, exchanges that accompany sex and include money, gifts, and services. Indeed, the materiality of every-day sex is an important element of Kenyan sex economies, past and present.

Ethnicity has played an important role in coastal sexual economies from the very beginning. Ethnic welfare associations actively regulated female sexuality in towns (for Nairobi, see L. White 1990, 190–94). Throughout the 1950s and 1960s in Mombasa, associations such as the Kakamega Society (of the Luhya ethnic group), the Kipsigis-Nandi Union, the Luo Welfare Society, the Taita-Taveta Union, and the local Coast African Cultural Society invoked the colonial Vagrancy Act (which prohibited unemployed men and women from living in towns) to repatriate prostitutes of their respective ethnic groups to their native areas. The predominantly male members of these associations believed that women engaged in transactional sex "spoiled the name of the tribe." Seeking to control "their" women, the groups also ethnicized women's sexualities, regulating them through ethnic categories of control. Furthermore, in towns, the ethnicities of prostitutes and clients played an important role in determining the exchange value of sex. For example, urbanites believed that men of certain ethnic groups had more money or paid better than others for sexual services, while women of certain ethnic groups offered better sexual services or were more exotic than others (L. White 1990, 107–9).

Transactional sex of various kinds was of critical importance to the effective running of a predominantly male, migrant labor economy. But with the decline of the national labor market in the mid-1970s, sexual economies did not disappear. To the contrary, coastal sex economies have flourished since then (Kibicho 2009; Omondi 2003; Tami 2008). The coastal town of Mtwapa became a haven for all kinds of transactional sex. As European retirees mostly from Germany, England, and Italy bought land and built properties in what had initially been a small Giriama village, Mtwapa quickly turned into Kenya's infamous "Sin City." Expatriates—known among residents as Kenya Kimbo, that is, "the cooking fat of Kenya" (Kimbo is a local brand name for cooking fat)—fueled a large market for casinos, discos, and nightclubs. In August 2008, a columnist with the *Standard*, a major national newspaper, observed that Mtwapa was "one of the fastest growing urban centers in Kenya." With "large apartments and commercial buildings . . . sprouting off the ground in virtually every corner," the town was "enjoying a building boom." The columnist wondered, "Where is the money coming from and why isn't the same happening in other towns?" "The answer," he suggested, "is loud and clear: sex, mainly between beautiful local girls and boys, and elderly Europeans . . . of German and British origin."[7] In 2010, a Kenyan journalist remarked that Mtwapa was a place of "unforgettable fun, sin and loads of cash." Animated by strippers, exotic dancers, streetwalking prostitutes, gays and lesbians, and "tourists [who] shamelessly come to seek casual sex," Mtwapa, he wrote, "comes to life, with sin that can put Sodom and Gomorrah to shame."[8] By 2011, administrators of the Kilifi and Mombasa Districts, at the borders of which the town is located, fought over its territorial incorporation, in no small part because of its spectacular revenues from the sex economy. Samburu men became key actors in the growing sex economies of Mtwapa and, if to a lesser extent, also in other coastal towns such as Ukunda (Diani Beach), Watamu, and Malindi, where similar sexual economies arose. Because Mtwapa was situated close to major beach resorts on Mombasa's North Coast, many young men strategically chose to rent rooms and live there. In 2008 and 2011, I joined Samburu men on their seasonal trips to Mtwapa to learn how they organized their lives, how they met tourists, and how their relationships unfolded.

PERFORMATIVE LABOR AND ETHNO-EROTIC FANTASY IN TOURIST ENCOUNTERS

Samburu men who arrived for the first time on the coast believed that it was relatively easy to produce value from their ethnic identity and bodily appearance. In 2008, a young man told me he had heard that "in Mombasa, a mzungu can fall in love with you, even if you don't talk to her." Many other young men who decided to migrate to the coast shared this belief. Upon arrival on the coast, however, they soon realized that things were not so simple. In order to be successful in doing business with the whites (M: *lbiashara o lmusunku*), Samburu migrants had to learn first how to become what they called morans of business (M: *lmurran loolbiashara*) (fig. 10). This involved learning the routines of life on the coast, how to bargain with curio traders for the handicrafts they would resell at the beach, how to bribe the officers of the Kenya Tourist Police for access to beaches, and how to enter the networks of beach vendors, with their rules, commissions, and benefits. It also involved learning to interact with tourists, to speak English and Swahili, and to have basic conversations in German and Italian. Most important, men also had to learn how to perform moranhood in ways that appealed to tourists.[9]

"The beach is our university," said Paul, a twenty-six-year-old man I met in 2011 in Mtwapa. He and I were sitting on Bamburi Beach in the shadow of his souvenir display table—what beach traders called a "show." He normally sat by his show, from nine in the morning until dusk. Sometimes, hours would pass before any tourists stopped by, so he did not mind my sitting with him. "You know," he said, "here at the beach, even those of us who have never

10. A "moran of business" talks to tourists in front of his display table ("show"). On the right, other beach boys wait at a respectful distance to approach the tourists. Bamburi Beach, April 2011. (Photo by the author.)

gone to school, we begin to speak the language of the whites [English], to learn some math, and how to write. The beach is like a school for us." Paul first arrived on the coast in 2005. He had never attended school and spoke neither Swahili nor English at the time. Upon arrival on the coast, he rented a room in Mtwapa with another Samburu man, an age-mate who belonged to the same clan. At first, Paul obtained a poorly paid job as a watchman for a German-owned restaurant. This gave him time to adjust to his new social environment and learn about life on the coast. Six months later, he was well prepared to begin working at the beach. "I took the savings I had from my wages as a watchman and bought bead necklaces and bracelets. I also ordered this big table," he said, pointing to his "show." "Then I applied for a beach permit and started working here."

Paul's show stood in the midst of numerous souvenir stands of Kamba and Giriama traders and was no more than a hundred meters away, on either side, from the displays of other Samburu men. Because of the tight competition that existed among these traders, Paul quickly learned that it took skill to attract tourists to his display and to persuade them to purchase his handicrafts. But by the time I met him, six years after he had begun migrating to the coast, Paul was already a role model for other Samburu men at the beach. They often tried to emulate his charm and friendliness in their dealings with tourists. My friends suggested that I spend some time with Paul if I wanted to learn how morans did business with tourists.

Every morning before going to the beach, Paul wrapped a red cloth around his waist, tightened a few colored bead strings around his neck, and placed seven thick bead bracelets on each forearm. He also placed two strings of beads in an X across his bare chest and some silver chains at his ankles. He wore his hair long, braided, and decorated with ribbons and beads in a fashion that tourists were likely to recognize from travelogues and postcards. While at the beach, he also carried a spear and a club. Like other Samburu men, Paul sought to distinguish himself from other beach boys and be appealing to tourists.[10] "These clothes make all the difference," he told me when, after I had spent a whole day with him at his souvenir stand, I pointed out how easy it was for him to gain tourists' attention.

When I asked Mary, a real-estate agent from England who had married a moran, why female tourists were more fascinated with Samburu men than with other beach boys, she explained. "It is because tourists consider Samburu are adhering to the pure ethnic culture, because they are still wearing the beautiful costume. Without any shadow of a doubt, if the Samburu went to the coast in jeans and dirty T-shirts, there would be no interest whatsoever. I can assure you of that." Mary recalled laughing at how other tourists would get upset when they saw Samburu wearing wristwatches or carrying mobile phones. "That's because tourists like to think that they discovered a pure vein of rich culture, the Victorian noble savage." While Mary was more critical of tourist fantasies than other women I interviewed, she also admitted her own attraction for the moran's appearance. "I remember when I first saw Samburu at the beach," she said. "I was fascinated. I had never seen anything quite like this. And, it really is beautiful, you know."

Paul was aware of the seductive power of the Samburu moran. When tourists approached his show, he stood up and adopted an erect bodily posture, with his chin raised and his chest thrust out. He immediately recognized tourists as German, Swiss, Italian, or British, calling out greetings in their respective languages. If he sensed that the vibe was right, he would call out endearing greetings to women, such as "Ciao, bella!" (Italian: Hi, beautiful!) or "Wie geht's, meine Schöne?" (German: How is it going, my beauty?).

He also smiled and joked while playfully looking women in the eye. This contrasted sharply with Paul's otherwise laid-back character and grumpy mood. Such gestures and intimacy were important, he explained.

> When the tourists come, you know, there are some who just like you when you're smiling, talking, and joking with them. You're dressed like a Maasai-Samburu. Then you can sit with them and talk, talk. They ask you how you live, how your people live. There are some who have read about the Samburu and Maasai, and they know. So they ask you about the culture, and you tell them. They want to know about your culture.

If smiling, joking, and talking were ways of showing friendliness toward female tourists and performing as a member of an exotic culture, they also opened up opportunities for other kinds of intimacy. When women asked Paul if they could photograph themselves with him, he always accepted, nodding and uttering a definite "Of course." He came forward and, with a gentle touch, hugged his interlocutor. He brought his face very close to hers, or he rested his head against hers, smiling. Denise, a Frenchwoman who now lived in Kenya, recalled what attracted her to Samburu men at the beach. "I think the natural beauty, the care they put in their appearance, that's what's attracting many white women. The fact that Samburus are not nervous, that they are quiet in the way they are speaking, polite, too, that is an advantage for them. Traditional Africa is on the way to being lost forever, and the Samburu tribe, still living very deeply inside it, could become a myth for many tourists. So tourists love to see the morans." As Syndey Kasfir (2002, 382) writes, "Travelers are shocked the first time they see flesh-and-blood *lmurran* [morans] walking about with spears . . . interrupting their linear notions of progress and inserting what logically belongs to the past into the present." "This apparent temporal displacement," Kasfir argues, makes "real *lmurran* into walking signs of themselves, as if they had stepped out of the pages of an illustrated nineteenth-century exploration account" (ibid.).

Paul told me that encounters with tourists at the beach could sometimes turn into erotic play. "There are some women who are crazy, you know, especially the Germans. They pull up your loincloth: 'Do you wear underwear?' They check. You say: 'Yes, I have.' And other women, they want to teach you how to swim. So you pretend you don't know. When you go into the water, they touch you down there. And that's how you begin to approach the tourists." Performing a certain innocence in matters of modern leisure, such as swimming, while claiming knowledge of matters of traditional culture were key ways for young men to heighten their erotic appeal while also creating opportunities for erotic proximity and sexual play.

By skillfully performing a moran persona that appealed to tourist ethno-erotic fantasies, young men sought to establish the possibility of intimacy and, therewith, a return of cash, whether through the immediate sale of souvenirs or longer-term intimacies. I think of such embodied acts as "performative labor." Describing tourist sexual economies in Brazil, Gregory Mitchell (2015, 5) defines *performative labor* as "the work of constructing, presenting, and maintaining facets of identity." The term refers to how embodied enactments of sexualized identities work through desire and affect to insert participants into specific racialized and gender subject positions while enabling monetary exchange (50–55). For Brazilian gay sex workers, Mitchell shows, performative labor involves "careful adjustments of the body—cruising on the beach, the game of eyes, feigned indifference, a flexed muscle, a careful jutting of the hip to accent the *bunda* (ass), finding just the right amount of macho pegada [swagger] for the particular client" (55). Such performances are *labor*, Mitchell argues, because "the value of the performance is entirely in the social capital [the performer] can acquire" (218). Samburu men in tourism knew well that their success depended on the quality and skill of their performance, and they consequently tried to improve their skill continuously.

Men like Paul produced an eroticized ethnicity through such skillful performance, in the very intimacy of the bodily encounter as tourists judged the authenticity of their performance. As Sara Ahmed (2000, 15) points out, "Differences are not marked *on* the stranger's body, but come to materialise in the relationship of touch between bodies." As encounters reopen prior histories of encounter with Others, they also urge their subjects to redraw boundaries and reiterate difference in order to sustain a distinct subjectivity (44). At the beach, young men's performances and their intimate encounters perpetually regenerated the ethnic and sexual difference congealed by the figure of the moran. A female tourist I met on Bamburi Beach told me that she liked "Samburu men" better than the other beach boys, because "they are much warmer and friendlier. . . . They are not pushy like the others." Here, as Ahmed suggests, "marking out of the boundary lines between bodies" involves "differentiating *between others*" "by telling the difference between this other, and other others" through subjective histories of intimate encounter (8, 44). Tourists who encountered Samburu morans at the beach sought ways of differentiating them from "Kenyans" and other "Africans." Meanwhile, Samburu men hoped to perform moran masculinity in ways that allowed

11. Moran dances at a beach resort in Bamburi, July 2008. (Photo by the author.)

tourists to recognize them as distinct from other beach boys and as more authentic intimate partners.

Traditional dance shows represented another venue in which Samburu men used skill to perform moran masculinity as an eroticized emblem of their identity (fig. 11). Several times a week during the tourist season, groups of up to twenty Samburu men performed traditional dances on the terraces or in the restaurants of tourist hotels. One evening in April 2011, I joined Paul and other men for a dance performance at the Bahari Beach Hotel—a four-star oceanfront tourist resort. I was friends with the leader of their dance group, and he usually negotiated with the guards of these gated hotels to allow me to attend their performances. A few minutes before the performance, Paul and the other men changed out of their beach attire and put on a special red cloth that the leaders of the dance group requested them to wear. Meanwhile, on the terrace, the DJ announced to some fifty tourists seated at tables, "The Maasai have arrived."

"Ladies and gentlemen," the DJ called, "before I invite the Maasai to entertain us with their hunting songs, let me ask you a question. Do you know why the Maasai wear red?"

After a long moment of silence, he answered his own question: "It's because the Maasai like to be feared by lions, and lions are scared of red."

The audience laughed and applauded.

"The songs you will see tonight are songs that these Maasai warriors sing when they go to hunt a lion. Let's give them a big welcome!"

Accompanied by applause, the performers walked onto the dance floor, singing in high-pitched tones. For the next thirty minutes, they performed some seven dances, clapping their hands, shaking their chests, and jumping up rhythmically. When Paul and a few other more experienced dancers jumped, they skillfully displayed their bodies, tightly wrapped in the red cloth. Paul glanced playfully at women sitting in the audience.

Popular tourist discourses of the exotic moran informed the encounters between different actors in the dance show. For his part, the DJ tried to intensify the links between "Maasai warriors," the bodies of the performers, the red color of their cloth, the mythical lion hunt, and the African wilderness through riddles and stories—another kind of performative labor—that branded the show and produced its exotic value. Members of the audience took advantage of the proximity of the dancers to photograph or film them. Meanwhile, the performers displayed their bodies erotically, thus enacting the kinds of scenes that tourists had most likely already encountered in travel guides, on banners at airports, or on postcards sold in souvenir shops. In all these instances, popular representations of the Maa moran mediated the practices of the different actors. Actors drew on dominant discourses of the alterity of the moran, if in different ways, to make their encounters meaningful.

Before their last dance, which Samburu call *shiptamen*, the dancers went into the audience and invited women to join them on the dance floor. Paul took advantage of this opportunity to go up to one of the two women with whom he had been interacting. Extending his hand, he asked her to join him in the dance. The woman, who until then was taking pictures, left the camera on the table, grabbed Paul's hand, and followed him onto the dance floor. In Samburu, *shiptamen* is a dance with significant erotic connotations. As men and women dance, facing each other in a line and holding hands, touch is an expression of the sexual desire of the dancing partners for each other. At tourist resorts, men used the choreographic structure of the same dance to interact with female tourists in intimate ways. For the dancers, playful smiles, intense glances, and soft touches were all part of a skillful and pleasurable performance that could potentially endear them to their foreign dancing partners. In such mixed dances, Bruner (2005, 85) explains, wilderness is "replaced by the benign and safe African tribesman." In this way, "the Maasai . . . become pleasant primitives" who are "tourist-friendly" (87). But the erotic possibilities of *shiptamen*—the exuberance and pleasure of bodily contact—may also open up discursive histories of difference. In the ambiguity of the encounter, the dance substituted sensuous engagement for the distant tourist gaze and shifted the locus of alterity, if only temporarily, away from the visual idiom and onto the sensuality of touch. The dance thus made the tribal performer into a potential intimate partner.

Following the show, the DJ announced a "Maasai market." The performers returned to the dance floor with spears, shields, necklaces, bracelets, or beaded sandals for sale. Some of them placed their handicrafts on the floor, while others walked in between the tables and mingled with the tourists. They had fifteen minutes to persuade tourists to purchase their merchandise. As men were not usually paid for their dance performances, this short time was the only opportunity Samburu men had to make any money for the evening. (Hotel managers felt that providing the dancers with this time in the presence of the tourists was, in fact, enough "payment" for their performances.) Paul used this occasion to return to the table of the woman with whom he had danced, introduce himself, and try to sell her some of his handicrafts.

When the dancers and I reconvened in front of the hotel at the end of the performance, Paul was very excited. Not only had he sold a shield to the woman with whom he had been dancing, but she had promised to visit him the next day at his beach stand. Visibly satisfied, Paul offered to pay the bus fare back to Mtwapa for all members of the group. Notably, speculation and hope in the proximity of foreigners also represented moments of pleasure and self-enjoyment for men like Paul. The delights of such encounters, as Don Kulick observes (1998, 183), are often conspicuously absent in studies of sexual transactions, which typically depict "sex workers" as merely instrumental in their engagements with potential clients. By contrast, a focus on encounters reveals not only how these men performed an eroticized ethnicity for tourists but also how, in the process, they came to experience their identity in new ways—for example, as a valuable thing that fascinated foreigners. As tourists watched their exotic performances with fascination, men also engaged in a pleasurable consumption of the moran masculinity they performed. Meanwhile, tourists approached Samburu men with their own desires and fantasies.

DESIRABILITY, DIFFERENCE, AND ROMANCE: EUROPEAN WOMEN IN KENYA

"At home in Germany, I myself don't have any problems with my age," Anna said. She was fifty-nine in 2011, when I interviewed her. "I go to discos, to concerts, I never think: 'Are you allowed to do this, because you are long past that age?' People might see me as an old broad [G: *alte Schachtel*]. But I certainly don't. I like to travel and enjoy myself." I met Anna through Paul. During the three weeks of her vacation, she would stop by Paul's show at the beach every day at lunchtime to bring him sandwiches and fruit. She liked to joke, saying that she had "stolen" the food from the buffet of the resort where she was staying. Then, as he ate, she would sit on the sand next to him. One day, Anna arrived while I was sitting with Paul by his show table. Paul introduced me to her and told her that I was doing research, and that she could talk with me in German. The pair had been dating, on and off, for the past two years. But Anna did not speak English, and Paul's German was basic. "We speak a lot past each other," Anna later told me. "He often does not understand me, and I don't understand him. But I like that he tries to speak German. It is important that at least one of us learns the other's language." Anna and I quickly connected over the topic of my research. She had read all the memoirs published in German by white women in relationships with Samburu men, and was very eager to share her impressions. Since I had read many of the same books, we talked about them. Later, I also interviewed Anna more formally about her own experiences and desires as they related to Kenya.

I asked Anna what she liked about Kenya. "There is something unique," she responded. "Kenya still has flair. This is about the people themselves. Despite the obsession with money, there is a certain easiness about life, it's okay to be childish, to enjoy yourself. And this is, of course, what makes people charming." It was Sunday, and we were sitting on a public beach north of Mombasa, where many mostly middle-class Kenyans sunbathed and picnicked. "Just look at this," she said, pointing all around us. "People like to enjoy themselves." Then she brought up the topic of local men:

> Here, they approach a woman with warmth, and they know that the white woman falls for that, because she probably misses that in Germany. It is true that the woman does help the man financially. But the man also gives something back to her. She can look consciously at her life and say that at the age of fifty or so, life is not yet over. There is warmth. And women fall for this. Even

if I have a few more years than Paul, I still fall for this. And one misses that at home sometimes. Because, with fifty, a woman there is . . . oh, well.

The issue of age came up repeatedly in our conversations about her experiences in Kenya. Anna, like other women I interviewed, explained that Kenyan men more generally gave them a unique opportunity to feel young and desirable, despite their age. "In Europe, as you know, men look for young, thin women, even when they themselves are old. So for a woman, it is more difficult to date at a certain point in her life." While Anna was critical of the masculine sense of entitlement that allowed elderly European men to turn down women of their own age, she also cherished the possibility of having younger partners herself. But she worried that others would judge her. "My son and I are very close," Anna told me. "So I told him about my trip and that I had sex with Paul. He said, 'Mama, are you still so clever? Are you still like before?'" Anna laughed. Then she said, "He maybe meant to say I should slow down." I noticed that aging was a difficult topic for her. "You know, if I were to have a younger partner in Germany," she explained, "everybody would point the finger at me and judge me. But Kenya is different. In Kenya, it is okay. Nobody cares about age differences."

Notably, then, what Anna consumed in Kenya was, in part, an image of herself as a more desirable woman who was in charge of her own sexual pleasures. And this in spite of what people at home, including her son, may have thought about her decisions relative to her age. If Anna was to embody a desirable femininity, it was important for her to believe that traveling to Kenya allowed her to escape Western ageist ideologies. It was also important for her to imagine that in Kenya, "people enjoy[ed] themselves" and that there was "a certain easiness about life." Such Othering fantasies allowed Anna to imagine being seen as desirable in ways she could not be at home. Sexual commodification, as anthropologist Anne Allison (1994, 21–22) argues, offers the possibility of a transformed subjectivity, for "the customer is not only purchasing one thing or an *other*, but is also paying to become one other as well."

Historically speaking, women like Anna, who come from a lower-middle-class background in Europe, have not always been able to travel and engage in intimate relationships abroad. Throughout the past few decades, a set of social and economic transformations have intensified and expanded such possibilities of mobiliy and consumption for some women in Europe. These transformations included the growing feminization of labor following de-industrialization; the reorganization of family life around practices of individual economic speculation and entrepreneurialism; market conversions of feminist ideas of women's rights and freedoms into new fantasies of emancipatory consumption; and—significantly—shifting discourses about race and culture as central terms of both citizenship and commodification (see Partridge 2012; El-Tayeb 2011). In his movie, *Paradise: Love* (2012), Ulrich Seidl captures evocatively this historical moment. Teresa, the movie's main protagonist, is a fifty-year-old Austrian who earns money as a social worker. She lives with her daughter in a relatively small apartment in what looks like a suburban social housing project. In a tense relationship with her adolescent daughter and visibly disenchanted with her daily life, Teresa travels to Kenya by herself to rest and rediscover herself through sexual intimacy and romance with local beach boys. In sharp contrast with her living arrangements at home, in Kenya, Teresa can afford to stay at a luxorious beach resort, eat in restaurants, and have fun. In Kenya, she also rediscovers herself, if only fleetingly, as desirable and attractive in the eyes of younger men. Although she remains suspicious of these men's desire for her—and her recurrent deceptions increasingly turn into racist derisions—her quest for intimacy becomes an important avenue to reinventing herself through the youth, masculinity, and racial Otherness of these men.

Like Teresa, my informant Anna had a lower-middle-class income in Germany. She worked as a manicurist in a beauty salon and rented a small apartment in suburban Frankfurt. She had never married, and her adult son now lived with his own family. For Anna, her ability to save money, travel, and enjoy herself were important ways of asserting her independence and her desirability, away from potentially judgmental friends and relatives at home. "When I'm in Kenya," Anna said, "I feel that I am in my world." She told me she had first visited Kenya in 1982. At that time, her Swiss fiancé—a university professor—had entered rehab with a severe drug addiction. In order to encourage Anna to break up with him and move on with her life, he bought her an all-inclusive vacation at a Kenyan beach resort. "The moment you get off the plane in Mombasa," she recalled him promising, "you will forget all about me." Though she did not want to travel at first, Anna was fascinated with Kenya. She stayed in a luxurious hotel, sunbathed at the beach, took a boat tour in the ocean, and went on a three-day safari at a wildlife reserve. During that trip, she met Danny, a Kikuyu beach boy with whom she eventually had a ten-year relationship. Anna estimated that throughout the 1980s, she had visited Kenya over twenty times. She stayed in Danny's home in Mtwapa, and they traveled together across the country. "I always paid for everything," Anna recalled, "because he did not have money. So he was my 'companion'

[G: *Begleiter*], as it were." "Through Danny," she continued, "I went deeper into the African culture." After ten years, Anna decided to end the relationship. "At some point, something broke between us. One doesn't know what it is. It just happens. We never fought or anything." In the following years, she traveled to Cuba and Jamaica, where she had other romantic relationships.

Anna did not return to Kenya until 2009. That year, her son had bought her a DVD of the movie *The White Masai*. "I liked the movie," she remembered. "But it made me nostalgic for Kenya. Because I had been here for so many years in the past, I had so many memories." The movie, she said, also made her nostalgic for the Samburu "warriors" she had often seen on her previous trips. "I had seen Samburus in Mtwapa in those days, in the 1980s," she recalled. "But I had no contact with them. They were very shy and they held themselves back. Of course, one has to look when one sees them. They make wonderful appearances [G: *wunderbare Erscheinungen*]. So I used to look at the warriors. But I did not know any of them." When Anna finally returned to Kenya, she encountered Samburu morans at the beach and in the evening entertainment program of her hotel. Paul—as it happened—sold souvenirs by the ocean in front of her resort. One evening, Anna invited Paul for dinner at a restaurant, and so they began a long-term, long-distance relationship. "I asked him where he was from," Anna recalled. "And he said Maralal. So I had to laugh. Because that was the reason why I came to Kenya. Because I saw the movie about Maralal and Samburu [*The White Masai*]. So we went together to Maralal. It was very spontaneous. Although I am now older, I said to him that if your family has nothing against seeing that you are together with me, then we shall go." Since then, Anna has traveled to Kenya twice per year to spend time with Paul. Because locals were not allowed to enter tourist hotels, she would rent a motel room in Mtwapa, where she and Paul could spend a few hours to have sex.

The desire to acquire a more authentic self through cultural difference prompted women like Anna to initiate relationships with Samburu morans rather than with other beach boys. Anna had returned to Kenya in 2009 because a movie had rekindled her fascination with Samburu morans. Other European women I interviewed came from very different backgrounds and had quite different experiences. However, they all invoked cultural difference, in one way or another, as a critical component of their desire for Samburu men. While most women met their partners on the coast, at the beach, in hotels, or in discos, these relationships also unfolded beyond tourist resorts. Some women traveled to northern Kenya to visit their partners' families. Others paid for their partners to visit them in Europe. Over time, women who had intimate relationships with Samburu men often saw themselves as having come to embody cultural difference in various ways. This perception added a sense of authenticity and value to their lives. On the Kenyan coast as well as in Nairobi and Maralal, it was relatively easy to recognize some of the foreign women who had relationships with Samburu men, because many of them wore colorful traditional bracelets and necklaces. Anna, too, wore three Samburu bead bracelets (M: *marnani*) on each wrist and one bead chain on each ankle. These beads indexed, as it were, the cultural difference she had come to embody. To display this acquired difference, some women commonly introduced themselves to other whites as Maasai or Samburu. "I lived with a Samburu for over eighteen years. I am a Samburu woman now," said Denise, a woman from France, by way of introducing herself to me in 2005. Other women introduced themselves as "white Maasai" or "mzungu Maasai," invoking the title of *The White Masai* book and movie. Intimate relationships with morans could thus transform the consuming subject, allowing her to "become different." Sara Ahmed (2000, 125) has pointed out that such "fantasies of becoming" affirm the subject's possibility of transforming herself through proximity to cultural Others. Consuming racial and cultural difference was a way of becoming a "white Maasai," that is, embodying the authentic experience of a Maasai or Samburu livelihood, without relinquishing privileged racial and material status.

In these significant ways, consumers of difference were also producers of difference—they participated in making the racial, ethnic, cultural, or sexual Otherness they desired. But intimacies with Maasai and Samburu men also allowed women to reinvent their whiteness—or to experience their whiteness in new ways. While many of the women I spoke with emphasized that Samburu and other Kenyan men desired them *because* they were white (see Helga's statement below), they claimed whiteness *with a difference* in relation to other tourists in Kenya or friends and relatives at home—they were not just white women but white Maasais. While the desire to expand whiteness through the embodiment of difference is premised on white privilege, women I spoke with did not see themselves as racist. Quite to the contrary. They imagined their relationships with Kenyan men as performances of their nonracism. An Englishwoman recalled with horror how, when she and her Samburu partner traveled to London and attended a family function, her sons and grandchildren looked at her and her partner with disgust. "They are all racist," she told me. "I will never forget how they looked at us. I said to myself: I'd rather live here in Kenya than be subjected to that kind of judgment in England."

However, while some of these women saw themselves as nonracist, it is important to ask how ideas of race figured in their desires. The possibility of becoming Other—or embodying racial, ethnic, and cultural difference—as a way of reasserting whiteness has a long history in Western primitivist fantasies. However, in the present, shifting discourses of race and multiculturalism in Europe and the global North multiplied venues for pursuing such consumptive fantasies. In Germany, England, the Netherlands, and other western European countries, rising politics of autochthonous belonging have played out through populist anxieties over immigrants and refugees (Geschiere 2009; Partridge 2012). In this context, racial and cultural difference became iconic of nonbelonging—of multiple non-European elsewheres. As Fatima El-Tayeb (2011, xxviii–xxix) argues, postindustrial Europe is characterized by a dominant discourse of "political racelessness"—a form of collective amnesia that erases Europe's long engagements with racial Others and depicts contemporary Others as merely "new arrivals." According to this logic, race is not a European problem. However, at the same time, the presence of nonwhite people in contemporary Europe gives rise to new erotic ways of experiencing whiteness. For example, as Damani Partridge (2012, 72–75) shows, in Germany white women who pursue relationships with black men sometimes experience these intimacies through their power to bestow citizenship—through marriage—upon men who otherwise don't belong. Women thus become "street bureaucrats," and black men "are empowered by a female gaze that erases their invisibility, giving them a status as extra-visible subjects" (76). In this context, fantasies of becoming Other—so central to multicultural forms of consumption—work to reproduce global racial hierarchies and essentialist geopolitical equations of race and culture with territory and belonging.

In Kenya, European women's desire for cultural difference was often also premised on a desire to overcome that difference and eventually build lasting romance, love, mutual care, and kinship. Several of the women I met on the coast and in Samburu sought to create spaces and relations through which to overcome some of the barriers of cultural difference and experience the comforts of shared desires and affects. Recall Helga, whom I introduced at the beginning of this chapter. I met her in Samburu in 2010 through my friend Elise. In my interview with Helga, she recalled that she had suffered intense trauma after losing her husband in a car accident in Germany five years prior. "I loved my husband very much," she said. "We always did everything together, and we had a simple but beautiful life." After he died, Helga became very sick. "I was like a ghost," she recalled.

I wasn't really there. After the funeral, they told me to go home fast, before I lost consciousness. They had me on IV drips for a while. Then some months passed, but I was still very sick and angry. So the doctor told me, "If you want to get well, you must go away from here, far, far away. You cannot be always reminded of your husband. Just go!" So I realized that that was the best solution. I had only one aunt in town, but I had lots of friends. Now I decided to let go of them, as they would always pity me and remind me of all my suffering. So I went to Thailand, to India, and then to Kenya.

While in Kenya, Helga decided not to return home. She rented an apartment on the coast, where she made new friends among the locals and expats.

In a way, Helga said, she desired to recreate the home and romance she had lost—or some imitation thereof. In the years that followed, she had intimate relationships with different Samburu and other men on the coast. "They all told me that I was beautiful," she recalled, "that I had a baby face, and that they wanted to be with me. I believed them at that time. I was foolish, perhaps." Now she disliked beach boys. She said that they were all annoying, that they wanted women for money, and that they were very disturbing. But if she had to choose, she said, she preferred Samburu beach boys over others. "When a Giriama sees a mzungu," Helga explained,

> he will call you from one kilometer away. Then Giriamas will disturb you, and it is very hard to get rid of them. But the Samburu are very polite. They come close to you, greet you, and ask you if you want to buy this or that. If you say "No, thank you," they just go and leave you alone. They are not annoying like the Giriama. The problem with the Samburu beach boys is that they love white women. They don't like their Samburu women. No. They like white women. And when you are alone as a woman, then that can be annoying.

When I met Helga, she had started a relationship with Jackson, a moran from Lorosoro, and had moved to Samburu. She used the money she obtained from renting out her apartment in Germany—some 600 euros per month—to support herself, Jackson, Jackson's mother, and his younger siblings and to build a house in the village. During my fieldwork, Helga and Jackson became my close friends.

Because Helga liked to ask for my opinions on design ideas for her new home, she often asked me to join her on her shopping sprees in Maralal, where she bought fabric, carpets, furniture, kitchen appliances, and other things. For her, imagining and making a home was more than just build-

ing a cozy space to live in. It was about creating a space in which to cultivate a sense of romance, privacy, and intimacy while sharing food, stories,
and warm moments with Jackson. Several other European women I met in
Kenya were extensively preoccupied with making homes. This involved, according to their respective means, building or renting houses in which to live
with their local partners, either permanently or during their vacations, and
making these spaces feel homey. For Janet, an Englishwoman who lived in
Mtwapa and was much wealthier than Helga, building a home for herself and
her Samburu partner became a never-ending process. She designed houses
and gardens, hired contractors and purchased building materials and household goods, only to move into the new house and immediately begin envi-
sioning another. In the past twenty-five years, she had built five or six houses.
What was at stake for women like Helga and Janet was a process of self-
making through a fantasy of romance and attachment to a home.

Moreover, for them homes also meant kinship. While a few younger
European women had their own children with Samburu men, others thought
that adopting or sponsoring children was a way to become part of local kin
groups. As Denise, a woman from France, explained, "For the Samburu, if
a woman does not have children, she is worth nothing." She continued, "I
was operated of [ovary] cancers some time ago, so I cannot have children.
But I took care of two boys from the family." Denise sent these children to
school, paid for their clothing and food, kept them in her house, taught them
French, and took them on vacations to safari parks across Kenya. Through
raising children, helping families with food, medical care, and school fees, or
taking care of their elderly, women hoped to build lasting affective ties and
kinship. Helga took great care of Jackson's mother, a woman she addressed
as "mama" and to whom she felt deep attachment.

However, as Helga and other women sought to actualize their desire for
romance, homeyness, and kinship, they sometimes came to perceive the cultural difference they had initially wanted as impeding love and real intimacy.
Like Anna and Paul, Helga and Jackson had something of a communication
problem. Helga spoke little English, and Jackson had only a very basic knowledge of German. Although they had devised their own way to communicate
through a mixture of English, German, and Maa words structured by English
syntax, they soon made it a habit to ask me to mediate their conflicts. Once
every two weeks or so, when they traveled to Maralal for groceries, they
stopped by my house and, over tea, complained to me about their problems
with each other.

One time, Helga said in German, "We walk on the street and I want to shop, and he has no patience. He leaves me there and walks away. What is it with Samburu men? Why can't they respect women?"

Understanding what Helga was complaining about, Jackson addressed me in Swahili: "My brother, I am telling her all the time that in our culture, as a moran, I am not supposed to walk with a woman on the street. That is very shameful. People will laugh at me."

After I translated what Jackson said, Helga snapped angrily at him: "*Scheiße* [shit] culture! People must change. That is a very backward culture."

"Culture is not *Scheiße*," Jackson retorted, laughing. "Why call culture *Scheiße?*"

The fight ended with Jackson drinking tea quietly while Helga complained loudly of how "Samburu men" believed they were "very special" and "so much better than women."

This moment shows how Helga and Jackson reimagined and relocated cultural difference in their everyday intimate engagements with each other. For Helga, being able to walk with Jackson through the streets of Maralal was an important part of what she saw as a romantic relationship. On other occasions, she also complained to me that Jackson would leave her at home alone all day while he hung out with his age-mates, or that he would not care to have long conversations with her. For her, however, hanging out, talking, eating, and sleeping with each other were all important parts of a romantic relationship. As Helga gradually learned about Jackson's temperament and preferences, she sometimes described these as how Samburu men typically were. Meanwhile, Jackson invoked "culture" to quiet Helga down, thus participating himself in a process of self-essentialization. It was a very common perception in villages and small towns throughout Kenya that, when two unrelated people of the opposite sex walked together in public spaces, they were probably involved in a sexual relationship. In coastal towns, men like Jackson had no problem walking with European women or even holding hands with them, because these forms of public intimacy were common in areas inhabited by tourists. But in Maralal, they worried that relatives, age-mates, or former schoolmates would laugh at the age difference between them and their European partners. Helga was in her sixties, while Jackson was twenty-seven. Jackson, therefore, invoked "culture" to explain his behavior in a way he hoped would not offend Helga. As they both invoked cultural difference, they also renegotiated and extended difference through their everyday intimacy.

This, then, was a central paradox of some women's desire: they desired morans for their cultural difference at the same time that they hoped to transcend that cultural difference and live out romantic fantasies of cohabitation and family. Women like Johanna, Anna, and Helga searched not merely for an authenticity that was bounded in time and space, but for an extension of that authenticity through long-term intimacies that made them feel desirable and different. Desiring simultaneously the cultural difference for which their partners stood and a cultural common ground for their relationship, they often became frustrated with their partners and with themselves. This central contradiction of desire prompted women to reevaluate continuously the meanings of their intimacies and the loci of cultural difference (Meiu 2011). This in turn made intimacies more slippery, more fragile. Furthermore, men and women navigated the slipperiness of intimacy by regenerating, in different ways, cultural difference. Whether or not Samburu men liked to kiss, hold hands, be told what to do, and so on were questions women variously addressed as they began relationships with these men. Newly discovered loci of difference—in Helga's case, Samburu men's not liking to walk with women—did not remain private. Women in relationships with morans often advised each other about their partners. Other women published memoirs. In these ways, intimate encounters actually shaped discourses of Samburu cultural difference and ethnosexuality.[11] But intimacies also remained in excess of such discourses; for such discourses could not fully represent or anticipate the complexity of women's concrete experiences.

"YOU HAVE TO ASK FOR MONEY": NEGOTIATING SEX, ROMANCE, AND COMMODIFICATION

To speak of ethno-erotic economies is to emphasize that racial, ethnic, and cultural alterity as well as ethnosexuality emerge through commodification, exchange, and consumption. Negotiating the role of monetary exchanges in relation to sex, love, and romance was probably the most salient way in which Samburu men and their foreign partners sought to work out central contradictions in their intimacies. For morans of business, their performance of ethnosexuality necessarily involved making bodily intimacies render a return of cash. Yet in some cases, it was also important to actively dissociate sex and romance from monetary transactions so as not to disturb women's fantasies of authentic intimacy.

Tiras, a twenty-eight-year-old Samburu I interviewed in Mtwapa in 2008, recalled his first intimate relationship with a tourist eight years earlier, when he had just arrived on the coast. "This lady, she was from Germany," Tiras recalled.

She was not that old. She came to my "show" at the beach, and we stayed there and talked. She liked me. She would bring me things to eat, like biscuits. At lunchtime, she'd bring me a soda. So she approached me like that. "Tomorrow," she told me, "we meet at the beach." I said OK. So in the morning, I went to the beach. I met with her, and we talked about the Maasai, Samburu. And she said, "Oh, me, I like Maasai. Oh, I want to marry a Maasai. Would you want me to be your girlfriend?" I said yes. So she told me to wait. She went to the hotel, got some money, and took me shopping. She thought I never wore trousers [*laughs*]. So she took me to the shopping center to buy me a pair.

Later that night, Tiras met the woman in a bar. They drank cocktails and then went walking on the beach. "Then she started kissing me and touching me. She asked: 'Can I play with you?' I said OK. Then we started having sex on the beach. She came with European condoms in her dress. So we had sex." Tiras continued to see her over the next months and also visited her in Hamburg once. "She liked to have sex, to hang out, walk," Tiras said. "But then, with time, money became a problem. Whenever I asked her for money, she said: 'Oh, I am working for my money. I also have things to pay for in Germany. I don't have money.' Then I said: 'Ah, OK, then I get another woman and we're finished.'"

In his recollection, Tiras initially depicted himself as passive in relation to his German partner, who, as he saw it, approached and seduced him. He thus described himself as desirable and attractive in ways that reasserted the aura of his ethnosexuality. But he also portrayed himself as innocent in ways that echoed tourists' ethno-erotic fantasies of the primitive moran. Tiras was, in fact, neither innocent nor passive. When he realized his partner did not offer him the money he had expected, he promptly ended the relationship.

At least two things, Samburu men knew, held value for tourists: their culture—usually reflected in the erotics of their bodily appearance—and their sexuality. Tiras recalled how, on his trip to Hamburg to visit his ex-partner, she had asked him to dress in moran attire every time they visited someone in the city. While Tiras was normally proud of his traditional attire, he recalled feeling deeply humiliated. "She was stupid," he said. "She wanted to show everyone that I was a poor, primitive man from the bush." But he put up with her requests, looking forward to the gifts of cash he would take back to Kenya. In addition to culture, Tiras perceived his moran sexuality, too, *as capital*. He explained, "You know, there are some mzungu women who read about the Samburu, like about Lketinga [from *The White Masai*] and about all the story of sex, this and that. So they already know what a Samburu does in terms of sex. And they want that experience." Yet what "that experience" was remained open to negotiation and imagination. Some men learned that to be commensurable with the commodity form, ethnosexuality had to be channeled through what seemed like a Western cultural sequence of sexual behaviors, beginning with foreplay, continuing with prolonged penetration, and ending in orgasm. "Some women don't like to have sex the way we do it in Samburu," Tiras explained, referring to men trying to have several orgasms quickly without foreplay or prolonged penetration. "They say: 'You make the woman to be less. You just have sex like a dog.' So when you have sex with a white woman, you have to kiss her. They will kiss you, suck you. And these things, we don't have in Samburu. Even in our school we didn't have these things. The first time I learned these things was in Mombasa." In my interviews, some men depicted themselves as more "modern" for having learned about kissing, touching foreplay, and oral sex. Other men, however, tactfully invoked their "culture" as a way to explain their own sexual preferences. What is noteworthy here is that regardless of the actual way in which sex unfolded, sexual intimacies held value because they cited fantasies of cultural Otherness and ethnosexuality.

In addition to culture and sexuality, there was also the issue of youth. Through moran ethnosexuality, the youthfulness of Samburu men's bodies also figured as capital. I asked Tiras why he thought his partner had to give him money for sex. So he explained. "Even you, when you stay with an old woman, you cannot stay like that. You have to ask all the time for money. Because, you know, she is using you. When you stay with an older woman, she feels young and beautiful. She behaves like a young lady. So you have to say: 'I have some problems. I need money.' Every day you ask her. So you have to know how."

"How do you know if a woman is willing to give you money?" I asked.

"In two days or three days, when you stay with her, you know," he said.

You can ask her for her help. You say, "I have a problem with my family. Can we send some things for the family?" OK. The first time, she tells you yes. And the second time, you say to her, "OK. In my life, you know, I don't have anything. I don't even have a bank account. I don't have a house. I don't have anything." And then, some, they tell you up front: "You know? I am not rich like you take me like . . . you are very expensive. You can look for another woman." So that time, you realize this woman is not serious for you. Because she will tell you, "No. You can look for another rich woman, because you are very expensive to me."

Note that the performance of moran ethnosexuality had to generate money. Men like Tiras invoked a normative assumption that, when sex involved a younger and an older partner, only the latter stood to benefit from sexual pleasure and from the possibility of feeling desirable. For this reason, many young men and women who had relationships with older partners, Kenyan and foreign alike, imagined these relationships as unequal intimacies. Indeed, the younger partners were sexual clients of sorts who enabled their sexual patrons to "feel young," to buy desirability, as it were. According to this logic, patrons had to offer a return payment in cash or goods for their clients' sexual services.

Men I interviewed emphasized that they never explicitly solicited money from women in exchange for sex. Such direct transactions, they explained, upset the fantasy of romance and love that some women entertained. As Tiras explained, "When a woman picks you up at the disco to have sex for one night, you don't have to ask her for money. She gives you right away. She just gives you some 2,000 shillings [about $25] or more. But those who want to stay with you, to marry you, that's a different story. There, you must ask." Samburu men did entertain foreign women for one-night stands. I also heard of young men having one-night stands with foreign gay men. But this occurred rarely—or, perhaps, covertly—as men feared that rumors of same-sex encounters could jeopardize their safety and respectability on the coast and at home. Such encounters did not render much money because they could not be prolonged into long-lasting relationships, lest men would be stigmatized as homosexuals. Most of them desired lasting relationships of intimate clientage to foreign women who were retired and thus, the men reasoned, had more money. In such instances, if the women did not offer gifts of cash themselves, men invoked family emergencies, health problems, and other issues as a way to demand cash. Once men had had one or more sexual encounters with their partners, they felt entitled to a return "gift" from them. Here, the language of reciprocity, gifts, and financial support hid a deeper perception of what men saw as commodified exchange. Although performing a dissociation between money on the one hand and sex and intimacy on the other, men were extending the dynamics of commodified exchange to intimacies that were not immediately recognizable as commodities by those involved.

Furthermore, through a return payment, ethnosexuality came into being in new ways as an effect of—rather than the raw material for—commodified exchange.[12] Cultural alterity and ethnosexuality were not the substance of the commodity but objects that emerged through market exchange, as concrete social actors made their encounters meaningful through older, colonial ethno-erotic fantasies. Cultural difference and ethnosexuality did not exist as such *in* the bodies of these men, but emerged in the process of their commodified exchange, as these men *performed* and *assumed* a certain identity and tourists *recognized* it (or not) for the real thing.

Although women I interviewed were aware of the economic inequalities between themselves and their partners, many imagined money and love as two separate domains and therefore spoke of their relationships as equal romances rather than patron-client relationships. They wished to sustain the idea that they were in equal relationships premised on love rather than material dependency. The most common theme in my interviews and informal conversations with many of these women was how constant demands of money from male partners impinged on their desires for romance, affection, and authentic intimacy. The authenticity of the men's desire came sharply into question when women debated the relation between money, love, sex, and culture. Interferences of money with sex, love, and romance often generated central contradictions in these relationships.

"I don't know how things will go with Paul," Anna told me at the end of her vacation, before returning to Germany. "There are always problems with money. I must say that I bought Paul many things, for him and his family. But sometimes I have to say, 'Well, sorry, that's it. I cannot do this all the time.' I also have my obligations at home, and I cannot leave so much money here. I am happy to part with some money while I am here. But I cannot send him money every month. One has to protect oneself from that." Meanwhile, Paul often complained to me that Anna teased him with low-value gifts such as clothes, drinks, and food, and refused to offer him more substantial amounts of money. "Can't she see I am poor?" he wondered out loud. "Why do I have to ask her? She sees I am at the beach every day, struggling to make a living. She says she has no money, yet she stays at the best hotel in the area." The nature of Paul and Anna's relationship was not clear to me at first. I knew that when foreign women visited Samburu men on the coast, the latter usually took time off from their business at the beach to spend time with them. But Paul did not. I eventually learned that Paul did not think of Anna as a long-term partner, even as he continued seeing her. I think Anna, too, did not envision a future with him, though she cherished their relationship and returned to see him, often twice per year. So Paul continued to work at the beach, hoping to meet a richer woman who would be willing to help him more substantially.

But even when women offered large sums of money to their partners, things did not always go well. While many women came from a middle-class background in Europe and often had to manage their budget very carefully while on vacation, other women enjoyed showering their partners with expensive gifts and cash. Janet, a woman born and raised in London, was in her midseventies and had lived in Kenya for the past twenty-five years. During this time, she had two consecutive long-term relationships with Samburu men. Although of a lower-middle-class background, Janet benefited from several pensions in England and so was rich by Kenyan standards. As mentioned earlier, she used her money over the years to build several houses in Mtwapa as well as two houses in Samburu (one for each of her partners). One day in March 2011, Janet invited me to her house, and while her male Kenyan servant prepared us tea, she showed me pictures of her partners. She pointed out name-label clothes and shoes she had bought for them and their friends, thick silver chains, golden rings with diamonds, and expensive cars. "They were beautiful boys," Janet recalled nostalgically, "always cheerful, always laughing, always joking. I loved to buy them things, to see how happy they were, and how they loved me because I took care of them." Giving was indeed pleasurable for Janet. Through such gifts, Janet and other European women performed their own cultural difference, as agents of Western modernity and civilization, in relation to their partners and their kin. Also through such gifts, women like Janet imagined themselves as independent and powerful. Being patrons, sexual or otherwise, to younger men sanctioned their desired self-images. Yet such gifts allowed women to make claims on the time of their partners. "Sometimes, when women give you money," Tiras explained, "they can give you, like, 20,000 shillings [some $250]. And then they begin calling you every ten minutes: 'Where are you? Why are you not answering the phone? Now, you are with another woman with my money?'" What Tiras perceived as women's attempt to control men also generated tensions and conflicts between partners. One of Janet's relationships ended after her partner beat her harshly. "He said he was the man," Janet recalled, "and I had no business asking him what he was doing and where he went." Here, then, was another contradiction that made intimacies slippery: men desired money from their female partners, yet they also felt that these gifts of money generated expectations that undermined their masculinity. This perceived gender reversal of power, as I show in the next section, characterized contemporary sexual economies in Kenya more generally. In this instance, however, it added further contradictions to the otherwise slippery intimacies between Samburu men and foreign women.

The pleasures, failures, and deceptions of commodified exchange were central to the production of the touristic moran, his sexuality, temperament, and behavior. In this sense, ethnic and sexual difference emerged not only through the commodity form but also at the limits of commodification, in the very ambiguous experience through which actors sought to render commensurable money, sex, romance, and cultural Otherness. Failed attempts to commensurate sex, money, and cultural difference often disturbed the intimate production and consumption of ethnosexuality. Intimacies would fail, because the object of initial desire did not correspond to women's fantasies in their full complexity. Intimacies would also fail because men's desire for money and goods conflicted with their ideals of independent masculinity. Nonetheless, intimate failures regenerated and transformed ethnic and sexual difference—and desires thereof—in myriad ways.

COASTAL CIRCUITS OF ETHNO-EROTIC
PLEASURE AND PATRONAGE

To understand what made intimacies between Samburu men and European women slippery and fragile and what informed the dynamics of commodified exchange between them, it is important to look beyond their immediate relationships. Samburu male migrants to the coast entered wider networks of sexual patronage and intimate commodification that shaped and were shaped by their relationships with foreign women. For example, Samburu men who obtained money through foreign partners could become sexual patrons of less wealthy Kenyan women. Meanwhile, those who did not have any foreign partners at a given time could become intimate clients of rich, older Kenyan women known as "big mamas." Such relationships could alternately enrich or impoverish young men, or merely help them make ends meet for a while. Like intimacies with foreign women, these relationships also drew on and reproduced commodified fantasies of ethnosexuality, if in different ways.

In Mtwapa, the financial power that came with being in relationships with foreign women enabled some young men to have intimate relationships with young Kenyan women. Samburu migrants referred to these women as mistresses (M: *sintan*) or "side plans" (S: *mipango ya kando*). They explained that whereas foreign women were "for money," "side plans" were for the pleasures of sex. Young men spoke at great length about these relationships when

12. Samburu men passing time on the streets of Mtwapa, July 2008. (Photo by the author.)

socializing with one another (fig. 12). Jadini, a Samburu in his midtwenties whom I met in Mtwapa in 2008, said that he did not mind having sexual relationships with bar girls, but he worried about long-term relationships with them. Like many Samburu men I spoke to, he thought that Kenyan women of other tribes were after male migrants' money, and that they also used sorcery to coerce their partners into sharing their savings with them. To illustrate his point, Jadini told me the story of Lelemana, an elder of the Lkuroro age set, who had been among the first Samburu to migrate to Mtwapa in the early 1980s. Lelemana had an elderly Swiss girlfriend who had moved permanently to the Kenyan coast. After her death, he inherited her villa. Soon thereafter, he married a young Kamba woman and remained in Mtwapa to live with her. Jadini pointed out that Lelemana had become extremely submissive to his wife, who controlled all his businesses. He saw this as proof that the woman had used sorcery to prevent Lelemana from returning home, to Samburu. More derogatorily, Jadini referred to such women as prostitutes (S: *malaya*), explaining that he did not want to be involved with any of them in the long run. Rather, like many other migrants, he hoped to return to Samburu and marry a woman whose family descent (M: *ntalipa*) he knew. Meanwhile, he said, mistresses were for pleasure.

It is important to note here that men who engaged in relationships with European women did not see themselves as prostitutes. However, they often spoke of Kenyan women engaged in sex-for-money exchanges as such. This is part of a wider local gendered imaginary, whereby men, unlike women, are

not blamed or criticized—at least not to the same extent—for their engagement in transactional sex. As Kamala Kempadoo (2001, 49) observed for the
Caribbean, this suggests "distinctly different gendered sites of power . . . for
men and women in the sex trade."

Ethnicity was a common way of fetishizing the sexuality of mistresses in
coastal Kenya. During the years they spent on the coast, male migrants desired to have sexual encounters with women of different ethnic groups. "Trying out the women of different tribes" (S: *kujaribu wanawake wa makabila to-
fauti*), they would say. This was an experience that adventurous young men
from rural areas hoped to undergo while living in towns. This was also a way
to embody a more sophisticated Kenyan masculinity premised on the objec-
tification and consumption of ethnicized feminine sexualities. The assumption was that women of different tribes had sex in different ways, offering
more or less pleasure (or different kinds of pleasures). A local underground
market of ethnic pornography had already capitalized on the desire of young
men to experience the ethnosexualities of different Kenyan women. On
fences and walls in Mtwapa, posters advertised "Adult DVDs" in "vernacular
Kikuyu, Kikamba, Luhya, Luo, Swahili," offering phone numbers for placing
orders. Men who did not own DVD players watched these films in public
video rooms after midnight. Jadini told me that he and his age-mates sometimes competed jokingly over who had slept with women of more ethnic
groups. Here, too, ethnicity offered various sexualities their exotic commodity value.

Samburu men who did not have foreign partners or who did not benefit too significantly from their relationships with them found an alternative
source of livelihood through relationships with "big mamas" (S: *akina mama
wakubwa*). These women were mostly Kamba, Kikuyu, and Giriama, but also
a few Samburu and Maasai. Some of them had initially arrived in Mtwapa
to work as domestic servants or bar girls, and eventually became wealthy
through relationships with foreign men. Whereas some of them were in
relationships with German, Swiss, Italian, or English male retirees, others
were older and had already inherited the houses and money of their deceased
European partners. Big mamas owned cars and businesses, hired maids, and
performed a certain middle-class status, such as driving their own cars, shopping at supermarkets, and working out in gyms. They also developed vast
networks of dependents. And some also initiated intimate relationships with
younger men, whom they supported materially for longer or shorter periods
of time.

In 2009, Jadini had two simultaneous relationships with a British woman and a German woman. With their financial help, he had rented a luxurious apartment with two rooms, running water, and electricity in a prestigious neighborhood of Mtwapa, and also enjoyed the luxury of taxi rides, restaurant meals, and disco nights with his friends. When I met him again in 2011, the European girlfriends he had been two-timing had found out about each other and abandoned him. Jadini had moved out of his luxurious apartment into the shacks, or the so-called Mtaa of Mtwapa. Under these circumstances, he soon accepted the intimate patronage of a big mama who had long been interested in him. She was a Kamba called Pamela. She had started off as a poor bar girl, and was now married to an elderly Swiss man to whom she had introduced Jadini as her brother. While Pamela's husband was in Switzerland, Jadini lived in their house. Using the monetary allowances from her husband, Pamela bought a new car and allowed Jadini to drive it and earn his own money as a taxi driver. For some male migrants, just like for the young women they pursued as "side plans," establishing intimate clientage to wealthy partners allowed them to subvert poverty, if only temporarily. They slept in the woman's house without paying rent and benefited from free food, new clothes, phone credit, and cash allowances. However, men like Jadini felt that—as with European women—relationships with big mamas were ways to both assert their masculinity through sexual desirability and undermine it. Jadini often complained to me, for example, that Pamela felt entitled to call his cell phone regularly and ask of his whereabouts. He also complained that he could not spend as much time at the beach anymore, and worried that his chances of meeting another European woman would therefore diminish. He explained that if relationships with big mamas allowed him and others to live a good life temporarily, it was ultimately through relationships with white women that one could hope to become rich.

Relationships between young men and big mamas replicated the hierarchical relations between foreign women and Samburu men. Indeed, migrants often spoke sarcastically of big mamas that "these women live just like the whites," in that they used their wealth to attract younger men and then "shamelessly" paraded their "boys" in public view. Young men who were not directly involved in such relationships were the most vocal critics of big mamas and the "boys" who consented to live with them. They explained that these relationships inverted ideal gender roles. As men became dependents of women, they emasculated themselves. For them, people believed, it was more difficult to negotiate ideal forms of assertive masculinity, premised on authority and control. Like foreign women, big mamas could control their male partners by requesting them to be home at certain hours, to not socialize with other women, and so on. On the coast and in Samburu, youth derogatorily referred to these men as "God's birds" (S: *ndege wa Mungu*), or, as it were, souls abandoned to faith. On the one hand, "God's birds" was a new name for the older category of "kept men" used in the colonial sexual economies of Mombasa. On the other hand, these men also embodied a form of dependent masculinity that was increasingly common across Africa following market liberalization.[13]

Ethnicity also played an important role in the intimate relations between big mamas and younger men. Big mamas desired Maasai or Samburu morans, invoking the stereotype of their sexual prowess or claiming that morans used traditional herbal medicines to be more virile. Over beer in a bar in Mtwapa, a forty-year-old Kamba big mama who had a Samburu boyfriend told me laughingly what she liked about morans. "Those ones, they don't know much," she said. "They only know that 'work of the bed' [S: *kazi ya kitanda*]." For the big mamas, as for European women, the possibility of having relationships with younger men who embodied a different, more exotic sexuality carried a particular appeal. But other Kenyans did not find Maasai or Samburu morans exotic or, for that matter, sexually desirable. For them, other forms of ethnic sexuality were more appealing.

The relationships between Samburu migrants and Kenyan women constituted an important context for the production of moran ethnosexuality. They also represented another important context, in which men and women extended commodity logics to their longer-term intimacies—an understanding that the sexual services of younger, more desirable partners required a return of value. Such relationships, finally, heightened an environment of speculation in which people employed sexuality in different ways toward social and economic gains. As these liaisons take place beyond tourist resorts, they usually remain invisible to anthropologists of tourism, who concentrate on tourist sites and local-tourist interactions. However, a focus on ethno-erotic economies takes us outside the tourist resort and brings to light the critical role of such wider networks of transactional sex in the making of ethnosexuality.

"WHITE MAMAS WANT FRESH MEAT": DEPLETION, SPECULATION, AND ETHNO-EROTIC REPRODUCTION

Samburu men's performances of moran ethnosexuality were riddled with uncertainty. Slippery intimacies, as we have seen, sometimes undermined the possibility of obtaining a lasting return of cash on performative labor. But as men tried to anticipate and foreclose the chance that their relations with foreign women would not work out, they faced additional challenges. If they migrated to the coast year after year without succeeding in sustaining relationships and accumulating wealth, they risked that with aging, they would no longer be attractive to foreigners.

One evening at the end of April 2011, I joined Paul at his show table on the beach. The tourist season was coming to an end, and he was quite sad.

"You know, I love my business," he told me. "But I don't want to do this for the rest of my life. If I become an old man and I am still at the beach, that would be bad." He continued:

> That elder who is called Loleku is my father's younger brother. He had left [Samburu] to come to Mombasa before I was born. And he is still here after all these years. He never went back home. And he is a Lkuroroi [man of the Lkuroro age set initiated in 1976]. He never married and has no children. Even if he goes home, he does not even have a homestead. If you go to Diani, you will see him. He still dresses like a moran. He makes a bit of money and then he drinks and chews khat [S: *miraa*]. It is very shameful! He is an old man, but he is still a beach boy.

Loleku was one of the many men who, despite having moved up the age-grade ladder and become elders, continued to live on the coast, dressing in moran attire, selling souvenirs, and dancing for tourists. Younger men called these elders "beach-boy elders" (M: *lpayian lobichboi*) or, when in Samburu, "elders of Mombasa" (M: *lpayian lo Mombasa*), as a way of questioning their respectability. Typically, beach-boy elders never acquired any wealth or had lost it to alcohol, gambling, or mistresses. They continued to live on the coast and returned to the beach in search of (further) life-transforming encounters with female tourists. But most of them managed to make ends meet only by working as watchmen or begging money off younger men.

When Paul first arrived on the coast in 2005, he was still a moran. That same year, however, his age set (the Lmooli) graduated to elderhood. Although Paul was now a junior elder, he continued to dress in moran attire and work at the beach. He explained to me that at twenty-six, he was still young and could pass as a moran. But he was visibly worried. He had had a few relationships with German women—including his unpromising relationship with Anna—but had yet to make or save enough money. If he returned home, he would need cash to build a house, buy cattle, and make a bridewealth payment for a future wife. As younger men of the new Lkishami age set were already taking over sexual economies on the coast, Paul felt that for him, time was quickly running out.

"White mamas want fresh meat," he explained to me in English, using a phrase that is now common in many sexual economies throughout the world.

As Paul saw it, foreign women did not care much about Samburu men's social and economic struggles but rather reduced them to their bodily appearances, their flesh. "Fresh meat" spoke thus of bodies whose value depleted with the aging process. In this context, beach-boy elders were by-products of a market that located ethnosexuality in the bodies of *young* men and excluded older men (Meiu 2015). For young men on the coast, beach-boy elders were a constant reminder that they had to act quickly. As the number of Samburu male migrants to beach resorts increased from one year to the next, men felt that their chances to produce wealth diminished considerably. I once heard a Samburu man advising another, "If you find a white woman once, hold on to her, because you will never find a second one again. Never!"

Kenyan men and women in coastal sex economies shared the sense that one had to act fast in the face of depleting possibilities of enrichment, which informed their pursuits of a future. Responding to their need to act on chance or heighten their luck, a diverse economy of magic and sorcery offered its services on billboards and posters along highways and town streets.[14] When I first visited Mtwapa in 2008, my research assistant, who had lived there for many years, advised me not to shake people's hands. Instead, he urged, I should offer my interlocutors a more "hip" closed-fist greeting. Handshakes, he explained, were extremely dangerous. Men and women rubbed their palms with "smearing powders" (S: *dawa ya kupaka*) purchased from Giriama witch doctors to make people they desired follow them blindly. I soon learned that the use of powders was widespread in the sexual economy of Mtwapa. While Samburu men often applied these before going to the beach and hotels, hoping to shake the hands of foreign women they desired, local women also used powders to attract rich boyfriends. It was commonly known that people greeted with the closed fist either when they suspected that the person they greeted had smeared powder on his or her palms or when they themselves had done so and did not want to deploy it until meeting the desired person. This knowledge made everyone into a potential user *and* victim of sorcery. Navigating everyday life in Mtwapa, my research assistant taught me, meant learning which ethnic groups were more likely than others to use such powders to gain control over the sexual desires and the wealth of others. As I described earlier, Jadini bemoaned Lelemana for having fallen prey to the sorcery of the Kamba woman who became his wife, emphasizing that the Kamba were among the most likely to use dangerous sorcery to gain sexual and material access to men. Sorcery markets promised to make social and economic value possible in a context in which its realization—whether through commodified intimacies or otherwise—was highly uncertain.

Like coastal residents who sold sorcery services, some aging Samburu men on the coast sought new ways to produce cash and authority by capitalizing on the speculative work of younger men involved in tourism. As unequal access to tourist money strained relations between young men and elders, some elders opened ethnic welfare associations that safeguarded access to and the proceeds from cultural and ethno-erotic commodification. These associations supervised Samburu migrants, managed their finances, and offered them benefits. At the time of my research, at least four associations operated along the coast: Samburu Moran Curio Dealer Association in Mtwapa; Samburu Self-Help Group in Watamu; Samburu Moran Traditional Dancers Association in South Diani; and Samburu Traditional Maasai Morans in North Diani. These organizations were registered with the Ministry of Gender, Sport, Culture, and Social Services and constituted "free enterprises," competing independently with private businesses without government subsidies. Elders who were association members obtained contracts with hotels and cultural villages and offered migrants the opportunity to participate in dance performances at these venues. They established links to political leaders on the coast as well as to the office of the Ministry of Tourism and obtained so-called beach operator permits for migrants. Moreover, they offered migrants small loans to help with start-up costs, money for health emergencies and urgent trips to Samburu, and various banking services that generated interest. At the beginning of every tourist season, migrants registered with an organization and claimed their savings and profit three or four months later, before returning home. Organization leaders withheld part of the profits at the end of every tourist season, keeping the rest of the money in a corporate account as collective capital for future investments. In controlling ties to the local administration, these elders claimed gerontocratic authority through the office of the organization. In stark contrast to the so-called beach-boy elders described above, these elders maintained some influence over morans. They mediated the fights between morans and occasionally sent young men who had misbehaved back to Samburu. In addition, these leaders tried to ensure that migrants spent their savings in Samburu, refusing, for example, to hand over their savings unless men boarded a bus for northern Kenya that very same day. In this sense, ethnic incorporation represented, not only a way for older men to cling to the earnings of morans in tourism and safeguard otherwise slippery contexts of intimacy, but also an institutionalized mechanism for redirecting tourist cash, albeit in uneven ways, toward building futures in Samburu.

The dynamics of ethno-erotic commodification informed a central tension between the seemingly equal participation of Samburu men of different age sets in the enterprise of sex and culture on the one hand and, on the other, the unequal market value of young men's bodies as opposed to older men's bodies. This tension pushed some senior men to the margins of sex economies, turning them into impoverished beach-boy elders, while pushing other senior men to incorporate ethnicity and derive profit from controlling access to markets of culture and ethnosexuality. The ensuing contradictions played out in complex speculative economies in which both sex and sorcery worked to produce futures.

COMMODIFYING INTIMACY IN
ETHNO-EROTIC ECONOMIES

Intimacies between Samburu men and European women are at the foundation of ethno-erotic economies. Intimacies emerged as young men performed moran masculinity and ethnosexuality at tourist resorts; as tourists encountered morans at the beach, in hotels, or elsewhere in coastal towns; and as they developed relationships with each other. A set of central contradictions animated these intimacies. Foreign women desired at once the cultural difference morans embodied and the possibility of overcoming some of this difference to enact fantasies of romance and love. Samburu men performed romantic attachments to women by dissociating their requests for money from sex and romance while not sustaining relations for long without some form of payment or material support. They also desired relationships with older rich women in order to build relations of clientage to them, yet felt emasculated by such arrangements. And men who aged and were supposed to gain authority and power in accordance with Samburu age-grade relations saw themselves devalued by a market that foregrounded young men's bodies as sexual commodities. All these contradictions conspired to make intimacies slippery, fragile, and uncertain. But they also made them a driving force in the regeneration of fantasies of cultural difference and ethnosexuality, because as intimacies failed, partners understood the failures as results of cultural Otherness. Cultural difference, more generally, and ethnosexuality, more specifically, emerged in various ways in exchanges of money and intimacy between Samburu men, European women, and Kenyan women.

These exchanges reached beyond tourism and were the basis of larger ethno-erotic economies.

In this context, the concrete ways Samburu men, foreign women, and Kenyan women produced and maintained intimate relationships both complicated and expanded logics of commodification associated with the neoliberal market. Elizabeth Bernstein (2007) argues that "bounded authenticity"—a form of transactional sex that is spatially and temporally delineated and finite, and whose value rests with the quality of the encounter—is emblematic of postindustrial capitalism. Yet as my ethnographic material shows, the opposite is also true. While one-night stands and immediate sex-for-money exchanges did occasionally take place between Samburu men and tourist women—or even Kenyan women—most of them sought to make intimacies more durable. Samburu men devised myriad ways to tame and stabilize such slippery intimacies and make their relationships with foreign women last. Some actively tried to frame monetary expectations as distinct from a possible return payment for sex and intimacy. Others purchased the services of sorcerers to heighten their chances of success. And still others built ethnic corporations to safeguard and draw profit from venues of ethno-erotic commodification. They all sought to make such intimacies into ongoing sources of value. Here, *pace* Bernstein, the challenge was precisely to find ways to prolong intimacies without jeopardizing their authenticity as opposed to bounding them off and presenting them as readily transactional. This suggests two things: first, that longer-term relationships were themselves infused with logics of commodification and exchange value, and second, that the *idea* of sex as a bounded commodity also worked as a principle for evaluating material returns in more lasting relationships. Recall, for example, that if a Samburu man had sex several times with a woman without a return payment in cash or kind, he easily ended the relationship, if he so wanted. In this sense, commodification itself took new forms—less immediately transactional, more spectral, more difficult to pin down.

Market liberalization, the retraction of the welfare state, and the rise of various forms of consumerism have coincided with a growing obsession with intimacy. Lauren Berlant (1997) observes a certain political reorientation in the United States, a move away from a public sphere as political community toward a privatized sphere of intimacy—domestic arrangements, relationships, love—as ultimate sites of emancipation. A certain optimism, Berlant argues, must remain crucial to this reorientation, precisely because, in the neoliberal context, poverty undermines for many the possibility of actualizing ideal forms of intimacy. The intimate is thus most invested with fantasy (Hemmings 2012). It also becomes a central site of self-making through consumption; hence the promise of the market to liberate us, if only we have the means to consume (Morris 2008; Povinelli 2006). Intimate commodification itself becomes a form of entrepreneurialism and a condition of citizenship and belonging in many places throughout the world. But at the same time, the meanings of commodification change. When Helga told Johanna at the start of this chapter that only prostitutes and beach boys ask their white partners for money, she was missing precisely how the relations she herself and those around her cultivated through love and care worked more and more by the logics of exchange value, yet appeared less and less in the form of what we conventionally recognize as a commodity.

4. Shortcut Money, Gossip, and Precarious (Be)longings

In every stock-jobbing swindle everyone knows that some time or other the crash must come, but everyone hopes that it may fall on the head of the neighbor, after he himself has caught the shower of gold and placed it in secure hands. *Après moi le déluge!*
—KARL MARX, *CAPITAL*

For me, one of the most brutal effects of neoliberalism in Africa is the generalization and radicalization of a condition of temporariness.
—ACHILLE MBEMBE, "AFRICA IN THEORY"

Money obtained through the commodification of moran sexuality has shaped social life in northern Kenya for the past three decades. In Samburu, men who returned from their seasonal trips to the coast crafted new styles of clothing, mobility, housing, and leisure. In villages and towns, people spoke at length about these men, at times criticizing them for pursuing transactional sex or sorcery, at other times trying to gain access to their resources. As some of these men accumulated, in a very short time, more money than labor migrants or traders could acquire in a lifetime, their wealth became a salient object of desire and derision. Contesting this wealth along with the respectability of its owners, men and women in Samburu reimagined what it meant to belong to local social worlds.

During a conversation with Mama Priscilla, a Samburu trader, I learned about some of the key issues of contention surrounding the wealth men produced through intimate relationships with foreign women. Her shop was located on one of the small streets of Maralal town. Women from neighboring villages stopped by every day to buy maize flour, sugar, cooking fat, or detergent. They often spent hours in the shop, sharing the latest news, complaining about rising prices, or gossiping about common acquaintances. They respected Mama Priscilla and enjoyed listening to her stories.

After graduating from high school in the early 1980s, Mama Priscilla married a police officer. In 1991 her husband died, and she moved from his village to Maralal to raise her two children on her own. She paid for their education by working as a maid. Now in her fifties, Mama Priscilla was very proud that her children were employed. She believed very strongly in education. Despite the fact that most high school graduates in the district could no longer find employment, her children's success convinced Mama Priscilla, as she often told me, that "studying is the only way to move forward in life." Every time I visited her, she invited me into the back of the shop to the small room in which she lived. There, she would proudly show me the gifts her children had sent her from down country: a DVD player or a new gas stove, an elegant blouse or a face cream, a watch or a purse. "They love their mother very much," she would conclude. "They know all I have been through for them."

Upon my return from one of my research trips to Mombasa, I went to visit Mama Priscilla. She asked me about her acquaintances on the coast, and then she said, "You know, I don't like those morans who go to Mombasa. Not at all. They all want to get rich fast. They don't want to study to improve their lives. No! They only want that shortcut money [S: *pesa ya shortkat*]."

"Shortcut money?" I asked.

"Yes, you know, that rushed money [S: *pesa ya haraka*] that you don't have to work for," she responded. "They use that sorcery of Mombasa to get whites [S: *wazungu*] fast, so that they get wealth. I know, because there were three morans in our family who went to Mombasa. They were all of the age set of my son. One of them had a car, a white woman, and was very rich. He got so rich that he forgot to go back to the witch doctor to pay his dues." Mama Priscilla paused as if to imply that what followed was self-evident:

"He lost everything. He became poor. And now, he also turned mad."

"All the wealth is gone?" I asked.

"All gone! Finished [S: *Kwisha basi*]!" She emphasized the loss by quickly rubbing her index finger across her lips from right to left while gently blowing out air. This was a common gesture in Kenya to point to the quick loss of fortunes. Although nobody could explain to me how this gesture signified loss more concretely, it was as if to point to riches which, like the index finger, came close to one's mouth, an icon of one's ability to consume and transform value in both positive and negative ways. But rather than being incorporated in ways that might nurture body and personhood, such riches came tantalizingly close, only to disappear.

Mama Priscilla recalled, "A few years ago, there was this other moran in our family, who had come back from Mombasa. He was just a young boy, but he had a car and a lot of money. Now, one day he drove by the front of my shop. Do you know how they drive?"

"Who drives?" I asked, wondering in what category she placed this man.

"These morans of Mombasa," she responded as she straightened her back, searching for the right position to impersonate their driving. "They wear sunglasses and they roll the window down. They hold the wheel with one hand and they put the arm out of the window, holding a cigarette." Mama Priscilla rolled her eyes, laughing. "Anyways, this brother of my son [his paternal parallel cousin] stopped the car in front of my shop to talk to someone. So I went out to greet him. But he pretended not to recognize me. He said: 'Who are you? Which family of ours? You are called Mama who?' Imagine! And this was someone who knew me very well. He grew up with my children. But their character [S: *tabia*] changes when they get all that money so fast."

Then, with some sort of satisfaction in her eyes, as if to say that moral wrongs don't go unpunished, she continued: "But guess what? The mzungu woman is gone, the money is gone, and he returned to the *shuka* [M, loincloth; here standing for 'poverty']. Finished!"

Mama Priscilla's story invokes motifs and motives, patterns of narration and formulas of moral criticism, that were common in Samburu. Many of my informants believed that education and employment, though inaccessible to the vast majority, were ways of "getting development," or stable wealth. At the same time, they saw going to Mombasa as a way of acquiring wealth quickly before, sooner or later, "returning to the *shuka*"—that is, discarding the "modern" trousers for the "traditional" loincloth, or losing wealth to poverty, development to backwardness. Mama Priscilla depicted the money acquired by men in coastal economies as distinct from the money of educated, employed men and women. At stake here, among other things, were the temporal rhythms of money's accumulation. Rather than being produced through long years of education and hard work, this money emerged through actions that took a "shortcut" between poverty and riches, social immaturity and adult respectability. Obtained suddenly, it subverted the ideal temporality of the life course, for as Mama Priscilla and other informants implied, a person should accumulate wealth and gain respectability only gradually throughout life. "Rushed money" or "shortcut money" both accelerated the normative pace of wealth accumulation and sidestepped life stages associated with the cumulative processes of self-making and social growth through schooling and laboring.

But this was not all. Some people also worried that transactional sex and sorcery replaced work (M: *lkasi*; from S: *kazi*), that is, mostly formal employment, as wealth-generating actions. Many Samburu referred to the money of Mombasa as "money of wrongdoings" (M: *shilingini e ngòk*) or "dirty money" (M: *shilingini chapu*). Younger people and those living in towns used Swahili idioms to describe this money more explicitly as "money of sex" (S: *pesa ya sex*) or "money of sorcery" (S: *pesa ya uchawi*). By contrast, they referred to money obtained through work as "money of sweat" (S: *pesa ya jasho*). They emphasized that the "money of Mombasa" and the goods purchased with it would evaporate quickly, whereas money of sweat could be converted into more lasting goods and relations. While these were highly contested categories of wealth, they indexed, respectively, negative and positive ways of producing livelihoods. And as I will show, they also named the perceived ability or inability of a particular kind of wealth to generate *nkishon*, or life force, and thus to expand itself and its owners both spatially (through growing families and social networks) and temporally (by lasting into the future).

In speaking about Mombasa morans and their money, Mama Priscilla and others reflected on what made morally positive forms of personhood and social value in the present. On the one hand, for Mama Priscilla, her shop, her children's education, and her wealth represented lasting outcomes of her hard work. The gifts she had received from her children were not only indices of her past struggles to provide for them but also evidence of her own capacity to build a future through their love and recognition. On the other hand, Mama Priscilla pointed out, her husband's brother's son, who had been in Mombasa, had engaged in morally questionable productive actions such as sorcery and transactional sex. The moral quality of these actions was centrally reflected in the man's "bad character" when he pretended not to be able to recognize a relative as close as his father's brother's wife, a kinship position Samburu classified as a mother as well. It was also reflected in the quick loss of his wealth, and in the general belief that "the money of Mombasa doesn't last" (S: *pesa ya Mombasa haikai*). This money could disappear for a variety of reasons. These included excessive consumption, quick redistribution, or, as I have shown in chapter 3, slippery intimacies that could lead quickly to conflicts between Samburu men and their foreign partners and end their relationships. But for Mama Priscilla, the transitory nature of this money was rooted in the immoral actions that generated it. At a time when the commodification of moran sexuality could produce, quite suddenly, more wealth than she and her children had succeeded to accumulate over many years of trade or employment, Mama Priscilla narrated this story to position herself and her wealth in a relation of moral superiority to the money of Mombasa and its owners.

I explore the money of Mombasa as a set of material and moral processes and representations of value in order to understand what this new category of wealth reveals about the making of social worlds and belonging in Samburu. By contesting the sources of money, the temporal rhythms of its production, as well as its moral and life-generating potentialities, various social actors articulated and negotiated the kinds of futures they desired, and assessed their own and others' moral character. But they also affected, to some extent, the concrete ways in which this money circulated within their district. As such, money produced through the commodification of moran sexuality shaped and in turn was shaped by the subjectivities of men and women in Samburu. I take subjectivity to refer to the desires, bodily dispositions, and perceptions of selfhood, style, space, and time. Meanwhile, I understand belonging as an intersubjective process through which people negotiate membership into a social group. In this sense, the emergence and transformation of subjectivities are anchored in processes of imagining and contesting morally positive forms of belonging. I ask: How did the money of Mombasa become visible to people in Samburu? How did sex, sorcery, and other seemingly immoral sources of money figure in relation to the perceived temporariness of the wealth and the moral worthiness of its owners? How did men who traveled to Mombasa display their wealth and circulate their resources at home? How did they position themselves in relation to local gossip? And how did other men and women perceive the desires and actions of these men? To answer these questions, I first show how Samburu men who migrated to the coast came to inhabit and perform a new category of masculinity in their home communities. I then describe how locals questioned the moral implications of these men's wealth and how, in the process, they reevaluated cultural templates of respectability and social value that served as criteria of belonging. Finally, I explore how young men who became rich positioned themselves amid local expectations of reciprocity, and how they devised new tactics for dealing with the gossip, scandal, and material demands of other locals. Such negotiations, we shall see, gave rise to new forms of kinship and attachment while producing new inequalities and exclusions.

"MOMBASA MORANS": STYLE, GOSSIP,
AND NEW SUBJECTIVITIES

In Samburu, the phrase "Mombasa morans" (M: *lmurran le Mombasa*) described young men who traveled regularly to tourist resorts to sell souvenirs,
dance for tourists, and meet European women. Not all of these men were
wealthy. Most of them, in fact, were not. However, the stereotype that Mombasa morans were rich originated in the great efforts of some of these men to
return to Samburu with significant amounts of money. Relatives, neighbors,
and age-mates expected them to have earned cash on the coast and to be able
to offer them gifts. Mombasa morans also needed money to live a good life
at home, before departing again for coastal tourist resorts. They desired to
buy fashionable clothes and to hang out with their friends in bars and restaurants. Therefore, those who did not save enough money during the tourist
season (at least $200–$300, during my fieldwork) often postponed making
the return trip. As a Samburu man once told me in Mtwapa, "You simply cannot go home without money." In turn, this imperative fueled the stereotype
that Mombasa morans were rich. "Beach boy / Rich boy," as the saying went
in Maralal.

Throughout the 1990s and 2000s, men who returned from the coast developed a distinct style of masculinity. They crafted particular ways of dressing, commuting, and spending time. In Maralal, one could easily recognize
Mombasa morans by their distinct attire (fig. 13). They wore blue jeans and
polo shirts, sunglasses, and expensive running shoes. They bought clothes
that displayed brand names such as Nike, Puma, or Reebok. They wore hairstyles associated with coastal youth, including dreadlocks or braids. Some
also wore gold chains, rings, or bracelets they had received from foreign partners. On the one hand, the clothing style of Mombasa morans indexed their
engagement with a world beyond the district. Indeed, they imagined themselves as more cosmopolitan than both the "morans of the bush" and educated youth, or the so-called *lkirda* (M: "those of the trousers"). On the other
hand, through their clothing style, Mombasa morans also claimed belonging
to local worlds: By wearing up to seven or eight traditional bead bracelets
(M: *marnani*) on each forearm, for instance, they showed that they belonged
to the moran age grade; that is, they were not just young men but distinctly
morans who were, if fact, *Samburu*.

During the months between tourist seasons, when Mombasa morans
lived in Samburu, many preferred to rent rooms in Maralal rather than stay
in the rural homesteads of their parents. Although they visited their fami-

13. Mombasa morans in Samburu, July 2011. (Photo by the author.)

lies, purchased livestock for family herds, and participated in the social affairs and rituals of their respective clans and age sets, they also spent much of
their time socializing with one another in town, eating in small restaurants,
listening to music, or attending parties. Their relative detachment from their
families' homesteads resonated with and was condoned by long-standing
ideals of moranhood. Samburu explained that morans should always provide for themselves and spend most of their time outside the homesteads of
their families.[1] Although, in the past two decades, numerous young men had
come to depend more strongly on the resources of their parents (Holtzman
2006), Mombasa morans who earned money independently invoked this
ideal proudly to determine how to dispose of their own time. Thus, Mombasa morans could spend less time at home and more time with one another.

    In Maralal, certain restaurants and bars came to be associated with
morans of Mombasa. In the early 1990s, a former Mombasa moran who had
become a wealthy politician and businessman opened a small motel bar called
Mtwapa Bar. The name of the establishment was suggestive of the fact that
both the owner and his current clientele had lived, at different points in time,
in the coastal town of Mtwapa. While in northern Kenya, young men who

lived in Mtwapa during the tourist season reconvened at Mtwapa Bar. There, they recounted events from their days at the beach and planned future trips to the coast. They also listened to Kenyan reggae and pop music, played pool, drank beer, chewed khat, and met with local young women.

Through these practices of conspicuous consumption, Mombasa morans made their wealth visible to others. And while many locals considered their spending excessive, the young men saw such consumption of both commodities and time as a way to craft and sustain relations of friendship and reciprocity with one another. For them, such relationships were not only beneficial but also pleasurable. Because these men shared their livelihoods both on the coast and in Samburu, they were more likely to understand and help one another. For example, when a Mombasa moran received money through Western Union from a partner in Europe, he treated his friends to meals, drinks, or taxi rides. In return, he expected similar treatment when another man in his group of friends obtained money. If one of them experienced a family emergency, the others supported him with cash, care, and labor.

As the numbers of Samburu men at tourist resorts grew significantly throughout the 1990s and 2000s, it became difficult for a Mombasa moran to know all the others. In Samburu, Mombasa morans formed networks of friendship according to the coastal towns where they lived during the tourist season. More specifically, men who lived on the North Coast (Mtwapa, Malindi, and Watamu) and those who lived on the South Coast (Diani and Ukunda) had different circles of friends. These groups also mapped, if only partially, on Samburu villages and lineage groups due to the fact that young men entered coastal economies by following their neighbors and immediate kin. So for example, men from the village of Siteti migrated primarily to the North Coast, while men from Lorosoro traveled to the South Coast. Despite belonging to different villages and lineages and traveling to different coastal areas, while in Samburu these men recognized each other, and were recognized by others as Mombasa morans because of their distinct style.

But the masculinities of Mombasa morans cannot be understood merely in terms of these men's performances and self-styling. In a context in which most local men and women did not have the resources to consume conspicuously, people used gossip, rumor, teasing, and folk songs to express both their desire and their disdain for these men. Indeed, Mombasa morans became salient objects of collective attention. Here, the self-styling practices of these men and the gossip of locals generated an indirect exchange that contoured the subjectivities of both gossipers and those about whom they gossiped. If Mombasa morans often preferred to socialize with one another, more so than with other locals, it was precisely because they perceived that the envy and gossip of others threatened their comfort and respectability.

"If people start saying that you are a beach boy, that is now very shameful," my friend Jackson explained to me in March 2011. I had asked him many times why he worried about what people said about him. So he decided to explain.

"How can you stay with other people and yet not care what they say?" he wondered in Swahili. "You know? Our people are sometimes *very primitive* [italicized words spoken in English]. They like to do a lot of talking. But they have not been anywhere else, and they don't know much. So if they see me with these clothes and with these bangles, they will say: [*in a dismissive tone*] 'Ah, this is a moran of Mombasa!'"

Jackson was in his late twenties. He had lived in Mombasa until 2009, when he met Helga, an expat from Germany (I introduced them both in chapter 3). Together with Helga—let us recall—Jackson moved back to Lorosoro to build a house.

"The other day, I was going with Helga to town," he began his story. "And our taxi broke down on that hill, in front of Maralal High School. So I got out of the car to help the driver repair it. And there were some girls in front of the school. And they started calling each other: 'Come! Come to see a beach boy!' That's what they were shouting. Seriously!" Jackson laughed. "And I could hear them. So I took a stone and threw it at them."

"So what's so special about a beach boy?" I asked.

"You know," he replied, "for them, in their minds, it's something very bad. It's like saying: 'Come and see a fag [S: *shoga*]!'"

Jackson was aware that his clothing style marked him as a moran of Mombasa and prompted what he saw as rude remarks from those he considered primitive, that is, naïve or noncosmopolitan locals. For him, calling someone a beach boy (in English, or using *bichboi* in Maa or Swahili) was shameful, for the noun implied a lack of respect. To call a young man a boy meant questioning his social maturity. But to call him a beach boy was to take the insult even further. Just like calling him a fag, this was a way to emasculate him publicly. For as some locals saw it, beach boys were, in fact, male prostitutes. Jackson had graduated in 2002 from the very same high school in front of which he now found himself insulted. He was familiar with the distinction that pupils, teachers, and other educated men and women made between building a future through education and employment and building a future through transactional sex. Following his graduation, at first Jackson had been employed as a soldier in the National Youth Service, and then as a

truck driver for a Nairobi firm. He had found both jobs stressful and poorly
paid, and decided to join some age-mates from his village on the south coast
of Mombasa.

Schoolgirls and other educated men and women in Samburu ridiculed
beach boys for sleeping with women who were their seniors. They invoked
the normative assumption that a man should only sleep with women his own
age or younger. On the coast, we shall recall, people ridiculed "God's birds"
(S: *ndege wa Mungu*) for having relationships with elderly women (see chapter 3). Similarly, in Samburu, youth enjoyed teasing Mombasa morans for dis-
regarding sexual boundaries of age or gender ideals of provider masculinity.
Jacinta, a waitress in a Maralal restaurant, told me in Swahili:

> Look at what these Mombasa morans are doing, just to get white people! *They
> are lowering their culture* [italicized words spoken in English]. What a shame!
> You know, sometimes these men even bring the old mamas home to Maralal.
> When I was working at this other restaurant, my friend Taitas came with an old
> mama from Mombasa. She was so old, this one. And I could not stop laughing.
> I called him and told him, "This is *too much*. How can you like this woman? She
> can be your grandmother." And he told me, "Jacinta, you are always so mean to
> me. You know I don't like her, but she has a lot of money, and she can help me."
> We usually laugh at these morans of Mombasa. We don't say that they "marry"
> [S: *wanaoa*, masculine, active verb] white women, but that they "are married"
> [S: *wanaolewa*, feminine, passive verb].

According to Jacinta, Mombasa morans emasculated themselves by consent-
ing to have sex with older women. Furthermore, by marketing themselves for
sexual purposes as Samburu morans, these men, she thought, "lowered their
culture." Many of my educated informants shared the logic and language
of Jacinta's narration (Meiu 2009). And Mombasa morans were well aware
of such narratives. Because Helga was Jackson's senior by over thirty years,
Jackson told me that he felt uncomfortable when he had to bring her to Maralal, for he anticipated that people would gossip. "People talk, you know," he
explained. "They say: 'Oh, how do you stay with that old woman? She's the
same age like your mother.' Even you, you cannot feel well when people talk
like that." Anticipating this kind of gossip, some Mombasa morans would
pay "plastic boys" (fig. 14)—that is, unemployed young men who occasionally guided travelers—to take their foreign partners shopping or show them
the town. This was one of the many ways in which these men anticipated and
acted on the possibility of local gossip.

14. A Mombasa moran and his European partner run into the "plastic boys" in Maralal, Samburu, 2011. Detail from a drawing by a Maralal high school pupil.

Gossip, rumor, and scandal are central modes for the production and alteration of belonging. Scholars argue that gossip is not only an efficient means for asserting the "unity" of a group in relation to its outsiders (Gluckman 1963), but also a way of dealing with emerging conflicts and contradictions and generating intimate alliances against oppressive political and economic hierarchies (Besnier 2009; Pietilä 2007; Scott 1990; Sparks 1985; L. White 2000). Focusing on the wider consequences of gossip practices, anthropologists argue that gossip is often employed as a political tool that can actively reshape social worlds. "Even though initially it is discussed in small informal circles," Tuulikki Pietilä (2007, 8) argues, "gossip usually reaches the ears of the subjects of the gossip sooner or later, in effect requiring them to respond in one way or another." In this sense, gossip represents a "metapragmatic discourse" (Silverstein 1993) through which social values, subject positions, and criteria of belonging are redefined by way of an "indirect dialogue" between gossipers and the subjects of gossip (Pietilä 2007, 8–9). Here, the subjectivities of Mombasa morans and the gossip of local men and women shaped each other dialectically. "Mombasa morans" named a new "subject position"—a cultural category of the self somewhat independent of the individuals who inhabit it (Boellstorff 2005, 10)—that synthesized everyday gossip and a self-designed style of consumption, mobility, and leisurely social-izing.

But local men and women did not use gossip or rumor simply to insult Mombasa morans. Although Jackson took offense when the schoolgirls had called him a beach boy, this was not necessarily the outcome that the schoolgirls intended. For young, educated women I interviewed, speaking of beach boys was a way to express not only disdain but also fascination, ad-miration, and desire. In the absence of stable employment, many educated men no longer made reliable boyfriends or husbands. What is more, like on the coast, numerous young men in Maralal and its environs had turned into God's birds, that is, souls left to faith, depending on parents or em-ployed (sometimes more senior) women for housing, food, and clothing. Young women told me they expected their partners to buy them gifts such as chains, bangles, cell phones, airtime, perfume, lipsticks, chocolate, and cakes. Without wages, many young men found it difficult to fulfill such ex-pectations. Hence, young women admired Mombasa morans for their access to cash and prestigious commodities. As I came to learn later, despite her criticism of Taitas, Jacinta considered him a dear friend and often received gifts of cash and goods from him. And she was not the only one. My research assistant Anna, a young, married schoolteacher who was well familiar with my research topic, delighted in ridiculing beach boys in my presence and em-phasizing their "bad character." Eventually, however, I learned that she had a secret affair with a moran of Mombasa who bought her a cell phone, clothes, and other gifts with money received from his European partner. By accepting these gifts, women recognized the Mombasa morans as desirable partners and reasserted their masculinities as potentially respectable.

If for European women the erotics of young Samburu men were primarily about their ability to embody cultural difference, for local educated women the erotic qualities of Mombasa morans rested rather with their cosmopoli-tanism, innovative style, and access to commodities. The gossip and teasing calls of local women conferred not only a mode of criticizing the morality of wealth and productive actions but also a pleasant and playful way of express-ing desire for these men and the power and wealth they announced through their distinct style. For some of these women, Mombasa morans con-gealed fantasies of good life, premised on access to money and prestigious commodities. Mombasa morans performed "distinction" (Bourdieu 1984) through their style, and sought to impress local women with their ability to consume. In turn, as salient targets of gossip, rumor, and teasing, these men became objects of desire and play for women who, through such playful talk, could more pleasantly inhabit the present. In the process, Mombasa morans and young women negotiated together—though often indirectly—what made desirable lives and futures.

While schoolgirls addressed Mombasa morans through mocking calls, "girls of the beads" (M: *ntoyie ee saen*)—that is, rural girls who did not go to school (Lesorogol 2008b)—indirectly addressed them through a particular genre of songs called *kakisha*. Kakisha were intimate songs that girls performed while they were among themselves, fetching firewood or water. Such songs could never be sung in front of male elders or in the homestead, for they aroused men. But girls always sang kakisha, expecting morans to hear them. They sang alone or in groups, and addressed their songs to individual morans or to their whole age set. As with gossip, through kakisha young women praised brave morans and shamed those who acted in ways deemed unmanly.[2] Beginning in the 1990s, numerous kakisha also targeted morans of Mombasa. Consider the following example:

Nairobi naishayie lmurran,	Nairobi took all the morans.
Mombasa natanga nkutuk.	Mombasa is an open mouth.
Kepuo Mombasa,	They went to Mombasa
Nepuo nkampo	And they went "abroad" (i.e., Europe)
Nelau nkishu nkitungat.	And the cows have no protection.
Engura nkaileer nkachau ninche?	Can you see the milky color of our cows?
Elepito Loldepiai.	The Pokot are milking them.

In these verses, the narrator depicts Mombasa as "an open mouth," referring to the power of this faraway place, unknown to rural girls, to attract young men. Morans had long traveled to Nairobi to work. More recently, however, Mombasa has been attracting even more young men. The open or empty mouth is an icon of greed, insatiability, and even cannibalism. In funerary rites, for example, the mouth of the dead has to be filled with fat, for an open, empty mouth is believed to "eat up" people or to call others to follow the dead to the grave. In this song, the narrator decries the way in which Mombasa, an imagined locus of economic power and an agentive "mouth," alienated the morans, leaving homesteads without herders. Because the morans' presumed role was to protect the cattle of their fathers, the girls questioned the importance of these men to the continuity of local worlds. Girls saw Mombasa morans as being at fault for the loss of cattle to raiders of the neighboring Pokot tribe.

Expectations of respectability and good manners associated with the girls of the beads demanded that these young women not look men in the eye or respond at length when asked questions. This prevented me from carrying out in-depth interviews with them. So I collected most of my kakisha songs from young married women, or "mamas of the beads," who could speak more openly with me given their marital status. Even so, when I would ask young women to sing kakisha so that I could record them, my requests were invariably met with laughter, embarrassment, and hesitation.

"You want me to sing you kakisha?" Mama Nailashe asked me disbelievingly. "Do you want all these neighbors of ours to think that I am mad?" I had asked Mama Nailashe to remember kakisha songs about Mombasa morans that she and her age-mates sang in the 1990s, when they had been girls. Although she eventually agreed to whisper some of these songs to me, her initial resistance pointed to the assumed inherent eroticism of kakisha that made its performance inappropriate in the domestic setting or in the presence of a young unmarried man.

Like everyday gossip or the teasing calls of schoolgirls, the moral messages of kakisha combined ridicule with admiration for Mombasa morans.

Natoye, kerepi ngari nenap lmurran naji lmalindi
Girls, we have to praise the car that is called Malindi [the Malindi Bus]

Tana kipal mikirep?
Or shall we stop praising it?

Amu keishayie lmuran lmooli neaku ntoyie nkolia mera.
Because it took all Lmooli [age-set name] morans, leaving girls "widows who are not [yet married]"

Natoyie mikisham lmuran loo lmooli tinirepi.
Girls, we don't love the Lmooli morans, though we praise them.

Meata naishopo namuka arubare te ngopi naapuo.
None of us puts on shoes to follow them to the places where they go.

Keshomo Lmooli Mombasa
The Lmooli went to Mombasa

Neraya nkishu ang Lpookot.
And our cows are being raided by the Pokot.

Anyo pasa pamabul ntolut paaku nanu erewa kini?
Why am I not the one to grow up to have these cows?

Keisupati nkishu ang le lkasin naa neja eitu nenjore,
[But] Our "cows of work" are beautiful and similar to the raided ones,

Amu tena shilingini epoui ayea ninche naikash alang neibukori lodo.
Because the money we get is better than pouring blood [through raiding].

These verses picture the departure of large numbers of morans of the Lmooli age set (starting in 1990) to the coast as an affront to the sexual order of village life. Unable to envision intimate relationships or future marriages to men their own age, young women called themselves "widows who are not (yet)" (M: *nkolia [na] mera*); that is, they became widows before even having had a chance to marry. As their sexual and reproductive futures became uncertain, their love for these men became ambivalent, for as the verses go, none of them goes through the trouble of putting on shoes to follow morans to the faraway places they go. But young women also admired Mombasa morans. Although in the past, most kakisha celebrated men who proved their bravery through cattle raids, these verses now suggest a certain ambivalence toward an older ideal of masculinity. They suggest that Mombasa morans bring money and purchase "cows of work" (M: *nkishu le lkasin*, that is, cattle obtained with money), and that these cattle are "beautiful and similar to the raided ones," making violent raids unnecessary. Young women also fantasized about the adventures of these men. Consider another example:

Oh, kore apa pabulu nang'enu mpari nabo aiputukunyo	Oh, long ago, when I was growing up [becoming knowledgeable], one day I was surprised.
Oh, peye na pare Lmooli lang kejo: 'Mombasa kipoito.'	Oh, when our Lmooli [age-set name] said: "We are going to Mombasa."
Nagira sila aibuk lkiiyo.	And I kept quiet and shed tears.
Nkai ai narok tanapa!	My black God, carry them! [protect them]
Nkai ai narok tanapa!	My black God, carry them! [protect them]
. . . .	. . . .
Oh, yentolimo tanaa ketintae loitalong'a ndeke nkare!	Oh, [you who went to Mombasa], tell us if there is somebody who took the airplane to cross the water [ocean]!
Oh, keitalang'a Lonkutere, lemeideli saye yoklorop.	Oh, Lonkutere crossed it [the ocean], [and] his upper-arm beads will not be tightened.
Oh, lemedeli saye meipima peipimuni ta mashini.	Oh, the upper-arm beads will not be tightened and his weight will not be measured on a scale.
. . . .	. . . .

Ntoye papa, kidek Nissan tanaa kipal mikidek?	Girls [of] our father, do we curse the Nissan or shall we not curse it?
Oh, tanaa kipal mikidek?	Oh, or shall we not curse it?
Oh, Nissan naishaye lmurran anap aya nkopi eishing'a.	Oh, the Nissan which took the morans to a place where they don't belong.
. . . .	. . . .
Oh, Nkai ai saidai lmurran montoki aitam ldama orok.	Oh, my God help the morans, don't give them the black sun [i.e., times of hardship].
Mombasa naishaye lmurran,	Mombasa took the morans,
Oh, neitulusu Mutwapa.	Oh, but mostly Mtwapa.
Oh, Jadini naaibooye lmurran kejo: 'Musungu kiranyie,'	Oh, Jadini protects the morans who say: "We are dancing with whites."
Oh, kejo: 'Musungu kiranyie.'	Oh, who say: "We are dancing with whites."
Oh, kiterepa ntoye to Lchingei,	Oh, we are praised by the girls in Lchingei,
Oh, nkashompa ta Mombasa.	Oh, and by the white women in Mombasa.
Oh, kemanyaa Lkugusi ana nkera Sirata Lalaigwanani,	Oh, Lkungusi lives like the children of Sirata Lalaigwanani,
Oh, Sirata Lalaigwanani.	Oh, of Sirata Lalaigwanani.
Oh, keimusunkui Losusana.	Oh, the brother of Susana is light-skinned.
Oh, Malindi eterekie lpapit,	Oh, he made his hair in Malindi.
Oh, keterea dei naing'asie metodolo te Irapa,	Oh, he made it, and [people] wonder as they see it in Irapa.
Oh, kejoito loshomo Mombasa: 'Iyioo eishi enyor musunku.	Oh, the man who went to Mombasa is saying: "We are loved by the whites."

Girls of the beads were both worried about and fascinated with morans who went to Mombasa. Kakisha songs, like the one above, expressed this ambivalence. Uncertain of whether or not to curse the vehicle—here, a Nissan—"which took the morans to a place where they don't belong," the narrator begins to enumerate her experiences with morans of Mombasa. On the one hand, the song suggests, there is nothing really bad about these men. Lonkutere, a man who went to Mombasa, eventually traveled overseas. Although locals might expect him to have suffered while being away from home, he is in very good health: he did not lose weight, as "his upper-arm beads" don't need tightening, and a doctor will not take his weight on a clinic scale, for he is not sick. On the other hand, the song satirizes the seeming infatuation of Mombasa morans. These men—so the song goes—snobbishly believe that they are admired by both the girls of their home village (here, Lchingei) and by the white women they meet in Mombasa. They are also spoiled by their luxurious lifestyle. Lkungusi, for example, lives "like the children of Sirata Lalaigwanani," an area of Samburu known to the girls for its spoiled infants. Furthermore, some of these men bring new styles to Samburu. The "brother of Susana," for example, had his hair styled in Malindi, on the coast, only to have people wonder at it in the Samburu village of Irapa.

"Do the girls sing a lot about morans who went to Mombasa?" I asked Jackson.

"Yes," he replied. "They do. I had not gone to Mombasa yet, at that time. But our *morijo* [senior members of the age set] had gone. And the fighting had started between the Samburu and the Pokot. So the girls sang: 'The morans have gone to Mombasa and the elders are looking after the cattle.' That is to insult the morans."

"And they sing that so that you can hear them?" I asked.

Yes. There are those who, if I have gone to Mombasa, they will sing that song about me. And other people will tell me, "You know what those girls are saying?" You feel very bad. During the raids in 2008, many morans came back because of those songs. One time, the girls recorded themselves on tape. And those who went to Mombasa took the tape with them. There, they went and they played it. *Haiiit* [expression of shock]! That was very harsh. Even I started to cry. I was crying tears, my brother. They were singing that the cows have gone, all of them, and the Lkishami [Jackson's age set, initiated in 2005] are in Mombasa. We felt very bad.

By questioning the respectability of morans, individually or as an age set, young women acted on the behaviors of these men. They framed their singing as a way of shaming these men into what they saw as morally positive ways of acting. But their songs, just like the mocking calls of schoolgirls or the gossip of locals more generally, were not simply meant to insult Mombasa morans. Kakisha songs also congealed young women's reflections and desires as they struggled to grasp new contexts of life and as they sought to position themselves in relation to the emerging styles and desires of the Mombasa morans.

Gossip, teasing calls, and songs about morans of Mombasa generated a "semi-public sphere," wherein, as Pietilä (2007, 9) argues, "concrete in-stances of gossip [and speech more generally] are part of a larger dialogue beyond the particular face-to-face situation." Through this dialogue, young women—whether schoolgirls or girls of the beads—crafted new desires for themselves and others while also shifting their expectations of masculine re-spectability. Men and women in Samburu did not merely evaluate the actions and wealth of the Mombasa morans in terms of preexisting templates of so-cial value, they also reflected on and reformulated those templates. Emerg-ing through this interchange of gossip and style, "Mombasa morans" repre-sent a new form of *masculinity*, a masculine subject position that synthesizes the contradictions between various desires, aspirations, and subjectivities.

Following Luise White's (1990) call to deconstruct the essentialist cate-gory of men and to theorize the complex processes through which men in African contexts are gendered, historians and anthropologists have explored how discourses, practices, and subjective experiences generated multiple, hierarchically ordered *masculinities* (Lindsay and Miescher 2003; Miescher 2005; Morrell 2001; Ouzgane and Morrell 2005; Richter and Morrell 2006; Silberschmidt 2001). Anthropologists also documented how, following neoliberal market reforms, social and economic transformations in Africa undermined the possibility of men to actualize hegemonic ideals of pro-vider masculinity (Groes-Green 2009, 2014; Honwana 2012; Hunter 2010; Mains 2011; Newell 2012; Ratele 2011). Building on this literature, I under-stand the masculinity of Mombasa morans as an outcome of the contradic-tions entailed in ethno-erotic economies. As men sell their ethnic sexuality to achieve masculine respectability, they subvert cultural expectations of work and sexual propriety, thereby engendering new, albeit deeply ambiva-lent, masculine subject positions.

Being a Mombasa moran, and herewith the subject of gossip, teasing, and songs, was a temporary subject position. Rather than a fixed identity, it was a nexus of multiple potentialities in the life of a man who, depend-ing on his skills and luck, could turn into a rich young man or, more tragi-cally, return to coastal resorts year after year, aging without having acquired substantial wealth. Men who were unsuccessful at tourist resorts eventually sought alternative ways to produce resources at home. Some traded goats and cattle. Others produced and sold charcoal. Although some of these men retained nicknames such as Lekost ("the one of the coast") or, more com-monly, Rasta (a nickname alluding to the Rastafarian hairstyles of coastal beach boys), they eventually abandoned the styles of Mombasa morans and were no longer subjects of gossip in the same way. By contrast, men who became rich made—along with their wealth—hot topics of gossip. Gossip about the money of Mombasa and the rich young men who brought it to the district allowed various social actors to assess how this new kind of wealth affected collective values and well-being, and how it enabled or undermined these morans' ability to belong to local worlds.

"THE MONEY OF MOMBASA DOESN'T LAST": CONTESTING THE WORTH OF MIRACULOUS WEALTH

Mombasa morans often returned to Samburu with enough money to invest in livestock and live a "good life" for a few months before returning to the coast. Few men managed to develop long-term relationships with one or several foreign women who agreed to support them with substantial amounts of cash. For those that did, however, the income could be substantial. Receiving money wires of $300 to $500 per month, in addition to financial support for the acquisition of property (some $20,000–$30,000 at a time), these men became some of the richest people in Samburu. Once they converted their dollars and euros into Kenyan currency, some were, in fact, millionaires. They often stopped migrating to the coast and used their money to build houses, acquire livestock and farms, buy cars and motorcycles, and open shops, lodges, and restaurants. For locals, this wealth was spectacular. Rich morans built large stone houses with three to ten rooms. By contrast, most people lived in small houses made of wood, mud, and dung (see chapter 2). Although rural areas lacked electricity and women walked long distances to fetch water, the households of these men had electricity generators, satellite dishes, and water pumps. Along the same dirt roads on which locals walked or biked for hours to reach market towns or relatives, rich morans drove Toyota Land Cruisers, Land Rovers, or motorcycles.

People were intrigued by how quickly such wealth materialized in the landscape of their district. Labor migrants and traders took many years to build houses of wood with iron-sheet roofs, and rarely could afford motorcycles, much less cars. Hence, locals wondered how young men—many of whom spent only short periods of time on the coast—were able to acquire such spectacular wealth so quickly. At the beginning of this chapter, Mama Priscilla described the money of Mombasa as "shortcut money" or "rushed money," or, as she explained, "[money] that you don't have to work for." My informants suggested that through such money, young men accelerated the usual rhythms of wealth accumulation and sidestepped actual work as a morally positive source of cash. "Rushed money" and "shortcut money" speak of a wider historical moment in which, as Jean and John Comaroff

(2000, 295) argue, "production appears to have been superseded, as the *fons et origo* of wealth, by less tangible ways of generating value." This is a context of rapidly shifting economic inequalities engendered by neoliberal reforms and a rising ethos of speculation and entrepreneurialism. In this context, anthropologists encounter, in different parts of the world, a new kind of wealth, variably known as "fast money," "hot money," or "quick money" (Osburg 2013; Walsh 2003; Znoj 2004). In many places, such money has given rise to salient moral contestations concerning the means and modes of economic production and social reproduction.

In Kenya at the time of my research between 2005 and 2015, fast riches made a hot topic of debate in mass media and everyday life. On February 23, 2011, the *Daily Nation*, a major national newspaper, published an opinion piece titled "Life Is Not a Beach: Time to End the 'Easy Money' Vicious Circle." In it, the author, a high school pupil from the Kenyan Coast, decries the desire of his peers for "easy money." He observes with disappointment the "widespread notion that you do not have to be educated to live comfortably," and notes that "locals are caught up in an endless pursuit of easy riches that mostly never happen."[3] On July 11, 2011, a piece in *Daily Kenya Living*, a magazine of the *Daily Nation*, described desire for quick wealth as iconic of the country's new generation: "Kenyan youth wants to swim in money, but their idea of work and a profession is different from that of their parents." The article warned that because "being wealthy is the number one ambition of Kenyan youth," there was also "a reason to worry: The generation is allergic to work."[4] The rhetoric resonated with what Max Weber ([1905] 2012, 11) described as a "Protestant ethic" anchored in "the *duty* of the individual to work toward the increase of his wealth." This "duty," Weber argued, "is assumed to be an end in itself." In Kenya, education, work, and gradual accumulation of wealth define middle-class belonging, even if sometimes only aspirationally and not as actual ways of doing things. Such values have also come to represent conditions of national belonging and respectability for middle-class Samburu living in towns.

For many Kenyans, fast riches vanishing as quickly as they appeared conferred concrete proof of the inherent immorality of their mode of acquisition. In Nairobi or on the coast, people spoke extensively of how the poor turned rich through dubious means, only to lose their wealth and "return" to poverty. So, too, in Samburu: people believed that "the money of Mombasa doesn't last." Every year, upon my return to the district, friends pointed out how one or another formerly rich Mombasa moran had sold his house, his car, or his cattle and ended up struggling to make ends meet. While everyone agreed that money ran out because white partners had ceased to support these men or because relatives and friends had continued to place high demands on their resources, they also wondered why Mombasa morans could not maintain and grow their wealth.

The money of Mombasa was not the only example of rushed money in Samburu. My informants often compared this money to the "money of the bomb blast." In the late 1990s, numerous Samburu and Maasai sought compensation in an international court case against the Kenyan Ministry of Defense and the British army. Land mines that had been abandoned by British soldiers training in northern Kenya had injured many of them. Other plaintiffs were relatives of men and women killed by such ammunition. In 2003, with the help of a British law firm, 233 people received compensations of some \$5,000 to \$20,000. They opened bars, stores, and lodges, built houses, and bought cars, becoming influential local traders and businesspeople. By 2010, however, many of them had spent their money and sold their businesses. Locals observed that like the money of Mombasa, the "money of the bomb blast" did not last, because it was rushed money or shortcut money, wealth that was not produced through a gradual process of work and accumulation. The *New York Times* noted on March 28, 2003, "Herdsmen that [had previously] walked everywhere were buying four-wheel-drive vehicles and carrying cell-phones." But, because "most of the herdsmen had never walked into a bank before" and some refused to attend a "training seminar on financial management," their money began disappearing. "Samburu millionaires fell from grace to grass," reported the *Standard*, a major national newspaper, on June 26, 2011; their "fortunes evaporated in seconds." As the article sarcastically noted, "Illiterate herdsmen who had not seen the inside of banking hall, and who had never gone beyond where their animals led them, were the new millionaires in town." But this "did not stop the herders from slumping back to poverty." Such narratives echoed old colonial stereotypes of Samburu "herdsmen" as irrational subjects who were, as a British district commissioner put it in 1921, "economically unsound."[5] Ridiculing the irresponsible squandering of wealth among Samburu, journalists reiterated the seeming alterity of Samburu livelihoods. As a British woman living in Maralal once told me, among the Samburu "there never has been a culture of money."

But whereas for outsiders "culture" easily explained why Samburu millionaires did not hold on to their riches, my Samburu informants offered more complex arguments. In narrating concrete cases in which the money of Mombasa disappeared, locals tried to grasp its origins and potentialities. Using gossip, they tried to work out *why* this money—just like the money of the bomb blast—vanished so quickly, and *why*, in the process of its depletion, it also affected the lives and well-being of its owners. Local gossip invoked and combined at least three sets of cultural logics about production, accumulation, and consumption: (1) notions of sorcery and blood consumption originating on the coast; (2) notions of sex, contagion, and materiality with an older history in Samburu; and (3) Christian ideas about labor, sweat, and theft that circulated in the Kenyan public sphere.

"This wealth will not last long, because everything that these guys have comes from sorcery [S: *uchawi*]," Jackson said of the new riches of two of his age-mates in the summer of 2011. He and I were sitting in the shade of his yet unfinished house in Lorosoro. With the modest help of his German partner, Helga, he had begun building the small dwelling two years prior. But because Helga struggled financially, he had only managed to build the exterior walls and the roof. In the meantime, his age-mates Meikan and Korendina, two other Mombasa morans from Lorosoro (whom I described in the introduction of this book), had each built a large house of stone in only few months. Jackson explained:

> I know for sure that Meikan got a *jini* [S: spirit] from a witch doctor in Tanzania. That's how he got Nora [a woman from Belgium]. But Korendina, I don't know. You know, both Meikan and Korendina were in Diani. They were at the beach. But Meikan became far richer than Korendina. He bought two big plots in town, and now he is building a lodge. He built a deep well on his plot to have water. Also, that house I showed you, it's his. He has a motorbike and that car you saw. But Korendina only built a house. Diane [Korendina's Scottish partner] also bought him a car. But he sold it. Some time back, he also had a wholesale in Kisima, but he closed it down. I think that he also has a *jini*, because, you see, he sold the car and his money started going away.

Jackson tried to make sense of the circumstances that led to the fast enrichment of his age-mates. He explained Meikan's spectacular wealth as having come through sorcery involving *majini* (sg. *jini*) spirits. But at first, he hesitated to claim that Korendina had also used sorcery. Nevertheless, realizing that Korendina's wealth "started going away," Jackson speculated that he, too, must have used a jini spirit. Here, sorcery became legible through symptoms of depletion. The depletion of wealth both exemplified and confirmed Jackson's conviction that money of sorcery would not last. "I'd rather build my house slowly and stay with it," he concluded. "I don't want those rushed things [S: *vitu vya haraka*]."

Majini sorcery represented the most common motive people invoked to explain why money of Mombasa did not last. In Samburu, this form of witchcraft was a recent phenomenon that people associated with the coast, the Swahili, and the Arabs. On the coast, Samburu said, people had long accumulated riches with the help of majini spirits. My informants perceived majini sorcery as more dangerous and more powerful than other kinds of sorcery. People maintained that it would bring abundant wealth faster than herbal medicines (S: *madawa*; or *miti shamba*) or the sorcery of Samburu occult practitioners. While elderly men and women spoke of majini in the most general terms, younger people narrated detailed stories of various men who owned majini. All perceived it to be mysterious and powerful, with some even fearing to mention the name of the spirits as such.

Putting together the stories I gathered from different informants, I learned that some Mombasa morans allegedly purchased majini from witch doctors in coastal Kenya and Tanzania. The contracting of a jini involved rituals that took place in caves or on top of graves. Once a jini owner, the novice had to regularly sacrifice birds and livestock, blood offerings (S: *sadaka ya damu*) to the spirit. The owner also had to follow certain taboos associated with a particular jini (e.g., owning cars that were red in color; avoiding certain foods; wearing specific colors on specific days; etc.). Some informants were convinced that although the owner might prosper for a while, sooner or later the spirit would increase its demands for blood offerings. Eventually, it could even demand the owner's parents or children. Unable to cope with these high demands, the owner would eventually go mad and die at the hands of the spirit.

Some informants explained that the objects that indexed the wealth of these rich morans most centrally—their money, cattle, cars, and houses—were imbued with a destructive power that threatened the lives and life force of others. Therefore, some men and women refused to accept gifts from rich Mombasa morans. One married couple I knew refused to allow their daughter to marry a man enriched in Mombasa, because they feared the bridewealth cattle would be purchased with money from the jini. Although they later consented to the marriage, when their daughter was unable to become pregnant, they had no more doubt that the man's jini had consumed their daughter's fertility. Similarly, men feared driving or riding in the cars of rich Mombasa morans. Said one man:

I would never buy a car from a man who I know was a beach boy. I wouldn't even drive it, if he asked me to. Those cars are not bought with clean money. He only told the white woman, "I want a car!" and he got it. That means that he used a jini. You will surely die in that car. You know, there was a man . . . who had been a beach boy in the South Coast. He bought a jini. The witch doctor told him that from that day on, he can never drive a white car, or he would die. All the cars he owned were red. He had some five red cars. And all his cars had accidents. But nothing ever happened to him. Those accidents would happen when he was away in France and someone else was driving them. Some of these people died. They were the *sadaka* [S, offering] for the jini.

Cars bought with money of sorcery were subject to the occult forces of their initial owners. Here, the car's red color expressed its association with the jini and the spirit's appetite for blood.[6] Indeed, a common way people died at the hand of a jini was when cars turned upside down, cutting their bodies open for the jini to consume their blood.

As part of a wider genre of gossip and scandal associated with the Mombasa morans, majini stories played an important role in helping men and women negotiate the social and moral criteria of belonging in the present. Such stories allowed locals to critique emerging inequalities and grasp the unpredictable dynamics of the circulation of capital in their district. This is probably what made majini narratives so appealing in a context where they had not existed before. Young men had exclusive access to an intimate economy premised on the commodification of moran sexuality, and therefore controlled the movement of its capital into and within their home district. What is more, in a context of widespread poverty in northern Kenya, the wealth of these men was highly visible to others. Hence, for men and women in Samburu, the money of Mombasa spoke, among other things, of the greed and immorality of these young, rich men. Janet McIntosh (2009b, 111) argues that among marginalized Giriama in Malindi, majini narratives facilitate a critique of the capital and spatial mobility of the wealthy and politically powerful Swahili. According to McIntosh, majini stories describe the "abandonment of a reciprocal, morally acceptable mode of personhood" as well as a "perverted relationship between labor and accumulation" (116). That is, "wealth seems to arrive and compound itself without being rooted in reciprocity or hard work" (ibid.). Similarly, Samburu saw the money of Mombasa as a morally problematic category of wealth, divorced from labor yet unpredictable in the rhythms of its appearance and disappearance. By criticizing young men and their money, Samburu emphasized the importance of reciprocity and recirculation as defining criteria of local belonging, and dismissed private modes of accumulation.

James Smith (2008, 105) argues that for the Wataita of southern Kenya, "the jini resembles... [the] commodity fetish, a purchased thing that appears to produce wealth out of nothing." Smith maintains that "by turning productive resources into consumer goods and destroying the means for the production of resources (e.g., maize, children, and livestock), majini help to make a world where Wataita are no longer the producers of value, but consumers" (107). The same can be argued for northern Kenya. As wealth emerged miraculously through the commodification of moran sexuality—in far greater quantities and more spectacular shapes than could ever be achieved through local means—majini narratives expressed people's fears of a world where they would fall prey to the desire to consume, without being able to generate resources of their own. To belong meant recentering generative forces, anchoring them in the district, and tying them to older social values.

In majini narratives, the fast enrichment of the few is premised on the future depletion of wealth in people and kind or, to put it differently, on the alienation of the many. The motive of blood extraction is common in majini narratives. It stands for the alienation of life and power: such spectacular wealth could emerge only through the appropriation of the life substance of others. Indeed, this argument has been common in many parts of Africa, past and present (Comaroff and Comaroff 1993; Geschiere 1997; McIntosh 2009b; J. Smith 2008; L. White 2000). In Samburu, the element of blood consumption was not restricted to the money of Mombasa. In 2009 and 2010, for example, accusations of large-scale blood-harvesting drives circulated widely after several men were found dead in the environs of Maralal, their bodies without blood. Like elsewhere in Kenya, locals suggested that devil worshippers transported blood to Tanzania for purposes of their own enrichment. According to this cultural logic, powerful centers located elsewhere—whether Nairobi, Tanzania, or Europe—alienated the generative life force of places and people like Samburu. To some extent, then, sorcery narratives emphasized how rising ethno-erotic economies turned alterity into a commodity by further solidifying an extant geopolitics of Samburu marginality, enriching a few Samburu who could associate with centers of power while further marginalizing the vast majority of locals.

But majini stories did more than just explain anxieties over alienation or the transience of wealth, or simply voice fears about the potential effects of the circulation of such wealth. They also expressed desire for the kinds of things that rich morans acquired. According to McIntosh (2009b, 119), "the implicit logic of the *jini* narratives may contain a thinly veiled longing for prosperity." Similarly, James Smith (2008, 108) argues that stories of majini "also imply that monetary wealth is seductive and erotic, that it opens a person to the dangers and promises of desire." For Jackson and other informants, gossiping about rich Mombasa morans and their wealth was a pleasurable pursuit. Their careful specification, precise enumeration, and detailed description of the riches of one or another man allowed them to express their own desires for acquiring similar objects, if only under different circumstances.

The ways in which Samburu understood the money of Mombasa combined logics about jini sorcery originating on the coast with older local notions of sex, contagion, and materiality. Some of my informants claimed to refuse gifts of money or goods from Mombasa morans, fearing that the self-depleting quality of these men's money would be transferred contagiously to their own wealth. One man who worked for the district administration made it a rule to turn down any gifts of money from such men. And on one occasion, I witnessed a Samburu woman refusing to drink a soda that a Mombasa moran had bought for her in Maralal. As with "bitter money" among the Luo of western Kenya (Shipton 1989) or the "money of shit" among the Nuer of South Sudan (Hutchinson 1996), Samburu said that money took over the qualities and substance of the things for which it was exchanged. For example, eating food purchased with the money of the bomb blast, some suggested, amounted to a cannibalistic consumption of the bodies of those for whom compensations had been received.[7] Consuming such unpropitious money or mixing it with the rest of one's wealth contagiously imparted its enervating qualities to a person's resources and life force. And while the money of the bomb blast perpetuated cannibalism, the money of Mombasa carried the substances of the sexual encounters for which it was exchanged.

"That money will finish here and now," Charlie, a junior elder, explained to me. "That money of sex does not live [S: *haiishi*, "nurture"], because it is like you are paid for it [sex]. Now, you take that payment of yours for sex and you give it to your child. That is like a curse that will follow you." Charlie maintained that the money obtained as a payment for sex "does not live" (S: *haiishi*, translated from M: *meishu*) or prosper (i.e., is depleting of "life force," *nkishon*). By suggesting that money obtained through transactional sex was cursed or that feeding one's child with that money was dangerous, Charlie pointed to more complex interconnections between sex, money, and life force.

Also known as "money of sex," the money of Mombasa threatened to rehearse incest, adultery, and other forms of "sex out of place." Food or other commodities purchased with money of sex were believed to perpetuate the forces and substances of the sexual act in which it originated. Accepting payment for sex was dangerous, as goods obtained in this way were unpropitious and could contagiously impart their self-depleting forces to persons, families, and their belongings. For example, when a male elder received cattle paid as a fine by a man who had adulterous sex with his wife or who impregnated his young unmarried daughter, he had to keep such cattle separate from the rest of his herd. Otherwise, the entire herd would lose its life force and die off. Samburu suggested that a sexual transgressor had to pay these "cattle of wrongdoings" (M: *nkishu ee ngòk*) to soothe the anger of an elder whom he wronged. For the recipient, the cattle of wrongdoings had, on the one hand, important symbolic and economic value. But on the other hand, they were unpropitious. These cattle carried within themselves the very substance of the adulterous act that called for their payment. Although they could be sold on the market, the money received in exchange could not be used to purchase food, because the substance of adultery would still be present in it. Sharing food purchased with money of sex with one's children, parents, and other kin to whom one was bound by a principle of sexual avoidance was tantamount to enacting an incestuous relation. Incest (M: *surupon*) was highly unpropitious and—through God's punishment—depleted life force. Such money could never "live" or "give life," that is, it could not nurture one's body, family, or wealth. To the contrary, it brought about depletion, madness, disease, and death. Note here how the substance of adultery imparted itself from the sexual act to the cattle received in its stead, to the money obtained for those cattle, to the food purchased with that money, to the family members who consumed that food, and so on.

Moreover, many Samburu regarded the sexual relationships between young men and elderly women as bad (M: *keturno*), for as Charlie told me, they "go against our culture": "In our culture a younger man is not to sleep with an older woman." Contrary to Charlie's statement, however, the relationships between Samburu morans and European women echoed older patterns of adultery and more recent inversions of gender roles in Samburu. Under current economic hardships, adultery was in fact very common in the district. As impoverished households relied on gifts circulated through extramarital sex to supplement the domestic resources, adultery came to erode the respectability and authority of elders (see chapter 6). Meanwhile, so-called God's birds, or young men supported by wealthier, more senior women, were also increasingly common. Nonnormative intimacies circulated money, but simultaneously tainted it. The commodification of sex was accentuated through local forms of intimacy, whether adultery or cohabitation. Hence, money of sex was increasingly common. Mombasa morans merely exacerbated these trends, converting sex into material wealth, more intensely and more spectacularly than others. In the eyes of some locals, then, money of Mombasa was the product of moral transgression.

Finally, Samburu believed that "sex out of place"—that is, sex performed outside the ideal space-time of domesticity and kinship—mobilized dangerous forces in ways that could not always be foretold. As in other East African contexts (Beidelman 1997; Heald 1999), for Samburu, sex harnessed powers that carried multiple potentialities. Women had long used sex out of place in the ritual context of collective fertility ceremonies (see discussion of *ntorosi* and *lopiro* ceremonies in chapter 6). If drawn on in the context of collective rituals, these powers could bring about life force and fertility for the communal good. However, if they were mobilized accidentally or for individual gain, those involved could be jeopardized. Everyday engagements in sex out of place could bring about disease, madness, or even death.[8] In a way, the money of Mombasa also played with these powers of sex out of place. And, like the cattle of wrongdoings, money of sex did not last.

In this sense, money of Mombasa spoke centrally of anxieties over the contagious and polluting forces associated with sex and its generative power. It also spoke of anxieties over social reproduction and the possibility of durable collective belonging. In speaking about the money of sex, informants grappled with a historical moment in which social reproduction and economic production came to be entangled in new, complex ways. In Samburu, sex was already a central site of social anxieties and moral dilemmas. Some informants emphasized that the rise of the money of sex was symptomatic of a crisis of social reproduction. Indeed, they understood the rapid spread of HIV/AIDS as an outcome of the perceived erasure of idealized moral boundaries between the domestic space and its outside (M: *aulo*), between marriage and adultery, between reproductive sexuality and sex as a new means of economic production. With reported HIV infection rates in Samburu reaching, by some estimates, 2.3 percent of the total population, locals associated the pandemic with the potential failures of sex as a key idiom of attachment—to each other and to life. In this context, narratives about the money of sex explored the limits of moral forms of intimacy and the potentialities of transgression. Could money of Mombasa really enable men to build families, sustain relations of kinship to clans and age set, and flourish in the future? Or was this money actually exhausting such relations?

Not everyone believed that sex-for-money exchanges were unpropitious. Men and women with scarce resources engaged in various forms of transactional sex themselves. Mombasa morans shared money with local women with whom they had intimate relationships, and with friends, family members, and various people who worked for them. Some of these men and women accepted and actively requested the material support of rich Mombasa morans. In such circumstances, they argued—quite conveniently, perhaps—that the negative forces of the money of Mombasa could only affect its owners. When I asked my research assistant Anna about people who refused the gifts of Mombasa morans, she laughed. Anna herself had an affair with a rich Mombasa moran and accepted various gifts from him. She pointed out that "those who refuse money, because they say it's money of Mombasa, they are just not hungry." Indeed, as the money of sex circulated more intensively in the district, some people considered it a legitimate alternative to otherwise absent resources. At other times, however, Anna, too, criticized the money of Mombasa and distinguished it from her wages as a teacher, which were "money of sweat."

Another commonly invoked reason for why money of Mombasa did not last was its origin in what people perceived to be the exploitation by Samburu men of their European partners. Obtaining money from these women, town-based informants suggested, was a form of stealing (S: *kuiba*), lying (S: *kufanya uongo*), or cheating (S: *kudangania*). According to them, money of Mombasa did not emerge through one's own "sweat," or legitimate labor, but through fake claims and forged stories. Other informants were more explicitly critical of what they saw as the false personas men performed in Mombasa in order to attract tourists. "The boy probably went here to school and used to wear pants," a young man told me in the summer of 2005, "but there [in Mombasa], they put the loincloth and take the spear to find white people." Performing a colonial stereotype was part of what locals perceived as cheating foreigners out of cash. Like sex, cheating and stealing were unpropitious actions that imparted infertility and self-depletion through contagion. People believed that cattle stolen on raids, for example, while prestigious tokens of courage for morans, would not prosper and, if mixed with the rest of the herd, could deplete its life force and lead to its extinction. Similarly, money of theft, lying, and cheating was self-depleting wealth. Echoing once more the Protestant ethic of honest work, lying and cheating figured as illegitimate means of wealth.

And yet at the same time, what counted as money of sweat, or morally legitimate wealth, was increasingly murky. For example, charcoal production, a common way of acquiring cash in the environs of towns, was not considered to yield durable wealth. It did not generate money of sweat, despite the hardship of the physical labor involved in making and transporting charcoal. As one elder explained to me, the money of charcoal (M: *shilingini e kuni*; S: *pesa ya makaa*) did not last because it was "stealing from the government." Others emphasized that producing charcoal was unpropitious, for it attracted the curse of the trees that a man had to cut (rural Samburu say that a person may kill a specific type of animal or plant eight times. The ninth time, that type of animal or plant will curse the person or kill him/her). Samburu also said that the money from brewing chang'aa was unpropitious, for it was based on the immoral act of intoxicating others. While people engaged in these activities acknowledged that they were unpropitious, they also emphasized that the goal of providing for one's children excused the means. Money of sweat referred more generically to money obtained though trade and employment. Yet in particular instances, even these forms of wealth production were open to contestation and moral accusations in everyday gossip.

By combining cultural logics associated with coastal sorcery, local reproduction, and middle-class respectability, gossip about the money of Mombasa revealed ongoing attempts to reimagine what it meant to be Samburu and to belong both to the district and to a world beyond it. A general shared sense that collective life force was depleting itself—or, to put it differently, that people were not as alive as they could be, or that they did not prosper enough—fueled locals' preoccupation with the new kind of money that shaped their worlds. On the one hand, such money reasserted locals' perception that an older set of ideologies of alterity was working to marginalize them further in the geopolitical order of the district, the state, and the market. On the other hand, by associating this money with the failures of sexuality—the failure to maintain proper divisions between economic production and social reproduction—locals also criticized their attachments to one another. If propitious kinship held sex in its generative place, money now crossed lines of propriety, turning sex into food, prostitution into kinship. And while it would be quite easy to argue that locals simply dismissed the actions and money of rich Mombasa morans, a more nuanced analysis shows how such dismissals also entail desire. Locals longed for the abundance and prestigious commodities of these men. They also enjoyed reflecting on how elastic the limits of the possible had become. Ethno-erotic economies animated these dynamics, expanding the meanings of belonging in different ways. If at the beginning of my fieldwork in 2005, people criticized money of sex as incompatible with domesticity and commensality, by the time I concluded my research for this book in 2015, this attitude changed. "Money is money," one elder told me then. "It doesn't matter how it comes to you. You eat it just the same."

"THE SPEECH OF A PERSON
CAN MAKE A TREE DRY UP"

Rich Mombasa morans carefully considered the potential effects of everyday gossip regarding their styles and wealth in Samburu. A central element of these men's subjective experiences was the fear of shame and loss of respectability at home. Shame (M: *anyit*, S: *aibu*) undermined one's ability to claim respect (M: *nkanyit*, S: *heshima*), and diminished one's possibilities of producing and expanding durable networks of kinship, patron-client relationships, and friendships. Shameful actions marked a person as morally corrupt, mean, and unfriendly, or as what locals simply called a *laroi*, a worthless man.

But young big men—that is, men who acquired money through relationships with foreign women—also worried about the potential impact of others' talk on their own well-being. Some of these men pointed out to me that gossip could be used to sever relations of reciprocity and care. Men who had European partners were always worried that people might spread rumors that would jeopardize their relationships with the foreigners. Rumors that a man was interested only in a white woman's money, that he was misusing her gifts, that he had married locally, or that he was planning to do so often persuaded European women to abandon their partners and cut off ties of material support. Gossip could directly jeopardize intimacies that were already quite slippery, as I have shown.

In addition, men invoked a common belief that the speech of others could affect the life force of those spoken about. *Nkutuk*, or speech—also meaning "mouth" or "language"—represented a medium for voicing desires and emotions in ways that had material effects on people and objects. Through spoken blessings or curses, for example, one gave material form to the desires or emotions generated in the stomach, thus propitiating or depleting the life force of others (Straight 2007b, 96–106). The elders taught children from an early age to use speech economically. "Walk fast on your foot, but not on your tongue" (M: *Sarsara te nkeju nimisarsar te Inkejek*), they advised, cautioning children that as another proverb says, "The speech of a person can make a tree dry up" (M: *Keitoi nkutuk e Itungani Ichoni oshal*). That is, the careless voicing of wishes and wants, admiration and anger could affect the bodies and belongings of others.

Speaking about others was thus a particularly powerful act. The Maa verb for "talking" about someone or something is *a-imaki*, which also means "to reveal" or "to expose." If many people in many places continuously "exposed" the same person through speech, this kind of speech could affect that person in negative ways. Lesepen, an elder I interviewed, told me of how, as a moran, he had been so brave and beautiful that girls praised him in their kakisha songs and people spoke of him with admiration. Because of that speaking— *a-imaki*—Lesepen eventually went "mad" for a while. He headed off to live alone in the bush for more than a year. Looking back at the events of his youth, Lesepen explained that the way in which people spoke of someone who had desirable qualities—beauty, skills, prosperity, and wealth—involved admiration, love, or even envy, a set of affects called *kemuntet*. When many people spoke of persons and their wealth with kemuntet, those whom they spoke about, along with their belongings, would lose their generative life force. Lesepen recalled how a rich labor migrant who had worked for the government built a house and acquired a large herd of cattle in Samburu. But as people started talking of him with kemuntet, he began drinking, sold all his properties, and became poor. Unlike sorcery and witchcraft, however, speaking of someone with kemuntet was an unintentional act. The presence of kemuntet could be realized only a posteriori, once its effects had already materialized.

In short, speech—whether gossip, scandal, or kakisha songs—not only shamed those whom it described and (indirectly) addressed, but also risked affecting their life force, their ability to sustain themselves and grow along with their wealth. While many believed that the money of Mombasa was short-lived given its origins in sex, sorcery, and theft, men who returned from Mombasa with money often invoked other people's jealousy and malicious talk—songs and scandal, rumors and gossip, *a-imaki* and *kemuntet*—as behaviors that threatened their wealth and well-being. How, then, did men with wealth position themselves in relation to these collective discourses and affects?

HOLDING ON TO WEALTH: SPEED, ENCLOSURE, AND THE NEW SPACE-TIME OF BELONGING

So-called rich morans (M: *lmurran ltajiri*) or young big men (S: *vijana wa-kubwa*) sought to limit the extent to which poorer relatives, age-mates, and neighbors could interfere in their lives. They hoped to prevent incessant requests for financial help, the refusal of which could easily lead either to the quick depletion of their wealth or to further dangerous gossip. Aware of former young big men who had lost their riches very quickly, young big men understood the conditions of their wealth to be extremely fragile. For them, it was important to act cautiously and devise new tactics for navigating everyday expectations in their communities. For example, by driving motorbikes or cars and living in homesteads with tall fences and locked gates, some of these men hoped to defer the loss of their wealth and negotiate more durable resources and respectability.

On an early field research trip to Samburu, I rented an apartment in the house of Repale and Vera. Repale, a Samburu moran in his early twenties, and Vera, a Swiss woman in her fifties, had married recently and built the house together. With over eight rooms, three bathrooms, and two kitchens, theirs was one of the largest houses in the area. It was equipped with indoor plumbing, electricity, and a satellite dish. A tall brick wall surrounded the compound. I had known Repale and Vera for two years when they offered to rent me an apartment in their house. A few weeks after I had moved in, however, Repale and I argued. Men and women from the nearby village of Siteti, where I was doing research, often stopped by to visit me. Because Repale and Vera kept the gates locked and their watchdogs loose at all times, visitors (who did not have cell phones and hence could not send me text messages) waited patiently at the gate until I happened to walk out. One time, Repale became angry.

"You know," he told me, "I don't like these people from the village to hang out at my gate all the time. These people bring trouble, and that is not good." I explained to Repale that my visitors were friends I had known for years. "I know these people, too," he retorted. "They are blacksmiths [M: *nkunono*]. These are very dangerous people." He invoked a common stereotype that blacksmiths were unpropitious, because—so the popular belief goes—they contagiously imparted to others their alleged inability to prosper and accumulate wealth. They were also said to have a potent curse that could impoverish others. Although this might have worried Repale to some extent, I suspected he also recognized among my visitors several elders who had once been wealthy young big men like he was, but who had lost their wealth and now lived in abject poverty. "I like to have my privacy," Repale explained. "We are very busy. You know? We don't have time for these people coming and disturbing us all the time. When these elders come, they just sit there and talk, 'y-e-e-e-e-s, y-e-e-e-e-s,' without any purpose." Repale sarcastically impersonated the elders' slow way of talking to emphasize their supposed inclination to waste time. "They don't understand we don't have time for that. Even my father, when he comes here, I tell him that I am busy. Otherwise, it is hard to get anything done."

Repale explained his desire for privacy as a way of being in charge of his own time. By contrast, he suggested, people of the villages (M: *ltungana le nkang*) liked to waste their time and the time of others. But Repale's desires for privacy and for saving time also seemed to be linked to deep anxieties about the fragile relations on which his wealth was premised. The impoverished elders at his gate likely reminded him of the conviction many people had that "the money of Mombasa doesn't last." How was he to manage the thin line between polite sociality and dangerous socializing when the future of his wealth was at stake?

With Vera's material support, Repale had become one of the richest men in the district. Vera had built the house with her own money, but shared the title deed with Repale. She also bought him two Toyota Land Cruisers. With gifts of money from Vera, Repale bought a four-acre plot of land in his village and a tractor for agricultural work. He also started a cattle farm and a construction firm, and opened a small wholesale shop in town. Together with Vera, Repale employed a maid, a watchman, a driver, and a farm manager. He occasionally also hired rural elders to herd his cattle and work on his farm.

Repale engaged in a set of practices that set him apart from other young men of his age and marked him as a wealthy and powerful big man (S: *mkubwa*) in the district. He usually wore tailor-made pants, shirts, and running shoes. He also wore an expensive wristwatch and silver rings. Wherever he went, he carried his BlackBerry phone in his hand. On a typical weekday, he ran errands between the administrative offices of the district, local NGOs, his cattle farm, and his shop. Unlike the vast majority of men and women in town, who walked to the market, the shops, the post office, or the bank, Repale drove his Toyota Land Cruiser everywhere he went. Evenings, he met friends and business partners at an expensive club in town, where they drank beer, smoked, and played pool. Twice a year, he went on vacation with Vera to a safari park in Kenya or to Switzerland. Repale's ability to conspicuously consume prestigious commodities marked him as a "young big man," that is, a man who, though still chronologically young, was already powerful and wealthy. Eventually, like other young big men, he entered politics, becoming a regional councillor with the local government administration in Samburu.[9] In fact, in Kenya the notion of the big man had long been associated with the formal domain of politics and autocratic corruption.[10] To understand Repale's stakes in the conflict described above, it is important to analyze more closely how his desires and sense of style informed his subjectivity.

By keeping his gates locked and his dogs loose while at home or driving around in his car, Repale sought to maintain his privacy and save time. These practices were common not only among young big men but also to some extent among headmasters, development workers, and businessmen who likewise enjoyed a significant income. They all used the relative enclosure of homes and cars as a way to deter other people from impinging on their daily routines, incessantly asking for financial help, and wasting their time. They all invoked time as a precious commodity.

"Time is everything," my university-educated research assistant once told me. "If you like to waste time, it is hard to achieve anything." He made this remark when we were transcribing an interview I had with a rural Samburu woman. On the recording, she was complaining about how Samburu who worked in the administration offices in Maralal treated her badly. She said they often pretended not to speak Maa to avoid having to deal with her. My research assistant defended the office workers:

> Time is very precious when you work at the offices. You only have so many hours to complete your work, then one hour for lunch. When these people [rural men and women] come to the offices, they cannot get straight to the point. They say first: [he switches from Swahili to Maa] *Hello, my son? Everything is fine? What is your news? What clan do you belong to? Whose family do you belong to?* And they just waste your time. So you just want to get rid of them fast.

By using the pretense of not speaking Maa, along with using the closed spaces of large homes, offices, or cars, employed men and women sought to avoid having their time impinged on by others. (Recall how, in the beginning of this chapter, Mama Priscilla's classificatory "son" pretended not to recognize her when she greeted him on the street.) In this way, office workers and businessmen also disposed of the time of the poor, who would wait for hours in front of their homes and offices to talk to them or ask for a favor. It is important to note that the everyday practices of spatial enclosure and time preservation were premised on privileged access to money and goods such as cars, fences, gates, or offices. All across Kenya, enclave-like homesteads with iron gates guarded the privacy of the nouveaux riches. The warning Fierce Dog (S: *mbwa kali*) painted in block letters on gates, actual watchdogs and watchmen, electric fences, and complex alarm systems heightened a sense of enclosure and inaccessibility to the houses of the wealthy. It is noteworthy that although Repale had also built a house in his village, he preferred to live in the house he had built with Vera near the town of Maralal. This allowed him to maintain some distance from expectations of reciprocity associated with rural life. Indeed, this was a tactic that numerous other young big men

15. Houses of young big men near Maralal, Samburu, 2011. (Photo by the author.)

employed (fig. 15). As Jackson explained it to me, "these men want to avoid being bothered by their neighbors and their families all the time."

If enclave-like homesteads protected the privacy of their owners while at home, private vehicles allowed the rich to navigate between places while maintaining a sense of privacy and more efficiently controlling their own time. "Being in a car is being in a different level altogether," Daniel, a Samburu development worker, explained in English. "That is why many people who have cars prefer driving through town rather than walking." He continued:

> You see, when you walk from home to the office in the morning, you are always late, because all these people stop you and want to greet you. . . . You cannot walk without talking to them. You see, me now, I am using a motorbike. But it is not because I don't like to walk. . . . It is because otherwise so many people would stop me. Sometimes, when I am very busy, I even use my car to go to work.

Daniel understood driving a motorbike or a car as a way to manage expectations of courtesy in ways that did not undermine one's good manners. A person who walked was supposed to stop and engage in polite conversation with others on the road. But driving a vehicle provided an excuse for avoiding customary courtesy. When I once jokingly mocked Repale for driving his car to his neighbors' house, he got defensive, replying, "It is a time issue. I cannot waste time stopping to talk to everybody on the road."

While many people with stable income sought some degree of enclosure through homes and cars, that enclosure had to be carefully negotiated. Daniel explained that keeping the gates locked while at home was also a sign of greed and selfishness. It showed the owner's lack of desire to interact with others. Such behavior could not only jeopardize the owner's respectability but also attract dangerous talk and even curses. A person should always be willing to welcome unexpected visitors, offer them tea, and listen to their problems and demands. Similarly, when driving, one had to stop the car and talk to people from time to time. If an acquaintance were to flag the driver down, it was only polite for him to roll down his window and chat for a few minutes. If the enclosure of homes and vehicles was a strategy to produce time without compromising respectability, it also had to maintain a certain degree of openness. If, however, enclosure undermined the possibility of interaction and reciprocity with others, people could easily read it as antisocial behavior par excellence. Speedy cars with tinted windows prevented bystanders from knowing whether or not the driver had seen them in the first place. Because I never owned a car while I was in the field, I often walked long distances to town or to the villages where I worked. On these occasions I often heard people comment on or gossip about the owners of cars that raced by.[11] Similarly, homesteads with high fences, locked gates, and watchdogs could prevent people from knowing whether the owner was at home.

Young big men like Repale were aware of the moral significance of generosity. In this sense, contrary to how others perceived them, they did not seek to produce complete enclosure and isolation from others. However, rather than invest substantially in relationships with people who were poor— including members of their lineages, clans, and age sets—they sought to develop friendships and reciprocal relations with other powerful and wealthy big men. Repale's closest friends, for example, were other former Mombasa morans who had also become young big men and kept their wealth. He also maintained strong friendships with councillors, government inspectors, school headmasters, and NGO directors. These men occasionally drove to one another's houses for barbeques or hung out at expensive safari clubs, to which poor acquaintances had no access. While young big men engaged in relations of reciprocity and commensality with men who shared their socioeconomic standing, they sought to distance themselves from neighbors and relatives who were poor. They worried that the poor could deplete their wealth with constant requests for material support as well as with gossip. If the "money of Mombasa" did not last, many young big men believed it was in no small part due to the requests and envy of less fortunate people in the district. By maintaining a degree of distance from poorer people, and socializing more with men of their own status, young big men sought to prevent their wealth from running out. But they also enjoyed spending time with people who would not judge them for how they had obtained their wealth and who shared their life experiences, in one way or another.

These new ways of producing space and time shaped everyday relations of kinship, reciprocity, and belonging. In her analysis of houses as loci of kinship, Janet Carsten (2004, 36) underlines the importance of a "processual understanding of kinship," with "a greater emphasis on the way kinship is *lived*" (emphasis in the original). Carsten argues that it is important "to understand kinship in particular contexts through the things that people do and the everyday understandings that are involved in living together" (37). A focus on the lived experience of everyday kinship also brings to light important aspects of how young big men reconfigured the space-time of kinship in Samburu. Through everyday practices of enclosure and time preservation premised on access to cash, they distanced themselves from poor relatives and neighbors and came into greater proximity to one another. In this way, they reshaped what E. E. Evans-Pritchard ([1940] 1969, 109–10) might have called the "structural distance" between different social categories. Evans-Pritchard argued that among the Nuer, social space is measured not like "real" space but in terms of the structures of kinship relations. "A Nuer village may be equidistant from two other villages, but if one of these belongs to a different tribe and the other to the same tribe it may be said to be structurally more distant from the first than from the second" (110). With echoes of Evans-Pritchard, but moving beyond a structural-functionalist language, we can understand young big men's everyday practices of kinship as generating new social spaces wherein distances are mapped more strongly along lines of material inequality rather than patrilineal descent.

Reciprocity along lines of descent and age-set relations had long represented a safety measure for livestock economies in northern Kenya. Such networks offered livestock owners the possibility of replenishing herds depleted by raids, drought, or disease (Anderson and Broch-Due 1999). With growing unemployment, the spread of HIV/AIDS, the effects of land privatization, and high population density in the Samburu highlands, relations of reciprocity with friends, age-mates, neighborhoods, lineages, and clans gained renewed importance for the poor. They represented forms of what Rosalind Morris (2008) has described as generalized practices of risk insurance in times of hardship. While young big men seemed to reject the egalitarian aspirations of lineages, clans, and age sets, their poor relatives, neighbors, and age-mates came to emphasize more strongly the moral implications of such kinship relations. I shall elaborate on these reconfigurations of the space and time of belonging in chapter 5 in relation to ritual and the life course.

MIRACULOUS WEALTH, NEW SUBJECTIVITIES, AND PRECARIOUS BELONGING(S)

Money of Mombasa refers to a category of resources, representations, and practices that emerged in Samburu with the commodification of moran sexuality. As young Samburu men encountered novel, seemingly miraculous possibilities of enrichment at tourist resorts, their relative wealth generated new inequalities and new moral dilemmas in northern Kenya. From a strictly demographic vantage point, migration to Mombasa was not a large-scale phenomenon: by 2010, during the tourist seasons, about one thousand Samburu men were on the coast. And while most Mombasa morans returned to Samburu with money, only some acquired the spectacular riches of the young big men. Thus, one could certainly argue that the activities of these men were not statistically representative of livelihoods in Samburu. I do not argue that they were. Nor, for that matter, do I think that these demographics somehow undermine the social significance of these historical processes. Quite the contrary: the desires, styles, and resources of Mombasa morans have come to reverberate, often in unexpected ways, throughout the social life of northern Kenya. People spoke about these men and their money extensively, sometimes even in parts of the district where nobody migrated to the coast. Money of Mombasa appeared suddenly and spectacularly in Samburu, prompting locals—far and wide—to desire and deride it, fear it and fantasize about it. Gossip, in these contexts, was not idle talk. Rather, it was a way of contesting and reimagining what constituted durable social value, what actions and outcomes garnered recognition and respectability, and what it meant to belong to local social worlds. As men and women envisioned desirable futures by positioning themselves in some relation to the money of Mombasa, they also reimagined and remade themselves as moral persons.

Emerging at the intersection of ethnosexual commodification and the moral expectations and material predicaments of contemporary livelihoods in Samburu, the money of Mombasa linked, as it were, the different parts of ethno-erotic economies. As money, desires, and beliefs circulated between coastal tourist resorts and Samburu towns and villages, they reconfigured social worlds. Indeed, wealth and desire shaped each other dialectically: the wealth of men who migrated to Mombasa prompted locals to articulate their various desires through gossip, while local gossip shaped how Mombasa morans and young big men disposed of their wealth. Drawing on complex ideas about durability and depletion, sex and sorcery, "money of sweat" and "shortcut money," various social actors negotiated how wealth could circulate, and how people's actions could sustain or undermine it.

The dialectical relationship between wealth and desire gave rise to new bodily dispositions and space-time configurations, as well as everyday configurations of kinship and belonging. In other words, it gave rise to new *subjectivities*. Jacques Lacan (1978, 38) argued that the subject "is the desire of the Other." For Lacan, the Other—with a capital *O*—is not another person or a disenfranchised set of subjects but a "cultural system of meaning" (Dean 2000, 1) entailed in language, social expectations, and "techniques of normalization" (17). For Lacan, the subject—never fully fixed, never fully stable—perpetually seeks itself in the recognition of the Other. Or, to put it differently, "the subject desires only in so far as it experiences the Other itself as desiring" (Žižek 2006, 42). Desire and, with it, subjectivity are not readily open to anthropological inquiry, for they evade what Judith Farquhar (2002, 57) has critiqued as the "symbolic logic of the concrete," wherein "explanatory power about signification seems to be gained at the expense of the poetry—the flavors and pleasures—inherent in everyday reality." Rather, anthropologists may "read" (to use Farquhar's term) desire and subjectivity from the surfaces of mundane life. In this sense, gossip, narratives, songs, and bodily dynamics of space and time are loci of desire and subjectivity. These constitute the Lacanian Other—a set of surfaces that may be "read" for desire and subjectivity. In this sense, local gossip tells us as much about the subjectivities of Mombasa morans and young big men as the actual practices of these men tell us about the subjectivities of gossipers.

So what kinds of subjectivities emerge through and around the money of Mombasa? And what do they tell us about the reconfiguration of belonging in Samburu? Following market liberalization in Africa and elsewhere, economic possibilities shift rapidly, while "wealth appears ever more proximate, but ... remains mostly inaccessible to the vast majority" (Makhulu, Buggenhagen, and Jackson 2010, 18). Life becomes a "tactical mode of being-in-the-world" (12), a speculative effort to produce some sense of permanence in the face of what Achille Mbembe calls "the generalization and radicalization of a condition of temporariness" (Shipley 2010, 659–60). Under these circumstances, capital—as we saw with the money of Mombasa—moved into Samburu suddenly before it disappeared again, quite quickly, through consumption and redistribution. The subjectivities that emerged in this context were premised on a desire to grasp this "condition of temporariness" through ideas about sorcery, depletion, or pollution. But as the next chapter will show, subjectivities also emerged through a desire to convert miraculous wealth into more durable forms of social value associated with marriage, age grades, and kinship. Such attempts emerged from what anthropologist Annette Weiner (1992, 7) described as "the need to secure permanence in a serial world that is always subject to loss and decay." According to Weiner, "Enormous energy and intensity are expanded in efforts to transmute or transcend the effects of deterioration and degeneration and/or to foster the conditions of growth and regeneration" (ibid.). In this context, however, belonging itself became precarious. As the temporariness of wealth—its miraculous appearance and disappearance—undermined the production of durable social worlds, how best to produce such worlds was itself a question that saturated local pursuits.

5. Marriage, Madness, and the Unruly Rhythms of Respectability

To the young man who closes his eyes to the parting of clouds and lets what
is beyond come in. . . . To the endless clock machine in the god body of the
young man who closes his eyes as the light sweeps him to eternity.
—CLIFTON GACHAGUA, *MADMAN OF KILIFI*

Early in my fieldwork, I was very interested in how Samburu perceived
the money of Mombasa and its owners. But as I continued my research, I
quickly realized another side to the story—namely, how this money could be
converted into the social value of belonging. A central claim of this book is
that the commodification of moran ethnosexuality shaped and was shaped
by how Samburu imagined belonging in northern Kenya. If, for example,
cultural expectations associated with the age grade of moranhood allowed
young men to leave local communities in search of money, the money they
brought back, in turn, reshaped these expectations. As we have seen, Samburu perceived money of Mombasa with ambivalence. This money, they
knew, could bring forth miraculous wealth quite suddenly and abundantly,
but it could also pollute wealth and make it disappear—just as rapidly and
unexpectedly. Thus, locals longed for access to such money that would allow
them to live better lives and fulfill various social and economic obligations,
but they also loathed it. They tried to keep it at bay, worried that it might
contaminate resources and relations and deplete their life force. Young men

who made money through intimate relationships with foreign women saw their wealth and respectability threatened by other locals who continuously requested their material support or gossiped about them. They, too, thought that this money usually did not last. "This money is the devil himself," one man who had lost his wealth told me. "It is very dangerous." Aware of the inherent temporariness of the money of Mombasa, then, men sought to transform it into durable forms of social value that, they hoped, would grant them attachment to local worlds: they invested in ritual, marriage, and kinship. But in doing so, they created new conflicts over belonging. And solving these conflicts, as this chapter will show, meant reimagining what it meant to belong and to be respectable.

Lekarda was in his late twenties when I met him in July 2008. Between 1996 and 2006, he migrated to Mtwapa every year. With the money he acquired through relationships with two German women, he returned to Samburu, built a house, opened a small grocery store, purchased cattle, and began cultivating maize. When I visited Lekarda for the first time at his home in Siteti, I thought that he was less wealthy than some of the other "young big men" I knew. His house was quite modest. A three-room structure with wooden walls and an iron-sheet roof, it more closely resembled the homes of labor migrants than the large stone villas of enriched Mombasa morans. He also did not own a car or a motorcycle. But Lekarda was less interested in big houses, cars, and motorcycles than in pursuing the respectability, prestige, and authority associated with local idioms of marriage and elderhood. In 2005, Lekarda's age set—the Lmooli—graduated out of the age grade of moranhood. In 2008, only three years since his initiation into elderhood and to everyone's surprise, Lekarda paid bridewealth and married not one but two young Samburu women.

It was unusual for a man to take more than one wife at such an early age and in such a short time. Men with limited material resources found it difficult to marry at all. Unable to fulfill bridewealth payments or finance wedding ceremonies, many chose to cohabit with their partners while deferring ritual obligations indefinitely. In addition, polygyny had become more of an ideal of prestigious masculine elderhood—an imagined cultural expectation of the past—than an actual common occurrence of the present. Indeed, in Siteti, Lekarda's village, only four men were in polygynous marriages, and all of them were senior elders in their sixties and seventies. In this context, Lekarda's actions stood out sharply. To those who struggled to catch up on wedding ceremonies, bridewealth payments, and other obligations of elderhood, he seemed to rush ahead of his age-mates and accelerate the temporal rhythms of his life course. Meanwhile, other men even younger than Lekarda started using money acquired in coastal economies to marry and become elders while quite young, still in the age grade of moranhood.

Men and women I interviewed perceived such premature marriages and early polygyny as problematic ways of "rushing" or "speeding up" the course of life. Many worried that the commodification of moran sexuality generated inequalities that transformed ideals of marriage, aging, and the life course. Were young men like Lekarda getting ahead of themselves by acquiring the prerogatives of prestigious elderhood while still young? Did rushed marriages and early polygyny constitute durable alliances, or did they in fact amount to fragile and unstable families? Did such marriages allow men to convert their seemingly transitory wealth into more lasting forms of respectability and recognition, or did they merely perpetuate the unpropitious qualities of the money of Mombasa? And what did these marriages mean to women as wives, daughters, mothers, or mothers-in-law?

I began examining ideas and practices associated with rushing, speed, and temporality in chapter 4. There, I demonstrated how "rushed money" or "shortcut money" gave rise to new desires and subjectivities in Samburu. Young big men, for example, sought to speed up their daily routines by driving cars as a way to cope with the perceived dangers of everyday requests for financial support, and to prevent the depletion of their wealth. In this chapter, I turn to a different aspect of temporal acceleration: namely, actions through which young big men like Lekarda sped up the normative rhythms of social reproduction. Such actions subverted, if only momentarily, normative ideals of marriage, aging, and elderhood, opening up new possibilities for imagining and crafting futures.

As my informants struggled to grasp the implication of such subversive events, "madness" came to figure centrally in the stories they told of Mombasa morans and young big men. They posited madness as a very likely outcome not only of this rushing and speeding but also of failing to attend to the ritual obligations of the life course. In our conversations, my informants offered madness as the moral opposite of a propitious, fertile marriage. If marriage was iconic of reproduction, the perpetuation of the lineage in time, and positive social value more generally, then being mad indexed negative social value, the failure to reproduce, and therefore the impossibility of a future. Madness, in other words, was the Janus face of marriage.

When I returned to Samburu in the summer of 2009, people throughout the district spoke of Lekarda with dread and horror. The madman of Siteti, they called him, his name having become too unpropitious to be uttered.

They said that after Lekarda married his second wife, he gradually "turned mad." He stopped talking to people and seemed very troubled. In the fall of 2008, just a couple of months after I had visited him, he killed a man from his village. The two men had been drinking alcohol and smoking *bhang* (a lower grade of marijuana) when they started to argue. Lekarda hit his opponent on the head with a machete, killing him instantly.

That he killed another person, however, was not what made Lekarda mad in the eyes of others. Homicide was not an uncommon occurrence. Rivalries over property, lovers, adultery, and hurt pride often prompted younger men to attack age-mates, neighbors, or even kin. According to my interlocutors, they did not have to be mad per se to do so. But it was what Lekarda did post facto that persuaded many of his inherent madness: friends from Siteti told me that he decapitated the body of his opponent, slit his stomach, and drank his blood.

"I think he had a jini," Mama Tiras, a young woman from Siteti, said. "We used to see him slaughter goats every week. That's for the jini. You see?! I think it's the jini who took hold of him and made him do those things, drink that blood. It is the jini that made him mad. Back in the day, this man had been a very good person. But he wanted that rushed money, then he wanted to marry fast, fast, and with all that happiness, at the end, he turned mad."

According to Mama Tiras, men who accelerated the rhythms of their lives to achieve wealth and worth quickly through illegitimate means could easily speed out of control and go mad. As I will show, madness, among other things, was seen as an outcome of excessive desires, uncontrolled mobility, and failed sexuality. With the rapidly shifting inequalities engendered by ethno-erotic commodification, success could quickly turn into failure, respectability into a derided state of madness.

Only a few young big men I knew were understood to have turned into madmen. Nonetheless, madness served as a potent signifier of failure and cast a broad shadow. On the one hand, madness spoke of the moral failures of particular persons. Lekarda's desire to achieve respect and prestige quickly was, in fact, what informants like Mama Tiras invoked to account for his failure. That Lekarda had failed to acquire respectability and moral recognition was beyond question. After the police arrested him, each of his wives ran away. For many, the dissolution of his homestead and his marriages, like his madness, spoke of his irreversible failure to embody moral personhood and to produce positive social value. As a madman who had killed, Lekarda had become the absolute embodiment of *social* death.[1] On the other hand, madmen—their bodily presence and the rumors that they prompted—also spoke of the failures of collective life more generally. For onlookers, mad-men congealed widespread anxieties over the perpetuation of families, lin-eages, clans, age sets, and other categories of belonging as well as over the ability of these social groups to sustain life force. In this sense, despite the numerous stories that held particular persons responsible for their own mad-ness, there was also a strong sense that madness emerged with the failure of kin and age-mates to produce and sustain propitious forms of relatedness and belonging. A senior elder from a village near Siteti explained to me that Lekarda's madness was not merely the outcome of his own actions but also the product of a longer history of misdeeds in his lineage. Two of his male an-cestors had killed people. The so-called *ng'oki* of the ancestor's actions—their unpropitious omen—perpetuated itself in time to deplete the life force of de-scendants like Lekarda. Here, a person's failures were always also collective failures.[2] What is more, even though Lekarda's family dispersed, many be-lieved that his unpropitious deeds would continue to contaminate its mem-bers; his wives, children, and the children of his children would likely also go mad sooner or later. In short, then, madness was about both the personal and the collective failures of social value, inextricably linking the two.

Rushing and *failing* emerged in relation to and called into question nor-mative representations of respectability and the life course. To understand the implications of these dynamics of value conversion, I contextualize them in relation to the attempts of other Samburu to *slow down* or **turn back time** in order to *catch up* on normative obligations of marriage and elderhood. As various people sought to understand what was going wrong in their lives, they often imagined a "return to culture"—to *lkereti*, or "the normal way of doing things"—as some kind of guarantee of social value. Here, representations and practices associated with clans and lineages, age sets and age grades, mar-riage and bridewealth, played a crucial role in promising to anchor moral per-sons and collectivities. What ensued was a dialectical relationship between subversive events and normative representations of marriage, elderhood, and the life course that transformed respectability and belonging, some-times in unexpected ways.

DEFERRING RESPECTABILITY: BRIDEWEALTH DEBTS AND "COME-WE-STAY" MARRIAGES

At the same time that men like Lekarda sought to speed up the rhythms of their life course, numerous other men and women in Samburu had to *slow down* and *catch up* on the expectations of marriage and elderhood. Many of them increasingly worried about the moral foundations of families, lineages, clans, and age sets as they saw poverty and their growing reliance on new means of livelihood undermine older, hierarchical relations between men and women, the young and the old. In particular, people contested how recent ways of making a living affected older templates of marriage, life course, and intergenerational relations. They worried about the growing number of indefinite deferrals of bridewealth payments, wedding ceremonies, and other important life cycle rituals.

Increasingly since the early 2000s, young men and women were living together and having children, but postponing weddings and bridewealth payments. Lacking the material means to realize ideal forms of marriage, they hoped nevertheless to gain some respectability by having children and establishing a home (M: *nkang*). Men had long used the period of their moranhood to accumulate cattle and cash, hoping that once initiated into elderhood, they would be able to pay bridewealth, marry, and settle down. In the 1990s, however, more and more junior elders had to postpone marriages because they had not acquired sufficient wealth by the time they had become elders. People used the Maa idioms of *lmaachani* (sg. *lmaachai*) or *lkiriko* (sg. *lkirikoi*) to speak of these men. A lmaachai was a man who did not have a family despite being an elder by age-grade status, but the word also referred more generically to a "pauper" or "idler." An lkirikoi, by contrast, was not necessarily a pauper but a man who had become unpropitious by virtue of not having married and fathered children in time. By custom, the likiriko were not allowed to join other elders in collective blessings, because people believed that the lkiriko's anger and envy toward others would turn their blessings into curses.[3] Young men explained that to be called lmaachani or lkiriko was very shameful, but to die unmarried and childless was even worse. Samburu would not bury a dead unmarried man, or *laingoni*, in a homestead, as they would bury, for instance, a respectable owner of a household (M: *lopeny nkang*) or a mother with children; instead, they typically abandoned a *laingoni* in the bushes. If the man died in a hospital, the family either refused to claim the body from the mortuary or buried it in a town cemetery, a place they considered no more dignified than the bushes. For to bury a laingoni close to one's homestead was to impart his unpropitious, nonreproductive state to its other inhabitants. With the rise of AIDS-related deaths over the past two decades, deaths of unmarried young men without offspring became common in the district. Such deaths reminded young men and women that respectability itself had become uncertain.

Yet as much as young men feared dying before getting married, marriage required vast resources that remained inaccessible to many. A man had to be able pay bridewealth of some six to ten cattle (depending on the custom of the lineage of the bride, as well as on the material possibilities of the groom), gifts of cash and commodities, and wedding expenses. Bridewealth payments were a key step toward the legitimization of marriage. In addition, the groom had to provide the wedding ox (M: *rikoret*), which he had to kill in front of the bride's house. The ritual killing of the wedding ox irreversibly sealed the marriage. What is more, following the wedding as such, the couple had to perform other ceremonies, such as *lmenong*, that aggregated the couple to elderhood and domestic life (I shall say more about *lmenong* later).

Lacking the material means to organize weddings and pay for bridewealth, young men and women produced alternative forms of intimacy and relatedness. They sustained relations of sex and gift exchange beyond the time that a man was a moran. Extramarital pregnancies also became more common as an increasing number of young women went to high school and lived in towns. Because people considered the pregnancies of young unmarried women unpropitious, mothers once helped their daughters to abort in secret. In the present, however, at least some young women sought to keep extramarital pregnancies, hoping that their offspring would cement ties of kinship to male partners and offer them a more secure livelihood. Like in other parts of Africa (for example, in South Africa: Hunter 2010, 145–46), giving birth out of wedlock allowed young women to demand material support from men and their families and sometimes secure the promise of a future marriage.[4] My household surveys showed a growing number of young single mothers residing with their parents across the district. Many of these women produced cash independently by brewing chang'aa or participating in women's microfinance projects, including various forms of petty trade and farming. They also took care of their parents and supported them financially. "Before, it was sons who took care of the parents," a senior male elder from Siteti once told me. "Now, more and more, it is daughters."

However, extramarital pregnancies and illegitimate children could undermine a young woman's ability to marry and become a respectable wife in the future. Women who became pregnant in school were expelled. People called them "broken girls" (M: *ntoyie naataroitie*). Young men called unmarried women with children *treila* (sg. *treilani*), a Maa neologism originating in the English noun *trailer* and alluding to the fact that these women would bring illegitimate children into the homestead of their future husbands. Because they already had children, their future husbands would kill a ram instead of an ox for the *rikoret* ritual on their wedding day. This was, of course, less prestigious and undermined women's respectability. Moreover, the stigma of unmarried women with children sometimes extended to the children themselves. Called "children of a girl" (M: *nkera ee ntito*), such children were unpropitious to the homesteads in which they lived and were excluded from different clan rituals.

In this context, young men and women who came of age in the late 1990s and the early 2000s sought alternative pathways to respectability through what young people—most of them educated—called "come-we-stay" marriages (using the English words in Maa or Swahili).[5] They began cohabiting either in the man's father's homestead or, also quite commonly, in the woman's father's homestead, according to where they could obtain access to land and other resources. There, they would build a separate house and have children. Although fathering children prevented men from falling into the category of lmaachani or lkiriko, it did not make them respectable elders, for they had not yet undergone important rituals. Because these young men were still in the age grade of moranhood, they were, in principle, not allowed to undergo wedding ceremonies or father children until they participated in the *lmuget le nkarna*, or the "ceremony of the [age set's] name," and became junior elders. But because many men lacked the resources to build normative families, "come-we-stay" marriages were for them a fair alternative to becoming lmaachani and lkiriko. Similarly for young women, such relationships were alternatives to being "broken girls" or concubines with diminishing marriage prospects. But such unofficial marriages did not grant women full respectability either, because a respectable woman was not supposed to give birth before her husband had ritually killed the wedding ox and paid bridewealth for her. Although elderly men and women recalled that similar types of marriages had existed in the past, they viewed them with great ambivalence.[6] In a meeting of the male elders of the Lmaarato subclan in September 2010 in Siteti, one senior elder complained, "Nowadays, we have seen . . . that the Lkishami [age set of morans] began 'marrying' [M: *ayama*] before the 'ceremony of the name.' It was not like that before. These 'marriages' must be stopped!" Early in my fieldwork, elders told me that during the "ceremony of the name," the elders would curse to death all the morans who had fathered children: "May the family of the transgressor turn to ashes!" (M: *Nkang e lperet taa nkuron*), the elders would say. But as the year of the ceremony approached and "come-we-stay" marriages became prevalent, elders grew reluctant to curse the young men. Some understood that young men and women were merely trying to cope with the hard times of the present. A senior elder from Siteti, whose eldest son cohabited with a young woman in his homestead, explained, "In the past, somebody could become an elder

188

[by age grade] and not have children. He would become an lmaachai. So it is better for you to have children when you are still young."

Although wedding ceremonies (M: *nkinyama*) and bridewealth (M: *nkauti*) were increasingly delayed, the very promise of having a wedding and paying bridewealth in the future remained crucial to men's and women's quests for respectability. Wedding ceremonies eventually took place once men underwent the ceremony of the name, became junior elders, and also saved some cash. In the absence of wealth, however, families sometimes substituted a ram (M: *rikoret e nker*) for the ritual wedding ox (M: *rikoret*) and renegotiated the amount of the so-called *lmongo lenkolong*, that is, the cash equivalent of a bull that the groom had to give to the bride's parents for wedding expenses. The groom still paid a gift of cash or "fine" (M: *pain*) of some KSh 1,000 (about $13) to the parents of the bride and bought blankets for the bride's father and his brothers. But, for many, the central components of bridewealth—some six to ten cattle—continued to be deferred indefinitely. They became bridewealth debts (M: *silen e nkauti*).

In the context of widespread bridewealth debts, the very promise of bridewealth informed most families' desires for a brighter future, although they did not know when to expect to receive a bridewealth payment. Bridewealth debts were not new, however. As Parker Shipton (2007, 125) argues, "[all] across Africa, marriage is conducted on something like an installment plan," with "the stretching of bridewealth debts across generations," in fact binding affines (kin related through marriage) in relationships of mutual entrustment. In Samburu in the past, the six to ten cattle that made up the central component of the bridewealth were considered but a first installment, with additional cattle to be paid when the future daughters of the newlyweds would bring in further bridewealth. By contrast, in the present, most bridewealth payments had turned into bridewealth debts.

My informants explained that ideally, patrilineal kin would contribute cattle to one another's bridewealth payments and would circulate among themselves the cattle received as bridewealth for their daughters.[7] In such a context, patrilineal kinsmen normally had high stakes in sustaining marriages. For if marriages broke apart, they would have to return the cattle they had received from a particular bridewealth payment. With the decline of cattle herds, however, clan mates were less likely to contribute livestock to one another's marriages. Under these circumstances, marriages dissolved more quickly in instances of conflict. When mistreated by husbands, women were more likely to abandon their marriages and either return to their own lineages or run to towns. In the relative absence of bridewealth payments, husbands could not make legitimate claims for the return of their runaway wives (M: *ntomonok nashomo kitala*). At the same time, with the growing number of runaway wives in the district (cf. Holtzman 2009, 222), some elders became reluctant to accept immediate bridewealth payment for their daughters when such payments were possible. They feared that they would have to return the payments sooner or later, if women ran away and marriages dissolved. An elder told me that accepting bridewealth had become like "eating stolen beasts" (M: *anya nyamu*), that is, benefiting from gifts without repayment, or engaging in what Marshall Sahlins (1972) called "negative reciprocity."

People with limited material resources also deferred other important life course ceremonies. Most significant among these was the ceremony of *lmenong*. By custom, each married couple had to organize and undergo the rituals of lmenong in the early months of their marriage. Lmenong also referred to the ritual prohibition according to which young men, once initiated into moranhood, could no longer eat food seen or touched by women. The purpose of the ceremony with same name was to end this ritual prohibition once men became elders and married. The ceremony involved, among other things, the construction of the "white house" (M: *nkaji naibor*), a hut in which the wife fed her husband milk "for the first time." This act brought husband and wife together in a food-sharing relationship that supplemented their sexual relationship and more fully sealed their marriage. Because the costs of an lmenong ceremony were sometimes as high as those of a wedding, many men since the 1990s have chosen to postpone it. Even so, an lmenong had to be performed before one's children grew up and were initiated through circumcision. Eventually, as more and more elders actually circumcised their children without having done the lmenong, they appeared to desynchronize life course ceremonies. Some women, for example, worried that their children would die following circumcision because of the father's failure to complete rituals in a proper sequence.

During the time of my research, elders often debated instances in which individuals and families had performed rituals in the wrong order or could not perform the rituals of elderhood, as they still lagged behind on the rituals of their youth. In 2010 in Siteti, for example, the elders postponed for weeks the burial of a fifty-year-old woman who had died in the Maralal Hospital. Because her husband had not done an lmenong ceremony, she could not be buried in his homestead. But the husband would not accept the shame of burying his wife in the town cemetery. So while the woman's body remained at the mortuary, the elders organized a makeshift lmenong ceremony (performed over the coffin). Only then did they return the woman's body to be buried in her husband's compound. In this context, elders felt frustrated with their inability to complete ceremonies and rituals in an ideal sequence. In another instance, at the beginning of my fieldwork, I saw a senior elder run away from his home right before the time of our scheduled interview. When I asked one of his sons why he had left, the son replied, laughing, "My father talked to that neighbor of ours you interviewed yesterday. And the neighbor told him you asked if he had done his lmenong. My father was ashamed to be asked that question, so he ran away."

As the vast majority of rural Samburu struggled to envision alternative ways of earning a living, they imagined the past as an ideal time of proper relations of kinship and age, equal access to communally owned land, abundant monthly remittances from labor migrants, and most important, large herds of cattle. These idioms represented ideals of livelihood, sources of respectability, and central modes of local belonging, because in the past they had allegedly allowed people to marry, pay bridewealth, build families, and perform important life cycle rituals and ceremonies in a proper order. In the present, however, these ideal forms of life and belonging seemed unattainable, and the absence of wealth compelled people to postpone important rituals indefinitely while also questioning pathways to respectability. In this context, the future itself became uncertain.

SPEEDY RITUALS AND EARLY ELDERHOOD: ACCELERATING THE RHYTHMS OF RESPECTABILITY

Several Mombasa morans accumulated wealth rapidly, became big men, and gained some of the privileges of elderhood while relatively young. While Lekarda, whom we met in the beginning of this chapter, married two wives early in his elderhood, other men began marrying while still young morans. By paying bridewealth and performing wedding rituals ahead of their agemates, they hoped to anchor their wealth and authority in the respect and social recognition associated with elders. Take the example of Sakaine. When I interviewed him in 2008, he was twenty-three and already the richest man of Siteti.

When Sakaine was a child, his family was poor. His widowed mother did not own livestock, so the family of seven subsisted on a small income from her producing and selling charcoal and brewing chang'aa. Through a local NGO, Sakaine eventually found a foreign sponsor to pay his high school tuition. But then the headmaster reassigned Sakaine's sponsorship to one of his own children. No longer able to afford tuition, Sakaine dropped out of school. He hoped to find a way to earn money quickly to continue his edu-cation. Around the same time, in 2005, he was initiated into the age grade of moranhood as part of a new age set of the Lkishami. Following their initia-tion, many Lkishami went off to Mombasa to find foreign women. Motivated by his age-mates and seeking money for tuition in order to finish high school, Sakaine decided to go to Mombasa, too. After only six months, he met Elise, a German in her fifties. Elise and Sakaine began a long-term, long-distance relationship, with Elise visiting Kenya twice a year and occasionally paying for Sakaine to visit her in Germany.

Sakaine soon became a big man in Siteti. Elise sent him money regularly through Western Union, which he used to invest in properties in the village. He built a luxurious, five-room stone house with a spacious veranda, an elec-tric generator, a satellite dish, and a grand sheet-metal gate. In Siteti there was no electricity, and most people lived in traditional houses covered with roofs of mud or bark. The otherwise well-off labor migrants built modest houses of wooden posts and rusty iron-sheet roofs. In stark contrast, Sakaine's house had an imposing presence. He also owned more than one hundred head of cattle and some three hundred goats and sheep. A survey I carried out in 2010 among twenty-one households of Siteti showed that most families did not own cattle (0.38 head per household) and had only a few goats and sheep (8.3 head per household). In addition, Sakaine fenced some four acres of land on which he cultivated maize and beans. He also opened a small shop in the village, supplying locals with sugar, maize flour, soap, detergent, paraffin, and other commodities. Finally, Sakaine bought a motorcycle and a Land Rover, which he drove when visiting friends in the village or shopping in town. Soon he developed a vast network of clients—mostly impoverished elders—whom he employed to herd his cattle, weed his farm, clean his compound, or guard his gate. Sakaine's neighbors and relatives spoke of him ambivalently. They often pointed out to me that "this young man is a big man" (S: *huyu kijana ni mkubwa*) or that "he is a rich moran" (M: *kera ninye lmurrani ltajiri*).

A few weeks after I had interviewed him, Sakaine came by my house with a friend to invite me to his wedding. His news took me by surprise. I knew that according to custom, a moran was not allowed to marry for several years. He explained that he did not wish to "waste time being useless" like his age–mates, and that "our culture is all about wasting time." His friend supported his point of view, saying, "This is why Samburu people will never be modern, because they like to waste time, waiting around without a purpose." Echo-ing state development discourses of being-in-time, Sakaine and his friend saw the desire to speed things up in life as part of being "modern," an onto-

16. Morans bringing the bridewealth cattle to the bride's parents' home at Sakaine's wedding, July 2008. (Photo by the author.)

logical position that contrasted with how "Samburu culture" disposed of time. This desire was also a product of Sakaine's anxieties that perhaps Elise would one day stop supporting him with money. After all, he was well familiar with former young big men who had lost their wealth, forced to return to the beach in search of more tourists. With access to the necessary resources, he decided to pay bridewealth (fig. 16) and marry the daughter of a regional councillor, another big man who, like Sakaine, had once been a beach boy in Mombasa. Many people attended the wedding, a large festivity that combined Samburu ritual and moran dances, several meals, an open bar, a disco night, and speeches by the big men of the region.

Sakaine's decision to marry and become an elder ahead of his age-mates generated scandal. In particular, his choice to perform the ritual killing of the wedding ox sparked controversy among the elders of Siteti. As a member of the moran age grade, Sakaine would not normally be allowed to kill the wedding ox until his age set performed the ceremony of the name, and only after the leader of the age set, the so-called *launoni*, himself married. Because the ceremony of the name was not going to be performed for about five more years (and the *launoni* would not even be chosen until then), the elders thought that Sakaine was bending the timing of age-grade rituals.

"This is wrong, my friend," Ldoroni, a junior elder, told me on Sakaine's wedding day. "This is not the way our tradition is supposed to be. Now that they have money, they just do as they please."

"Why don't the elders stop him?" I asked.

"The elders are also after money," he explained. "If you have money, you decide how you want it to be. But it's wrong. The whole thing is just to show how big he is."

According to Ldoroni, the elders' desire for money, like Sakaine's desire to become an elder ahead of time, corrupted the temporality of age-grade rituals. This case was particularly upsetting to Ldoroni. Like numerous junior elders of his age set, he cohabited with his partner while continuously deferring bridewealth payments and the killing of the wedding ox because he lacked the necessary material resources. By contrast, Sakaine was able to fulfill these expectations long before they were supposed to take place.

Accelerating access to the privileges of elderhood through early marriage was not a new phenomenon. So-called age-set climbers (M: *lailepi*, sg. *lkailepi*) had long existed in Samburu. They were orphaned morans blessed by elders to "climb" (M: *a-ilep*) an age set in order to marry and take over family responsibilities. In contrast to age-set climbers, men like Sakaine took it upon themselves to become elders.[8] Also unlike age-set climbers, these men sought to climb an age grade without climbing an age set as well. So while their age set was in the age grade of moranhood, they stood out for being the first members of the age set to claim elderhood. Age-set membership was often premised on the collective interference of the age cohort with the life of each one of its members. But young big men, because of their wealth and power, were no longer subject to age-set control. As a Samburu woman put it, "a rich moran only listens to himself, and that pulls him out of his age set." Elders called such a man a "transgressor," using the Maa noun *lperet*. In the past, *lperet* referred to a moran who married his girlfriend against the will of her parents. The moran would come to the girl's house and kill the wedding ox under the cover of night. This usually occurred after the girl's father had promised her in marriage to an elder. Elders of the clan usually cursed transgressors to death during the *lmuget* ceremonies. More recently, elders also used the term *lperet* to speak of morans who fathered children in "come-we-stay" marriages, and those like Sakaine who performed rituals reserved for elders.

In the years following Sakaine's wedding, young big men increasingly followed his lead. In doing so, they subverted what others invoked as long-held ideals of aging. They used their wealth to skip ahead of their age-mates and "buy" their way up the age-grade ladder. Their actions placed them in an ambivalent relationship with other members of their age set. On the one hand, these men's actions "pulled them out of their age set"—that is, they no longer depended on the support and moral recognition of their age-mates.

In the early 1990s, members of the Lmooli age set still sought to exercise control over those members who acquired wealth through European women and eventually stopped abiding by the moral expectations of moranhood. One man told me how his age-mates whipped him during an age-set meeting for "having become proud," though this was the only story I heard of such a meeting during my fieldwork in the 2000s. On the other hand, rich Mombasa morans and young big men came to be seen by their age-mates as patrons of sorts, men with resources who, by virtue of their membership in the age set, could be called on to support them with money. In this context, young big men occupied an ambivalent position in their age sets.

Embodying the contradictions between age grades and wealth accumulation, young big men engendered what I wish to call *queer moments* in the temporalities of aging. I use the adjective *queer* to refer to ways of being-in-time that subvert normative temporal expectations. My use of *queer* resonates here with that of Kenyan English speakers, for whom the adjective is taken to mean "disobedient," "odd," or "out of place." But it also resonates with queer theorists' discussions of nonnormative ways of being-in-time, or "queer temporalities" (Freeman 2007; Halberstam 2005). As they desynchronized competing ways of aging, young big men produced moments that revealed—if only momentarily—the hegemonic workings of normative expectations of age. By making elderhood a commodity, they challenged the kinds of time expected to go into its achievement. They showed how elderhood was possible without long periods of waiting or without the *gradual* accumulation of wealth—and they did this at a time when, in the absence of wealth and work, other people experienced an excess of time and could do little *but* wait. In becoming elders while in their early twenties, young big men subverted normative temporalities of aging and the life course.

I speak of queer *moments* rather than "queer temporalities" to underline that the queerness of these practices of age was *momentary*. Rather than sustain an ongoing "queer time," or "the potentiality of life unscripted by conventions of family, inheritance, and child rearing" (Halberstam 2005, 2), "queer moments" emerged from (hetero)normative reproductive desires and often facilitated arguments for the reiteration of normativity. As young big men used their money to subvert the ritual time of age grades, poor elders more strongly reiterated the normative time of ritual aging. By asserting the unpropitious nature of the young big men's actions, elders could more tightly control the time of poorer morans. Elders also benefited financially from instances of "transgression." Following Sakaine's wedding, they capitalized on their ritual power and allowed many other young big men to marry early in exchange for a monetary "fine" (M: *pain*). These queer moments therefore regenerated the importance of elderhood, albeit in a new, commodified form.

The actions of young big men like Sakaine also affected women's life course and respectability in significant ways. The ability of these men to pay bridewealth up front, at a time when most people traded in bridewealth debts, made it more likely that some parents would intervene in their daughters' lives and push them into marriages in order to obtain money and cattle. For others, these marriages were problematic, for they undermined long-term expectations of exchange, reciprocity, and accountability between affines. When bridewealth was paid instantly and definitively, marriages were contracted more like commodity exchanges, foreclosing, at least partly, the possibility of ongoing demands from affines. Furthermore, while some young women desired to be married to young big men, others had to marry them against their will.

The mothers of these young women also encountered new dilemmas. "I had decided to go to the police," Mama Jasiti said, recalling a conflict in her family a year prior. I visited Mama Jasiti in January 2011 at her home in a highland village. Together with her husband and young children, she lived in a large hill top compound. Her small house was made of branches and plastered with clay and dung. While sitting inside at the hearth, we chatted over a cup of hot tea. "I was going to report what had happened to that daughter of mine called Jasiti," she continued.

Mama Jasiti's husband and his brothers had decided to marry Jasiti to a young man named Taitas. With Jasiti's blessing, Taitas asked her father for her hand in marriage. The father and his brothers quickly agreed, noting that Taitas was very rich. He had made a lot of money through a long-term relationship with a Swiss woman he had met at one of the coastal tourist resorts. Taitas offered to make all the bridewealth payments up front, but requested that Jasiti drop out of school and join him in his rural house. Mama Jasiti did not agree to her daughter's marriage, for she was imagining a different future for her. She wanted her daughter to finish school and attend the teachers' college.

"They were not supposed to take her out of school," Mama Jasiti protested. "Well, I stayed, and then I said, 'Tomorrow, I will go to the police. I will go to report, tomorrow.'"

But before Mama Jasiti had a chance to walk to the Maralal Police Station, other women from her village intervened. They explained to Mama Jasiti that her daughter, like most educated women in the district, would most likely not find employment after graduation and would struggle to make a living.

"The women stopped me," Mama Jasiti recalled. "They said, 'Why do you want to prevent your daughter from living a good life?'"

Learning of Mama Jasiti's anger, Taitas offered to pay ten times the customary bridewealth fee or "fine" for a total of KSh 10,000 ($150). In doing so, he hoped to "soothe" the heart of his future mother-in-law. Eventually, Mama Jasiti agreed to the wedding, if only halfheartedly. Although she never fully reconciled with what had occurred, she told me proudly that Taitas and her daughter now lived in a large, luxurious stone house, and owned a car and a large herd of livestock. She had just returned home after visiting them for a week.

If we are to approach Mama Jasiti's dilemma as engendered by and conducive to a set of *queer moments*, we begin to recognize how the subversive actions of young big men generated conflicts and contestations through which markers of respectability were reworked. Taitas drew on his newly acquired wealth to marry Jasiti while she was still in school. But he did so against Mama Jasiti's will. Because Taitas had wealth, the elders no longer considered the fact that, in order to marry, Jasiti would have to abandon her education, an otherwise important source of prestige and potential future income. Eager to obtain bridewealth more quickly (probably so they could deal with their own debts), the elders consented to the marriage. In the process, they overrode Jasiti's mother's customary authority over her daughter and created a conflict involving many clan members. Yet the subversiveness of this situation was but *momentary*: it lasted only as long as it unsettled notions of respectability associated with schooling and expectations of gendered parental authority. Not only did Jasiti's father and his brothers undermine Mama Jasiti's authority, but so, too, did Mama Jasiti undermine her husband's and future in-laws' authority over their daughter by threatening to go to the state authorities. If only temporarily, these actions brought out central contradictions in the contemporary dynamics of marriage, filiation, and gender relations. They also created a space for their possible reimagination. Such moments contained the potential for what Jose Esteban Muñoz (2009) has called "not-yet-conscious futures"—that is, multiple future-making possibilities inherent in the material and moral circumstances of the present. Some of these "not-yet-conscious futures," Muñoz argues, may sidestep the hegemony of normative reproductive imperatives. But these destabilizing dynamics may also call for the production of a new normative. As other women persuaded Mama Jasiti to submit to the elders' decision, they kept her authority—as a senior wife of her husband's clan—within the confines of what they thought was respectable. At the same time, however, young women's respectability came to be reimagined, away from schooling and toward new possibilities for a good life. Here, the extent to which individuals could push the limits of the doable and craft new pathways to respectability came sharply into question. Yet at the limits of the doable lay the haunting threats of failure.

SPEEDING OUT OF CONTROL: MADMEN, UNANCHORED MOBILITY, AND THE FAILURES OF SEXUALITY

Madness figured centrally in stories Samburu told about the young big men. Quick access to cash, people thought, led some of these men to lose self-control: they drank alcohol, had sex with prostitutes, acquired HIV, and eventually went mad and died. Or so people said. Be that as it may, narratives of madness offered a commentary on marriage, family, and reproductive sexuality in the present. Everyday stories of madness and madmen illustrated the consequences of not attending to matters of reproduction and belonging in ways locals considered propitious. As various social actors read the bodies of the mad and told their stories, they posited madness as a salient, ongoing threat to the making of collective futures. Madmen (M: *lmaadai*, sg. *madai*) embodied the haunting possibility of social failure: their very presence reminded onlookers of the fragile nature of respectability and life force.

Consider, for example, the story of Tangan. I first saw Tangan on the streets of Mtwapa in April 2011. At that time, I did not know his name. He was in his early thirties and, by age-grade status, a junior elder. Yet his appearance was hardly that of a respectable elder. He walked through the streets of Mtwapa completely undressed. His hair was long and shaggy. Although most of the time he sat quietly on the edge of the street, there were also times when he had violent outbursts. On such occasions, he ran toward women on the street and, in a loud voice, accused them of having infected him with AIDS and threatened to rape them in return. Women usually ignored him, laughing as they walked past him. They all knew that this young man was "cheesy," as youths would say. That is, he was mad.

A few months later, I saw Tangan again, this time in Samburu. He was walking through Maralal. Friends told me that Tangan's older brother, a Mombasa policeman, had brought him back home so their elderly mother could care for him. This was not the first time that Tangan's brother had brought him home. But on all previous occasions, Tangan ran off and eventually found his way back to the coast by hiking or climbing on trucks. This time, however, the situation was different. Tangan had developed tuberculosis, which in combination with AIDS, many thought, announced his imminent death. His brother brought him to their village for what he probably thought would be Tangan's final days. Tangan's mother found it difficult to care for him at home and would hospitalize him in Maralal every now and then. His sister, Mama Sempen, was my neighbor in Maralal. She told me that the last time I had seen Tangan on the streets of Maralal, he had run away from the hospital. She was both saddened by her brother's situation and ashamed of it.

Mama Sempen was a widow raising two young children on her own. I visited her one day to ask her about her brother. She agreed to share his life story with me. Looking at the floor and tossing a handkerchief in her hands, she recalled the days when her brother's troubles had started.

"He finished the secondary [high school]. After the secondary, he went to Nairobi to work in the National Youth Service as a soldier. Everything was going very well with him."

Mama Sempen paused. She sighed.

"After a while, he saw that he could not make much money in the military. He wanted to make money faster. He did not want that small, small money he got in the Youth Service. He wanted that shortcut money."

Mama Sempen explained that Tangan had seen his elder brother become rich by marrying a German woman he had met on the coast. Indeed, by the mid-1990s, the brother had moved temporarily to Germany. So Tangan decided to go to the coast, hoping he would meet a tourist and follow in his brother's footsteps. However, he was not as fortunate as his brother. He struggled to make ends meet by selling souvenirs and sometimes also working as a night watchman to supplement his income. Later, however, with the help of his brother and some European girlfriends of his own, Tangan opened a barbershop in Mtwapa.

"It was called Afro-Kinyozi," Mama Sempen recalled. "It was very smart."

As soon as he began making money, however, trouble started. Tangan had a relationship with a Giriama woman. Mama Sempen said that after her brother moved in with "the Giriama," as she called her, he stopped visiting his family in Samburu and no longer sent money to his mother. Although by age grade he was already a junior elder, his sister pointed out, Tangan had not married and lived as a "pauper." What is more, Mama Sempen said that other Samburu would often see him at the bars with different women. "He was spending all his money on them." Then, in 2009, he began falling sick very often. When he went to see a doctor, he tested positive for HIV. Immediately afterward, Tangan "went mad."

"I don't know what it was that made him mad," his sister said. "Was it the shock of having AIDS? Or was it the witchcraft of the women of the coast? I really don't know."

Soon, Tangan's barbershop went bankrupt and he lost all his savings.

For Mama Sempen and other Samburu, Tangan's story spoke to the perceived failures of reproductive sexuality in the present. Young men with money, they reasoned, were exposed to the dangers of conspicuous consumption and promiscuous sex—namely, witchcraft and AIDS. Women of ethnic groups living on the coast—Giriama, Digo, and Kamba—figured in their stories in moral opposition to Samburu women. While the former were seductresses interested in the money of male migrants, the latter anchored men in relations of family and kinship and thus made ideal wives. And, whereas a certain degree of sexual enjoyment was expected of men who were morans, junior elders like Tangan were expected to begin a home of their own by marrying and settling down. Their sexuality had to be rooted less in self-enjoyment and more in the work of reproduction, of growing (M: *abulu*) their lineages. But Tangan was still on the coast some five years after becoming an elder. Not only did he enjoy sex with multiple women, but he also took his sexuality to the market, as he occasionally had sex with tourists for money. He had postponed returning home and settling down to elderhood. Sexual promiscuity and commodified sex undermined Tangan's ability to become a respectable elder. Instead, his sexual excesses depleted his life force and brought disease, madness, and a quick progression toward death.

For my informants, madness could have many causes, including curses; bad omens caused by one's own actions or those of ancestors or kin; envy and jealousy; revenge and witchcraft; the failure to complete certain rituals in specific sequences; and much more. In the present, the failures of reproductive sexuality also figured centrally in stories about madmen, which told of madmen themselves born of adulterous encounters, men and women bewitched by jealous partners, and rich men manipulated by greedy women. The madmen that walked along the streets of Maralal or through neighboring villages reminded locals daily of the dangers of excessive wealth and sex. Walking in public spaces either *un*dressed, like Tangan, or *over*dressed (wearing several layers of clothes), with long beards and dirty, long hair, madmen's bodily appearance indexed antisociality and their resignation from the pursuits of respectability—in short, social death.

The failed sexuality of madmen was understood to manifest itself in, and be partly an outcome of, uncontrolled mobility. Tangan walked around Mtwapa "without a purpose," and whenever his family brought him home to Samburu to anchor him, as it were, he found his way back to the coast. Madmen, Samburu said, refused to stay put. They refused to belong. They ran away from their families and roamed around uselessly; unlike moral persons who engaged in the making of resources and respectability, they did not seem to pursue anything. Indeed, their state echoed and intensified their initial lack of sexual and social rootedness. In the normative order of things, mobility had to be anchored in the fixity of the *nkang*, or homestead, of marriage, family, and children. The stability of the homestead and the family tempered masculine and feminine mobilities, employing movement for collectively recognized ways of leading a good life and belonging. Men engaged in trade or labor migration returned to and invested in their homesteads and families. Likewise, women who traveled to town markets and other places returned to their houses and hearths. Those elders who were mobile without being anchored at the same time risked speeding out of control.

To better understand this implicit cultural logic, consider the following practice. In Samburu, it is said that several men cannot travel in a car or a pickup truck with only one woman, lest the car speed out of control and have an accident. Therefore, if several men find themselves in vehicle with only one woman, they must place an average-size stone in it before departing. While my informants could not elaborate on the logics behind the practice, to me these logics parallel those of the uncontrolled mobility and unanchored sexuality of the madmen. As wives, women anchor men's movements, offering them a stable home. The home itself is anchored in the stones of the hearth—the locus of its fertility and life force (Straight 2007b, 74–75). Men without women (or with not enough women) are dangerously mobile. They can lose themselves in the speed of their own mobility and become mad or die. When entering the distinct spatiotemporal realm of the car (recall Daniel's statements in chapter 4 that describe the car as occupying a realm of its own), men must bring along a stone—a symbol of fixity and of a woman's hearth—to anchor the car's movements. Similarly, unattached madmen can be said to speed out of control and thus be left in a perpetual state of chaotic movement. People alluded to this logic more explicitly, for example, when they nicknamed one Maralal madman "Concorde," after the high-speed aircraft that made global headlines when it crashed in France in 2003.

If uncontrolled mobility figured as both a condition for and an outcome of madness, the excessive movements of those who risked going mad were still driven by the pursuits of respectability and belonging. Madness, by contrast, marked a space and time in which movement lost its social intentionality. Socially dead, madmen were merely waiting for their physical demise. In Samburu, many understood AIDS and madness as entangled bodily signs of morally negative social value. Those who refused to test for HIV feared that their knowledge of a positive status would make them mad. Mama Sempen, for one, told me that she preferred not to know her HIV status. Of persons suffering from AIDS-related illnesses (which locals read by the appearance of marked emaciation), just like of those who were "mad," people would say *meisho niche*—or, as English-speaking Samburu would translate it, "they are not alive." More accurately, however, the verb *a-ishu* refers to the ability of people, animals, and goods to be sources of life force. *Meishu ninche*, then, translates specifically as "they do not give life" or "are devoid of life force"; the lack of life force marked a process of continuous self-depletion. AIDS was called *mbiita*, literally "wasting away." Therefore, both AIDS and madness marked nongenerative, self-depleting states of being that ended in death.

Madness worked here as a representation of personal and collective failure that recaptured and reclaimed an imagined normative status quo. Stories about madmen pointed, if in different ways, to the limits of the doable—that is, the lines beyond which subversive actions and moral transgressions became social failure. It is not my interest here to tell what *is* beyond madness as a representation. Nor, for that matter, do I have the data to do so. Medical practitioners and development workers in Samburu often explained what people called madness as chronic depression, mental disability, or schizophrenia. Yet these categories do not capture the work that narratives of madness do. For such narratives allow social actors to negotiate the limits of moral acceptability while also stigmatizing and marginalizing those they see as mad. Beyond the limits of acceptability, there is failure: persons become nonpersons, and life depletes itself.

Judith Halberstam (2011, 23) explores failure as a "way of life" associated with "modes of unbecoming." Failure is, among other things, "a refusal of mastery, a critique of the intuitive connections within capitalism between success and profit, and a counterhegemonic discourse of losing" (12). For Halberstam, failure may also become "the map of political paths not taken, though it does not chart a completely separate land" (19). By thinking of madness as the failure of social life—or rather as a representation thereof— invocations of madness work to foreclose what Muñoz (2009) calls the potentialities of "not-yet-conscious futures" inherent in the material and moral conditions of the present. More specifically, when narratives about madness concern the failures of sexuality and uncontrolled mobility, they work to exclude alternative configurations of sex, intimacy, and sociality. And most important, this happens precisely as part of the expansion of ethno-erotic economies, when the commodification of moran sexuality opens up myriad new possibilities of attachment. In other words, madness works ideologically to reinforce the significance of marriage, family, and reproductive sexuality at the very moment when people perceive these categories to be reconfigured by economic transformations and new styles of accumulation and consumption. Madness works here as a shifting category that allows men and women to renegotiate legitimate pathways to normative respectability rather than displace such ideals.

Between marriage and madness, then, a space of experimentation and new possibilities of belonging emerged. If marriage and the prerogatives of elderhood were not easy to achieve through normative pathways, what other ways were there? And how might such alternative pathways—however subversive—ultimately regenerate rather than displace normative ideals of marriage, family, and elderhood? In dealing with these implicit challenges, Samburu crafted new articulations of marriage and elderhood and, therewith, new modes of attachment to local social worlds.

TURNING BACK TIME AND CATCHING UP: BEACH-BOY ELDERS

While young big men used their money to rush into elderhood, impoverished men in coastal economies often advanced to the age grade of elderhood without having accumulated any wealth. Some of these elders postponed returning to Samburu for many years, to avoid the shame and humiliation of being unmarried and, therefore, unpropitious *lmaachani*, or paupers. By the time of my field research, some of these men had lived on the coast continuously for up to twenty-five years. They called Samburu their home and imagined a better time in their futures when they would be able to return to their villages, catch up on ritual and social obligations, and become respectable elders.

At the beach, impoverished elders tried to *turn back time*, as it were, and return (M: *a-chukunye*; S: *kurudi*) to being morans in order to produce resources associated with an age-grade status they had come to inhabit too soon. We already encountered the "beach-boy elders" or "elders of Mombasa" in chapter 3. These were men who, though already in the age grade of elderhood, dressed in the attire of young morans in order to attract tourists. Less popular with tourists than the younger men, these beach-boy elders

often worked also as watchmen to make ends meet. Few managed to accumulate wealth, but others used their savings to invest in respectability and a
good life at home.

Remember Ltarsia, whom we met in the introduction of this book. Born
near Mount Nyiro in the far north of Samburu District, Ltarsia was initiated
into moranhood in 1976 as part of the Lkuroro age set. He spent the following years herding cattle. Following severe droughts in the late 1970s, all the
cattle of Ltarsia's family died, so the family migrated to the southern highlands and settled in Siteti. In Siteti, Ltarsia saw that many of his age-mates
had begun traveling to the coast. He decided to join them in 1982. Although
he had never gone to school and spoke only the Maa language, at the beach
he quickly learned Swahili and a bit of English. But unlike some of his age–
mates, who became rich, Ltarsia only managed to earn enough to live, send
money to his parents, and save cash for a bridewealth payment. None of the
relationships he had with foreign women allowed him to accumulate wealth.
In 1990, as a new age set was initiated into moranhood, Ltarsia's age set was
promoted to elderhood. No longer a moran, Ltarsia continued to dress in
moran regalia and go to the beach. A few years after his initiation into elderhood, Ltarsia married a Samburu woman and fathered four children while
still living in Mtwapa. In 2000, he returned with his family to Siteti. In eighteen years at the coast, however, he had saved only enough money to build a
small, bark-covered wooden house and establish a herd of some fifty goats.
Although he had been an elder for ten years by then, he still had not performed important parts of his wedding ceremony, including his lmenong.

When I first met Ltarsia in 2008, the chances for him to "catch up" on his
life course ceremonies were slim. He had already sold off all his livestock and
was struggling to make ends meet by producing and selling charcoal. "This
elder is just a beach boy" (M: *kera ele payian bichboi ake*), a man from Siteti told
me, referring to Ltarsia. Recall that to speak of a man—and even more so of
an elder—as a beach boy was to infantilize and disrespect him (see chapter 4).
Although Ltarsia had stopped migrating to the coast, other villagers invoked
his past to explain his current situation. When I asked a Samburu woman
what she thought of beach-boy elders, she told me, laughing:

Nowadays, my child, we have those elders who have gone to Mombasa. There,
the Lkuroro [age set of elders] believe that they are still morans. They haven't
seen that people have left them behind long ago. [*laughing*] Are the Lkuroro
still morans up to now? Let God hate me if I am lying. Don't they understand
that age sets pass with circumcision? The Lmooli [age set] were circumcised,

even the Lkishami were circumcised, and the Lkuroro are still in Mombasa.
They are still morans. And they are very old men. They are lost.

Many men and women I interviewed used similar narratives to ridicule what
they perceived as the beach-boy elders' attempt to defy the linear flow of
time by refusing to acknowledge that people had moved on and "left them
behind" (M: *keshomoki ninche*). Such narratives undermined the respectability
of these men. Also called "the lost ones" (M: *loimina*), beach-boy elders re-
versed the clock of aging and were lost to their forward-moving relatives and
age-mates at home. Here, "being left behind" meant gradually losing claims
to belonging.

Like the young big men, beach-boy elders subverted normative temporal
expectations through the very practices by which they hoped to fulfill them.
They also corrupted sexuality. During elderhood, when male sexuality was
supposed to be about the domestic processes of social reproduction, beach-
boy elders took their sexuality to the tourist market for economic production. Elizabeth Freeman (2007, 159) points out that "queer time" emerges
at the intersection of "marginalized time schemes" and "disavowed" erotic
practices. In this context, *pace* Halberstam (2005), queer temporal moments
do not have be about a deliberate attempt to oppose reproductive normativity—for example, when a subculture refuses to live by normative expectations of reproduction and life course—but may emerge as people articulate
normative desires through subversive means.

But, unlike other "beach-boy elders" who were ashamed to return home
because they lacked the resources to marry and start a family, Ltarsia began
to catch up on the prerogatives of elderhood. When I saw him again in September 2010, he had acquired some cattle and stopped drinking. "He was
alive" (M: *keishu niniye*), as people would say—that is, he was healthier, pros-
perous, full of life. He also wore new, clean clothes and a new "godfather hat"
(i.e., cowboy hat)—a quintessential marker of elderhood. Over a cup of tea in
his homestead, he spoke to me proudly of his recent achievements. I learned
that he had become deeply invested in the rituals organized by his age set and
one of the most vocal defenders of such ritual expectations. As I described
in the opening of this book, Ltarsia used his otherwise modest resources
to host the blessing ceremony for the morans of Siteti. He thus invested in
modes of collective belonging that would grant him recognition and support
in the future. And, having struggled to achieve respectability locally, Ltarsia
now defended its principles also.

That the ceremonies of marriage and elderhood played such a central role in the making of belonging, relatedness, and respectability in Samburu was partly an outcome of the new, open-ended possibilities of ethno-erotic commodification. Here, the ritual economies of Samburu promised durable and morally legitimate forms of life and attachment. They also promised inclusion and support within local communities. Yet local ritual economies—not unlike the "casino capitalism" that defines a neoliberal economy of speculative gambling (Comaroff and Comaroff 2000)—often exhausted the material resources of individuals before they had a chance to catch up with their heavy requirements. Some Samburu men spent all their savings trying to resynchronize the life course rituals of their parents and lineages as a condition for their own future marriages and elderhoods. Without such a ritual resynchronization, their own future lives would be devoid of life force and the ability to thrive. But sometimes, they too lost their money before they could even begin investing in their own wedding ceremonies and bridewealth payments.

Consider the example of Jadini, a young man I met in Mtwapa in 2011. Jadini spent most of the wealth he had accumulated through relationships with two foreign women on trying to fix his parents' marriage. His father had never paid bridewealth for his mother, nor had he performed any of the wedding rituals. In fact, his parents had not lived together for many years. However, if Jadini was to craft respectability for himself as a member of his father's clan, he could not be a so-called child of a girl (M: *nkera e ntito*), or an illegitimate child; rather, he had to craft belonging to his father's clan. Moreover, Jadini wished to repair his father's respectability. Not having married, his father could not claim to have "grown" his lineage, for his children belonged—albeit unpropitiously as "children of a girl"—to their mother's clan. To become respectable, Jadini's father had to pay bridewealth retroactively and secure the belonging of his children to his line of descent through the appropriate rituals.

"I was worried for my father," Jadini told me.

If he had died, nobody would have agreed to touch his body. I said, "No, my father cannot stay like that." I talked to my mzungu and asked her to help me. She gave me money. So I organized the wedding for my father. I got 150,000 shillings [about $1,900]. I bought cows. I went to Maralal and picked up my mother. She had been living there for many years, separated from my father. I took her to Wamba to my father. There, I've done all those ceremonies, everything: the *rikoret*, the *lmenong*. Everything. We also sent cattle to her family as bridewealth.

Unlike other young big men who sought to acquire houses, cars, and businesses, Jadini's priorities were somewhat different. He chose to invest first in
setting straight the ritual obligations of his parents as a condition for his own
belonging. To many Samburu, this was seen as the better way of doing things.
Jadini hoped that once he had fixed the marriage of his parents, he would be
able to marry himself. Like Sakaine, whom I introduced earlier in this chapter, Jadini wanted to use his resources to pay bridewealth, hold wedding ceremonies, and become an elder while still in the age grade of moranhood. However, soon after he had financed the marriage of his parents, his European
partners abandoned him and cut their financial support. When I saw Jadini
last, he was drinking heavily. With his age set due to begin marrying soon, he,
too, worried that he would become a beach-boy elder.

SUBVERTING THE RHYTHMS OF RESPECTABILITY

The rise of ethno-erotic economies and the times of economic hardship that
sustained them shaped how people imagined and actualized pathways to respectability and belonging in Samburu. Whereas numerous men and women
struggled to catch up on ritual obligations associated with marriage and
elderhood, young big men enriched through relationships with European
women fulfilled such obligations long before they were due. Divorcing the
privileges of elderhood from older ideas about gradual wealth accumulation
and long periods of waiting, young big men commodified access to elderhood
and questioned the kind of time necessary for its achievement. Meanwhile,
beach-boy elders sought new ways to catch up on the ritual obligations of
an elderhood they had come to inhabit before acquiring the necessary resources. All these men struggled to participate in a ritual economy that
would, so they thought, grant them respectability and recognition at home
and anchor them in local worlds in ways that were durable and meaningful.
To do otherwise was to risk losing life force and becoming a madman or a
living dead man. Fearing failure, young big men, beach-boy elders, Mombasa
morans, and other Samburu subverted, albeit in different ways, the means
and temporal rhythms of marriage, elderhood, and respectability.

Nonetheless, this did not lead to the abandonment of older templates
associated with age grades, age sets, rituals, and kinship. Even as young big
men, for example, no longer had high stakes in age-set relations, age sets did
not fade in importance. To the contrary, age sets now provided poorer men
with strong ties of reciprocal support and allowed them to claim what they
could now frame as morally superior forms of elderhood. Anthropologists
Paul Baxter and Uri Almagor (1978, 20) argued that "economic individual-

ism and age-setting are probably incompatible." They anticipated that "East African age-set and generation-set systems . . . seem doomed to extinction or, at best, to be preserved . . . in a reserve for tourists to wonder at uncomprehendingly" (23). However, as we have seen, with the rise of ethno-erotic economies, age grades and age sets emerge in new ways, their rituals more commodified, their age cohorts more markedly shaped by rapidly shifting inequalities.

As these men tried to get the best out of ethno-erotic capital and local belonging through marriage and age-grade relations, they came to embody the contradictions of multiple competing temporal rhythms of their life course. At once accelerating and inverting the ideal ritual time of age grades through the bodily time of ethno-erotic capital or the time-producing wealth of the big man, these men subverted the temporalities of aging. They performed what Freeman (2007, 159–62) describes as embodied sensations of asynchrony or of time being "out of joint" with normative temporal expectations. Neither fully youth nor fully elders, young big men and beach-boy elders sustained temporal contradictions arising from the expectation that a gradual wealth accumulation should be simultaneous with a gradual process of social aging. As these men navigated volatile economic contexts through competing notions of age, time, and the life course, their contradictory practices opened up new future-making possibilities in the material conditions of the present.

However, at the same time that such subversive practices created the potentiality for alternative futures and new ways of attachment, they also generated arguments for the reproduction of a hegemonic status quo. Beach-boy elders, young big men, and madmen came to my attention because men and women in Samburu spoke about them at length. Through such talk, they actively questioned the respectability of these men and reasserted ideal forms of aging, even when these were no longer available to everyone. Furthermore, even if young big men and beach-boy elders subverted age and time—as did many poor rural Samburu, for that matter—their desires for particular kinds of social value were, by and large, normative. Thus, rather than speak of "queer temporalities" as embodied practices actively *opposed* to a reproductive normativity (Halberstam 2005), I use "queer moments" to refer to subversive means and outcomes of otherwise normative desires.

In prompting us to reflect on how various social actors speed up or out of control, slow down or try to catch up, the analytic of queer moments reveals an important aspect of belonging in ethno-erotic economies. Queer moments demonstrate the dialectical relationship between the commodification of moran sexuality in intimacies with foreign women and the ways in which people imagine and actualize respectability and attachment to social worlds in Samburu. A set of major contradictions drive this central dialectic on which ethno-erotic economies rest. As money of Mombasa circulated widely in northern Kenya, it intensified attempts to both subvert and diversify and also stabilize and normalize the means of belonging. People desired both to incorporate the foreign capital of ethnosexual commodification and to exclude those who, pursuing this kind of money, took new, unruly pathways to respectability. They hoped both to expand the limits of acceptable belonging—to make the circulation of this money possible—and to fix it, keep it in check, and anchor it in the boundaries of custom.

The rise of ethno-erotic economies led thus to the inflation of ritual economies in Samburu. As young big men, beach-boy elders, and others turned to ritual as a means of belonging, rural elders found that their collective ritual expertise and power was itself a commodity in high demand. They could fine those who subverted ritual expectations and normalize subversions as "transgressions" in order make their blessings necessary. If ritual economies were central to negotiating local belonging, they also became—as the following chapter will show—key modalities for crafting belonging to a world beyond Samburu.

6. In a Ritual Rush: Crafting Belonging in Lopiro Ceremonies

The rush is the affect of a speculative economy.
—ROSALIND MORRIS, "RUSH/PANIC/RUSH"

Rituals reveal values at their deepest level . . . and since the form of expression is
conventionalized and *obligatory*, it is the values of the group that are revealed.
—MONICA WILSON, "NYAKYUSA RITUAL AND SYMBOLISM"

The ideal rhythms associated with age grades, the life course, marriage, and
reproduction in Samburu were out of synch with the actual pace at which
different people could fulfill these social obligations. Men participating in
coastal sexual economies merely pushed these temporal asynchronies to new
extremes, moving either too fast or too slow, turning back and forth in seemingly unruly ways, or speeding out of control and going mad, while trying to
become respectable elders. As many locals depended on these men's cash,
ritual itself—an important means for acquiring belonging—became more and
more like a commodity, and access to its privileges became more sharply divided by new inequalities. These transformations expanded the range of possible ways to belong. But they also produced anxiety and uncertainty over
the meanings of belonging. For rural Samburu—many of whom had been further marginalized in this context—new challenges emerged. To gain recogni-

tion and access to resources within the state and a wider global political and economic arena, it was important that they acted collectively. But how could they gain collective recognition and respectability in Kenya and beyond when unequal access to money undermined the very possibility of maintaining a set of shared criteria for belonging? Furthermore—to return to a question that I raised in the introduction—how could they be respected in this larger world when what they were recognized for was, in part, their allegedly excessive ethnosexuality? And how could they imagine collective belonging when money produced through the commodification of moran ethnosexuality now fueled local economies and undermined the respectability of Samburu, nationally and internationally? To understand how Samburu articulated these questions and what solutions they imagined, I turn to a set of clan rituals that took place in the district during the time of my fieldwork.

One evening in December 2010, the Kenyan television channel Citizen announced that Samburu had begun organizing ceremonies called lopiro. In the previous weeks, I had attended two such ceremonies. I had learned that every fourteen to eighteen years, clan groups from different regions in Samburu held lopiro ceremonies within a few weeks or months of one another. During lopiro, married men and women danced, ate, and exchanged gifts. At the center of lopiro was a particular form of adultery—or what Samburu called *loloito*—that involved younger men and the wives of more senior men. Through these ceremonies, these men and women promised to put an end to their relationships and retire to respectable elderhood.

According to the Citizen report, lopiro was a "dancing competition," an opportunity to build "clan unity," a way to "bring the rains," and a "Samburu way of celebrating Christmas." The report mockingly asked, "Why is it that people who live primitively have not yet grasped the precise meanings of Christmas?" This Othering rhetoric was not new to me, given how often Samburu people served as prototypical examples of radical Otherness in the national media. But what surprised me at that time was that the report did not mention adultery, despite the central role it plays in lopiro. Kenyan journalists have long been fascinated with what they see as the oddities of Samburu sexuality. Newspapers and magazines often feature young Samburu men with many lovers, old men who married underage girls, or sensationalist accounts of how cultural backwardness and promiscuity were responsible for the prevalence of sexually transmitted infections among Samburu. Why, then, did the Citizen journalists not mention adultery? Had they missed it in their conversations with locals? Or did their interviewees purposefully withhold such information, knowing how it would be used?

Certainly, the suppression of explicit references to sex was very important in lopiro. When I attended my first lopiro ceremony, I had been visiting Samburu for over five years. Although at that time I did not encounter any references to lopiro, either in the field or in the literature on the region, I had learned that matters of sexual intimacy were not readily discussed among members of different age and gender groups. One encounter during a lopiro ceremony helped me understand some of the implications of sexual secrecy.

I was talking to four women I had known for several months. They were senior wives who had organized the ceremony. I asked them about the links between lopiro and adultery. "You know, lopiro is very much about that kind of relationship," Mama Lmarai said, prompting her age-mates to laugh with embarrassment. I asked the women if everybody who participated in lopiro knew about these relationships. "Everybody knows," Mama Lmarai explained. "That is something that Samburu know." She later added, "That is something that continues with every generation." Meanwhile, another woman arrived—Mama Mbenesi. She had not met me before. Upon hearing what the women were talking to me about, she opened her eyes wide in shock. "You stupid women!" she started scolding them. "Why do you tell the white man our secrets? Have you any idea where he will take these things?" With a dismissive wave of her hand, she turned her back on us and left.

Veiling sex in secrecy or revealing it through speech had two important implications for negotiating belonging, both locally and to the world outside Samburu. First, in lopiro, knowledge about sexual intimacies was embedded in symbols and sensibilities that did not need to be verbalized—at least not for those who belonged to the scene of the ritual as such. For them, concealing sex was an important task. In everyday life, loloito was a central reason for conflicts between husbands and wives, juniors and seniors, the rich and the poor. Speaking openly about adultery could refuel these conflicts. Moreover, to speak of sex was a highly erotic act. People understood desire and speech as material extensions of persons that "touched" the bodies of others, thus mimicking the act of sex. When junior men and more senior married women spoke to each other of sex, speech dangerously rehearsed adulterous acts. Even among themselves, women rarely mentioned the word *adultery*, speaking instead in hushed voices of lopiro's secrets (M or S: *siri*).

Second, if knowledge of adultery was for the participants implicit in the ritual itself, these matters remained largely concealed from the foreigners—tourists, NGO workers, and journalists—who attended the ceremonies. Revealing such secrets to foreigners, as Mama Mbenesi suggested, was problematic. Samburu were well aware that foreigners were fascinated with their culture, bodies, and sex lives. In Samburu, stories abounded of books authored by foreign women about their intimate relationships with local young men, and of movies based on such books (Meiu 2011, 103–4). Many locals felt that such productions embarrassed them both in Kenya and internationally. Unsurprisingly, some participants in lopiro were worried about revealing sexual matters to foreigners.

In lopiro, sexual secrecy had to do both with moral expectations of sexual propriety and with concerns over perpetuating ethnic sexual stereotypes. For Mama Mbenesi, the fact that senior wives had spoken explicitly to me, a younger man, about these secrets reenacted the very intimacies the ceremony sought to end. But my being a *white* man also prompted Mama Mbenesi to worry that her age-mates might further fuel the Western fascination with Samburu sex lives. Many Samburu shared her concern. Amid economic uncertainty, they worried that such stereotypes might jeopardize their opportunities to build a future as they tried to access material resources by crafting durable relations to one another, townships, the state administration, and powerful countries abroad. Conscious of the dangers of reproducing ethnic sexual imaginaries, I wish to interrogate precisely how sexuality came to figure in Samburu politics of ethnic belonging. Notwithstanding Mama Mbenesi's concern, reflecting on matters of sexuality is crucial to rethinking the possibilities of belonging in contemporary Samburu.

Participants in lopiro dealt in various ways with the contradictions between, on the one hand, contemporary moral and material dilemmas of social life in the district and, on the other, stereotypes of their sexual Otherness that circulated widely in Kenya and on the global market. Lopiro synthesized these contradictions into new visions of collective belonging. What, then, can lopiro tell us about how ritual actors positioned themselves in relation to globally circulating discourses of their sexual alterity? How did they imagine social life in relation to new inequalities? And how did the actions of participants in lopiro represent their relations with their ethnic group, their region, the state, and the global market?

RUSHING TO THE RITUAL: DESIRE AND FEAR IN LOPIRO CEREMONIES

It was in early December 2010 that I attended my first lopiro ceremony. Peter, a Samburu teacher, called to inform me of "a very important festivity" that was expected to begin in his village the following day. He insisted I join him and his wife at their rural home, explaining that I could learn a great deal about Samburu culture by attending the ceremony. Peter was in his late thirties. He had graduated from the Teacher's Training College, and was the headmaster of a primary school. He had married Nasieku, a former school-teacher who now ran a small shop. Peter and Nasieku had four children. They owned a spacious, five-room house in a middle-class residential neighbor-hood of Maralal. They also owned livestock, which they had entrusted to Peter's relatives in his village. Ever since Peter began tutoring me in Maa lan-guage some years prior, we have become close friends. Often, he invited me to join him on his visits to his rural home to attend ceremonies, to see his par-ents, or to check on the livestock. On these visits, Peter proudly introduced me to his clan mates as his "pupil from America," and enjoyed talking to me for long hours about Samburu ceremonies, kinship, and age sets.

At the time he invited me to attend the lopiro of his clan, Peter had been very sick for more than a year. He had esophageal cancer. A few weeks be-fore lopiro, his cancer metastasized in the liver. He had lost a lot of weight, his liver became visibly enlarged, and his eyeballs became dramatically pro-nounced in his emaciated face. Now he was walking slowly, his thin body resting on a wooden cane, and he put great effort in every word he uttered. On the morning of the ceremony when I arrived at his house to pick him up in a hired taxi, Peter wore one of his best suits, which was now too large on him. His wife, Nasieku, and another woman from the neighborhood were running through the house looking for clothes and beads, joking and laugh-ing. They were in a hurry to get ready for lopiro. Peter himself was impa-tient. "Let's go, let's go!" he urged. "Otherwise we will miss the beginning." I remember thinking that there was something almost sinister in our rush that day. Hurrying seemed amplified by the fear of what we now all knew was Peter's quickly approaching death.

As our taxi approached the site of the ceremony, we saw men and women arrive in large groups from all sides, singing and laughing. "Drive to where that tall flag is!" Peter urged the driver, pointing to the ceremonial flag that had been raised to mark the site of lopiro. Peter, Nasieku, and I looked out the windows of the car. We noticed that for the purposes of the ceremony, all the junior elders—Peter's age-mates—were dressed in clothes and decora-tions characteristic of the morans. "Hey, look," Nasieku laughingly pointed out. "All the Lmooli [the junior elders' age-set name] have gone back to being morans!" Peter nodded. "It's as if they haven't aged at all, after all these years," he said. He looked on, smiling. Some three hundred people were already dancing around the ceremonial flag; their voices resounding through the thick bushes, their rhythmic jumping shaking the ground. "This ceremony," our driver observed, "is the biggest I've ever seen."

Peter and I walked through the crowd. I felt uneasy as I realized that his relatives and friends were greeting him with unconcealed horror in their eyes. After seeing him, some women put their hands over their mouths in shock, then hurried off to mingle with the dancers. On our previous visits, locals had always shaken his hand with the deference and respect usually granted to a headmaster. This time, however, they did not shake his hand. It was as if Peter's body had become contagious with death—its emaciation a sign of failure and depletion and a source of fear in the midst of a ceremony meant to generate life force, fertility, and a sense of trust in the future. When Peter went off alone, Mama Naserian, a local woman I knew well, confessed her horror to me: "*Haiiit* [expression of shock]! He is very sick!" Then she sighed. "It's that 'thing' [M: *ntoki*] which is now killing all our people," she said, as if the name of the ailment had itself become contagious. She meant AIDS. Then Mama Naserian, too, was off to the flag, laughing, singing, and dancing. For Peter and his age-mates, the ceremony provided an opportunity to buy time by ritually reverting to the days when they were all young morans. Thus, they sought to "make life" or "give life" (M: *a-ishu*) and revitalize their relations. Meanwhile, however, for many of the participants in the ceremony, Peter's body was a horrific reminder that they were running out of time, that AIDS "is now killing all our people," and that the future was quickly closing down on them. Hence, everyone seemed in a hurry to dance, sing, and laugh, as if to make a future possible and perceptible in the present.

The dynamic interplay of desire, fear, and rushing offers an important lens through which to examine the wider significance of lopiro ceremonies for their historical context. How did participants in lopiro articulate their desires for a collective future? How did historically specific fears and anxieties play into the ritual imagination of belonging? And what kinds of belonging did people imagine in this context? Lopiro ceremonies took place in times when, as we have seen in previous chapters, sex had become a new, morally dangerous source of miraculous wealth, and foreign commodities, through their unequal distribution, had come to transform relations of gender, age, generation, and kinship. In this context, AIDS became a symptom of the moral failures of persons and families, and a symbol of their perceived inability to embody generative life force. In lopiro, anxieties about sex, commodities, fertility, and life force translated into fear over the possibility of not belonging or the possible disconnection of people from resources circulated by the state and the market.

After attending the lopiro of Peter's clan, I attended two more lopiro ceremonies and gathered extensive information about a fourth. These ceremonies attracted large numbers of participants—people from different villages who, though belonging to the same clan, did not always know one another. People I had not met previously—like Mama Mbenesi—might have imagined that I was a traveler, a development worker, or someone's sponsor. But when I talked with them and they sensed that I shared some of their knowledge about ritual and local issues, they opened up to me and engaged me in long, in-depth conversations about lopiro. In the months following the ceremonies, I carried out short interviews with some twenty men and women who organized lopiro for different clans, as well as daylong interviews with five ritual specialists (M: *kursai*). In addition, my thinking about lopiro developed during long hours of conversation with my research assistants and my friend Elly Loldepe, a Samburu anthropologist.

BRINGING THE PAST INTO THE PRESENT: DRAMA OF ADULTERY IN LOPIRO CEREMONIES

To understand what role sexual intimacy played in imagining and crafting collective belonging in Samburu, it is important to examine how people performed lopiro ceremonies and explore the moral dilemmas at their core. A lopiro lasted four days. On the first day, participants planted a flag in front of the homestead where the ceremony was being held. Throughout the following three days and nights, they ate and danced around that flag. On the fourth day, they exchanged expensive gifts. The ceremony involved two sets of ritual actors: male junior elders and the wives of a preceding, more senior set of elders—the fire-stick elders. Informants pointed out to me that some members of these two age-gender cohorts might have had sexual relations, beginning when the men were morans and the women young wives.

Lopiro began with a ritual reversion of time as the participants attempted to inhabit the time when their adulterous relationships had begun. During the ceremony, the junior elders dressed with the clothes, beads, and head decorations specific to morans. In addition, they applied red ocher (M: *lkaria*) to their necks and heads like the morans. Because the junior elders had given up this attire several years prior, when they had graduated from moranhood in 2005, the sight of them dressed as morans provoked laughter among participants. Like the beach-boy elders I described in previous chapters, who dressed as morans to attract tourists, junior elders who adopted this attire for lopiro also amused onlookers. For the duration of the ceremony, junior elders were expected to observe culinary and spatial prohibitions otherwise associated with the morans. For example, they were prohibited from consuming food seen or touched by women (a prohibition known as M: *lmenong*) and from eating inside the homestead or unaccompanied by age-mates. In this sense, junior elders, most of whom were husbands and fathers, figured in ritual as unattached morans of the "bush," that is, young men who had to spend most of their time outside the homestead. In lopiro, as my interlocutors put it, these elders "went back" (M: *kechukunie*) to being morans, a temporal reversion they cherished with nostalgic enthusiasm.

Similarly, the wives of fire-stick elders smeared red ocher on their necks and wore feathers in their headdresses, both signs of youthfulness. They also wore more strings of beads around their necks than usual. Although most of these women had been married for over twenty years, during the ceremony people addressed them as *nkaibartak*, that is, young wives who had just moved into their husbands' homestead. In this way, my interlocutors said, women, too, "went back" to an earlier stage of their married lives. Therefore, lopiro turned back time—or brought the past forward—by one or two decades, when men were young morans and women newly wedded wives, to engage with unsettling histories of intimacy. Ritual time-traveling, as we shall see, was a way of repairing the past and revitalizing the present.

The wives of fire-stick elders told me that they had begun planning the lopiro in secrecy. First, they chose two women from among themselves to represent them in the ritual roles of Mama Lopiro (M: *ngoto lopiro*) and her Maid of Honor (M: *nchapukera*). Then they secretly chose two younger men to represent the age set of the junior elders in the ritual roles of Mister Lopiro (M: *lpayian lolopiro*, also S: *bwana lopiro*) and his Best Man (M: *lchapukera*). The men and women chosen to play these roles had to be known for their exemplary moral conduct. Together, these four ritual actors reflected ideals of reciprocity and commensality as well as complex ideas about propitious, life-generating numbers (Rainy 1989, 810–11).

Women announced their intentions to organize lopiro several months before the actual ceremony. They did so by ritually "stealing" a personal belonging from the junior elder they had designated to be Mister Lopiro. This ritual took place during another ceremonial occasion that brought together the local clan group. Then, as men and women danced together, Mama Lopiro snatched a possession of Mister Lopiro's and ran off with it. In the past, this would be a decorative feather from the man's headdress. In the Maa language, *lopiro* (pl. *lopir*) means "feather." From there comes the name of the ceremony. But more recently, this belonging could also be a walking stick, a hat, or a wristwatch. Once the women took this object—now generically referred to as a "feather"—they began singing a song to inform everyone that through this gesture, they had initiated a lopiro ceremony. After this ritual, word went around the district that in a certain clan, "the women have taken the feather." Together with the junior elders, the women now persuaded clan members to donate money to buy large quantities of food and gifts.

The ritual act of "taking the feather" from a junior elder had strong erotic connotations. In a mundane context, taking an item from another person and holding on to it expressed one's affective attachment to that person. People believed that personal belongings are imbued with one's bodily substance—smell, sweat, or dirt (all known as M: *latukuny*)—and thus are extensions of one's embodied personhood (Straight 2007b, 69–93). Holding on to someone's belonging was similar to holding on to that person. The ritual of taking the feather expressed women's desire for their lovers. But it also indexed an everyday convention by which women could "steal" (M: *a-purr*) a possession from a secret lover as a way to invite him "to pick it up later," thus creating a context for intimacy. In Maa, the verb *a-purr* can be used interchangeably for "steal" and "seduce" (Spencer 1965, 148), suggesting how appropriating a personal belonging can both express affection and invite intimacy.

On the morning of the ceremony's first day, hundreds of junior elders walked together to the house of Mama Lopiro. They carried a flag (M or S: *bendera*) made out of one or two pieces of fabric and a wooden pole. Upon arriving, the men planted the flag outside Mama Lopiro's compound, where it remained for the four days of the ceremony. Once the flag was raised, the wives of fire-stick elders took it into their possession, surrounded it, and defended it, day and night, for the duration of the ceremony (fig. 17). The women explained that the junior elders now intended to "steal" the flag and run off with it. Whenever men walked by the flag, women hit them with their walking sticks, to everyone's amusement. On the last day of the ceremony, in the early afternoon, all the junior elders gathered and walked toward the flag to "steal" it from the women. A big ritual fight emerged between the junior elders and all the fire-stick elders' wives, now surrounding the flag to defend it. The women hit the men with their sticks and pushed them away from the flag while other clan members and their guests watched, entertained. After a while, the women had to "lose" the fight and allow the men to uproot the flag and, eventually, walk away with it.

The flag, in its own way, also spoke of the secrets of adultery. On some level, the flag indexed the "feather" that the women had stolen from the junior elders. Like the feather, the flag belonged to the junior elders, but the

17. Women defend the flag of Iopiro, December 2010. (Photo by the author.)

women held and defended it. A woman suggested to me that "the flag represents the relationship [S: *uhusiano*] between the mamas and these elders." In
some clans, participants made the flag from two pieces of cloth, explaining
that one piece represented the junior elders and the other the wives of the
fire-stick elders. Also, participants inscribed on the flag the names given by
their clan to the respective age sets of these men and women. In this sense,
the flag tacitly publicized the "secret" of adultery. A ritual specialist told me
that the flag "is borrowed culture from colonialism." Indeed, the colonial administration had used flags to designate the sites of its political rallies and to
make these events "official." Since the 1950s, following the administration's
lead, morans have used flags to mark the sites of their dances. In Iopiro, the
flag marked the location of the ceremony and also "officialized" its public
secrets, if only to those in the know.

The ritual fight between junior elders and the women on the last day of Iopiro had other important connotations. When asked why the women fought
the men for the flag, a woman explained, "The mamas don't want these relationships to end. They love these young men and don't want it to be over."
In light of this logic, by fighting to obtain the flag, the men actually tried
to snatch a bodily extension of themselves from the hands of the women,

thus withdrawing themselves from these relationships. In daily life, a man's snatching his personal belonging from a mistress—whether beads or a cell phone—indicates his wish to terminate their relationship.

The ritual trajectories of the feather and the flag marked at once a temporal reversion and a fusion of the social categories of morans and the young wives. By taking the feather, women invited junior elders to follow them back in time to when their relationships had started, at the quintessential place of adultery, in the bushes beyond a wife's compound. When junior elders arrived at Mama Lopiro's house and planted the flag outside her homestead, they expressed their desire for intimacy. They acted as seducers of wives, sneaking through the bushes onto an elder's homestead, thus overturning boundaries of moral order. Junior elders erected the flag in the bush just as, in everyday life, morans would plant spears in the ground on the site of a sexual encounter, to warn others to stay away. In this sense, in lopiro, the feather and the flag represented what anthropologist Victor Turner (1967, 28, 31) called "dominant symbols," that is, unifiers of "disparate significata" and "fixed points" of the ritual event. The feather and flag congealed the collective passions and conflicts of adultery. By the flag, wives of fire-stick elders danced along with men who—at least for the purposes of the ceremony—figured as their secret lovers. They held these men's hands and, to everyone's amusement, sang verses that satirized their husbands:

Mayieu nanu iyie; nayieu ake lpayian obaiye lkaria!	I don't want you [my husband]; I only want a man who [recently] left the red ocher [i.e., a younger man who has recently been a moran]!
Mayieu nanu . . . Lkuroroi chapu ong'ou nkaji muna abake etuo apa.	I don't want . . . a dirty Lkuroro [husband's age-set name] whose house smells like alcohol long after he left.

Fire-stick elders reacted angrily to their wives' decision to organize lopiro. One elder described these ceremonies to me as "idiocies of the women." I also heard that after women of different clans took the feather, their husbands carried out long debates, wondering, "Why have the stupid women started these old idiocies again?" The wives of fire-stick elders usually anticipated that their husbands would be angry, so they waited to organize lopiro until their husbands had aged enough, so that "they would not have [impulsive] hearts" (M: *meata ninche ltauja*). It quickly became clear to me that by initiating lopiro, women were acknowledging that at least some among them had had intimate relationships with these younger men, and they also were inviting these men to enact their everyday relationships in the ritual drama of lopiro.

At first sight, lopiro exemplifies what Max Gluckman (1954) called "rituals of rebellion," which seemingly overturn social order while, in fact, reproducing a status quo. Lopiro worked ideologically to reinforce patrilineal values by ending adultery. To achieve this, the drama of adultery was first enacted in public view. However, *pace* Gluckman, lopiro did not merely reinforce a social order but generated a space and time in which participants could imagine and contest multiple possible futures. Participants in lopiro engaged with the historical dynamics of intimacy and desire as a way to reenvision and revitalize their relations with one another and an outside world. To understand this, it is important to examine what adultery meant, and what role it played in people's everyday lives.

WHAT MAKES ADULTERY?
INTIMACIES, COMMODITIES, AND LIFE FORCE

Samburu referred to adultery as *loloito*, a noun that derives from the gerund of the Maa verb *a-lo*, "to go" (*a-loito*, "going"), and connotes a perpetual state of movement. From the point of view of male elders, loloito presupposed the uncontrolled (often invisible) sexual mobility of wives, morans, and other male elders as they snuck into each other's compounds or secretly ran off to meet in the "bushes." These intimate mobilities subverted "healthy separations" (Straight 2005, 93–94) between the homestead and the bush, juniors and seniors, the lineage and its outsiders, and thus often challenged the respectability of male elders, who were responsible—individually or as a group—for controlling the boundaries of sexual propriety. Not all extramarital intimacies, however, counted as loloito. For example, relationships between men and concubines, widows, and runaway wives or, until quite recently, those between a woman and her husband's "best man" at the wedding were not loloito. Nor, for that matter, were all forms of adultery equally problematic. Adultery between a man and his age-mate's wife was less contentious, for example, than adultery between a moran and his elder's wife.

Following research in Samburu between 1958 and 1960, Paul Spencer (1965) came to see adultery between morans and young wives as an outcome of the structural contradictions inherent in the "gerontocratic system." Although elders did not allow morans to marry, girls their age were married to junior elders or as second or third wives to more senior elders (137, 137n1). Under these circumstances, through adultery, morans continued relationships with women of their own age while challenging elders' authority and impressing age-mates with their courage (146). For women, relationships with morans contained an element of rebellion against husbands whose authority often seemed unjust (227–28; see also Ott 2004, 137; Straight 2005, 96–97, 99). While everyone knew that this form of adultery existed with every generation, conflicts often arose when elders discovered particular instances of adultery involving their wives. In this sense, what counted as a most salient form of adultery were those intimacies that threatened the hegemony of senior men and their seeming rights in women's sexuality (cf. Llewelyn-Davies 1981, 348; see also Goody 1956).

British colonial administrators formalized the power of senior men to control adultery and thus, to some extent, "subsumed women's voices to male domination in matters of domestic discord and resolution" (Kanogo 2005, 53). Male labor migrants, for example, began turning to native courts and the local police as a way of dealing with the adultery between morans and their wives. Meanwhile, Christian notions of shame and sexual propriety resignified, if only partially, the meanings of loloito. In some contexts, loloito came to be associated with excessive adultery or prostitution (Wanyoike 2011, 191).

More than a simple rebellion against senior men, loloito was also about love and the pleasures of secrecy. As one woman explained to me, "When you are married, the husband no longer treats you in a special way. So you keep something on the side, for your own heart." Part of the pleasures of adultery derived from its being a secret. Adultery was a way to cheat (M: *a-sap*) or steal (M: *a-purr*); it was something one had to cover (M: *a-iyop*; among the Maasai, the derivative *enkyiopo* also refers to adultery). Secret lovers (M: *sintani*, pl. *sintan*) were not just sexual partners but also conversation partners—people with whom one felt comfortable. When a Samburu tells you that "you stretch your legs like in a lover's house" (M: *iche nkeju anaa lotii nkaji e sintan*), it means you are perhaps too comfortable in a particular situation (Da Ros, Pante, and Pedenzini 2000, 26).

In the past four decades, adultery intensified an older convergence between sex and commodities. Secret lovers have long exchanged gifts of milk, meat, beads, and money. These were important material tokens of love, affection, and attachment, part of what Mark Hunter calls "the everyday materiality of sex" (2010, 179–80). Growing inequalities and the proliferation of cash and commodities in rural domestic economies fueled new patterns of adultery (Holtzman 2009, 171, 206). With the strong decline of cattle economies, rural elders found it more difficult to access cash, and sometimes did not meet their families' daily needs for food, tea, or soap, or their wives' desires for perfume, telephone credit, shoes, or clothes. At the same time, men employed as soldiers, police officers, teachers, councillors, traders, or NGO workers, or men married to European women could access such commodities more easily. In this context, sexual intimacies played out more and more through the logic of commodity consumption. Wives could deny their husbands sex if they did not remit money to feed their children, and long-term mistresses claimed cash remittances from their male partners. Like elsewhere in Kenya, educated Samburu women began referring to their secret lovers as "side plans" (S: *mipango ya kando*), a phrase that suggests the importance of material support in addition to—or as part of—erotic pleasure and love.

If sex was generally held to propitiate fertility, health, and well-being, and mothers often encouraged their married daughters to seek lovers as a way of "mixing the herd" (Straight 2005, 97) or giving birth to diverse children, Samburu also believed that adultery was unpropitious (M: *ketolo*). Adultery "mixed the blood" of different households and risked affecting the life force and well-being of those involved (ibid.). It could harm a woman's pregnancy, childbirth, and lactation (99) or, if the female partner came from an unpropitious lineage, lead to the impoverishment or death of a woman's lover or husband (Ott 2004, 136). Thus, another, much less common word for *adultery* I encountered in Samburu was *nkirengenyicho*—a noun derived from the verb *a-irenge*, "to give or mix blood." Furthermore, the unpropitious qualities of adultery passed through objects exchanged for sex. Money received as a gift in exchange for sex was "money of wrongdoings" (M: *shilingini e ngʼok*). Recall that using such money to feed one's family was like inviting the family to partake in the sexual acts in which that money originated—a quintessential act of incest (M: *surupon*) (see chapter 4). Such mixings of blood, sex, and commodities depleted life force, making people and things un-alive (M: *meishu*), in a sense of perpetual self-depletion.

HIV infections, which have been rising in Samburu since the 1990s, only cemented people's perceptions that moral, reproductive sexuality was eroding.[1] Many of my informants were convinced that AIDS is a form of self-depletion prompted by the unpropitious mixing of blood, sex, and commodities in the recent past. Rural men and women perceived AIDS as a "foreign" illness originating in the uncontrolled mobilities of labor migration, prostitution, and everyday adultery. They associated it with the gradual depletion of life force, visible through the loss of bodily weight (Wanyoike 2011, 156). By 2010–11, AIDS signaled that something was going awfully wrong with sex and commodities in the present, lending urgency to organizing lopiro. "There was something bad the elders were seeing," Mama Nabulo explained. She had been the Maid of Honor of the lopiro ceremony of her clan. "If people were to continue with this story [of adultery], something bad would happen."

INTERSECTIONS OF SEX, FEAR, AND FERTILITY IN LOPIRO

But here is an interesting twist to the story. Childless women or those who had not given birth in a while believed that sex with junior elders during the ritual time of lopiro would restore their fertility. When Peter and I were in the car on our way to the lopiro ceremony of his clan, I kept questioning him about the significance of this ceremony, which I did not know much about at the time. Respectfully lowering his voice so that Nasieku would not hear him, he told me that lopiro dealt with the issue of adultery, and that it angered the fire-stick elders very much. "[They] used to hate lopiro," he said. "They hated it very much, because during lopiro, these mamas [wives of the fire-stick elders] were allowed to have sex with these young men [junior elders], and their husbands were not allowed to go there." Peter heard of this kind of ritual sex in the early 1990s, when his clan organized its previous lopiro ceremony. But at that time he was a moran, and like all morans, he was not allowed to attend. In the meantime, however, things had changed. Peter emphasized that "because so many people have now died of AIDS, the elders said that all mamas must be home before the dark."

Indeed, in some lopiro ceremonies I attended, women took an active role in banning ritual sex as a way to curb the spread of AIDS. They knew that the disease had claimed many lives in Samburu. So for them, ritual sex risked further depleting collective life force. A ritual reversion in time was therefore an opportunity to engage not only with the beginnings of adultery within a generation but also with the beginnings of the epidemic in Samburu. "You saw that lopiro of ours?" Mama Nabulo asked me a few days after the ceremony had ended. "The [fire-stick] elders hated it that we have taken the feather. They started worrying about it . . . You know, now, there is that 'thing which makes our bodies fear' [M: *ntoki natureyeki sesen*]." She meant AIDS. "Now, we told the elders from whom we took the feather that there will be none of that [ritual sex]. Those were traditions of the people of the past." Not all women would have agreed with Mama Nabulo, however. Women who did not have any children were less likely to abandon ritual sex than those who were already mothers. For barren women (M: *nkolipi*; pl. *nkolipiono*), the desire to gain fertility, conceive, and become respectable wives sometimes surpassed the fear of AIDS. Ritually transposed into the past, then, participants in lopiro sought both to relive the time when they had been young, attractive, and adventurous and to set straight things which had gone wrong during those days. But inhabiting the past also carried the possibility of reinforcing the very mistakes that have had haunting effects on the present. Would lopiro generate propitious belonging, or would it reproduce old sources of conflict and depletion?

Some participants in the ceremony witnessed the threads of their ritual actions coming apart right when they were struggling to carefully weave them together. Let us recall the horror and panic that Peter's thin, sickly body had generated upon our arrival at the lopiro of his clan. Like Peter, many other wealthy members of the clan had arrived that morning at lopiro from Maralal town, driving their own cars or riding in hired taxicabs. Among rural Samburu, cars have long been associated with the circulation of resources in and out of the district. These circulations were often beyond the control of rural elders and therefore key objects of ritual intervention in lopiro. Since the 1990s, cars and other vehicles have also indexed the circulation of venereal diseases, especially AIDS. In a kakisha folk song of the 1990s, girls threatened to curse cars for taking morans away from the district to Mombasa, and for having them return with gonorrhea, "a disease . . . they have taken from an Italian woman." Cars symbolized the unpredictable movements of both commodities and disease from an imagined core of the world economy: through Mombasa to the global North—a place generically called *nkampo* (from S: *ng'ambo*, meaning "abroad"). When Peter and I arrived at the lopiro, many cars were pulling up to park near the ritual flag, thus— accidentally, perhaps—intruding on the main stage of the ceremony. Turned back in time to engage, among other things, with the emergence of AIDS in their lives, ritual actors might have perceived Peter's arrival as a symbolic reenactment of the mythical arrival of that disease in the district. Like Peter, AIDS had arrived by cars from centers of political and economic power to "[kill] . . . all our people." Peter's arrival in a car as well as his being accompanied by a white anthropologist indexed his engagements with a more powerful foreign place. It was as if he had benefited from the "lands of the foreigners" (Rutherford 2003), and—like the Mombasa morans—eventually returned to his native home to bring disease. In this sense, his accidental infringement upon the ritual scene of lopiro might have come unexpectedly for many participants. Yet they nevertheless acknowledged Peter before quickly moving on. Ritual action remained deeply uncertain as desire and fear collided in its very performance.

CLAN, COUNTY, AND CORPORATION: BELONGING TO THE STATE AND TO THE WORLD

By and large, contemporary lopiro ceremonies dealt with the dilemmas of increasingly impoverished and politically marginalized rural Samburu. Unlike Peter, who benefited from a permanent salary and could afford a middle-class lifestyle in Maralal, men and women in his rural home struggled to obtain cash by trading small livestock, brewing and selling chang'aa, trading charcoal, or requesting cash remittances from better-off relatives in Maralal, Nairobi, or Mombasa (see chapter 2). On our visits to his village, Peter carried several banknotes of KSh 50 (less than $1) in the right pocket of his suit. When relatives or clan mates complained about lacking medicine, cooking fat, or maize flour, he took out a banknote or two and pressed it in their palm with a warm handshake. Nasieku did the same for the women of Peter's clan. Meanwhile, men and women in rural communities sought to multiply and intensify affective relations with wealthier relatives and friends as a way to make ends meet. But because wealthier relatives living in towns, including former Mombasa morans who were not young big men, often failed to send money to rural relatives, elders worried. They knew that the creation of a livable future required access to "foreign" resources, that is, goods from outside Samburu District, through which to sustain lineage, clan, and age-grade relations. The most viable way for Samburu to claim resources in the arena of the state and the market was by being recognized through their ethnic identity. However, for many rural people, lack of resources seemed to undermine the possibility of sustaining the very relations of belonging that they thought of as defining their identity. As relatives with permanent sources of income, like Peter, or the rich, young big men moved to towns and sought social value in tailor-made suits, large houses, and taxi rides, rural elders feared that the relations of kinship which sustained propitious life would fade away.

How were people to claim recognition from the Kenyan state and foreign sponsors when the very foundation of what they saw as Samburu ethnicity—belonging through kinship, age relations, and more—was undermined by unequal access to resources? How were they to foreclose adulterous relationships, and forego the proliferation of ethnic stereotypes of sexual promiscuity, when extramarital relations circulated commodities that were otherwise inaccessible to many households? And how could they assure that political recognition would give all of them access to resources rather than refuel existing inequalities?

The lopiro ceremonies I attended coincided with the writing and pro-mulgation of a new constitution of Kenya in 2010. Pursuing economic lib-eralization reforms, Kenyan legislators drafted a constitution that decen-tralized state administration and distributed political power to regional governments. This reform, they thought, would stimulate local forms of eco-nomic production and attract foreign donors. In the former administrative order, the government appointed the leaders of provinces and districts. In the new order, the residents of the county would elect their own leaders.

The Samburu District had been administrated first by British colonials and later by members of more dominant Kenyan ethnic groups. The new order offered Samburu the possibility of taking more active control of their politico-economic affairs. Locals thought that capitalizing on Samburu ethnic identity and cultural heritage and on the "exotic" savannah landscape of their territory would help them develop tourism as a main source of reve-nue. Not incidentally, Samburu businessmen eventually used footage from the 2010 lopiro ceremonies on DVDs to advertise their county to investors in Europe. But if the future Samburu County was to become an "ethnic cor-poration" (Comaroff and Comaroff 2009), how, in the new order, could re-sources be made to circulate more widely and also encompass rural commu-nities?

As people began competing over the emerging possibilities of the new order, rural elders quickly turned to their respective clans. Members of larger clans hoped to use their demographic advantage to elect one of their own in the position of county governor (C. G.). Smaller clans sought to forge alli-ances with one another and with larger clans to gain seats in the County As-sembly. In preparation for the elections of March 2013 (when the district would officially become a county), the leaders of different clans summoned all their male elders to secret meetings. To coerce clan mates into pursuing their decisions, elders used the traditional curse (M: *ldeket*) (on the elders' use of the curse more generally, see Spencer 1965, 184–209). They threatened to curse to death any clan member who would not comply with their decision to elect a particular candidate. Youth in towns, businessmen, and others viewed this emerging clan politics with great skepticism. In the face of these contes-tations, rural male elders soon realized that if their political strategies were to be effective, then re-creating identification with and devotion to the clan was an urgent imperative.

Lopiro ceremonies constituted ritual occasions to regenerate affective ties of belonging among clan members, including town-based relatives. Although male elders were at first furious with women who initiated lopiro ceremonies, they soon found these ceremonies ideal contexts for political mobilization. As inequality, adultery, and disease undermined claims to political recognition and as clans began competing with one another for political alliances and economic connections to the state, lopiro emerged as sites where elders mobilized clan membership to achieve new goals. Samburu who were members of parliament, councillors, and others also turned to lopiro, hoping to gain the support of particular clans for their upcoming campaigns for positions in the county administration. They sponsored and attended these ceremonies and gave speeches that they hoped would build electoral support. But could Samburu elders really come together as what they called one flock (M: *mboo obo*) when conflicts over adultery and limited access to money not only divided them but also fueled ethnosexual stereotypes?

For elders, the possibility of political engagement in matters of government administration and, hence, access to foreign resources depended on their clan's ability to effectively fashion itself as a law-abiding representative unit of Samburu. Rural elders' turn to clan politics as well as the organization of lopiro ceremonies most likely emerged from Samburu's deep anxiety over their increasing political and economic marginalization. This state of affairs was echoed by Frantz Fanon ([1952] 2008), who wrote that the colonial subject is permanently faced with a fear of "abandonment." Unable to "take pleasure in his insularity," he must seek recognition through the very same hegemonic structures that are the source of his oppression and marginalization (3, 33). "Others have betrayed and thwarted him," Fanon noted, "and yet it is only from these others that he expects any improvement of his lot" (55). In a dialectical process akin to the Hegelian master-slave relation, the colonial subject "wants to have himself recognized" by the structures that he belongs to, and thus recognizes those structures as sources of salvation (199). Thus, for the colonial subject "there is only one way out, and it leads to the white world" (33). Similarly, for rural Samburu in postcolonial Kenya, to imagine a future was to be recognized by external hegemonic structures, such as the state and the market, and thus to gain access to resources and rights. But, *pace* Fanon, rural Samburu did not seek herewith to have "white skins" by producing worlds that mimicked those of Kenya middle classes or more powerful countries abroad—what Fanon (29, 80) described as a "desire for lactification." Rather, they sought to engage the Kenyan state and the global market through the mediating frame of their local modes of belonging, and thus to reproduce these local attachments.

ADULTERY, ETHNOSEXUALITY, AND
THE POLITICS OF BELONGING

As ritual actors publicly engaged in unsettling aspects of their intimate lives, they also had to position themselves in relation to enduring discourses of their ethnosexuality that have long shaped their terms of belonging to the colonial and postcolonial state. Adultery figured centrally in how colonials imagined Samburu ethnosexuality, and it also informed colonial strategies of control and reform. Spencer argued that "when the tribe came properly under British protection and inter-tribal fighting was no longer necessary for survival," the conflicts between male elders and morans were amplified, in part, because of adultery: "The Kiliako [age set initiated in 1921] were . . . the first age-set to devise songs which were unintelligible to the [male] elders"; through these they planned sexual encounters with the elders' wives (1965, 148). Meanwhile, Spencer suggested, "the Kimaniki [age set initiated in 1948] have been troublesome, committing adultery as never before" (ibid.). Responding to a perceived rise of adultery, male elders collaborated with administrators to devise new ways to curb such intimacies (Simpson 1996). Charles Chenevix-Trench noted that although "the African Court Elders were all illiterate" and "ignorant of the laws of evidence," they were "terrific experts on adultery" (1964, 144). In 1956, for example, they received the support of the administration to ban a song genre called *ntoo*, through which they thought morans arranged meetings with their wives, using secret sexual idioms (Spencer 1965, 147). In this way, adultery became a key marker of sexual alterity and a central site for inscribing colonial disciplinary power.

Lacking written sources on lopiro's history and with only a few vague oral recollections recorded during my research, it is difficult to assess how the colonial politics of adultery shaped the ceremony. The younger men and women I interviewed told me lopiro has been around since time immemorial. But some of my elderly interlocutors suggested that lopiro emerged only toward the end of colonial rule. Even if the latter were right, however, lopiro in its current form must have emerged from older ritual events that were brought together in new ways. Numerous ritual elements I encountered in lopiro have existed in Samburu in the past and also among other Maa-speaking ethnic groups.[2] Furthermore, unlike other clan ceremonies, such as initiations, lopiro was not mandatory for every generation. Hence, it could be that some of my interlocutors had not encountered it in their youth.

Be that as it may, there is some historical evidence that the colonial politics of adultery in the mid-twentieth century shaped some aspects of lopiro.

Some elders suggested that lopiro in its current form emerged from what had been, in the first part of the twentieth century, various ceremonies that brought together two or more clans.[3] At that time, reproducing solidarities between clans had been much more important, for it allowed different clans to collaborate in mobilizing militarily against more powerful, neighboring ethnic groups. In the late-colonial context, as the colonial state took over matters of security, clans started competing with each other over the political favors of state administrators. Colonials used clans as categories of control, appointed chiefs for each, and favored individual clans according to their elders' ability to control their women and morans. The colonial emphasis on clans generated new kinds of competition between different clans, and intensified elders' commitment to emphasizing clan solidarity. These factors played an important role in transforming what had once been older inter-clan ceremonies into the intra-clan ceremony of lopiro. But more evidence is necessary to prove this with certainty.

Through the discourses on Samburu adultery, reformists not only posited a certain Samburu ethnosexuality but also shaped the strategies of control and the terms of recognition through which administrators, Samburu elders, women, and morans claimed and contested belonging to the polity. In this sense, lopiro synthesized the old and the new—rituals of belonging and colonial discourses of adultery and ethnosexuality. This dialectical relationship between ethnosexuality and belonging also shaped how Samburu men and women eventually came to craft belonging. As rural Samburu sought to reimagine their relations to the state and the market, discourses of sexual alterity continued to shape the conditions under which they belonged. Lopiro responded to these conditions to set in order the moral foundations of collective life. I will return now to the rituals of this ceremony to show how its participants repositioned sex and commodities according to what they imagined were desirable forms of belonging.

RITUAL INTERVENTIONS ON SEX AND COMMODITIES

The most spectacular part of lopiro was the ritual exchange of commodities on the fourth day of the ceremony. After the junior elders uprooted the flag, all participants entered the homestead of Mama Lopiro. A senior elder recited a blessing and prayed for the fertility and life force of the clan. Then, Mama Lopiro and the Maid of Honor, representing all the wives of the fire-stick elders, came to the front. They held out the "feather"—in this case, a hat—that they had "stolen" from Mister Lopiro. Shivering visibly with emotion, the women returned this object to Mister Lopiro, thus indicating that the adulterous relationships between their respective age-gender cohorts had come to an end. Then the main ritual actors exchanged expensive gifts. Mama Lopiro and the Maid of Honor gave Mister Lopiro and the Best Man a motorbike and a bicycle, respectively (fig. 18). The women also gave them tailor-made neotraditional garments, snuffboxes, decorated clubs, and helmets. Junior elders then gave Mama Lopiro and the Maid of Honor strings of beads, white fabric decorated with beads, red skirts, beaded leather belts, shoes, purses, wallets, umbrellas, and leather covers for their cell phones (fig. 19). The four main actors also exchanged gifts of cash, from about $350 to $700 in Kenyan currency.

We may interpret these ritual exchanges in three ways. First, we may see them as attempts to redirect desires from sex to commodities. As the main ritual actors violently "shivered" (M: *keikirikira*), a senior elder, acting as master of ceremonies, encouraged them—over a microphone—to calm down. Then he praised each gift in Maa, joking and entertaining his audience:

> Elders! Elders! We are seeing motorbikes right here in front of us. We are seeing bicycles and other beautiful decorations. Just look at these things! These [are] things that the [junior] elders will use to go into politics. These [junior] elders will campaign in politics. Thank you so much, women! . . . These children of ours [referring to the women] have produced something very beautiful here. We have seen a motorbike that is worth thousands. We have seen a bicycle that is worth a lot of money. Clap your hands! Clap your hands, Lorokushu [clan name]!

Presenting and praising every item, the master of ceremonies encouraged these two age-gender cohorts to rejoice in the pleasures of the commodities, which he offered in lieu of the pleasures of ritual participants' secret intimacies. Although commodities that circulated through adultery disrupted reproductive sexuality, it was through commodities that sex could be contained within the family. In this sense, substituting commodities for sex more readily served the purposes of clan politics. This ritual appropriates modalities of power that, in the present, circulate widely throughout Africa. Rosalind Morris (2008, 212), writing of South Africa in the time of AIDS, argues that the "substitution of commodity consumption for sex" is a wider trend that allows for the "multiplication of avenues of transference" of desire and opens up new possibilities of satisfaction and pleasure (see also Singer 1993, 37–38).

Second, we may see the gift exchange as an attempt to reconfigure how

18. Junior elders receive a motorbike and a bicycle from the women during lopiro, December 2010. (Photo by the author.)

19. Women receive gifts of fabric from the junior elders during lopiro, December 2010. (Photo by the author.)

foreign commodities circulated and shaped the Samburu's lived worlds. These commodities had long been present in Samburu. "These are beautiful things," one woman told me. "People like these things because they are fashion [M: *pachon*]." But because they were not accessible to everyone, these commodities also spoke of the district's new inequalities. Motorbikes, tailor-made clothes, and large sums of money were common among the businessmen and political leaders in towns. In rural areas, however, they were the privilege of a few rich people, among whom the richest were often the so-called young big men in relationships with European women. These men often failed to circulate wealth in ways that included poorer kin and agemates. Fearing the depletion of their own wealth, young big men typically engaged in reciprocity with other young big men, excluding poorer households. In lopiro, rural men and women responded to these new patterns of commodity circulation. For the organization of the ceremony and for the gifts exchanged between the four main ritual actors, all married men and women of the clan had to contribute money (about $5–$10). But the young big men were asked for the highest contributions (about $30–$50). In this way, rural men and women sought to reroute cash through channels that emphasized clan solidarity. After the ceremony, the four main actors redistributed this money as small cash gifts to the poor families of their clan. They did this even though, in an everyday context, locals considered the young big men's cash the money of wrongdoings, because it originated in the tourist commodification of moran sexuality. But by rerouting this money through lopiro for the collective good, they purified it of its unpropitious qualities.

Finally, we may interpret the ritual gift exchange as a way of anchoring commodities in the homestead and mobilizing their imagined power to produce recognition and belonging in a wider world. The homestead (M: *nkang*) iconically indexed the ideal polygynous family unit, headed by an elder. But the homestead was also a marginal place in relation to an imagined center of economic power. Hence, in lopiro, the Samburu homestead figured in moral opposition to the outer places of the bush, the market, and the state.[4] By bringing expensive commodities and exchanging them in the middle of the homestead, ritual actors not only anchored the powers of these goods in kinship but also made kinship attachments central to their belonging to a world beyond Samburu. As the master of ceremonies suggested, the exchanged commodities were beautiful things that "the elders will use to go into politics"—referring here to formal state politics (S: *siasa*). Moreover, during the gift exchanges, junior elders placed multiple high-denomination banknotes (KSh 1,000) into the headdresses of Mama Lopiro and her Maid of Honor,

20. Junior elders place banknotes in Mama Lopiro's headdress, Samburu, August 2011. (Photo by E. Loldepe.)

allowing money thus to transmit its regenerative capacities to the women who sought fertility (fig. 20). In this way, ritual actors transformed foreign commodities into new sources of reproduction and life force. The poetics of these rituals suggest a world in which foreign commodities do not need to alienate rural Samburu or remain morally opposed to propitious forms of belonging, but—to the contrary—could potentially come to sustain it in various ways.

Throughout the second half of the twentieth century, the ritual exchanges of lopiro grew spectacularly in proportions. The goods' exchange value as well as their quantities grew with every cycle of the ceremony. If in the 1970s participants exchanged cloth, tobacco, and soap, by the 1990s they added bicycles. In 2010, they included motorbikes, and participants were trying to purchase cars and pickup trucks. The inflation of the gifts' value and the intensification of the ritual around the commodity exchange were triggered, in part, by two sets of desires. First, members of different clans tried to outdo each other by offering higher sums of money and more expensive, more numerous gifts, as well as organizing larger, more conspicuous ceremonies. The prestige of each clan relative to others was centrally reflected in the proportions of its lopiro. In the context of the clan politics engendered by the new administrative order, lopiro ceremonies became important statements of power and claims to recognition for their organizers. Second, a lopiro congealed the clan's material power in relation to a larger world inhabited by its members. This world was constantly transforming, at once intensifying the circulation of commodities and excluding the poor from their consumption. In this context, clan members mobilized resources, purchased expensive commodities, and threw large ceremonies as a way to challenge the sharp material inequalities that informed mundane life—its unsettling patterns of desire and disease—in Samburu. And because these inequalities have risen dramatically in the last few decades with the effects of land privatization, the decline of cattle economies, the rise of unemployment, and the commodification of moran ethnosexuality, so too have lopiro ceremonies.

THE RITUAL RUSH: EROTIC PERFORMANCE AND COLLECTIVE BELONGING IN LOPIRO

Ritual constitutes a central mechanism for the production of belonging in Africa and beyond. Structural-functionalist anthropologists theorized ritual as a central means of social reproduction and political organization. Ritual, they argued, perpetuates the polity by alleviating internal conflicts and contradictions and by cultivating emotional devotion to collective values and representations (Gluckman 1954, 1962; Leach 1954; Lienhardt 1961, Middleton 1960; V. Turner 1967, 1969; M. Wilson 1959). Sexual intimacies played an important role in enforcing or subverting power and authority, and therefore sex has long been a central object of ritual intervention (Beidelman 1997; Heald 1999; Kratz 1994; V. Turner 1967). More recent studies approach ritual as a deeply historical and inherently multivocal practice through which subjects create social worlds by negotiating moral and material transformations, emerging possibilities and exclusions, and identities and inequalities (Argenti 2007; Bloch 1986; Cole 2001; Comaroff 1985, Hunt 1999; Ngwane 2004; Thomas 2003; H. White 2004). I suggest that rituals may constitute powerful ways of building what Mimi Sheller (2012) calls "citizenship from below," that is, employing embodied performances to negotiate inclusion into various political and economic arenas.

If ritual represents a way of acting out claims to belonging, its rhythms and affects tell important stories about the kinds of belonging that participants desire. Participants in lopiro sought to produce clan solidarity, fertility, and life force while reshaping desires for sex and commodities. But ritual action often seemed to fail just as it was unfolding. This, then, generated fear and anxiety among participants. Recall how, in the beginning of this chapter, Peter and Nasieku had been in a hurry to get to the lopiro, as if to get away from Peter's quickly approaching death. Similarly, participants in lopiro were in a rush to dance, laugh, and intensify the very speed of ritual action when faced with the signs of its failure. Peter's sick body, like the bodies of "madmen" or the discovery of breaches of ritual abstinence during lopiro, prompted people to turn their backs on and literally run away from what they saw as possibilities of the ritual's failure. Fear of failure was also a fear of collective abandonment and further marginalization. It was as if, ritually turned back in time, people were now quickly running out of time. So people rushed to engage ritual more fully, more intensively.

Rosalind Morris argues that "the rush" has become an affective orientation, which works through risk discourses, to displace panic (2008, 208–9, 223). In the context of a retracting labor market and the AIDS epidemic in South Africa, panic in the face of death incited people to speculate on possible futures and to hurriedly invest in some sort of social value (ironically, in the case of South Africa, death insurance schemes). Morris argues that "the rush is the affect of a speculative economy" (209), an embodied subjective orientation informed by both risk and panic. Similarly, in lopiro, fear and panic in the face of collective abandonment generated an embodied rush to make an ethnic future more readily perceptible.

In a rush to leave unpropitious occurrences, objects, and relations behind and more quickly project themselves into a desired future, participants in lopiro created a sense of what Victor Turner called "communitas" (Turner 1969, 94–165) in the affective and sensual dimensions of their dances and ritual exchanges. Jafari Allen (2011) offers the term *transcendent erotics* to refer to "a sensuous practice that includes the deployment of sexualities pitched and styled to play various games more effectively or to at least less painfully experience physically or materially marginal circumstances" (95). In this sense, Allen argues, "erotics can be a catalyst for the creation of community" (99). A "transcendent erotics" transpired in the dances and rituals of lopiro, as people sought to imagine and live an alternative experience to their current predicament. In this sense, the "erotic" in *ethno-erotic economies* speaks, not solely of how tourists invested the bodies of young Samburu men with sensuality and sexuality, but also of how desire, fear, and rushing intersected in the material and affective textures of ceremonies like lopiro. Such erotic intersections carry the potential of imagining and actualizing collective belonging in myriad new ways. In lopiro, belonging emerged precisely from this eroticized ritual play in which a strong desire for political recognition and an acute fear of abandonment generated an embodied rush and therewith a sense of affective attachment to people, places, customs, and imagined futures.

Lopiro ceremonies expressed, among other things, anxieties of rural Samburu men and women in the face of their increasing political and economic marginalization. They provided political engagement with a particular social and economic context in which the commodification of ethnosexuality reshaped the lives of many Samburu. Samburu have long dealt with colonial representations of their ethnosexuality and tried to imagine futures *through* and *around* them. Representations of ethnosexuality also shaped their terms of belonging to the colonial and postcolonial state. During my research, postcolonial subjects engaged in something like lopiro attempted to grasp the contradictions of living at once for the self and for the Other, at once through local expectations of respectability and well-being and stereotypes of ethnosexuality and cultural Otherness.

ONCE THE RUSH HAS PASSED: EPILOGUE

Only one week after the lopiro ceremony of Peter's clan had ended, I was once more in one of the many cars and hired taxis that were driving people from Maralal to Peter's village. Peter had died, and we were taking his body to his father's compound for burial; the elders of his clan had already dug his grave. Local clan members might have perceived the arrival of Peter's body— once more by car—as pointing yet again to their increasingly fragile relation with an outside world that claimed their young men and returned—by vehicles—disease and death.

In the middle of his father's farm, schoolteachers, businessmen, local councillors, and young big men from town stood around Peter's coffin and gave speeches to one another in English and Swahili, languages spoken by only a few of his rural relatives. Local clan members stood to the side, by the bushes on the margins of the farm, as the wealthier, more influential guests from town took over the central scene of the ritual. I read this spatial arrangement as pointing to how the imaginaries of the previous week's lopiro remained, in fact, utopian. The desires of the lopiro participants to tame the circulations of commodities, to undo inequalities, and to generate moral relations of belonging sat in sharp contrast to the inequalities informing the funeral guests' grouping. But it would be wrong to say that the ritual had ultimately failed. During the meal that followed Peter's burial, locals remembered the lopiro with great enthusiasm and joy. "Hai-ai-ai, what a beautiful ceremony it was!" Mama Naserian recalled. "Our people have done something beautiful indeed." As Mama Naserian saw it, something had transpired from the lopiro of the previous week into the present. Maybe it was the fact that, even if they could not really affect directly—or, at least, not as quickly as they would want—current inequalities or circulations of sex, commodities, and disease, members of the local clan group were all together, sharing their historical predicament, even as they dug Peter's grave and prepared the food for his funeral.

Conclusion

Locked in this suffocating reification, I appeal to the Other so that his liberating gaze, gliding over my body suddenly smoothed of rough edges, would give me back the lightness of being I thought I had lost, and taking me out of the world put me back in the world.—FRANTZ FANON, *BLACK SKIN, WHITE MASKS*

On a Friday evening in March 2011, a group of Samburu men departed for their dance performance at the Bamburi Beach Hotel, south of Mtwapa. While the dancers waited in front of the hotel to be allowed to enter, a European woman approached Boniface, a young moran, asking if she could take his picture. After she photographed him, she thanked him and left. But Boniface called after her, hoping she would purchase some beads from him. Seeing this, Lkeseyion, an elder of the Lkuroro age set—the fire-stick patrons of the morans—scolded Boniface for disturbing the tourist. "Don't upset the mzungu, or else we will all get in trouble with the hotel," he supposedly said. Boniface got angry and snapped at the elder: "Is she the mzungu of your mother? Or, why are you telling me what to do?" A fight ensued. Elders of the Lmooli and Lkuroro age sets fought with the morans of the Lkishami age set until the hotel security guards intervened.

The following evening, I joined the same group of dancers at the Bahari Beach Hotel. Tension was brewing among them. They walked in small groups of two or three at a distance from one another. Before entering the hotel for the scheduled dance performance, the dance-group leaders—two junior elders—called for an emergency meeting in front of the resort. They had been absent the previous evening, and so asked to be told what had happened. Everyone sat down on the lawn by the hotel gate. Different men stood up, one by one, and spoke. Lkeseyion and other elders said that the morans were disrespectful, and that they were causing trouble for everyone in the group. Meanwhile, Boniface and other morans blamed the elders for compromising their chances to meet white women. After listening to both parties, one of the leaders, Jeff, stood up. He was angry. "Stop arguing over who is an elder and who is a moran!" he said, gesturing violently with his knobkerrie. "If you want to destroy our business, why don't you all go and work as watchmen? Here in Mombasa, there is no difference between the Lkishami, the Lmooli, and the Lkuroro. Those are things of home [M: *ntokitin ee nkang*]. If you want to call us all morans, call us all morans! If you want to call us all elders, call us elders! We are all morans. We are all elders. We are all the same. So just stop arguing over these things."

For this dance-group leader, performing touristic moranhood at beach resorts and sustaining access to hotels and cultural villages were not immediately compatible with the age-grade relations that were otherwise so central to belonging in Samburu. As an elder and a fire-stick patron of the morans, Lkeseyion thought he was more entitled than anyone else to scold Boniface for what he thought was inappropriate behavior. And he expected Boniface to remain quiet and defer to his authority as a fire-stick patron. At coastal resorts, elders complained that morans were more disobedient and disrespectful than they would have been at home. They explained the morans' behavior as a result of both their financial independence and the poor moral standards of coastal life. Meanwhile, young morans like Boniface laughed at elders like Lkeseyion who, for purposes of tourism, proudly dressed as morans decades after they had become elders. These young men explained that they refused to accept the authority of these "beach-boy elders," because they did not consider them morally exemplary or respectable. To emphasize this point, morans on the coast often used the expression "There are no elders in Mombasa. All the elders are at home" (M: *Metii lpayeni Mombasa. Netii lpayeni pooki nkang*).

Performing moranhood for tourist consumption entailed a set of erasures necessary for reproducing the possibility of this very kind of performative labor. Such erasures entailed, among other things, the temporary bracketing of generational inequalities and differences. The fact that, on the coast, elders dressed as morans when they performed for tourists reflected this momentary concealment of differences in age-grade status. As one of the group's leaders, Jeff made this explicit when he told the dancers that for purposes of business, "we are all the same." In other words, dancers were expected to leave behind—in the privacy of their lives back home in Samburu—claims to age-set belonging and gerontocratic authority. Bringing such claims to the coast could jeopardize their access to tourist money.

Yet Jeff's words reflect a central irony inherent in the commodification of moran ethnosexuality: while men involved in tourism were expected to put aside differences of age and generation and see themselves as equal, they were anything but equal in matters of age. There are at least two reasons for this. First, men who were physically young were more appealing to tourists and had much higher chances of finding foreign partners to sponsor them. As men aged, however, their ability to embody desirable ethnosexuality depleted itself irreversibly. Beach-boy elders knew that relative to younger men, they stood little chance of finding foreign partners for transactional sex or marriage. Sidelined by a global sexual economy that located value in youthful bodies, they tried nevertheless to make some money by dancing and selling souvenirs. Second, with the rise of the commodification of moran ethnosexuality, age sets and age grades gained novel importance for Samburu. In this context, people associated age sets and age grades with durable forms of social value, that is, with practices and relations that sustained life and prosperity over long periods of time. So people turned to age relations, and for different reasons: young big men wished to convert their wealth into the respectability of elderhood; beach-boy elders wished to save face, as it were, vis-à-vis locals who questioned their respectability; and rural men and women (as they affirmed in lopiro ceremonies, for example) hoped to anchor themselves in local social worlds and amplify their chances for better lives in the future. Samburu, then, had to navigate the emerging contradictions between sexual markets of male youthful bodies, the growing importance of customary forms of age and generation, and the subversive means through which different people produced respectability.

The irony entailed by these social dynamics of age and generation is emblematic of the contradictions that are generated by and, in turn, drive ethno-erotic economies. One such contradiction lies in the fact that those engaged in ethno-erotic commodification—whether directly or indirectly—must reconcile two sets of competing orientations. On the one hand, they are oriented toward an outside world whose recognition and resources are necessary for the reproduction of their own local worlds. On the other hand, they are oriented toward forms of autochthony and ethnoregional belonging that define good, auspicious life, their ability to reproduce and thrive. This double orientation resonates, in part, with what Frantz Fanon ([1952] 2008) described as a binary racial consciousness. For Fanon, this type of consciousness emerges when the black colonial subject desires the recognition of his white master as a condition for his own being and emancipation. Colonial subjects are thus split between an existence for the self and an existence for the other; they desire to be recognized by the very same structures that are the source of their oppression, and they fear the possibility of being abandoned by power. For, Fanon said, "the black man cannot take pleasure in his insularity." For him, "there is only one way out, and it leads to the white world. Hence the constant preoccupation with attracting the white world, his concern with being as powerful as the white man" (33). Somewhat similarly, postcolonial Samburu desire the recognition of the state, the global market, and the global North as a condition for a collective future. This is a world that Samburu perceive as external to their own local worlds, yet a world that is richer and more powerful than they are. While not always white per se (e.g., the postindependence Kenyan state), this outer world is nevertheless structured by "White Global supremacy" (Pierre 2013). And it is in and around such global racist hierarchies that the postcolonial subjects I described in this book sought to make a living, gain political influence, and access economic resources.

Yet the desire of Samburu men to have intimate relationships with white women is much more complex than what Fanon ([1952] 2008, 45, 85) described as "hallucinatory lactification"—a desire to "whiten skins" or "become white" through the love and recognition of a white partner. Although some Samburu men in relationships with European partners no doubt enjoyed the desirability and influence that they sometimes acquired vis-à-vis local women and others, their desires for European partners cannot be reduced to a Fanonian "hallucinatory lactification." For they did not seek to "whiten skins" as such—whether by appropriating what they saw as Western culture or otherwise. Rather, they sought to reproduce, if in new ways, attachments to ethnic regions through custom, kinship, ritual, and respectability. These modes of attachment, seen from afar, marked Samburu as racial, ethnic, and cultural Others in relation to foreigners and other Kenyans. But these attachments were also about much more than what these outsiders cared for or even understood. While tourist markets, for example, valued Samburu dances and moran sexuality, Samburu's investments in ritual, clans, age sets, and life force pointed to a desire to sustain social worlds that were autochthonous. It is suggestive, perhaps, that Samburu referred to those who departed from some of the principles of such attachments—for example, middle-class Samburu—as "black whitemen" (M: *musunku orok*).

The idiom of the white blackman worked as a critique of those who seemingly disinvested themselves from custom and localist belonging. And it also made custom central to autochthonous attachments—a prerequisite for appropriating emerging flows of global capital and power.

Although global white supremacy is a condition of the possibility of ethno-erotic economies, the latter cannot be adequately understood if reduced to racial binaries. Rather, as I have shown, ethno-erotic economies are based on a set of multiple shifting lines of inclusion and exclusion that continuously transform subjectivities and attachments in unexpected ways. Samburu District, let us recall, has long been marginalized within both the colonial and the postindependence Kenya—nearly cut off from state welfare or investments in infrastructure and security. Unlike southern Kenyans, those living in northern regions had relatively minimal opportunities to engage in labor or the national market economy. Colonial and postcolonial ideologies of cultural and sexual Otherness legitimized, in part, the marginalization of northerners like Samburu. But with growing markets of ethnosexuality and culture since the 1980s, some Samburu found new means of empowerment and livelihood by performing their ascribed and assumed Otherness. Able to accumulate more wealth than unemployed youths elsewhere in Kenya, young big men formed a new center of power and authority in the north. They thus subverted to some extent the state's politics of ethnoregional marginalization. Yet they also engendered new criteria of exclusion. Because moran ethnosexuality was the privilege of *young men*, it disqualified from the outset women, older men, and non-Maa people more generally from participating in ethno-erotic exchanges. Those who were left out from these new economic possibilities struggled to gain access to the resources of young big men. Some women became their mistresses or wives, others worked as their housemaids. Male elders sought to obtain money by granting rich morans the ritual initiations that they desired or, in coastal towns, by leading ethnic associations and managing the finances of Mombasa morans. Other elders worked for young big men as watchmen, herders, farmers, drivers, or construction workers. Thus, men and women made this money circulate more widely in Samburu, constantly drawing and shifting lines of exclusion. By reflecting on the moral value of this particular money, they also expanded the reaches of ethno-erotic economies.

Locals needed access to the money of the Mombasa morans and the young big men; conversely, these men needed access to kinship relations and rituals that would grant them respectability and belonging in Samburu.

But even as young men found themselves privileged by a global sexual economy, the fact that they had sex for money weakened their claims to inclusion in Samburu social worlds. Samburu, in villages and towns, at first distanced themselves from and questioned the moral qualities of the money, styles, and livelihoods of the Mombasa morans. Associating these men with the unpropitious powers of "sex out of place" and coastal sorcery, they were reluctant to grant them too quickly the privileges of full membership in the social worlds of their regions. Locals used gossip, scandal, or satirical folk songs to inform these men—if sometimes only indirectly—that their actions and desires were not readily acceptable to locals, or quite compatible with the social worlds locals wished to build. Finding themselves somewhat excluded within the ethno-region to which they wished to belong, these men entered a Faustian bargain of sorts with those whose recognition and respect they sought. Together, they struggled to reimagine what respectability and belonging meant, and how money produced through ethno-erotic exchanges could be converted into valuable relations and attachments. This Faustian bargain—its exchanges of money, care, intimacy, and respectability—articulated different parts of ethno-erotic economies, bringing coastal tourist markets and northern ethno-regions, among other social spaces, into an open-ended dialectical relationship.

In thinking of ethno-erotic economies as premised on and driven by a set of dialectical relationships, I do not wish to posit that such economies constitute an integrated system. Quite to the contrary. I chose this approach, first of all, because *dialectics* refers to an analytical method that underscores how, at particular moments in time, different discourses, practices, desires, and cultural representations come into various contradictions with one another. Such contradictions then generate new forms of sociality and subjectivity, but also new paradoxes, disarticulations, and conflicts. The point here is not to think of such phenomena as systemic, bounded, or static, but precisely to challenge such presuppositions by emphasizing their open-ended, relational transformations. Second, dialectical thinking also allows for a critique of hegemonic suppositions inherent in social and cultural phenomena. In a time when commodity logics deepen essentialist understandings of people such as Samburu—their ethnicity, culture, and sexuality—and fetishize their difference (i.e., presenting it as something that is within them and has little or nothing to do with global history, the market, or the state), it is crucial to explore how different phenomena affect or transform one another while synthesizing longer histories of material and ideological contradiction.

A dialectical exercise, then, as Steven Caton (1999, 15) points out (drawing on the Frankfurt school), helps identify how a certain phenomenon "seems to be engaged in a criticism of its *own* hegemonic project."

::::

At the beginning of my research, I struggled to grasp why Samburu men did not migrate to Europe, as had so many other young men and women from Kenya and elsewhere in Africa. I wanted to understand why most of them preferred to return to the marginal areas of northern Kenya, and why they invested so much money and energy in forms of custom and respectability that initially worked to exclude them. That other Samburu made significant efforts to incorporate these men in their social worlds puzzled me, especially because they did not seem to agree with their sexual economic pursuits. Part of the answer, I eventually learned, lay with the fact that young men who made money through foreign partners could more easily acquire authority and prestige in the economically marginal areas of northern Kenya than they could, say, on the coast, in Nairobi, or in Europe. Many of my informants thought that if they were to go to Europe, they would work menial jobs and live in relatively marginal circumstances. But in Samburu—precisely because of the region's long history of political and economic marginalization—their money had higher value. It was also due to this history of geopolitical marginalization that the money of these men became an important—though not unproblematic—resource for many poorer locals. And so, converting money into belonging and belonging into money, Samburu intensified their struggles to define ethno-regional attachments and autochthony.

A turn toward autochthonous or ethno-regional belonging represents an important outcome of globalization and the market reforms of late capitalism. "In Africa," Peter Geschiere (2009, 21) argues, "this penchant for 'community,' tradition, and 'chiefs' seems to be a logical consequence of a drive towards decentralization. If one wants to bypass the state and reach out to 'civil society,' local forms of organization and 'traditional' authorities seem to be the obvious points of orientation." "What is at stake," Geschiere claims, "is less a defense of the local than efforts to exclude others from access to the new circuits of riches and power" (26). Furthermore, in some African contexts—as elsewhere in the global South—postcolonial subjects have discovered that their ethnicity and culture carry market value. The commodification and incorporation of ethnic identity and cultural difference, John and Jean Comaroff (2009, 142) argue, "without doubt, opened up new means of producing value, of claiming recognition, of asserting sovereignty, of giving affective voice to belonging; this, not infrequently, in all-but-total absence of alternatives." In this context, the commodification identity drives a turn toward ethno-regional belonging, and this kind of belonging becomes a source of marketable identity.

Sexuality makes matters even more complex. For when sexuality converges with ethnic and cultural identity in the commodity form (to produce ethnosexual commodities), it often undermines the possibility of individual or collective belonging. In East Africa, sexual morality has been pointedly contested as a principle of citizenship in recent scandals over gay rights and sex workers' rights. Notions of sexual propriety associated with religiosity, nationalism, and development are criteria of middle-class belonging and—by extension—moral citizenship. Daily, the national media features instances of sexual "perversion"—promiscuity, incest, adultery, bestiality, and rape—as inherent threats to middle-class respectability, life course, and family values. In this context, questions of sexual respectability grew in importance both to local forms of belonging and to the collective belonging of Samburu to the state and the wider world. Here, as Desiree Lewis (2011, 211) argues, "to belong as citizens, we must have legitimate and 'natural' sexual roles to play. When we step out of these roles, we become unnatural, Westernized and traitorous." Ethno-erotic economies, then, were driven by a contradiction of belonging: to survive and to belong, one had to sell sex, yet selling sex undermined one's possibilities to belong.

As more and more young men participated in coastal economies, performing a touristic moran persona and selling ethnicity through the figure of the moran, being Samburu became a matter of positioning oneself in relation to the moran and his ethnosexuality. In other words, ethno-erotic commodification produced ethnic identity *as* sexual difference and made "being Samburu"—if only in part—a form of sexual subjectivity. What is more, ethno-erotic commodification dialectically shaped collective belonging in Samburu, among men and women who did not participate directly in tourism. Participants in lopiro ceremonies, for example, envisioned a sense of ethnoregional belonging by engaging with the moral and material effects of ethno-erotic commodification on their lived worlds. Because they perceived the relations between sexuality and commodities as jeopardizing their ability to build futures through kinship, ritual actors sought to anchor sex in lineage relations and to domesticate foreign commodities in ways that would amplify rather than deplete the life force of families and clans. What is important in lopiro is that "being Samburu" was not only about making and sustaining lineage, clan, and age-set relations but also about internalizing a certain orientation—a certain moral stance, if you will—toward sexuality and its commodification. Being Samburu, then, was about being in a world that is partly structured by the commodification of Samburu ethnosexuality.

::::

I began this book—much like the field research on which it is based—with a set of questions about belonging. I wanted to explore what kinds of belonging are possible for Samburu as their ethnosexuality became a global commodity, and how the commodification of moran sexuality shaped what it meant to belong to social worlds in northern Kenya. My ethnographic journey, however, introduced a set of new themes that are important in clarifying what belonging is all about and how it becomes visible to the anthropologist. What ensued as part of the contradictions of ethno-erotic economies were a set of asynchronies, queer moments, intensifications, and disinvestments that, for the anthropologist, can capture quite strongly how struggles over autochthony and ethno-regional belonging unfold in concrete terms.

The analytic of *temporality*, for example, captures quite powerfully how struggles over belonging played out, and how the dynamics of inclusion and exclusion were negotiated as part of rising ethno-erotic economies. First, notions of time were central to the production of cultural and sexual alterity. State leaders, development workers, and Kenyan middle classes invoked a modernist ideology of unilineal time to legitimize the geopolitical and economic marginalization of Samburu in postcolonial Kenya. Considering them "backward" and "primitive," they expected Samburu to catch up and become modern. Yet when Mombasa morans acquired houses, cars, and other tokens of modern lifestyle and middle-class respectability, national newspapers and street gossip questioned precisely the *time* that went into the production of such wealth. The idiom of "shortcut money"—a kind of money that would not last because it did not originate in legitimate labor, or "sweat"—reflects a cultural logic wherein advancing on an imaginary temporal axis of development requires a slow, gradual expansion of labor. According to this logic, those who took shortcuts subverted the temporality of development and, in the process, undermined their own ability to belong both to regional social worlds and to Kenya's middle classes. The fact that they turned poor as fast as they had become rich served as proof of their sexual immorality and cultural backwardness.

Second, the temporal qualities of *durability* and *temporariness* were driving forces of struggles over belonging. If the money of Mombasa did not last, as informants would say, this was not merely because of the deeds of its owners.

For the intimacies through which ethnosexual commodification took place were themselves fragile and slippery. They required that young men dissociated—in time—requests for money from acts of romance or sexual intimacy. Yet this did not always work as planned. Meanwhile, those who had relationships with European women and obtained money from them sought to make their wealth last by slowing things down. They dwelled in enclave-like homesteads, resided more often in towns rather than villages, and drove in speedy cars to avoid requests of money and support from kin. They thus tried to stop the internal clock of such self-depleting wealth. But with an excess of (devalued) time on their hands, poor Samburu could wait for hours in front of the gates and cars of young big men to ask for financial support. Here, a desire for durable wealth and a general economic condition of temporariness characteristic of neoliberal capital informed various practices of being-in-time.

Third, as the spectral nature of wealth made belonging itself uncertain, a set of temporal intensifications emerged—a rush to belong, to make durable attachments possible, and to project a collective future in Samburu. Men and women who organized lopiro ceremonies transposed this *rush* into the temporalities of ritual itself. Lopiro ceremonies turned back time, to repair the past and make possible a better future before sexual immorality, HIV/AIDS, and abandonment by the state and market would annihilate life in Samburu. Young big men, beach-boy elders, and others were in a similar rush to attach themselves to local worlds. This rush to belong led to a set of temporal asynchronies, or what I called queer moments. Young big men sped up their initiation into elderhood, while beach-boy elders sought to turn back time, dress as morans, and—like other poor Samburu—eventually catch up on the ritual obligations of elderhood. Their acts at once subverted, played with, and pushed the limits of belonging while producing affective attachments in new ways.

Speeding, rushing, turning back time, and catching up are temporal dynamics that emerged here from an intensified desire to belong, and to do so sooner rather than later. Therefore, negotiating belonging involved a temporal politics—an attempt to orchestrate multiple competing temporalities.[1] Henri Hubert ([1905] 1999) pointed out long ago that because the rhythms of time are always experienced as plural, humans everywhere struggle to reconcile the tensions between different competing "calendars" (for discussion, see James and Mills 2005, 7–9). Here, temporality is not merely a product of structural circumstances but also inheres in the concrete practices through which people produce and embody time (Bourdieu 1977; Munn

1992). In the context of ethno-erotic economies, the temporalities of sexual commodification (the time between romance and requests for money; the passing of tourist seasons; the depleting youthfulness of the male body, etc.) intersected with the temporalities of state development and middle-class respectability (ideology of progress and cultural backwardness; the ideal life course of the wage laborer; etc.); and those of Samburu kinship (age-grade time; aging through a gradual wealth accumulation; etc.) to make negotiations over belonging into attempts to orchestrate, attune, or synchronize multiple competing temporal rhythms. The unruly rhythms of respectability and the queer moments they engender, for example, reveal how belonging is about much subtler processes and everyday attempts to align the rhythms of social action (Bourdieu 1977) rather than simply about being either included or excluded.

And while people negotiated the rhythms of belonging, new social and cultural transformations crystallized in their everyday lives. For instance, the logics of commodification now expanded the domains of belonging and infused them more strongly with exchange value. Age grades, kinship, and ritual—the very criteria of ethnoregional belonging—gained some sort of monetary value. The relationships between Mombasa morans, young big men, their European partners, and African mistresses and "big mamas" (sexual patrons) all followed implicit logics of value tied to youthful bodies, cultural difference, romance, and more. So, too, the relationships between Samburu migrants on the coast and their wives and kin at home. Elders, we shall recall, commodified ritual initiations as young big men wished to become elders before their time; and young big men refigured bridewealth as commodity exchange by paying it fully up front to foreclose as much as possible further requests from affines. These logics of commodification were made explicit in lopiro ceremonies, in which participants acted on commodities to make them do the work of social reproduction. In this sense, the concept of ethno-erotic economies makes problematic classic Marxist divisions between realms of economic production and social reproduction. Ethno-erotic economies maintain both transactional sex and kinship relations, both intimacy and money, both tourist hotspots and marginal ethnoregions in the same conceptual space, united—as it were—in the Faustian bargain of belonging and ethno-erotic commodification.

Ethno-erotic economies are not a new phenomenon. Ethnicity has played an important role in the commodification of sexuality in Kenyan towns since the advent of colonial rule. But following the effects of market liberalization, ethno-erotic commodification intensified, generating ever-growing networks of monetary and intimate exchange. Globalization, the rise of international tourism, and the growing prevalence of transnational sexual intimacies fueled Kenyan ethno-erotic economies. In this context, contemporary economies were structured by different logics of production and exchange than they had been in the past. In those days, Kenyans engaged in commodified ethno-erotic exchanges around relatively stable markets of labor in towns (L. White 1990). Women and men who sold sex produced wealth gradually, siphoning money from the wages of labor migrants. In the present, by contrast, ethno-erotic exchanges became for some Kenyans primary sources of economic production. Furthermore, unlike older ethno-erotic exchanges that were based on the temporalities of the wage economy, sex-for-money exchanges in the present took the form of speculation characteristic of neoliberal capitalism (see Comaroff and Comaroff 2000; Weiss 2004). For postcolonial subjects, ethno-erotic economies promised both instant wealth and abject poverty, sometimes in a maddening alternation. In the absence of employment, then, the commodification of ethnosexuality sustained a real potential of rapid enrichment even for those who, in fact, continued to live in poverty. It sustained the capability to include and exclude different people at different times.

Acknowledgments

Ethno-erotic Economies is the outcome of many collaborations, friendships, and relations of affective and intellectual kinship. The book is not only *about* belonging but also a product of my own relations of belonging—various temporary and long-term attachments—that have inspired and anchored my academic trajectory over the years. The idea for this book came to me suddenly in 2005 while I was living in Kenya's Samburu District, trying to learn Maa language and become familiar with the social worlds of the district's regions. During my time in Kenya, many friends and research interlocutors welcomed me into their lives and helped me understand their struggles, desires, and values. They have generously offered me their time, thoughts, and knowledge, and oriented me toward topics I wasn't always prepared to explore. This project had initially started with a somewhat narrow focus on the representation of Samburu dances in tourism. But my friends and mentors in Samburu taught me to ask wider questions and to look beyond what seemed immediately relevant at a particular moment in time. It is thus that I became interested in sexuality, kinship, gender, age, and generation, and ended up spending time both in Samburu villages and towns and at coastal tourist resorts. I am deeply grateful to Mohamed Abdilahi, Leah Kimaru, Paul Lekararo, Paul Simon Lekembe, Linah Lelemoyog, Mary Lelesiit, Bakuni Lempisikishoi, Christopher Saruni Lenarongoito (†), Richard Lengeiyia (†), Joyce Lengeiyia, William Leparkiras, Elly Loldepe, and many, many interviewees whose names I shall not mention, for purposes of confidentiality. To all I say, *ashe oleng naa*. In Nairobi, the Sang family welcomed me into their home on numerous occasions—driving me to and from the airport or the *matatu* shuttle for Maralal—and Richard Ambani helped me navigate the dusty shelves of the national archives.

For much of what I have learned about Africa, social theory, and the powers of a daring ethnographic and historical imagination, I am forever indebted to Jean and John Comaroff. Their devoted mentorship, most patient guidance, and unparalleled energy and enthusiasm have provided me with the most propitious attachments through which to grow and thrive. For me, their kinship remains, as Samburu would put it, *keishu* (life-giving) in more ways than one. Jean shepherded me with patience throughout my work, always making time to discuss anything from complex theory to the ethnographic nuts and bolts of my fieldwork. John taught me how to become a professional scholar, to articulate my ideas in coherent yet exciting ways, and to read classic texts generously for theoretical inspiration and innovative argumentation.

At the University of Chicago, Jennifer Cole has been for me an invaluable model of disciplined academic work thorough ethnographic research and a well-grounded style of anthropological argumentation. Her expertise on issues of sexuality, gender, generation, and kinship and her commitment to exploring and reflecting on the numerous and nebulous conjunctures of ethnographic writing have inspired me tremendously. I was also very fortunate to work with Nancy Munn, who gave me invaluable advice from the time I began conceptualizing this project. Nancy read and discussed with me numerous drafts of various chapters in this book. Her devotion to the detail of ethnographic writing and argumentation and her ideas about value, temporality, and sociality have shaped my work substantially. Judy Farquhar taught me always to reflect on the limits of my conceptual vocabulary, to make the obvious strange, and to venture into conceptual fields that would seem otherwise forbidden. Ralph Austen, Rachel Jean-Baptiste, William Mazzarella, Constantine Nakassis, Emily Osborn, François Richard, and Michael Silverstein offered valuable feedback on my work. For devoted moral support and enlightening critiques of my writing in its early stages, I thank Filipe Calvao, Mark Geraghty, Larisa Jasarevic, Julia Kowalski, Kate McHarry, Victoria Nguyen, Carly Schuster, Gabe Tusinski, and Joshua Walker. My conversations with Rob Blunt, Beth Brummel, Anne Ch'ien, Lauren Coyle, Claudia Gastrow, Casey Golomski, Anna Jabloner, Fred Ketchum, Erin Moore, Paul Ocobock, and Jay Sosa have inspired me over the years. In 2011–12, Linda Zerilli welcomed me in the University of Chicago's Center for the Study of

Gender and Sexuality and provided me with an ideal space to think and write. Since the time I lived in Chicago, Anita Hannig has been an invaluable friend and interlocutor, encouraging me through every step of this project. At Concordia University in Montreal, my former mentors and, later, colleagues— Andrew Ivaska, Christine Jourdan, and Anthony Synnott—encouraged me to do field research in Kenya and helped me articulate the purpose of such research. To all I am deeply grateful.

Paul Spencer, the first anthropologist to work in Samburu (1958–60), remains to me a tireless ethnographer and an inspiring friend and mentor. We spent whole days, from early in the morning until late in the evening, talking about Samburu kinship and history at his house in Somerset, England. He generously shared his early ethnographic data with me, and also read and commented on drafts of my work. A few years ago, when I visited the descendants of his adoptive Samburu clan, the Pardopa-Lorokushu, rumor spread quickly throughout the area that "Paul's grandson" had come to look for his family. Despite my explaining otherwise, people there came to know me as "Paul's grandson." Paul and I joked about this matter often. But, as he had once written somewhere, jokes are no joking matter. Paul died in August 2015, just when I was concluding my fieldwork for this book. Rest in peace, *akuiya lai.* You will be missed.

Steven Caton, Peter Geschiere, Christian Groes-Green, Dorothy Hodgson, Janet McIntosh, and Gregory Mitchell have all read earlier drafts of this book very closely and provided eye-opening critiques and suggestions. They helped me to see more clearly the wider conceptual and political implications of my ethnographic material, and to articulate these implications more strongly in my writing. At Harvard University, my colleagues Robin Bernstein, Kerry Chance, Biodun Jeyifo, John Mugane, Pauline Peters, Laurence Ralph, Brandon Terry, and Lucy White have also read different chapters of this manuscript and offered most constructive critiques and suggestions. In addition, other anthropologists, including Mwenda Ntarangwi, Charles Piot, Jonathan Skinner, Rupert Stasch, and Dimitrios Theodossopoulos, offered helpful critical feedback on various drafts of my work. Conversations with Byron Good, Michael Herzfeld, and Sydney Kasfir have also inspired this work.

I wish to thank my editor, Priya Nelson, for believing in this book project from the onset. No doubt, her warm encouragements have made the process of writing and revising this book so much more pleasurable. I also wish to thank Ellen Kladky, Dylan Montanari, and the anonymous peer reviewers at the University of Chicago Press. My deepest gratitude goes to my graduate students, Renugan Raidoo and Kevin Tervala, for their tireless work in helping me to prepare this book for publication, and to Kim Greenwell and Sandra Hazel for their careful editing of the text.

My family's love and care have given me a sense of belonging when I needed it most. My grandmother, Rodica Drăghia, has encouraged my passion for ethnography since I was a teenager and has always offered me tremendous moral support, if lately over the phone from Romania. My parents, Liliana and George Meiu, visited me in Kenya while I was conducting my fieldwork and always looked out for me. Raphaël Schroeter, my partner, has stood by me in the long, tiring hours of research and writing, and reminded me persistently—as he still does—how it is all worthwhile. Thank you.

I acknowledge grants from the Social Sciences and Humanities Research Council of Canada (#752-2009-0092) and the Fonds québécois de la recherche sur la société et la culture, Quebec (#135285), that enabled me to carry out field research in Kenya and write up first drafts of this book. A grant from Harvard's Weatherhead Center for International Affairs enabled me to organize a book manuscript workshop in May 2015, and funds from Harvard's Faculty of Arts and Sciences covered additional costs related to the preparation of this manuscript. Substantial parts of chapters 5 and 6 were published earlier in *Ethnos* (Meiu 2015) and the *American Ethnologist* (Meiu 2016). I wish to thank these journals for permission to reproduce this material as part of the current book.

Notes

1. The national currency of Kenya is the Kenyan shilling (KSh). Unless other-wise indicated, all references to amounts of money are given in US dollars.

2. In the Maa language, the proverb reads: "Nkai, iwa yeiyo ai o papa lai, niking'uaki laji lai."

3. Calabashes, as extensions of embodied personhood, figure widely in the prac-tices of rural Samburu. For a detailed discussion of how calabashes and other household objects relate to the bodily substance, life force, and well-being of their owners, see Straight (2007b, 69–93).

4. Africanist anthropologists document the implications of young men's and women's desire to immigrate to Europe and North America in relation to citi-zenship, kinship, and economic exchange (Buggenhagen 2012; Coe 2013; Cole and Groes-Green 2016; Piot 2010, 77–96).

5. Tourists came to Kenya as early as the 1900s (Kibicho 2009, 63), but their numbers boomed in the last decades of the century. Following independence in 1963, the government of Kenya embraced tourism as a main path to eco-nomic development, and established the Kenyan Tourism Development Cor-poration (1965) and the Ministry of Tourism and Wildlife (1966). Throughout the 1970s, the number of visitors leveled at 350,000 per annum. However, fol-lowing global economic reforms, the number increased twofold in the 1980s (Schoss 1995, 36–38). Throughout the 1990s and early 2000s, the number of tourists visiting Kenya each year increased further (by 94.4 percent), reaching 1,361,000 in 2004 (ECPAT n.d., 3). In the following years, tourist arrivals fluc-tuated. They fell sharply following the postelection violence of 2008, tourist

kidnapping incidents in late 2011, and the terrorist attacks on Nairobi's Westgate Mall in 2013. However, in 2011, the number of tourists in the country reached an all times high of 1,750,000 (World Bank, http://data.worldbank.org/indicator/ST.INT.ARVL?locations=KE, accessed December 15, 2016).

6. Kenya Cultural Profiles website, www.enchanted-landscapes.com (accessed October 22, 2004; the site has been discontinued).

7. Oscar Obonyo and Daniel Nyassy, "Moran Mania: The Good, the Bad, and the Ugly in the Commerical Use of Maasai Culture," *Sunday Nation Lifestyle* (Nairobi), December 12, 2004.

8. Vocative, "Beach Boys: Objects of Desire." http://www.vocativ.com/27673/beach-boys-objects-desire (accessed November 24, 2016).

9. Frank Mutulu (2014), "Kenya's Beach Boys," AfkTravel online, https://afktravel.com/57229/kenyas-beach-boys (accessed November 24, 2016).

10. For a critical discussion of the content of the book, see N. Berman (2005), Maurer (2010), and Meiu (2011).

11. The work of Bronislaw Malinowski (1927, 1929) in the Trobriand Islands and of Margaret Mead (1928) in Samoa are examples in this regard. For a critical summary of early approaches to sexuality in anthropology, see Lyons and Lyons (2004).

12. Rather than seeing race, ethnicity, and culture as objective realities, postcolonial theorists since the late 1970s have described them as discursive enunciations within the global politics of inequality, marginalization, and exploitation. Homi Bhabha (1994), for example, shows how, as objects of discourse, race, ethnicity, and culture mediate forms of sovereignty and subjection and legitimize unequal access to material resources. In this sense, representations of the Other are far from disconnected from the people and places they describe (102–3); rather, such representations have material effects.

13. Obsurvative [pseud.], "Moran No More," *Wenyewe* (blog), December 20, 2016, obsurvative.wordpress.com (accessed March 21, 2015).

14. One can encounter this trend among Native Americans in the United States and Canada, indigenous people in Latin America and South Asia, and even the Maasai of Tanzania (Cattelino 2008; Hirsch 2016; Hodgson 2011; Shneiderman 2015).

15. I have changed the names of these locales in order to protect the confidentiality of my informants. Events and persons described in this book would otherwise be easily identifiable.

CHAPTER ONE

1.   Alex Kiprotich, "Samburu: The Land of the Unpredictable," *Standard* (Nairobi), June 26, 2011.

2.   Nyambesa Gisesa, "The Allure of Northern Kenya," *Daily Nation* (Nairobi), May 16, 2012, http://www.nation.co.ke/Features/DN2/The+allure+of+Northern+Kenya/-/957860/1406308/-/item/0/-/gr46caz/-/index.html (accessed December 16, 2016).

3.   Lieut Lytton, 1924, *Samburu District Annual Report*. Kenya National Archives, Nairobi, PC/NFD/1/9/1.

4.   Photographs by colonials, settlers, and travelers at the turn of the century depict large battalions of African warriors who were respectively Kikuyu, Pokot, Luo, Maasai, Nandi, or Kalenjin (Pavitt 2008, 19, 39, 43, 88, 92, 127, 230–31). Colonial postcards from the time depict portraits of individual Meru, Kikuyu, Nandi, or Maasai warriors. Warriors posed in various states of undress, their bodies smeared with fat or ochre and decorated with elaborate bead and wire adornments. In these photographs, bodily decorations and accessories that would eventually become associated exclusively with the Maa-speaking morans (e.g., spears, shields, long hair, or lion-mane headdresses) were common across regions and identities, albeit with differences of pattern.

5.   Since 1865, Maa-speaking Laikipiak have raided Samburu and pushed them out of the rich grazing lands of northern Rift Valley (Sobania 1993, 110). Meanwhile, consecutive epidemics of pleuro-pneumonia, smallpox, and rinderpest killed many people and decimated livestock (see also Kasfir 2007, 43; Spencer 1973, 154; Waweru 2012, 36–38).

6.   District commissioners appointed selected elders as chiefs (M: *laigwanak*) of their respective clans and, since 1936, as members of the Local Native Council and the Native Tribunal. Many elders were happy to collaborate with the colonial administration for one reason or another. Some were angry that they had lost cattle to levies imposed as a consequence of the actions of morans. Others saw the colonial state as a new source of material resources, power, and authority.

7.   H. B. Sharpe, 1936, *Annual Report, Laikipiak-Samburu District*, Kenya National Archives, Nairobi, DC/SAM/1/2.

8.   These campaigns intensified at a particular moment of colonial rule. In the early 1900s, the colonial government divided and subdivided the British East Africa Protectorate into provinces and districts—more or less along lines of ethnicity—and appointed British administrators to govern each division and keep subjects within its bounds. During World War I, colonial rule in Sam-

buru District became laissez-faire, and many Samburu took advantage of the relative absence of administration to move their livestock into the grasslands of the Leroki plateau, a highland area that bordered on the farmlands of the white settlers in the Laikipiak District (Simpson 1994, 518–72). White settler families hoped that the colonial government would grant them the plateau for agricultural farming. Samburu, however, hoped to use Leroki as seasonal pasture for their cattle. Throughout the following decades, the colonial administration had to mediate between settlers and Samburu in their competition over Leroki. Recurring raids and murders by morans in the twenties and thirties prompted settlers to appeal to the government to take repressive security measures against Samburu. Following the murder of a white settler by Samburu morans in 1931, the colonial government initiated drastic measures to reform moranhood and keep Samburu within the borders of their district.

9. Unknown author, 1936, *Political Report Samburu*, Kenya National Archives, Nairobi, DC/SAM/3/2.

10. Unknown author, 1951, *B.C.M.S. Executive Board of the Mombasa Diocese*, Church Missionary Society Archives, Birmingham University, MS47/Box 26.

11. See, for example, "Moran Systems, 1931–1941," Kenya National Archives, Nairobi, DC/KJD/2/1/7.

12. C. F. Atkins, 1935, *Laikipiak District—Annual Report*, Kenya National Archives, Nairobi, DC/SAM/1/2.

13. See, for example, J. M. B. Butler, 1950, *Monthly Intelligence Report—Samburu*, Kenya National Archives, Nairobi, DC/SAM/3/4.

14. J. M. B. Butler, 1952, *Handing Over Report—Samburu*, Kenya National Archives, Nairobi, DC/SAM/2/1.

15. For a discussion of the participation of morans in the movie, see Kasfir (2007, 45).

16. For a discussion of Leni Riefenstahl's work in East Africa, see Meiu (2008).

17. Nigel Pavitt's (1991) coffee table book on the Samburu sells widely in tourist bookstores throughout Kenya.

18. As international travel became more accessible to the middle classes in Western Europe, the East African Tourist Travel Association, established in Nairobi in 1948, advocated for wildlife conservation, gradually replacing colonial hunting safaris with wildlife viewing and photographing safaris (Akama 1999, 13–14; Schoss 1995, 97–120). Kenyan tourism thus came to be anchored in a visual spectacle of diverse wildlife and exotic landscapes (K. Little 1991; Schoss 1995, 285–330). Following Kenya's independence in 1963, the government established the Kenya Tourism Development Corporation (1965) and

the Ministry of Tourism and Wildlife (1966) in order to stimulate the growth of the national tourist industry.

19.   In the early 1970s, Samburu morans also danced for tourists in the town of Namanga, on the border with Tanzania (Paul Spencer, personal communication, February 19, 2011). However, I found no further information on this in my interviews with elderly Samburu performers.

20.   See Hassan Huka and Karanja Muchiri, "4-Year-Old Bride for the Price of Beaded Necklace," *Daily Nation* (Nairobi), January 27, 2010, http://www.na tion.co.ke/News/regional/-/1070/850622/-/8pe6rd/-/index.html (accessed November 27, 2016).

21.   Opinion column, "NTV Story about Girl Sex Slaves in Samburu a National Shame," *Daily Nation* (Nairobi), October 28, 2012, http://www.nation.co.ke /oped/Letters/NTV-story-about-girl-sex-slaves-in-Samburu-a-national -shame/-/440806/1605432/-/view/printVersion/-/wv1i3t/-/index.html (accessedNovember 27, 2016).

22.   Following Kenya's independence in 1963, an emerging political class of Afri-can elites initiated five-year development plans, investing in education, health services, water resources, roads, and electricity. These development plans represented central mechanisms through which the state incorporated people into the national economy and extended control over its population. The official discourse depicted development (S: *maendeleo*) as a material temporal passage from tradition (S: *-a kienyeji*) to the modern (S: *-a kisasa*). In the face of what they saw as a wide gap between their own, "modern" cultural values and the values of the poor, these new elites hoped, as the members of the New Kenya Party put it in 1959, that "there may rapidly emerge from the poorer majority people having *similar interests* and *similar ideals* to those more economically advanced" (quoted in Leys 1974, 43, my emphasis). From this perspective, development was about a process of cultural reform and political control that would enable the transformation of the material relations of production and the increase of profit in the national economy. For a critical reading of development ideologies in Kenya, see J. Smith (2008).

23.   See Plus News, "Camel Clinics Bring Condoms to Nomads," CABSA, August 31, 2010, http://www.cabsa.org.za/content/camel-clinics-bring-condoms -nomads-31810 (accessed on November 27, 2016).

24.   Philip Mwaiko, "Changing Faces of Maasai Moran," *Sunday Magazine* (of the *Standard* [Nairobi]), August 10, 2008, pp. 4–5.

25.   For similar instances of sex with foreigners as "national shame" in Senegal and Madagascar, see Ebron (2002, 171–73) and Cole (2008).

CHAPTER TWO

1. For a discussion of the movie *The Air Up There* as well as Samburu participation in it, see Kasfir (2007, 293–308).

2. For a discussion of the movie *The Ghost in the Darkness* and Samburu participation in it, see Askew (2004) and Kasfir (2007, 293–308).

3. Straight (2007b, 216) translates *nkishon* as "the life that is visible to others and is passed to one's children through inheritance."

4. Discussing Samburu relations of descent, Spencer (1965, 71–76) distinguished analytically between the hair-sharing group (i.e., a minor lineage), the lineage, the subclan, the clan, the phratry, and the moiety. However, Samburu distinguished more generically only between two categories: (1) the *ntipat* and (2) the *lmarei*. English-speaking informants translated *ntipat* with "extended family" and *lmarei* with "clan." Unlike Spencer, I am not pursuing a structural analysis of social organization; therefore, for purposes of this study, I follow my interlocutors' mode of classification. Clans and subclans were not territorial units. In their actual living arrangements, clans and subclans were spread out across the district and lived intermixed in different regions. However, in every region there were higher concentrations of one clan over another, so that each clan had several "hot spot" locations throughout the district. Spencer (20) referred to families of the same clan living in the same area as a "local clan group." The local clan group played an important role in the everyday lives of its individual members. The senior men and women of this group mediated conflicts between its members, organized rituals and ceremonies, and were bound by obligations of mutual trust and reciprocity. In townships, local clan groups also played a central role in neighborhood relations, business relations, and ceremonies.

5. For example, girls who came of age during my fieldwork identified with the Lkishami age set, calling themselves "girls of the Lkishami" (M: *ntoyie ee Lkishami*) or simply *Nkishami*, using the feminine prefix *n-* instead of the masculine prefix *l-* for the name of the same age set. Once they became married wives (M: *ntomonok*), women became part of the age set of their husbands (Straight 2007b, 31–32, 74–75; see also Kawai 1998). For example, if an Nkishami girl was married as a second wife to a man of the Lkuroro age set (which was very common), she became an Nkuroro. The wives of a certain age set related to each other as age-mates and addressed each other as "co-wives" (M: *nkaini*). They acted, therefore, as an age set with important ritual and political roles. See chapter 6 for an example of women acting collectively as an age set.

6. Following the economic transformations animated by the global politics of late capitalism, Brad Weiss (2004, 5) argues, "there is a sense, across the [African] continent (and undoubtedly beyond), that these transformations do have a cumulative, interpenetrating significance." For example, gambling-like speculation and entrepreneurialism replace labor as bases of economic production; the politics of youth, generation, and civic society replace politics of class; and there is "explosion not only of new commodity forms, but of whole new modes of consumption" (ibid.). For a more detailed discussion of the social, economic, and political implications of neoliberal reforms in Africa, see Comaroff and Comaroff (2000), Ferguson (2006), Makulu, Buggenhagen, and Jackson (2010), and Piot (2010).

7. For a discussion of land adjudication processes in Kenya, see Bates (1989), Galaty (1992), McCabe (1990), and P. Little (1992).

8. Controlled grazing schemes in the highlands since the 1950s had already forced families who owned large numbers of livestock into the lowlands (Spencer 1973, 179–91; Lesorogol 2008a, 39–42). Previously, people had migrated seasonally from the lowlands to the highlands in search of pasture and water for their cattle.

9. For example, when Chinese investors began drilling for oil and building a highway in the eastern part of the district in 2009, the government forcibly evicted local residents from the area.

10. Land adjudication also produced unequal opportunities for men and women. With a few exceptions, all registered members of group ranches were male elders. Because policymakers operated with a stereotypic image of the Maa pastoralists as a deeply patriarchal people, they placed men at the forefront of land policies, making them the rightful owners of land (for a similar case among the Maasai, see Hodgson 2001; Talle 1988). Women always held important customary rights in the cattle herds of their husbands (Spencer 1965, 53–58), but the same rights did not extend to landownership. As daughters and wives, women lived and worked on the farmlands of their male kin without any customary rights to owning, inheriting, or selling land. In theory, women could use civic courts to obtain inheritance rights in the land of their parents. But because the land was still held collectively by male elders registered in group ranches, the subdivision of land was a matter of the elders' decision, and inheritance was regulated through customary law.

11. Typically, women denied their husbands rights over money obtained for chang'aa, calling it money of the childrrn (M: *shilingini enkera*). Custom entitled husbands to one or two free glasses of chang'aa from every batch brewed

by their wives, but they had to pay for additional glasses. In this way, as Holtzman (2009, 205) observes, brewing allowed women "to circumvent male control of cash [and] to make desired purchases."

12. People also refer to sex using the verbs *a-rrag* (literally, "to lie down," polite form), *a-ikinyie* (to fuck, vulgar form), or *a-rubbo* (literally, "to beat," vulgar form).

CHAPTER THREE

1. Africanist anthropologists and historians have explored at length intimacies and sexualities in relation to money, goods, and the economy (Cole 2010; Groes-Green 2014; Foley and Drame 2013; Hunter 2010; Magubane 2004; Mojola 2014; Nyamjoh 2005; Nyanzi et al. 2005; Tade and Adekoya 2012; L. White 1990).

2. Studies of tourism rarely question how ethnicity and sexuality are products of a world beyond tourist resorts. Some scholars see the identities of hosting peoples as raw material to which tourists add value in the process of consumption (e.g., Hinch and Butler 1996; M. Smith and Duffy 2003). Others see hosts' identities as "staged" performances that locals employ strategically to make money before returning to their "real" lives "backstage" (e.g., MacCannell 1976; M. Smith and Duffy 2003). Anthropologists of tourism draw on postmodern critiques of culture and identity to offer a more complex approach. Rather than take culture and identity as a priori realities, they focus on how these emerge in the interactions between "guests" and "hosts" (Bruner 2005; Burns 1999; Gimblett 1998; K. Little 1991; V. Smith 1977; Urry 1990). However, by focusing almost exclusively on categorizing and comparing social life within tourist resorts, anthropologists of tourism omit the complex implications of these sites for the larger contexts in which they exist. Similarly, studies of "sex tourism" coin elaborate comparative typologies for "sex tourists," "sex workers," and their transactions (e.g., Bauer and McKercher 2003; Bishop and Robinson 1998; Clift and Carter 2000; Kempadoo 1999, 2001; Kibicho 2009; Ryan and Hall 2001) without examining how sexual commodification shapes the lives of actors outside the tourist encounter. Anthropologists writing on "sex tourism" have critiqued essentialist comparative analytics by describing more complex lived realities (Brennan 2004; Cabezas 2009; Frohlick 2013; Jacobs 2010; Padilla 2007), but they still focus primarily on tourist locales and their actors.

3. I found numerous references to the "male prostitutes" of Mombasa in the letters and documents of the colonial and early post-independence administration, stored at the Kenyan National Archives, Nairobi. References and brief

discussions of "male prostitution" in Mombasa and on the coast can also be found in G. Wilson (1957), Gachuhi (1973, 5–7), and Shepherd (1987, 251–52, 258–59). For a more general discussion of homosexuality in coastal towns, see Amory (1998). For a comparative case of same-sex relations in the context of early colonial labor migration, see Epprecht's (2004) discussion of "boy wives" in southern Africa.

4.   Letter from Bwana Obo Dini to the Town Clerk of the Municipal Council of Mombasa, March 7, 1966; Kenya National Archives, Nairobi, CQ/10/5—Prostitution and Brothels, 1958–1970.

5.   Ibid.

6.   Temporary wives are mentioned, for example, in the Draft for Annual Report, 1961, Kenya National Archives, Nairobi, CQ/10/5—Prostitution and Brothels, 1958–1970.

7.   "Hans," "Toy-Boys and Mtwapa's Property Boom," *Standard* (Nairobi), August 28, 2008.

8.   Kiundi Waweru, "Vivacious Life at Kenya's Sin Spot," *Standard* (Nairobi), December 17, 2010.

9.   For a more detailed discussion of trade networks in Kenya's coastal tourism, see Mahoney (2009).

10.   When Samburu morans began walking along the beaches in 1978, other so-called beach boys had already been active in the informal beach economy for at least two decades. Kenyans initially attributed the derogatory term *beach boy* to Kamba young men who had migrated to Mombasa in the 1960s to sell woodwork to tourists at the beach (Peake 1984, 82–124; Schoss 1995, 247). Mijikenda and Swahili young men from coastal towns and villages had also been active in the beach economy, enticing tourists to purchase everything from guided tours and souvenirs to drugs and sex. Many of these young men spoke different European languages, and some of them had adopted a Rastafarian style, wearing dreadlocks and listening to reggae music (Schoss 1995).

11.   By and large, postcolonial theorists have drawn on Foucault's notion of disciplinary power to locate cultural difference in the realm of discourse (Said 1978; Trouillot 1991). Meanwhile, queer critical race theorists have drawn on phenomenology and affect theory to locate racial, ethnic, and cultural difference in the realm of embodied encounters (Ahmed 2000; Holland 2012). My analysis shows that we need to bridge these two approaches through a dialectical understanding of discourse and encounter. For example, Homi Bhabha (1994, 121–31) draws on both Foucault and Freud to argue that in the face of the ambivalence of actuality (practice, encounter, and so on), colonial discourses must perpetually "reinscribe" cultural difference (for a critical discussion of

this argument, see Caton 1999, 9–10). As I have shown, however, concrete histories of embodied encounter do more than simply trigger the "reinscription" of difference. They also transform and relocate the particular contents of difference. The dialectics of intimate encounter and discourse are open-ended, carrying multiple potentialities for the making of ethnosexuality and cultural alterity.

12.   John and Jean Comaroff (2009, 20) make a similar argument about ethnicity, suggesting that its commodification is a source of its reproduction.

13.   For example, in Madagascar, the *jaombilo* are young men who become partners of women enriched through marriages to Frenchmen. Cole (2010, 141) shows that in a particular urban cultural context, *jaombilo* seemed to bargain away their masculinity, because they accepted being dependent on women. For a similar case in Senegal and Mozambique, see Nyamnjoh (2005) and Honwana (2012, 95–98).

14.   In the sexual economies of Mtwapa, several types of sorcery for the purposes of love and intimacy were associated with different ethnic groups. For example, my informants pointed out that sorcerers (S: *waganga*, sg. *mganga*) of the Giriama and the Digo ethnic groups sold herbal medicine (S: *miti shamba*), the Swahili sold *majini* (S., sg. *jini*) spirits for purposes of love and money, and various up-country people sold "witchcraft with mirrors" (S: *uchawi wa vyoo*), using reflections to influence potential intimate partners from afar. Even when the actual sorcerers were not of those ethnic groups, distinct sorcery practices remained by and large ethnicized.

CHAPTER FOUR

1.   The prohibition of morans eating food seen or touched by women, known as *lmenong*, played an important role in removing young men from domestic economies, whether to decrease competition over scarce food resources (Holtzman 2003, 234) or to avoid adultery and intergenerational conflicts (Spencer 1965).

2.   Elderly Samburu I spoke to recalled, for example, how, with the growth of labor migration in the 1950s, girls used kakisha songs to ridicule men who wore pants. In response to such songs, labor migrants used to take off their pants in buses, upon arrival in the district, to avoid further ridicule. But girls also used kakisha to influence the outcomes of important political decisions in which they otherwise had no say. In 1996, following armed cattle raids by Turkana on western Samburu, many Samburu families lost their livestock and moved to the highlands. People recalled vividly how Nacham, a girl of the Lokumai clan with a beautiful voice, started singing a kakisha that shamed low-

land morans for abandoning their cattle instead of retaliating the attacks of the Turkana. She sang, "God, why don't you change me to be a Turkana girl, so that all the dotted cows of the Samburu would be brought to me?" Lowland morans, so the story goes, were so ashamed and humiliated by this girl's song that they defied the elders' orders, hired trucks, and returned to the lowlands to fight with Turkana raiders.

3. "Life Is Not a Beach: Time to End the 'Easy Money' Vicious Circle," *Daily Nation* (Nairobi), February 23, 2011.

4. Kamau Mutunga, "No Apologies, We're Material Youth in a Material World," *Daily Kenya Living* (magazine of the *Daily Nation*), July 18, 2011.

5. E. N. Erskine, *Handing Over Report*, 1921, Kenya National Archives, Nairobi, PC/NFD/1/9/1.

6. Sorcery was legible from the color of the cars. Red cars indexed sorcery, as redness was a sign of blood. Meanwhile, vehicles were signs of mobility and extraction. These signs had long converged to index illegitimate means of wealth production in East Africa. Luise White (2000, 127) shows that during colonialism, urban East Africans associated red cars with occult forms of blood extraction that benefited the rich and powerful. Red cars thus indexed attempts to draw surplus value through occult means.

7. Straight (2002, 13) makes a similar argument about money obtained through the sale of *mporo* marriage beads. Women's beads, like other personal belongings, contained their sweat, scent, or dirt—their so-called *latukuny*—and therefore represented bodily extensions of themselves. Selling these beads meant jeopardizing one's life force and well-being. Men who prospered from such sales were said to lose their wealth fast, for they "cannibalized" the bodies of others.

8. For example, rural Samburu said that if a woman engaged in sexual intercourse with her husband or with a man of his age set (himself a classificatory husband) in the bush, she would have children with disabilities or other problems. Here, the bush figured as a place of adultery, where a woman met lovers (that is, not her husband or his age-mates, who all classified—for this purpose—as husbands). By sexually transgressing these boundaries of space, a woman mobilized forces that affected her and her offspring in unforeseen ways. Similarly, urban Samburu said that if a couple had sex in a car, the next day the car would speed out of control and crash.

9. Since the late 1990s, several Samburu men who had acquired wealth through coastal tourism have used their money to sponsor their own election campaigns and become area councillors. These men invested money in building or renovating village schools or constructing water pumps as a way to pursue the

villagers' vote. They also invested money in political rallies, where they invited men and women to feast on food they provided and to express their wishes and concerns. On these occasions, they distributed small gifts of cash to the attendees and promised, once elected, to devise new ways of circulating cash to rural areas. They sought to redistribute their wealth in ways that allowed them to develop extended networks of patrons and clients. Ultimately, they hoped to obtain salaries as state-employed politicians and regenerate their wealth once their European partners no longer supported them financially.

10. Benefiting from access to the social and economic resources of the state, politicians-cum-businessmen depicted themselves as big men (B. Berman 1998, 330). Kenya's big men claimed authority by amassing wealth and generating vast networks of patron-client relations that were crucial to their economic and political standing. Addressed primarily as "big men" (S: *wakubwa*) or "respectable men" (S: *waheshimiwa*) and spoken of, at various times, as "the ones of Mercedes Benz" (S: *wabenzi* [in the 1980s]) or "bosses" (S: *wadoss* [in the present]), these men owned large houses in cities and in rural homelands and drove expensive cars. At political rallies (S: *baraza*) across the country, they distributed large sums of money to local spectators, and at various community fund-raisers (S: *harambee*) they tried to outdo one another through large gifts of cash. Big bellies revealed through unbuttoned expensive suits, upright bodily postures topped by "godfather hats" (cowboy hats), or flamboyant speeches delivered in a loud, confident voice became quintessential indices of the big men. To these one must add an excessive desire for sexual consumption reflected in multiple wives and mistresses, all of whom were showered with expensive gifts. Previously, African servants and clients had addressed their white male patrons as "big men," and villagers used similar phrases to speak of wealthy landowners. But unlike their predecessors, postcolonial big men also displayed their largesse through self-aggrandizing practices of conspicuous consumption (Blunt 2010, 3–5). While big manhood indexed the *spatial* dimensions of power (largesse, wealth, connections) and elderhood its *temporal* dimensions (old age, acquired wisdom, and ritual expertise), the two forms of masculine authority converged, if only partially, in the practices of postcolonial subjects. Big men sought to portray themselves as "elders" in order to enhance their power and authority. Jomo Kenyatta, the country's first president, fashioned himself as *the* elder (S: *Mzee*) of the nation. In response, elders of various ethnic groups soon offered to bestow "tribal elder" titles on different politicians and businessmen as a way of becoming their clients and protégés (see also McIntosh 2009a).

11. In such instances, vehicles engendered an "intersubjective spacetime" (Munn

1986, 10–12, 61–63). That is, the subjectivities of both drivers and bystanders emerged in a dialectical relation to each other and to the different spatial and temporal dimensions they came to inhabit in and around vehicles. In this sense, the driver and the bystanders became particular instances of what Jain (2004) has called "subjects of automobility," that is, subjects that emerge through the discourses and practices associated with vehicles. Like cars and motorbikes, large houses with high fences and iron gates constituted media that produced subjective experiences for both owners and those who waited, often for hours, in front of their locked gates.

CHAPTER FIVE

1. Homicide in itself made the slayer unpropitious. The slayer was said to have "eaten a person" (M: *ketama ltungani*) and thus to "have a bad omen" (M: *keata loikop*). Even if the slayer underwent ritual cleansing and paid bloodwealth (M: *nkiroi*)—neither of which Lekarda had done—he continued to have socalled *lmogiro*, or "unpropitiousness." This substance did not allow him to prosper, and made him and his descendants likely to go mad.

2. Bilinda Straight (2007b, 105) describes how a person's unpropitiousness "jumps the gap" between persons to affect others. In this sense, Straight speaks of "the radical intersubjectivity of Samburu persons."

3. This custom also existed among the Maasai (Llewelyn-Davies 1981, 341). In Samburu, during birth rituals, for example, women served the *lkiriko* food before anyone else so that they would not curse the newborn child. Then they asked all lkiriko to refrain from participating in the ritual blessings.

4. In the past, the family of a man who had impregnated a girl had to pay a cow called *nkiteng e morno* to the girl's father as punishment for his deed. In the absence of livestock, however, some families would now agree—though reluctantly—that the man could marry the girl.

5. The phrase "come-we-stay" is common throughout Kenya. I did not encounter this expression in Samburu at the beginning of my fieldwork, although the practice that it describes was already widespread. However, toward the end of my fieldwork—by 2015—the phrase was quite common among youths in both urban and rural areas. There was no equivalent word in Maa or Swahili.

6. Although I could not identify a contemporary Maa word for this type of marriage, elders pointed out that at the turn of the twentieth century, following devastating droughts, people had lacked resources to marry. Similar unofficial marriages existed at that time, and a woman in such a relationship used to be known as *mpos korom*. By the mid-twentieth century, this word came to mean "concubine"—a woman who lived with a man that was not her husband be-

cause he did not pay bridewealth for her. I heard some elders use this word to refer derogatorily to young women in come-we-stay marriages.

7. This mode of collecting and redistributing bridewealth cattle was common throughout East Africa (see Evans-Pritchard 1951; Gulliver 1955; Spencer 1965).

8. Similar instances of accelerated aging existed in other parts of Kenya throughout the twentieth century. Among the Maa-speaking Chamus of Lake Baringo, since the 1900s, age-set climbers have been young boys who, as a way of claiming rights in property, sought circumcision into moranhood long after the moran age set had been ritually closed (Spencer 1998, 181–89). Similarly, during colonialism, Kikuyu rich men in central Kenya paid an "ox of climbing" to become senior elders and gain political power (Lonsdale 1992, 345).

CHAPTER SIX

1. In rural areas, condoms were available only on the rare occasions when health workers distributed them to young men. In the absence of condoms, risk became an inescapable element of sexual intimacies. While most HIV-prevention campaigns emphasized abstinence, high levels of HIV infection often prompted Kenyan journalists to invoke the sexual alterity of Samburu people. (For a similar dynamic in the Trobriand Islands, see Lepani [2012].)

2. The competition between two age-gender groups, the mobilization of women as an age set in pursuit of fertility, or the symbolic role of the feather, among other things, can also be encountered in the Maasai *lolbaa* ceremony (Spencer 1988, 252).

3. Ritual specialists explained to me that lopiro brought together, transformed, and recombined ritual elements of older ceremonies such as *kishkish*, *nkijare*, and *ntorosi*. In *kishkish*, girls "stole" a feather from the morans of another clan or region by way of inviting them to organize a dance in the girls' area. In *nkijare*, married men and women of different clans gathered in a dance competition between different, alternating age-gender cohorts. Finally, in *ntorosi*, all "barren women" who resided in a certain area walked together for two months, singing songs, blessing other women in exchange for food, and forcing men they came upon to have sex with them. At the end of *ntorosi*, women would regain their fertility.

4. For a similar ritual symbolism of the homestead in different parts of Southern Africa, see Comaroff (1985, 214–16) and H. White (2004, 158–60).

CONCLUSION

1. For early anthropologists, time was a function of structural organization, categorized as respectively linear or cyclical and mediated by systems of kinship and political organization (Evans-Pritchard [(1940) 1969], 94–96, 249–51; Leach 1961, 124–36). By contrast, recent studies use *temporality* to capture more dynamic ways of being-in-time. I think of temporality as an embodied symbolic process unfolding in practice, through which people imagine themselves inhabiting a present in relation to various kinds of pasts and futures (Munn 1992, 115–16). Temporality reflects how large-scale structural and historical processes inform everyday life (cf. Gell 1992; James and Mills 2005; Hodges 2008).

Glossary

For all Maa-language verbs, I adopted a classification principle that is used in Maa dictionaries. Their infinitive form begins with the prefix *a-* (*a-bulu*, *a-purr*, etc.). Rather than alphabetize these verbs by their prefix, I alphabetized them by their root.

aibu. (S) Shame.

akina mama wakubwa. (M) Big mamas; rich women.

a-am. (M) To eat; to fuck (vulgar).

anyit. (M) Shame.

aulo. (M) Outside.

baringoi. (M) Song and dance genre.

beach-boy elders. A derogatory name Samburu use to speak of men who have been initiated into the age grade of elderhood, but continue to dress as young morans and to participate in coastal beach tourism.

bendera. (M/S) Flag.

biashara oo lmusunku. (M) Business with whites; beach trade with tourists.

biashara oo suom. (M) Business with small stock; goat and sheep trade.

a-bulu. (M) To grow; to make something grow.

bwana. (S) Man.

chang'aa. (M/S) Traditional home-brewed alcohol obtained through the fermentation of grains.

a-chukunye. (M) To return.

dawa ya kupaka. (S) Witchcraft powders; literally, rubbing medicine.

emutai. (M) Disaster.

fire-stick elders. Elders who are the ritual patrons of the morans and who are two age sets above them. They kindle the ritual fire that brings the morans' age set into being, and their name comes from the fire stick (M: *mpiroi*) used for this purpose.

a-ikinyie. (M) To fuck (vulgar).

a-ilep. (M) To climb.

a-imaki. (M) To talk of someone or something with desire; to reveal; to expose.

a-ishu. (M) To be alive; to thrive with life force.

a-jing silen. (M) To go into debt.

jini. (S) Spirit employed in witchcraft.

jua kali. (S) The informal economic sector; literally, "hot sun."

kabila. (S) Ethnicity, tribe.

kakisha. (M) Girls' song genre.

kazi ya kitanda. (S) Euphemism for sex; literally, "bed work."

keata loikop. (M) S/he has bad omen (because of having killed a person).

kemuntet. (M) Affect combining admiration, love, and envy.

keraisho. (M) Childhood.

keshomoki ninche. (M) They were left behind.

ketama ltungani. (M) S/he killed a person; literally, "S/he ate a person."

keturno. (M) It is bad.

-a kienyeji. (S) Traditional.

-a kisasa. (S) Modern; contemporary.

kotolo. (M) Unpropitious.

kubaki nyuma. (S) To be left behind.

kudangania. (S) To cheat.

kuiba. (S) To steal.

kufanya uongo. (S) To lie.

kursai (*sg.* kursa). (M) Ritual specialists.

kurudi. (S) To return.

kuvuta mbele. (S) To push forward.

laigwanak (*sg.* laigwanani). (M) Chiefs.

laigwanak lolmurran. (M) Moran chiefs (appointed by the colonial government).

lailepi (*sg.* lkailepi). (M) Age-set climbers.

laingoni. (M) Dead young man.

laji. (M) Age set; the noun is also used to refer more specifically to members of an age set that belong to the same clan.

lalashe. (M) Brother.

lamurrano. (M) Moranhood.

laroi. (M) Worthless man.

latukuny. (M) Bodily sweat; smell; dirt.

launoni. (M) Spiritual age-set leader.

lautani. (M) Male relative through marriage; in-law; affine.

lchapukera. (M) Best Man; ritual role in lopiro ceremonies.

ldeket. (M) Curse.

ldoinyio. (M) Highlands.

lkaria. Red ocher.

lkereti (*pl.* lkeretita). (M) Customs; traditions; "the normal way of doing things."

lkirda. (M) Educated men and women; literally, those of the trousers.

lkirikoi (*pl.* lkiriko). (M) A man who is unpropitious for not having married and fathered children long after his initiation into elderhood and who cannot participate in collective blessings for fear that his blessings would turn into curses toward others.

Lkishami. Name of the age set initiated in 2005.

Lkishili. Name of age set initiated in 1960.

Lkuroro. Name of the age set initiated in 1976.

lmaachai (*pl.* lmaachani). (M) A man who does not have a family despite the fact that, by age-grade status, he is already an elder; a pauper; an idler.

lmarei. (M) Clan.

lmasi. (M) Long hairdo associated with the morans.

Lmekuri. Name of age set initiated in 1936.

lmenong. (M) Ritual prohibition according to which during moranhood, a man cannot eat food seen or touched by women; the noun also refers to a ceremony through which this prohibition is lifted, and husband and wife are brought into a food-sharing relationship.

lmon'go. (M) Bull.

lmon'go lenkolong. (M) Bull or its monetary equivalent given by the groom to the bride's parents to defer wedding costs.

Lmooli. Name of the age set initiated in 1990.

lmurran loolbiashara. (M) Business moran; a polite way to refer to beach boys.

loimina. (M) The lost ones; noun used to refer to beach-boy elders.

Lokop. (M) Samburu; literally, "the one of the land."

lopeny nkang. (M) Homestead owner; family head.

lopiro. (M) A four-day ceremony that for each clan takes place every fourteen to eighteen years. At the center of this ceremony are the adulterous relationships between junior elders and wives of fire-stick elders, relations of clan belonging, and commodity exchanges.

lorere. (M) Tribe.

lpapayian lolopiro. (M) Mister Lopiro; ritual role in lopiro ceremonies.

lpayian lobichboi. (M) Beach-boy elders.

lpayiano. (M) Elderhood.

lperet. (M) Transgressors; men who marry as morans against the will of the elders.

lpurkel. (M) Lowlands.

ltungana le nkang. (M) People from villages.

lwenet. (M) Culture.

mabati. (M/S) Iron sheet; it can also refer to a house with an iron-sheet roof.

madai (*pl.* lmaadai). (M) Madman.

madawa. (S) Medicine; herbal remedies.

maendeleo. (S) Development.

maendeleoni. (M) Development.

malaya. (S) Prostitute.

manyatta. (S) Traditional homestead; word borrowed in Kenyan Swahili from a Maa noun that, in Maasai, refers to a moran village.

marnani (*sg.* marnai). (M) Bead bracelets.

mayan. (M) Blessing; it can also refer to a blessing ceremony.

mbele. (S) forward; in front.

mbiita. (M) HIV/AIDS; the noun comes from the verb *a-biita*, "to waste away."

mboo obo. (M) One flock; the phrase refers to social unity or cohesion.

mbwa kali. (S) Fierce dog.

mganga (*pl.* waganga). (S) Sorcerers; witch doctors.

mipango ya kando (*sg.* mpango wa kando). (S) Secret lovers; literally, "side plans."

mkubwa. (S) Big man.

Mombasa moran. Young men who migrate to coastal tourist resorts to sell souvenirs, dance for tourists, and find European partners.

moran. Kenyan English and Swahili noun for a young man who has been initiated, through circumcision, into the age grade of "warriorhood"; from the Maa noun *ilmurrani* (pl. *ilmurran*). A man becomes a moran between the ages of fifteen and twenty.

morijo. (M) Senior members of an age set.

mpos korom. (M) Concubine; female life partner for whom no bridewealth has been paid.

musunku orok. (M) "Black whiteman," referring to educated, middle-class Samburu.

mzungu. (S) White person.

nchapukera. (M) Maid of Honor; ritual role in lopiro ceremonies.

ndege wa Mungu. (M) "God's birds," referring to young men who depend on female sexual partners for material support.

ng'oki. (M) Bad omen from having killed a person. This omen is passed down from one generation to the other, depleting life force and well-being.

ngoto lopiro. (M) Mama Lopiro; ritual role in lopiro ceremonies.

nkaibartak (*sg.* nkaibartani). (M) Young wives.

nkaini. (M) Co-wives.

nkaji e mabati. (M) A house with an iron-sheet roof.

nkaji naibor. (M) Ritual hut constructed for the *lmenong* ceremony; literally, "a white house."

nkampo. (M) Overseas; abroad; from the Swahili noun *ng'ambo*.

nkanashe. (M) Sister.

nkang. (M) Home; compound; family.

nkanyit. (M) Respect.

nkauti. (M) Bridewealth.

nkera ee ntito. (M) "Children of a girl"; illegitimate children.

nkerashai. (M) A type of traditional house common in the Samburu highlands. It is made of wooden poles and branches and plastered with a mixture of dung and clay. Its layout can be rectangular or oval, and its roof is usually flat.

nkinyama. (M) Wedding ceremony.

nkiringenyicho. (M) Unpropitious sexual mixing; adultery.

nkiroi. (M) Bloodwealth.

Nkishami. Collective name of girls who came of age when the Lkishami age set was in the age grade of moranhood.

nkishon. (M) Life force; fertility; the ability to reproduce and prosper.

nkishu ee ng'ok. (M) Cattle of wrongdoings; cattle received by a man from another as reparation of adultery.

nkishu le lkasin. (M) Cattle of work; cattle purchased with wages.

nkolia. (M) Widows.

nkolipi (*pl.* nkolipiono). (M) Barren woman.

nkosheke. (M) Stomach; womb.

nkutuk. (M) Speech; language; mouth.

ntalipa. (M) descent; origin.

ntasim. (M) Medicine; ritual.

ntipat. (M) Lineage; subclan; a subsection of a clan.

ntito (*pl.* ntoyie). (M) Girl.

ntoki. (M) Thing.

ntokitin ee nkang. (M) Matters of home; private matters.

ntomonok (*sg.* ntomononi). (M) Married women.

ntomonok nashomo kitala. (M) Runaway wives.

ntoo. (M) song and dance genre.

ntorosi. (M) Women's fertility ceremony.

ntowuo. (M) Age set.

ntoyie ee saen. (M) "Girls of the beads"; rural girls.

ntoyie naataroitie. (M) "Broken girls"; girls who become pregnant before initiation.

pachon. (M) Fashion.

pain. (M) Fine.

pesa ya haraka. (S) Rushed money.

pesa ya jasho. (S) Money of sweat.

pesa ya shortkut. (S) Shortcut money.

pesa ya uchawi. (S) Money of sorcery.

a-purr. (M) To steal; to seduce.

raha. (S) Happiness; comfort; fun.

rikoret. (M) Ox killed by the groom on the wedding day by way of sealing the marriage.

rikoret e nker. (M) Ram substituted for the wedding ox in marriage ceremonies.

a-rrag. (M) To have sex; literally, "to lie down."

a-rubbo. (M) To beat; to fuck (vulgar).

rungu. (M) Knobkerrie; club.

sadaka ya damu. (S) Blood offering; sacrifice.

a-sap. (M) To cheat.

shilingini. (M) Money.

shilingini chapu. (M) Dirty money.

shilingini e chang'aa. (M) Money of chang'aa.

shilingini e kuni. (M) Money of charcoal.

shilingini e ng'ok. (M) Money of wrongdoings.

shilingini e nkera. (M) "Money of the children"; euphemism for money obtained through alcohol brewing.

shiptamen. (M) Name of a Samburu dance.

shoga. (S) Faggot.

shuka. (M) Loincloth.

silen. (M) Debt.

silen e nkauti. (M) Bridewealth debt.

sintan (*sg.* sintani). (M) Lover.

siri. (M/S) Secrets.

surupon. (M) Incest.

tabia. (S) Personal character.

a-tamaki. (M) To be eaten; to get fucked (vulgar).

treila (*sg.* treilani). (M) Unmarried women with children; Maa neologism originating in the English noun *trailer*.

uchawi. (S) Sorcery.

uchawi wa kioo. (S) Type of sorcery using mirrors to affect people at a distance.

uhusiano. (S) Relationship.

vijana wakubwa. (S) Young big men; rich young men in relationships with European women.

vitu vya haraka. (S) Rushed things; things obtained without work.

waheshimiwa (*sg.* mheshimiwa). (M) Respectable persons; term used to address rich, influential persons.

wakubwa (*sg.* mkubwa). (M) Big men; term used to refer to rich, influential persons.

wanaoa. (S) They marry (masculine form).

wanaolewa. (S) They are married (feminine form).

a-yama. (M) To marry.

young big men (*S:* vijana wakubwa). A term some Samburu use to refer to men who became rich through relationships with European women; also known as rich morans.

References

Ahmed, Sara. 2000. *Strange Encounters: Embodied Others in Post-coloniality*. Transformations: Thinking through Feminism. London: Routledge.

Akama, John S. 1999. "The Evolution of Tourism in Kenya." *Journal of Sustainable Tourism* 7 (1): 6–25.

Albuquerque, Klaus de. 1998. "Sex, Beach Boys, and Female Tourists in the Caribbean." *Sexuality and Culture* 2: 87–111.

Allen, Jafari S. 2011. *Venceremos?: The Erotics of Black Self-Making in Cuba*. Perverse Modernities. Durham, NC: Duke University Press.

Allison, Anne. 1994. *Nightwork: Sexuality, Pleasure, and Corporate Masculinity in a Tokyo Hostess Club*. Chicago: University of Chicago Press.

Amar, Paul. 2013. *The Security Archipelago: Human-Security States, Sexuality Politics, and the End of Neoliberalism*. Durham, NC: Duke University Press.

Amory, Deborah. 1998. "Mashoga, Mabasha, and Magai: 'Homosexuality' on the East African Coast." In *Boy-Wives and Female Husbands: Studies in African Homosexualities*, edited by Stephen O. Murray and Will Roscoe, 67–87. New York: St. Martin's Press.

Anderson, David, and Vigdis Broch-Due. 1999. *The Poor Are Not Us: Poverty and Pastoralism in Eastern Africa*. Eastern African Studies. Athens: Ohio University Press.

Argenti, Nicolas. 2007. *The Intestines of the State: Youth, Violence, and Belated Histories in the Cameroon Grassfields*. Chicago: University of Chicago Press.

Arnfred, Signe. 2004. "Re-thinking Sexualities in Africa: Introduction." In *Re-thinking Sexualities in Africa*, edited by Signe Arnfred, 1–33. Uppsala: Nordic African Institute.

Askew, Kelly M. 2004. "Striking Samburu and a Mad Cow: Adventures in Anthropollywood." In *Off Stage/On Display: Intimacy and Ethnography in the Age of Public Culture*, edited by Andrew Shryock, 33–68. Berkeley: University of California Press.

Bates, Robert H. 1989. *Beyond the Miracle of the Market: The Political Economy of Agrarian Development in Kenya*. Political Economy of Institutions and Decisions. Cambridge: Cambridge University Press.

Bauer, Thomas G., and Bob McKercher. 2003. *Sex and Tourism: Journeys of Romance, Love, and Lust*. New York: Haworth Hospitality Press.

Baxter, Paul Trevor William, and Uri Almagor. 1978. *Age, Generation and Time: Some Features of East African Age Organisations*. London: Hurst.

Beidelman, Thomas O. 1997. *The Cool Knife: Imagery of Gender, Sexuality, and Moral Education in Kaguru Initiation Ritual*. Smithsonian Series in Ethnographic Inquiry. Washington, DC: Smithsonian Institution Press.

Belliveau, Jeannette. 2006. *Romance on the Road: Traveling Women Who Love Foreign Men*. Baltimore: Beau Monde Press.

Berlant, Lauren. 1997. *The Queen of America Goes to Washington City: Essays on Sex and Citizenship*. Durham, NC: Duke University Press.

Berman, Bruce. 1998. "Ethnicity, Patronage and the African State: The Politics of Uncivil Nationalism." *African Affairs* 97 (388): 305–41.

Berman, Nina. 2005. "Autobiographical Accounts of Kenyan-German Marriages: Reception and Context." In *Germany's Colonial Past*, edited by E. Ames, M. Krotz, and L Wildenthal, 205–26. Lincoln: University of Nebraska Press.

Bernstein, Elizabeth. 2007. *Temporarily Yours: Intimacy, Authenticity, and the Commerce of Sex*. Chicago: University of Chicago Press.

Besnier, Niko. 2009. *Gossip and the Everyday Production of Politics*. Honolulu: University of Hawai'i Press.

Bhabha, Homi K. 1994. *The Location of Culture*. London: Routledge.

Bishop, Ryan, and Lillian S. Robinson. 1998. *Night Market: Sexual Cultures and the Thai Economic Miracle*. New York: Routledge.

Bloch, Maurice. 1986. *From Blessing to Violence: History and Ideology in the Circumcision Ritual of the Merina*. Cambridge: Cambridge University Press.

Blunt, Robert. 2010. "Of Money and Elders: Ritual, Proliferation, and Spectacle in Colonial and Postcolonial Kenya." PhD diss., University of Chicago.

Boellstorff, Tom. 2005. *The Gay Archipelago: Sexuality and Nation in Indonesia*. Princeton, NJ: Princeton University Press.

Bourdieu, Pierre. 1977. *Outline of a Theory of Practice*. Cambridge: Cambridge University Press.

———. 1984. *Distinction: A Social Critique of the Judgement of Taste*. London: Routledge and Kegan Paul.

Brennan, Denise. 2004. *What's Love Got to Do with It? Transnational Desires and Sex Tourism in the Dominican Republic*. Latin America Otherwise. Durham, NC: Duke University Press.

Bruner, Edward M. 2005. *Culture on Tour: Ethnographies of Travel*. Chicago: University of Chicago Press.

Budgor, Mindy. 2013. *Warrior Princess: My Quest to Become the First Female Maasai Warrior*. Guilford, CT: Globe Pequot Press.

Buggenhagen, Beth A. 2012. *Muslim Families in Global Senegal: Money Takes Care of Shame*. Bloomington: Indiana University Press.

Burns, Peter. 1999. *An Introduction to Tourism and Anthropology*. London: Routledge.

Cabezas, Amalia L. 2009. *Economies of Desire: Sex and Tourism in Cuba and the Dominican Republic*. Philadelphia: Temple University Press.

Carsten, Janet. 2004. *After Kinship*. New Departures in Anthropology. Cambridge: Cambridge University Press.

Caton, Steven C. 1999. *Lawrence of Arabia: A Film's Anthropology*. Berkeley: University of California Press.

Cattelino, Jessica. 2008. *High Stakes: Florida Seminole Gaming and Sovereignty*. Durham, NC: Duke University Press.

Chanler, William Astor. 1896. *Through Jungle and Desert: Travels in Eastern Africa*. New York: MacMillan.

Chanock, Martin. 2000. "'Culture' and Human Rights Orientalising, Occidentalising and Authenticity." In *Beyond Rights Talk and Culture Talk: Comparative Essays on the Politics of Rights and Culture*, edited by Mahmood Mamdani, 15–36. New York: Saint Martin's Press.

Chenevix-Trench, Charles. 1964. *The Desert's Dusty Face*. New York: W. Morrow.

Clift, Stephen, and Simon Carter. 2000. *Tourism and Sex: Culture, Commerce, and Coercion*. Tourism, Leisure, and Recreation Series. London: Pinter.

Coe, Cati. 2013. *The Scattered Family: Parenting, African Migrants, and Global Inequality*. Chicago: University of Chicago Press.

Cole, Jennifer. 2001. *Forget Colonialism? Sacrifice and the Art of Memory in Madagascar*. Berkeley: University of California Press.

———. 2004. "Fresh Contact in Tamatave, Madagascar: Sex, Money, and Intergenerational Transformation." *American Ethnologist* 31 (4): 573–88.

———. 2008. "'Et Plus Si Affinites': Malagasy Marriage, Shifting Post-colonial Hierarchies, and Policing New Boundaries." *Historical Reflections* 34 (1): 26–49.

———. 2009. "Love, Money, and Economies of Intimacy in Tamatave, Madagascar."

In *Love in Africa*, edited by Jennifer Cole and Lynn M. Thomas, 109–34. Chicago: University of Chicago Press.

———. 2010. *Sex and Salvation: Imagining the Future in Madagascar*. Chicago: University of Chicago Press.

Cole, Jennifer, and Christian Groes-Green, eds. 2016. *Affective Circuits: African Migrants to Europe and the Pursuit of Social Regeneration*. Chicago: University of Chicago Press.

Comaroff, J. 2007. "Beyond Bare Life: AIDS, (Bio)Politics, and the Neoliberal Order." *Public Culture* 19 (1): 197–219.

Comaroff, Jean. 1985. *Body of Power, Spirit of Resistance: The Culture and History of a South African People*. Chicago: University of Chicago Press.

Comaroff, Jean, and John L. Comaroff. 1993. *Modernity and Its Malcontents: Ritual and Power in Postcolonial Africa*. Chicago: University of Chicago Press.

———. 2000. "Millennial Capitalism: First Thoughts on a Second Coming." *Public Culture* 12 (2): 291–343.

Comaroff, John L., and Jean Comaroff. 2009. *Ethnicity, Inc.* Chicago Studies in Practices of Meaning. Chicago: University of Chicago Press.

Constable, Nicole. 2009. "The Commodification of Intimacy: Marriage, Sex, and Reproductive Labor." *Annual Review of Anthropology* 38 (1): 49–64.

Cooper, Frederick. 1987. *On the African Waterfront: Urban Disorder and the Transformation of Work in Colonial Mombasa*. New Haven, CT: Yale University Press.

Dahles, Heidi, and Karin Bras. 1999. "Entrepreneurs in Romance: Tourism in Indonesia." *Annals of Tourism Research* 26 (2): 267–93.

Da Ros, Achille, Virgilio Pante, and Egidio Pedenzini. 2000. *Proverbi Samburu = Samburu Sayings*. Bologna: Editrice missionaria italiana.

Dean, Tim. 2000. *Beyond Sexuality*. Chicago: University of Chicago Press.

Ebron, Paulla A. 2002. *Performing Africa*. Princeton, NJ: Princeton University Press.

ECPAT (End Child Prostitution, Child Pornography, and Traficking), UK. N.d. "Child Sex Tourism in Kenya." http://www.ecpat.org.uk/downloads/Kenya05.pdf, accessed November 24, 2016.

El-Tayeb, Fatima. 2011. *European Others: Queering Ethnicity in Postnational Europe*. Minneapolis: University of Minnesota Press.

Epprecht, Marc. 2004. *Hungochani: The History of a Dissident Sexuality in Southern Africa*. Montreal: McGill-Queen's University Press.

———. 2008. *Heterosexual Africa? The History of an Idea from the Age of Exploration to the Age of AIDS*. Athens: Ohio University Press.

———. 2013. "The Making of 'African Sexuality': Early Sources, Current Debates." In *Sexual Diversity in Africa: Politics, Theory, and Citizenship*, edited by S. N. Nyeck and Marc Epprecht, 54–66. Montreal: McGill-Queen's University Press.

Evans-Pritchard, E. E. (1940) 1969. *The Nuer: A Description of the Modes of Livelihood and Political Institutions of a Nilotic People*. Oxford: Oxford University Press.

———. 1951. *Kinship and Marriage among the Nuer*. Oxford: Clarendon Press.

Fabian, Johannes. 1983. *Time and the Other: How Anthropology Makes Its Object*. New York: Columbia University Press.

Fadiman, Jeffrey. 1976. *Mountain Warriors: The Pre-colonial Meru of Mt. Kenya*. Papers in International Studies, Africa Series, no. 27. Athens: Ohio University Center for International Studies, Africa Program.

Fanon, Frantz. (1952) 2008. *Black Skin, White Masks*. New York: Grove Press.

Farquhar, Judith. 2002. *Appetites: Food and Sex in Postsocialist China*. Body, Commodity, Text. Durham, NC: Duke University Press.

Ferguson, James. 1999. *Expectations of Modernity: Myths and Meanings of Urban Life on the Zambian Copperbelt*. Perspectives on Southern Africa. Berkeley: University of California Press.

———. 2006. *Global Shadows: Africa in the Neoliberal World Order*. Durham, NC: Duke University Press.

Foley, Ellen E., and Fatou Maria Drame. 2013. "Mbaraan and the Shifting Political Economy of Sex in Urban Senegal." *Culture, Health and Sexuality* 15 (2): 121–34.

Foucault, Michel. 1978. *The History of Sexuality*. Vol. 1. New York: Pantheon Books.

Fratkin, Elliot. 1994. "Pastoral Land Tenure in Kenya: Maasai, Samburu, Born, and Rendille Experiences, 1950–1990." *Nomadic Peoples* 34/35: 55–68.

Freeman, Elizabeth. 2007. "Introduction." *GLQ: A Journal of Gay and Lesbian Studies* 13 (2–3): 159–76.

Frohlick, Susan. 2013. *Sexuality, Women, and Tourism: Cross-Border Desires through Contemporary Travel*. Contemporary Geographies of Leisure, Tourism and Mobility. London: Routledge.

Fumagalli, Carl T. 1978. "An Evaluation of Development Projects among East African Pastoralists." *African Studies Review* 21 (3): 49–63.

Gachuhi, J. Mugo. 1973. "Anatomy of Prostitutes and Prostitution in Kenya." Working paper, University of Nairobi.

Galaty, John. 1992. "The Land Is Yours: Social and Economic Factors in the Privatization, Sub-division and Sale of Maasai Ranches." *Nomadic Peoples* 30: 26–40.

Gavaghan, Terence. 1999. *Of Lions and Dung Beetles*. Ilfracombe, England: Arthur H. Stockwell.

Gell, Alfred. 1992. *The Anthropology of Time: Cultural Constructions of Temporal Maps and Images*. Oxford: Berg.

Geschiere, Peter. 1997. *The Modernity of Witchcraft: Politics and the Occult in Postcolonial Africa*. Charlottesville: University Press of Virginia.

———. 2009. *The Perils of Belonging: Autochthony, Citizenship, and Exclusion in Africa and Europe.* Chicago: University of Chicago Press.

Gimblett, Barbara Kirshenblatt. 1998. *Destination Culture: Tourism, Museums, and Heritage.* Berkeley: University of California Press.

Gluckman, Max. 1954. *Rituals of Rebellion in South-East Africa.* Manchester: Manchester University Press.

———, ed. 1962. *Essays on the Ritual of Social Relations.* Manchester: Manchester University Press.

———. 1963. "Gossip and Scandal." *Current Anthropology* 4 (3): 307–16.

Goody, Jack. 1956. "A Comparative Approach to Incest and Adultery." *British Journal of Sociology* 7 (4): 286–305.

Graeber, David. 2001. *Toward an Anthropological Theory of Value: The False Coin of Our Own Dreams.* New York: Palgrave.

Gregory, Steven. 2007. *The Devil behind the Mirror: Globalization and Politics in the Dominican Republic.* Berkeley: University of California Press.

Groes-Green, Christian. 2009. "Hegemonic and Subordinated Masculinities: Class, Violence and Sexual Performance among Young Mozambican Men." *Nordic Journal of African Studies* 18 (4): 286–304.

———. 2011. "Philogynous Masculinities: Contextualizing Alternative Manhood in Mozambique." *Men and Masculinities* 15 (2): 91–111.

———. 2014. "Journeys of Patronage: Moral Economies of Transactional Sex, Kinship, and Female Migration from Mozambique to Europe." *Journal of Royal Anthropological Institutes* 20 (2): 237–55.

Hachfeld-Tapukai, Christina. 2004. *Mit der Liebe einer Löwin: Wie ich die Frau eines Samburu Kriegers wurde.* Bergisch Gladbach, Germany: Luebbe.

———. 2009. *Der Himmel über Maralal: Mein Leben als Frau Eines Samburu-Kriegers.* Bergish Gladbach: Ehrenwirth.

Halberstam, Judith. 2005. *In a Queer Time and Place: Transgender Bodies, Subcultural Lives.* New York: New York University Press.

———. 2011. *The Queer Art of Failure.* Durham, NC: Duke University Press.

Hardwick, Alfred Arkell. 1903. *An Ivory Trader in North Kenia: The Record of an Expedition through Kikuyu to Galla-Land in East Equatorial Africa; With an Account of the Rendili and Burkeneji Tribes.* London: Longmans, Green.

Haugerud, Angelique. 1997. *The Culture of Politics in Modern Kenya.* Cambridge: Cambridge University Press.

Heald, Suzette. 1999. *Manhood and Morality: Sex, Violence and Ritual in Gisu Society.* London: Routledge.

Hemmings, Clare. 2012. "Sexuality, Subjectivity . . . and Political Economy." *Subjectivity* 5 (2): 121–39.

Hinch, Thomas, and Richard W. Butler. 1996. *Tourism and Indigenous Peoples*. Issues in Tourism Series. London: International Thomson Business Press.

Hirsch, Eric. 2016. "Investing in Indigeneity: Development, Finance and the Politics of Inclusive Sustainability in Andean Peru." PhD diss., University of Chicago.

Hoad, Neville. 2007. *African Intimacies: Race, Homosexuality, and Globalization*. Minneapolis: University of Minnesota Press.

Hobsbawm, Eric J., and Terence O. Ranger, eds. 1983. *The Invention of Tradition*. Cambridge: Cambridge University Press.

Hodges, Matt. 2008. "Rethinking Time's Arrow: Bergson, Deleuze and the Anthropology of Time." *Anthropological Theory* 8 (4): 399–429.

Hodgson, Dorothy. 2001. *Once Intrepid Warriors: Gender, Ethnicity, and the Cultural Politics of Maasai Development*. Bloomington: Indiana University Press.

——. 2011. *Being Maasai, Becoming Indigenous: Postcolonial Politics in a Neoliberal World*. Bloomington: Indiana University Press.

Hofmann, Corinne. 2005. *The White Masai*. London: Bliss Books.

——. 2006. *Reunion in Barsaloi*. London: Bliss Books.

——. 2008. *Back from Africa*. London: Arcadia Books.

Holland, Sharon Patricia. 2012. *The Erotic Life of Racism*. Durham, NC: Duke University Press.

Holsteen, Melbourne Edward. 1982. "Continuity and Change in Samburu Education." PhD diss., University of Florida.

Holtzman, Jon. 2003. "Age, Masculinity, and Migration: Gender and Age among the Samburu Pastoralists in Northern Kenya." In *Gender at Work in Economic Life*, edited by Garcia Clark, 225–41. Lanham, MD: Altamira.

——. 2004. "The Local in the Local: Models of Time and Space in Samburu District, Northern Kenya." *Current Anthropology* 45 (1): 61–84.

——. 2005. "The Drunken Chief: Alcohol, Power and the Birth of the State in Samburu District, Northern Kenya." *Postcolonial Studies* 8 (1): 83–96.

——. 2006. "The World Is Dead and Cooking's Killed It: Food and the Gender of Memory in Samburu, Northern Kenya." *Food and Foodways* 14 (3–4): 175–200.

——. 2009. *Uncertain Tastes: Memory, Ambivalence, and the Politics of Eating in Samburu, Northern Kenya*. Berkeley: University of California Press.

Honwana, Alcinda. 2012. *The Time of Youth: Work, Social Change, and Politics in Africa*. Sterling, VA: Kumarian Press.

Hubert, Henri. (1905) 1999. *Essay on Time: A Brief Study of the Representation of Time in Religion and Magic*. Oxford: Durkheim Press.

Hughes, Lotte. 2006. "'Beautiful Beasts' and Brave Warriors: The Longevity of a Maasai Stereotype." In *Ethnic Identity: Problems and Prospects for the Twenty-First Cen-*

tury, edited by L. Romanucci-Ross, G. De Vos, and T. Tsuda, 264–94. Lanham, MD: Altamira.

Hunt, Nancy Rose. 1999. *A Colonial Lexicon of Birth Ritual, Medicalization, and Mobility in the Congo*. Durham, NC: Duke University Press.

Hunter, Mark. 2010. *Love in the Time of AIDS: Inequality, Gender, and Rights in South Africa*. Bloomington: Indiana University Press.

Hutchinson, Sharon Elaine. 1996. *Nuer Dilemmas: Coping with Money, War, and the State*. Berkeley: University of California Press.

Jacobs, Jessica. 2010. *Sex, Tourism and the Postcolonial Encounter: Landscapes of Longing in Egypt*. New Directions in Tourism Analysis. Farnham, England: Ashgate.

Jain, Sarah S. Lochlann. 2004. "'Dangerous Instrumentality': The Bystander as Subject in Automobility." *Cultural Anthropology* 19 (1): 61–94.

James, Wendy, and Daniel Mills. 2005. "Introduction: From Representation to Action in the Flow of Time." In *The Qualities of Time: Anthropological Approaches*, edited by Wendy James and Daniel Mills, 1–15. Oxford: Berg.

Jeffreys, Sheila. 2003. "Sex Tourism: Do Women Do It Too?" *Leisure Studies* 22: 223–38.

Kanogo, Tabitha M. 2005. *African Womanhood in Colonial Kenya, 1900–50*. Oxford: James Currey.

Kasfir, Sidney L. 2002. "Slam-Dunking and the Last Noble Savage." *Visual Anthropology* 15 (3–4): 369–85.

———. 2007. *African Art and the Colonial Encounter: Inventing a Global Commodity*. African Expressive Cultures. Bloomington: Indiana University Press.

Kawai, Kaori. 1998. "Women's Age Categories in a Male-Dominated Society: The Case of the Chamus of Kenya." In *Conflict, Age, and Power in North East Africa*, edited by Eisei Kurimoto and Simon Simonse, 147–67. Oxford: James Currey.

Kempadoo, Kamala. 1999. *Sun, Sex, and Gold: Tourism and Sex Work in the Caribbean*. Lanham, MD: Rowman and Littlefield.

———. 2001. "Freelancers, Temporary Wives, and Beach-Boys: Researching Sex Work in the Caribbean." *Feminist Review* 67: 39–62.

Kibicho, Wanjohi. 2009. *Sex Tourism in Africa: Kenya's Booming Industry*. New Directions in Tourism Analysis. Farnham, England: Ashgate.

Kimambo, Samantha. 2007. *The English Maasai and Other Truths*. Self-published. https://www.Lulu.com.

Kratz, Corinne Ann. 1994. *Affecting Performance: Meaning, Movement, and Experience in Okiek Women's Initiation*. Washington, DC: Smithsonian Institution Press.

Kulick, Don. 1998. *Travesti: Sex, Gender, and Culture among Brazilian Transgendered Prostitutes*. Worlds of Desire. Chicago: University of Chicago Press.

Lacan, Jacques. 1978. *The Four Fundamental Concepts of Psycho-Analysis*. New York: Norton.

Leach, Edmund. 1954. *Political Systems of Highland Burma: A Study of Kachin Social Structure*. Cambridge, MA: Harvard University Press.

——. 1961. *Rethinking Anthropology*. London: Athlone Press.

Lepani, Katherine. 2012. *Islands of Love, Islands of Risk: Culture and HIV in the Trobriands*. Nashville: Vanderbilt University Press.

Lesorogol, Carolyn K. 2008a. *Contesting the Commons: Privatizing Pastoral Lands in Kenya*. Ann Arbor: University of Michigan Press.

——. 2008b. "Setting Themselves Apart: Education, Capabilities, and Sexuality among Samburu Women in Kenya." *Anthropological Quarterly* 81 (3): 551–77.

Lewis, Desiree. 2011. "Representing African Sexualities." In Tamale (ed.) 2011, 199–216.

Leys, Colin. 1974. *Underdevelopment in Kenya: The Political Economy of Neo-Colonialism, 1964–1971*. Berkeley: University of California Press.

Lienhardt, Godfrey. 1961. *Divinity and Experience: The Religion of the Dinka*. Oxford: Oxford University Press.

Lindsay, Lisa A., and Stephan Miescher, eds. 2003. *Men and Masculinities in Modern Africa*. Portsmouth, NH: Heinemann.

Little, Kenneth. 1991. "On Safari: The Visual Politics of a Tour Representation." In *The Varieties of Sensory Experience: A Sourcebook in the Anthropology of the Senses*, edited by David Howes, 149–63. Toronto: University of Toronto Press.

Little, Peter D. 1992. *The Elusive Granary: Herder, Farmer, and State in Northern Kenya*. Cambridge: Cambridge University Press.

Llewelyn-Davies, Melissa. 1981. "Women, Warriors and Patriarchs." In *The Cultural Construction of Gender and Sexuality*, edited by Sheri Ortner and Harriet Whitehead, 330–58. Cambridge: Cambridge University Press.

Lonsdale, John. 1992. "The Conquest of Kenya, 1895–1905." In *Unhappy Valley: Conflict in Kenya and Africa*, edited by Bruce Berman and John Lonsdale, 1:13–44. Oxford: James Currey.

Lorway, Robert. 2014. *Namibia's Rainbow Project: Gay Rights in an African Nation*. Bloomington: Indiana University Press.

Lynch, Gabrielle. 2011. *I Say to You: Ethnic Politics and the Kalenjin in Kenya*. Chicago: University of Chicago Press.

Lyons, Andrew P., and Harriet Lyons. 2004. *Irregular Connections: A History of Anthropology and Sexuality*. Lincoln: University of Nebraska Press.

MacCannell, Dean. 1976. *The Tourist: A New Theory of the Leisure Class*. New York: Schocken Books.

Magubane, Zine. 2004. *Bringing the Empire Home: Race, Class, and Gender in Britain and Colonial South Africa*. Chicago: University of Chicago Press.

Mahoney, Dillon. 2009. "The Art of Connection: Negotiating the Digital Divide in Kenya's Curio Industry." PhD diss., Rutgers University.

Mains, Daniel. 2011. *Hope Is Cut: Youth, Unemployment, and the Future in Urban Ethiopia.* Global Youth. Philadelphia: Temple University Press.

Makhulu, Anne-Maria, Beth A. Buggenhagen, and Stephan Jackson. 2010. Introduction to *Hard Work, Hard Times: Global Volatility and African Subjectivity,* edited by Anne-Maria Makhulu, Beth A. Buggenhagen, and Stephan Jackson, 1–27. Berkeley: University of California Press.

Malinowski, Bronislaw. 1927. *Sex and Repression in Savage Society.* London: Routledge.

———. 1929. *The Sexual Life of Savages in North-Western Melanesia: An Ethnographic Account of Courtship, Marriage, and Family Life among the Natives of the Trobriand Islands, British New Guinea.* London: Beacon Press.

Mason, Cheryl. 1995. *White Mischief: The True Story of a Woman Who Married a Kenyan Tribesman.* Sussex: Summersdale.

Mason-Lekimenju, Cheryl. 2001. *No Ivory Tower.* Hampshire: Encompass.

Maurer, Elke Regina. 2010. *Fremdes im Blick, am Ort des Eigenen: Eine Rezeptionsanalyse von "Die weiße Massai."* Freiburg: Centaurus Verlag.

Mbembe, J.-Achille. 2001. *On the Postcolony.* Studies on the History of Society and Culture. Berkeley: University of California Press.

McCabe, J. Terrence. 1990. "Turkana Pastoralism: A Case against the Tragedy of the Commons." *Human Ecology* 18 (1): 81–103.

McClintock, Anne. 1995. *Imperial Leather: Race, Gender, and Sexuality in the Colonial Contest.* New York: Routledge.

McIntosh, Janet. 2009a. "Elder and 'Frauds': Commodified Expertise and Politicized Authenticity among Mijikenda." *Africa* 79 (1): 35–52.

———. 2009b. *The Edge of Islam: Power, Personhood, and Ethnoreligious Boundaries on the Kenya Coast.* Durham, NC: Duke University Press.

———. 2016. *Unsettled: Denial and Belonging among White Kenyans.* Berkeley: University of California Press.

Mead, Margaret. 1928. *Coming of Age in Samoa: A Psychological Study of Primitive Youth for Western Civilisation.* New York: William Morrow.

Meiu, George Paul. 2008. "Riefenstahl on Safari: Embodied Contemplation in East Africa." *Anthropology Today* 24 (2): 18–22.

———. 2009. "Mombasa Morans: Embodiment, Sexual Morality, and Samburu Men in Kenya." *Canadian Journal of African Studies* 43 (1): 105–28.

———. 2011. "On Difference, Desire, and the Aesthetics of the Unexpected: *The White Masai* in Kenyan Tourism." In *Great Expectations: Imagination, Anticipation, and Enchantment in Tourism,* edited by Dimitrios Theodossopoulos and Jonathan Skinner, 96–115. Oxford: Berghahn Books.

———. 2015. "Beach-Boy Elders and Young Big-Men: Subverting the Temporalities of Aging in Kenya's Ethno-erotic Economies." *Ethnos* 80 (4): 472–96.

———. 2016. "Belonging in Ethno-erotic Economies: Adultery, Alterity, and Ritual in Postcolonial Kenya." *American Ethnologist* 43 (2): 215–29.

Middleton, John. 1960. *Lugbara Religion: Ritual and Authority among an East African People*. Oxford: Oxford University Press.

Miescher, Stephan. 2005. *Making Men in Ghana*. Bloomington: Indiana University Press.

Mitchell, Gregory. 2015. *Tourist Attractions: Performing Race and Masculinity in Brazil's Sexual Economy*. Chicago: University of Chicago Press.

Mojola, Sanyu A. 2014. *Love, Money, and HIV: Becoming a Modern African Woman in the Age of AIDS*. Berkeley: University of California Press.

Morrell, Robert. 2001. *Changing Men in Southern Africa*. New York: Zed Books.

Morris, Rosalind C. 2008. "Rush/Panic/Rush: Speculations on the Value of Life and Death in South Africa's Age of AIDS." *Public Culture* 20 (2): 199–231.

Munn, Nancy D. 1986. *The Fame of Gawa: A Symbolic Study of Value Transformation in a Massim (Papua New Guinea) Society*. Cambridge: Cambridge University Press.

———. 1992. "The Cultural Anthropology of Time: A Critical Essay." *Annual Review of Anthropology* 21: 93–123.

Muñoz, José Esteban. 2009. *Cruising Utopia: The Then and There of Queer Futurity*. New York: New York University Press.

Mwakikagile, Godfrey. 2001. *Ethnic Politics in Kenya and Nigeria*. Huntington, NY: Nova.

Nagel, Joane. 2003. *Race, Ethnicity, and Sexuality: Intimate Intersections, Forbidden Frontiers*. New York: Oxford University Press.

Najmabadi, Afsaneh. 2005. *Women with Mustaches and Men without Beards: Gender and Sexual Anxieties of Iranian Modernity*. Berkeley: University of California Press.

Newell, Sasha. 2012. *The Modernity Bluff: Crime, Consumption, and Citizenship in Côte d'Ivoire*. Chicago: University of Chicago Press.

Ngwane, Zolani. 2004. "Real Men Reawaken Their Father's Homesteads, the Educated Leave Them in Ruins." In Weiss 2004, 167–92.

Nyamnjoh, Francis B. 2005. "Fishing in Troubled Waters: Disquettes and Thiofs in Dakar." *Africa* 75 (3): 295–324.

Nyanzi, Stella, Ousman Rosenberg-Jallow, Ousman Bah, and Susan Nyanzi. 2005. "Bumsters, Big Black Organs and Old White Gold: Embodied Racial Myths in Sexual Relationships of Gambian Beach Boys." *Culture, Health and Sexuality* 7 (6): 557–69.

Oddie, Catherine. 1994. *Enkop Ai (My Country): My Life with the Maasai*. East Roseville, NSW: Simon and Schuster Australia.

Omondi, Rose Kisia. 2003. "Gender and the Political Economy of Sex Tourism in Kenya's Coastal Resorts." Working paper, Moi University, Kenya.

Ong, Aihwa. 1996. "Cultural Citizenship as Subject-Making: Immigrants Negotiate Racial and Cultural Boundaries in the United States." *Current Anthropology* 37 (5): 737–62.

Osburg, John. 2013. *Anxious Wealth: Money and Morality among China's New Rich*. Stanford, CA: Stanford University Press.

Ott, Elisabeth. 2004. *Nkanyit und Gewalt: Häusliche Gewalt gegen Frauen in Samburu zwischen Tradition und Willkür*. Berlin: Weissensee Verlag.

Oucho, John O. 2002. *Undercurrents of Ethnic Conflicts in Kenya*. Leiden: Brill.

Ouzgane, Lahoucine, and Robert Morrell. 2005. *African Masculinities: Men in Africa from the Late Nineteenth Century to the Present*. New York: Palgrave.

Padilla, Mark. 2007. *Caribbean Pleasure Industry: Tourism, Sexuality, and AIDS in the Dominican Republic*. Chicago: University of Chicago Press.

Partridge, Damani J. 2012. *Hypersexuality and Headscarves: Race, Sex, and Citizenship in the New Germany*. Bloomington: Indiana University Press.

Pavitt, Nigel. 1991. *Samburu*. London: K. Cathie.

———. 2008. *Kenya: A Country in the Making, 1880–1940*. New York: W. W. Norton.

Peake, Robert Edmund. 1984. "Tourism and Alternative Worlds: The Social Construction of Reality in Malindi Town, Kenya." PhD diss., SOAS, University of London.

Perlov, Diane C. 1987. "Trading for Influence: The Social and Cultural Economics of Livestock Marketing among the Highland Samburu of Northern Kenya." PhD diss., University of California, Los Angeles.

Phillips, Joan. 1999. "Tourist-Oriented Prostitution in Barbados: The Case of the Beach Boy and the White Female Tourist." In *Sun, Sex and Gold: Tourism and Sex Work in the Caribbean*, edited by Kamala Kempadoo, 183–200. Lanham, MD: Rowan and Littlefield.

Pierre, Jemima. 2013. *The Predicament of Blackness: Postcolonial Ghana and the Politics of Race*. Chicago: University of Chicago Press.

Pietilä, Tuulikki. 2007. *Gossip, Markets, and Gender: How Dialogue Constructs Moral Value in Post-socialist Kilimanjaro*. Madison: University of Wisconsin Press.

Pigg, Stacy Leigh, and Vincanne Adams. 2005. "Introduction: The Moral Object of Sex." In *Sex in Development: Science, Sexuality, and Morality in Global Perspective*, edited by Vincanne Adams and Stacy Leigh Pigg, 1–38. Durham, NC: Duke University Press.

Piot, Charles. 2010. *Nostalgia for the Future: West Africa after the Cold War*. Chicago: University of Chicago Press.

Povinelli, Elizabeth A. 2006. *The Empire of Love: Toward a Theory of Intimacy, Genealogy, and Carnality*. Durham, NC: Duke University Press.

Rainy, Michael E. 1989. "Samburu Ritual Symbolism: An Adaptive Interpretation of Pastoralist Traditions." *Social Sciences Information* 28 (4): 785–819.

Ralph, Michael. 2008. "Killing Time." *Social Text* 26: 1–29.

Ratele, Kopano. 2007. "Native Chief and White Headman: A Critical African Gender Analysis of Culture." *Agenda* 21 (72): 65–76.

———. 2011. "Male Sexualities and Masculinities." In Tamale (ed.) 2011, 399–419. Oxford: Pambazuka.

Richter, Linda M., and Robert Morrell. 2006. *Baba: Men and Fatherhood in South Africa*. Cape Town: HSRC Press.

Roitman, Janet Lee. 2005. *Fiscal Disobedience: An Anthropology of Economic Regulation in Central Africa*. Princeton, NJ: Princeton University Press.

Rutherford, Danilyn. 2003. *Raiding the Land of the Foreigners: The Limits of the Nation on an Indonesian Frontier*. Princeton, NJ: Princeton University Press.

Ryan, Chris, and Colin Michael Hall. 2001. *Sex Tourism: Marginal People and Liminalities*. London: Routledge.

Sahlins, Marshall D. 1972. *Stone Age Economics*. New Brunswick, NJ: Transaction.

Said, Edward W. 1978. *Orientalism*. New York: Pantheon Books.

Sanchez Taylor, Jacqueline. 2001. 'Dollars Are a Girl's Best Friend? Female Tourists' Sexual Behavior in the Caribbean." *Sociology* 35 (3): 749–64.

Schoss, Johanna H. 1995. "Beach Tours and Safari Visions: Relations of Production and the Production of 'Culture' in Malindi, Kenya." PhD diss., University of Chicago.

Scott, James C. 1990. *Domination and the Arts of Resistance: Hidden Transcripts*. New Haven, CT: Yale University Press.

Sheller, Mimi. 2012. *Citizenship from Below: Erotic Agency and Caribbean Freedom*. Durham, NC: Duke University Press.

Shepherd, Gill. 1987. "Rank, Gender, and Homosexuality: Mombasa as a Key to Understanding Sexual Options." In *The Cultural Construction of Sexuality*, edited by Patricia Caplan and Gill Shepherd, 240–70. London: Tavistock Publications.

Shipley, Jesse Weaver. 2010. "Africa in Theory: A Conversation between Jean Comaroff and Achille Mbembe." *Anthropological Quarterly* 83 (3): 653–78.

Shipton, Parker MacDonald. 1989. *Bitter Money: Cultural Economy and Some African Meanings of Forbidden Commodities*. Washington, DC: American Anthropological Association.

———. 2007. *The Nature of Entrustment: Intimacy, Exchange, and the Sacred in Africa*. Yale Agrarian Studies Series. New Haven, CT: Yale University Press.

Shneiderman, Sara. 2015. *Rituals of Ethnicity: Thangmi Identities between Nepal and India*. Philadelphia: University of Pennsylvania Press.

Silberschmidt, Margrethe. 2001. "Disempowerment of Men in Rural and Urban East Africa: Implications for Male Identity and Sexual Behavior." *World Development* 29 (4): 657–71.

Silverstein, Michael. 1993. "Metapragmatic Discourse and Metapragmatic Function." In *Reflexive Language: Reported Speech and Metapragmatics*, edited by John A. Lucy, 33–58. Cambridge: Cambridge University Press.

Simpson, George L. 1994. "On the Frontiers of Empire: British Administration in Kenya's Northern Frontier District, 1905–1935." PhD diss., West Virginia University.

——. 1996. "Gerontocrats and Colonial Alliances." In *The Politics of Age and Gerontocracy in Africa: Ethnographies of the Past and Memories of the Present*, edited by Mario I. Aguilar, 65–96. Trenton, NJ: African World Press.

Singer, Linda. 1993. *Erotic Welfare: Sexual Theory and Politics in the Age of Epidemic*. New York: Routledge.

Smith, James Howard. 2008. *Bewitching Development: Witchcraft and the Reinvention of Development in Neoliberal Kenya*. Chicago Studies in Practices of Meaning. Chicago: University of Chicago Press.

Smith, Melanie K., and Rosaleen Duffy. 2003. *Issues in Cultural Tourism Studies*. London: Routledge.

Smith, Valene L. 1977. *Hosts and Guests: The Anthropology of Tourism*. Philadelphia: University of Pennsylvania Press.

Sobania, Neal. 1993. "Defeat and Dispersal: The Laikipiak and Their Neighbours at the End of the Nineteenth Century." In *Being Maasai: Ethnicity and Identity in East Africa*, edited by Thomas T. Spear and Richard Waller, 105–19. Oxford: James Currey.

Somerville, Siobhan B. 2000. *Queering the Color Line: Race and the Invention of Homosexuality in American Culture*. Series Q. Durham, NC: Duke University Press.

Spacks, Patricia Meyer. 1985. *Gossip*. New York: Knopf Doubleday Publishing Group.

Spencer, Paul. 1965. *The Samburu: A Study of Gerontocracy*. Routledge Classic Ethnographies. London: Routledge.

——. 1973. *Nomads in Alliance: Symbiosis and Growth among the Rendille and Samburu of Kenya*. London: Oxford University Press for the School of Oriental and African Studies.

——. 1988. *The Maasai of Matapato: A Study of Rituals of Rebellion*. Manchester: Manchester University Press.

——. 1998. *The Pastoral Continuum: The Marginalization of Tradition in East Africa*. Oxford: Clarendon Press.

Sperling, Louise. 1987. "The Adoption of Camels by Samburu Cattle Herders." *Nomadic Peoples* 23: 1–17.

Stoler, Ann Laura. 2002. *Carnal Knowledge and Imperial Power: Race and the Intimate in Colonial Rule*. Berkeley: University of California Press.

Stout, Noelle M. 2014. *After Love: Queer Intimacy and Erotic Economies in Post-Soviet Cuba*. Durham, NC: Duke University Press.

Straight, Bilinda. 2000. "Development Ideology and Local Knowledge among Samburu Women in Northern Kenya." In *Rethinking Pastoralism in Africa*, edited by Dorothy Hodgson, 227–48. Oxford: James Currey.

———. 2002. "From Heirloom to New Age Artifact: The Cross-Cultural Consumption of Mporo Marriage Beads." *American Anthropologist* 104: 1–15.

———. 2005. "In the Belly of History: Memory, Forgetting, and the Hazards of Reproduction." *Africa* 75 (1): 83–104.

———. 2007a. "House, Fire, Gender." *Material Religion: The Journal of Objects, Art and Belief* 3 (1): 48–61.

———. 2007b. *Miracles and Extraordinary Experience in Northern Kenya*. Contemporary Ethnography. Philadelphia: University of Pennsylvania Press.

Swamy, Gurushri. 1994. "Kenya: Structural Adjustment in the 1980s." Washington, DC: World Bank.

Tade, Oludayo, and Adeshewa Adekoya. 2012. "Transactional Sex and the 'Aristo' Phenomenon in Nigerian Universities." *Human Affairs* 22 (2): 239–55.

Talle, Aud. 1988. *Women at a Loss: Changes in Maasai Pastoralism and Their Effects on Gender Relations*. Vol. 19. Stockholm Studies in Social Anthropology. Stockholm: Department of Social Anthropology, University of Stockholm.

Tamale, Sylvia. 2011. "Researching and Theorizing Sexualities in Africa." In Tamale (ed.) 2011, 11–36.

———, ed. 2011. *African Sexualities: A Reader*. Oxford: Pambazuka.

Tami, Nicole. 2008. "Romancing Strangers: The Intimate Politics of Beach Tourism in Kenya." PhD diss., University of Illinois at Urbana-Champaign.

Thomas, Lynn M. 2003. *Politics of the Womb: Women, Reproduction, and the State in Kenya*. Berkeley: University of California Press.

Tignor, Robert L. 1976. *The Colonial Transformation of Kenya: The Kamba, Kikuyu, and Maasai from 1900 to 1939*. Princeton, NJ: Princeton University Press.

Trouillot, Michel-Rolph. 1991. "Anthropology and the Savage Slot: The Poetics and Politics of Otherness." In *Recapturing Anthropology: Working in the Present*, edited by Richard Fox, 17–44. Santa Fe: School of American Research Press.

Turner, Victor. 1967. *The Forest of Symbols: Aspects of Ndembu Ritual*. Ithaca, NY: Cornell University Press.

———. 1969. *The Ritual Process: Structure and Anti-Structure*. Symbol, Myth, and Ritual Series. Ithaca, NY: Cornell University Press.

Urry, John. 1990. *The Tourist Gaze: Leisure and Travel in Contemporary Societies*. London: Sage Publications.

Visweswaran, Kamala. 2010. *Un/common Cultures: Racism and the Rearticulation of Cultural Difference*. Durham, NC: Duke University Press.

Waller, Richard. 1993. "Acceptees and Aliens: Kikuyu Settlement in Maasailand." In *Being Maasai: Ethnicity and Identity in East Africa*, edited by Thomas T. Spear and Richard Waller, 226–57. Oxford: James Currey.

———. 2010. "Bad Boys in the Bush? Disciplining Murran in Colonial Maasailand." In *Generations Past: Youth in East African History*, edited by Andrew Burton and Helene Charton-Bigot, 135–74. Athens: Ohio University Press.

Walsh, Andrew. 2003. "'Hot Money' and Daring Consumption in a Northern Malagasy Sapphire-Mining Town." *American Ethnologist* 30 (2): 290–305.

Wanyoike, Pauline Nasesia. 2011. "The Perceptions of Rural Samburu Women in Kenya with Regard to HIV/AIDS: Towards Developing a Communication Strategy." PhD diss., University of South Africa.

Waweru, Peter. 2012. *Continuity and Change in Samburu Pastoralism*. Saarbrücken, Germany: Lap Lambert Academic Publishing GmbH KG.

Weber, Max. (1905) 2012. *The Protestant Ethic and the Spirit of Capitalism and Other Writings*. London: Penguin Books.

Weiner, Annette B. 1992. *Inalienable Possessions: The Paradox of Keeping-While Giving*. University of California Press.

Weiss, Brad. 2004. "Introduction: Contesting Futures; Past and Present." In Weiss 2004, 1–19.

———, ed. 2004. *Producing African Futures: Ritual and Reproduction in a Neoliberal Age*. Leiden: Brill.

White, Hylton. 2004. "Ritual Haunts: The Timing of Estrangement in a Post-Apartheid Countryside." In Weiss 2004, 141–66.

White, Luise. 1990. *The Comforts of Home: Prostitution in Colonial Nairobi*. Chicago: University of Chicago Press.

———. 2000. *Speaking with Vampires: Rumor and History in Colonial Africa*. Berkeley: University of California Press.

Wilson, Ara. 2004. *The Intimate Economies of Bangkok: Tomboys, Tycoons, and Avon Ladies in the Global City*. Berkeley: University of California Press.

Wilson, G. M. 1957. "Male Prostitution and Homosexuals: Appendix to 'Mombasa Social Survey.'" Unpublished mimeograph, Nairobi.

Wilson, Monica. 1959. *Communal Rituals of the Nyakyusa*. Oxford: Oxford University Press.

Wiszowaty, Robin. 2010. *My Maasai Life: From Suburbia to Savannah*. Vancouver: Greystone Books.

Zelizer, Viviana A.. 2005. *The Purchase of Intimacy*. Princeton, NJ: Princeton University Press.

Žižek, Slavoj. 2006. *How to Read Lacan*. New York: Norton.

Znoj, Heinzpeter. 2004. *Heterarchy and Domination in Highland Jambi: The Contest for Community in a Matrilinear Society*. London: Kegan Paul.

Index

A page number in *italics* refers to an illustration.

in Samburu, 15, 124; out of place,
164–65, 166, 243, 265n8
sex-for-money exchanges: in African
sexual economies, 99–100; asking
woman tourist for money, 124–25;
beyond tourism, 100–101; fantasy
of romance and love in, 125, 126, 128,
136; gendered expectations within
Samburu and, 89; gender reversal
of power associated with, 127–28,
131–32; respectability and, 65–66,
69; of Samburu men with foreign gay
men, 125; status of Kenyan state and,
64; unequal ages and, 124, 125. *See
also* commodification of sex; ethno-
erotic economies; money of Mombasa; prostitutes; transactional sex
sex tourism, 33, 100, 262n2
sexual alterity, 21–23; adultery as marker
of, for colonials, 228; globally circulating discourses of, 212, 229; modernist ideology and, 246; of morans,
59, 60, 64; performances driven by
fantasies of, 98. *See also* Otherness
sexuality: as construct, 21–22; gender
asymmetries in notions of, 89; recreational model of, 98–99
sexually transmitted diseases: criticism of morans by middle class
and, 40–41, 47, 60, 62; gonorrhea
in morans, 40–41, 60, 224; national
media interest in Samburu and, 210.
See also HIV/AIDS
sexual morality: delegitimization of
Samburu and, 63; policing of, in
global South, 27; struggles over belonging and, 27, 245. *See also* moral
concerns of Samburu
sexual secrecy, 210–12, 221, 228

sexual violence against young women,
59, 63
shadow economies of northern Kenya,
46
Sheller, Mimi, 234
shiptamen, 111–12
Shipton, Parker, 188
shortcut money, 140, 141–42, 157; cultural logic of development and, 246;
Tangan's story and, 198. *See also* fast
money; money of Mombasa
side plans, 128–29, 131, 222. *See also*
mistresses
Siteti: highland advantages of, 45; photo
of, *67*; as research site, 27
slave trade, 20
slippery intimacies, 38, 97–98; contradictions of, 122, 136; gender reversal
of power and, 127–28; quick loss of
money and, 142–43, 169, 247; seeking
stabilization of, 101, 137; uncertainty
of performative labor and, 132–33.
See also intimacy
Smith, James, 163
social reproduction: accelerated by
young big men, 182; beach-boy
elders and, 204; economic production and, 33, 158, 166, 169, 248; fast
money and, 158; money of sex and,
166, 169; ritual as means of, 234,
248
social value, templates of, 70–75
sorcery, 38; ascribed to Kenyan women
by male migrants, 129; condition of
temporariness and, 179; criticism of
returning men for using, 139, 140,
142, 143; loss of Mombasa money
and, 160–64; majini and, 160–64,
183, 264n14; red cars indicating,